T0261898

DRAFTING THE RUSSIAN NATION

JOSHUA A. SANBORN

Drafting the Russian Nation

Military Conscription, Total War,

and Mass Politics,

1905–1925

Northern

Illinois

University

Press

Published by the Northern Illinois University Press, DeKalb, Illinois   60115

Manufactured in the United States using acid-free paper

Design by Julia Fauci

Library of Congress Cataloging-in-Publication Data

Sanborn, Joshua A.

Drafting the Russian nation : military conscription, total war, and mass
politics, 1905–1025 / Joshua A. Sanborn

   p.   cm.

Includes bibliographical references and index.

ISBN 0-87580-306-7 (alk. paper)

1. Draft—Russia. 2. Draft—Soviet Union. 3. Russia—Politics and government—1894–1917. 4. Soviet Union—Politics and government—1917–1936.
5. World War, 1914–1918—Russia. 6. Soviet Union—History—Revolution,
1917–1921. I. Title.

UB345.R9 S25 2003

355.2′2363′094709041—dc21

2002071913

A portion of chapter 3 is adapted from "Family, Fraternity, and Nation
Building" by Josh Sanborn, from *A State of Nations,* edited by Ronald Suny
and Terry Martin, copyright 2001 by Oxford University Press, Inc. Used by
permission of Oxford University Press, Inc.

For Kim and Clay

Contents

Acknowledgments

I have received massive support in a number of ways during my work on this project. Some of this support has been financial. I have received grants from the University of Chicago, the John D. and Catherine T. MacArthur Foundation's Center for the Advancement and Study of Peace and International Cooperation, the Mellon Foundation, and the Social Science Research Council (with funds provided by a grant from the United States Department of State under Title VIII). I also benefited from the help of Lafayette College, which provided funding for me to hire Sarah Glacel, a very able research assistant, and gave me a semester off to finish the manuscript. The good cheer and hard work of the Lafayette librarians have enriched this project, as have the University of Chicago librarians and the many Russian archivists who helped me along the way. Thanks also to Mary Lincoln, whose energy and professionalism as editor at Northern Illinois University Press have made the task of turning a first manuscript into a first book more a pleasure than a chore.

My intellectual debts are greater still. Time is the most valuable commodity of the scholar, and colleagues have been extremely generous in donating that time to help me improve this book. Sheila Fitzpatrick, my dissertation advisor, has certainly spent more time and energy than anyone else in this regard. I fear my debt to her will never fully be repaid. Ron Suny has been a consistently kind critic, strong backer, and friend, for which I thank him. Michael Geyer's insights have enriched this book immensely. His energy and acumen never cease to amaze me. Richard Hellie also gave valuable advice, especially early on in the project. In addition to my professors at Chicago, I owe a lot to the large, smart, and engaging group of fellow graduate students who were there when I was. Tuesday nights at the volatile Wilder House workshops created, for me at least, a primary academic community. Matt Payne, Terry Martin, John McCannon, Julie Hessler, Golfo Alexopolous, Jon Bone, Julie Gilmour, Chris Burton, Matt Lenoe, Steve Bittner, Elena Pavlova, Alison Smith, Kirill Tomoff, and Jenifer Stenfors all provided moral as well as intelletual support. At Stephen F. Austin State University, I benefited from the advice and comments of Rafe Blaufarb, Scott Bills, and Troy Davis. Colleagues at Lafayette have also been generous, in particular the members of the junior faculty reading group: Paul Barclay, Andrea Smith, Neil Englehart, and Galen Brokaw. I am similarly grateful to many friends and scholars outside my circle of institutional ties. Peter Holquist, Eric Lohr, Nick Breyfogle, Eagle Glassheim, Gary Gerstle, and the two reviewers for Northern Illinois University Press read part or all of the manuscript at various points and gave excellent advice.

Last, but not least, my family provided financial, intellectual, and moral support. It was only through the sacrifices of my parents that my secondary and higher education choices were possible, and without my grandparents' generous gift in 1990, I would have been unable to go on the Stanford-Soviet Exchange Project, which changed my life in ways I never imagined at the time. My older brother Geoff has been a consistent intellectual and emotional touchstone. I hope he knows that I look up to him. My younger brother Ben got out of the "family business" of academe, but I try not to hold it against him. My in-laws have also been supportive of the new member of their family who seemingly spends every other decent vacation period in Russia.

There are many debts I owe to my wife, Kim, but I dedicate this book to her and to my son, Clay, for uncomplicated reasons. I simply love you so much.

DRAFTING THE RUSSIAN NATION

Introduction

But now thus saith the Lord that created thee, O Jacob, and he that
formed thee, O Israel. Fear not, for I have redeemed thee. I have called
thee by name; thou art mine.

—Isaiah 43:1

The extensive militarization of all aspects of state and public activity is
a law of modern war preparations. Woe to him to whom militarization is
merely metaphysics.

—Aleksandr Svechin, *Strategy*

The story of Russia's murderous twentieth century properly
begins on New Year's Day, 1874. It was on that day that Tsar
Alexander II definitively transformed the relationship between
political belonging and the production of violence by making
military conscription both universal and personal. The univeral
conscription decree signaled a substantial shift in the nature of
power and politics in the Russian Empire, and the decision to issue it was not taken lightly. Alexander's conservative advisors
had warned him that making military service a national duty
rather than a traditional one would weaken the social and military base of the old regime and hence his own power. In the
1860s, he listened to these conservatives and refused to countenance such a major change. But after the juggernaut national
army of Prussia defeated both Austria and France with surprising ease between 1866 and 1871, Alexander was willing to reex-
amine the issue. Three years of committee work and the tireless
efforts of War Minister Dmitrii Miliutin and Miliutin's associate
Nikolai Obruchev finally convinced the tsar that it would be
suicidal to ignore the lessons of recent wars. Alexander made
these lessons clear in his decree. Bismarck's Germany, he
claimed, had "proven" that "the strength of a state is not in the
number of its troops alone, but is primarily in the moral

and intellectual qualities of those troops. Those qualities only reach the highest stage of development when the business of defending the fatherland becomes the general affair of the people *(narod)*, when all, without distinction of title or status, unite for that holy cause."[1]

With this decree, Alexander reluctantly accepted the new military-political calculus that the rest of the continental powers had already adopted with the formative experience of the French Revolution and the recent Prussian military victories in mind. The logic of this new relationship between military service and political belonging articulated by progressive military officials across Europe was simple: (1) armies of national citizens were superior to standing armies separated from the population; (2) in wars between nationalized armies, larger armies still had an advantage over smaller ones; therefore (3) the security of the country depended on the broadest possible extension of military service and citizenship. In sum, as Alexander stated, armies and state power only become fully developed when the "business of defending the fatherland becomes the general affair of the people." In the more anxious words of Aleksandr Svechin cited in the epigraph: "Woe to him to whom militarization is merely metaphysics."

Though the logic of this new relationship was simple, nothing else about it was, especially in the Russian Empire. Alexander's decree started the process, but it did not end it. What did it mean to create a citizen-soldier in a country with only a weakly and unofficially developed notion of "citizenship," in a country in which most of those soldiers were only a bit more than a decade out of bondage? In the ethnically and socially diverse empire, could one even speak of a single "people" that could serve as a focal point for the new political ideology? Could one articulate the principles of modern nationalism within the confines of an autocratic political system? These were the difficult questions faced by military reformers and their growing number of allies in the late nineteenth century and early twentieth century, and these questions defined the project they set for themselves. That project was to create a strong Russian nation that would serve as both the basis and the justification for the expanded and invigorated Russian army. The project thus entailed the creation of a new political field that would increase both political participation and the production of violence by linking the two together. Mass politics would emerge with the mass army. Mass killing and mass death would quickly follow. It is my goal in this book to show that the nearly simultaneous appearance of mass politics and mass killing in Russia was not coincidental.

As the title of the book suggests, I argue that this connection between mass politics and mass killing was framed institutionally through the mechanisms of universal military conscription and more broadly by the ideology of the nation. Military planners "drafted the nation" in two ways. First, they drew up blueprints for a new, dynamic political community composed of independent men dedicated to the defense of their land and families. This community would be multiethnic and multi-class, and it would exist alongside the other nations of Europe. Second, they used the draft to gather millions of men into an army that was meant both to be a physical embodiment of the nation and a symbolic brotherhood of citizen-soldiers. These new institutional and ideological constructions were bold, dynamic, and ultimately enormously destructive. They were destructive, of course, for those who died in war and in incidents of state repression, but they also subverted both the autocratic regime in which they were developed and the radical Bolshevik regime that sought to succeed it. The institution of universal military conscription and the ideology of the nation undermined both these regimes by producing a powerful form of political subjectivity that contested the formal bases of both the tsarist autocracy and the new communist order: the national citizen-soldier. That subjectivity was produced through the dialogue between military officials and conscripts over the ideational principles of the community they sought to create and through the acts of violence that helped to define the national political form.

In the pages that follow, I will explore this relationship between the production of violence and the transformation of Russian subjectivity in detail. My approach is thematic and layered rather than chronological and strictly linear. Each chapter is intended to explore the basic question of the relationship between military service and the nation between 1905 and 1925 from a different angle. The argument will build cumulatively, not sequentially. As a result, I will plead here at the outset for a bit of patience from readers eager for exhaustive treatments of topics the first time they are mentioned. The structure of this book is such that questions hinted at in early chapters often find fuller treatment in later ones.

Chapter 1 outlines the explicit "high" and "low" politics of conscription. The focus is on the nature and form of the state's appeal to its citizens to perform violence for the nation and the dynamics of conscript response to that appeal. Over the course of the period under study, this dialogue fundamentally shifted its terms from one that was strictly confined to the question of duty to one that made explicit the rights and benefits that soldiers could expect in return for military service. This acknowledgment of reciprocal rights and duties on the part of both parties laid the basis for the new national compact that emerged during the years of total war.

The next two chapters address the fact of heterogeneity and the desire for homogeneity that Russian nation-builders, like nation-builders everywhere, struggled to come to terms with. Chapter 2 addresses the ways that both state and nonstate actors dealt with the "dilemma of difference" faced by a political community that stretched across two continents. I focus here in particular on ethnic and class differentiation and the complex ways that conscription policy sought both to acknowledge and eventually to efface the diversity of the realm. Chapter 3 explores ways that military planners attempted to build unity in spite of the fragmented nature of their society. They did so negatively by identifying and marginalizing domestic pariahs who fell outside of the categorical boundaries that marked the "people" who constituted the national community. But they also attempted to build positive cohesion among co-nationals by appropriating very personal and previously localized affinitive bonds, like kinship, for the national project.

In addition to these explicit nation-building projects, military men engaged in two other major campaigns that ultimately did as much to constitute the nation as did their attempts to deal with ethnic and class questions. Chapter 4 examines the first of these: the broad-based effort to nationalize masculinity across the country. Here I argue that military officials drove the process of normalizing a single, militarized form of masculinity. Masculine ideals became the content of the character of the citizen-soldier and thus provided a powerful basis of solidarity among men in uniform, a solidarity that was independent of their loyalties to the particular regimes that they fought to protect. Finally, chapter 5 examines violence itself. Through a study of the ways that soldiers were trained in violence, the way they practiced it, and the problems faced by those who refused to perform it, I argue that the production of violence should be seen as an autonomous force in the developments of the era. Violence was not dependent upon "identity." Instead, violence helped constitute political identities, a process we can see quite clearly in an examination of the institution of military conscription.

Military Conscription

Sovereigns elicit responses from their subjects in many different ways, but only rarely is this process so formally institutionalized as it is when young men are ordered to serve their country under arms. Military recruitment is a core state project that embodies and incorporates the ideological and "practical" aspects of domestic rule and foreign relations. The full spectrum of political relationships is exposed: authority is invoked, obedience made manifest, and the preeminence of the community over the individual is asserted. As a result, the nature of any political system is reflected, at least in part, in the way that its armies are formed.

The politics of military service has peculiar importance for national political systems, however. As I will argue more explicitly later in the book, the performance of and exposure to violence was consistently seen as the ultimate civic duty by most Russian political actors throughout the period under study. This sense of military duty as the primary national duty extends well beyond Russia's borders. It has been a fundamental touchstone of political belonging throughout the modern era.[2]

It was not, however, until the intellectual, technological, and institutional developments associated with the Age of Revolution that the military constellation of the early modern period (characterized by standing armies separated from the population and pledged to the interests of a small elite) began to give way to the military constellation of the high modern period (characterized by mass armies integrated with the population and pledged to support the interests of the "people"). This transformation began in the intellectual realm, with a spirited Enlightenment debate about the relative merits of standing armies and citizen militias. As a result of this broader debate, proposals for creating a nation-in-arms were significant even before the dramatic events at the end of the eighteenth century.[3] European monarchs were of course rather less enthralled with these proposals than were European intellectuals.

The Age of Revolution transformed these ideas into institutions and policies. The transformation began during the American Revolution. From the start, American revolutionaries linked soldiering with citizenship, but they generally held the belief that the proper performance of duty, whether civic or military, had to be voluntary.[4] That conviction suffered under the strain of war, as revolutionary leaders struggled to build a large enough volunteer force. Nevertheless, it was not until 1778 that the Continental Congress approved a coercive federal draft at the desperate urging of George Washington, and even Washington saw the measure, at the time, as only a short-term expedient. When the war ended, so too did conscription and indeed the federal standing army itself.[5]

The intellectual and institutional legacies of the eighteenth century were therefore still ambiguous in 1789. The events that definitively changed the dynamic of military service and civic belonging were the wars of the French Revolution. It was this set of struggles that, out of the hodgepodge of Enlightenment thought regarding liberty, duty, standing armies, and militias, crystallized the nation-in-arms around the figure of the citizen-soldier. Three moments were particularly important in this development. The first was on 20 September 1792, when French forces (some of them singing the "Marseillaise" and shouting "Vive la nation!") forced a Prussian retreat at Valmy, proving to those who hadn't paid sufficient attention to North American events that forces of citizens could in fact defeat professional standing armies. Johann Wolfgang von Goethe, accompanying the Prussian troops as an observer, told soldiers that night that from "this place and this time forth commences a new era in world history and you can all say that you were present at its birth."[6] Goethe's listeners must have thought him prone to exaggeration. The Prussian retreat was not a devastating loss (only one hundred Prussians were killed in the battle), and there was no particular reason why the revolution might not have yet been doused by the conservative European powers. Neither was this an unambiguous victory of volunteers over recruits; many of the French troops were in fact army regulars. Still, the attention paid to this victory and the subsequent victory over the Austrians at Jemappes did firmly place the feats of citizen-soldiers at the center of the developing revolutionary narrative.

The second moment was the declaration of the *levée en masse* on 23 August 1793. The act expanded the limits of the political/military class by defining tasks that men and women of all ages were to perform in the period of war. It also made clear that this would be a "forced" duty: the "French people" would be in "permanent requisition for army service." In addition, no one would be allowed to hire substitutes or avoid service for reasons of social or economic privilege.[7] This decree represented the true radicalization of both warfare and citizenship, because it directly challenged the fundamental basis of the era of limited political participation and limited wars. Those who supported the democratic urge at its heart hoped that the extension of military responsibilities to the whole populace would bring not only more equality and more justice, but also more peace, for democratic societies composed of militarily obligated men would avoid war whenever possible. No less a figure than Immanuel Kant argued in his 1795 essay "On Perpetual Peace" that lasting peace *required* the replacement of regular armies with armed forces composed of citizens.[8] This dream that universal military service obligations would lead to greater peace went unrealized. Instead, quite the opposite occurred. As armies grew larger, as societies and armies became firmly intertwined, and as the stakes rose with each war, so too did the destructiveness of this new, radical "modern" warfare. Indeed, the logic of universal conscription led not to peace but to ever more apocalyptic confrontations, as the increased ease with which soldiers could be replaced led to ever bloodier fighting.[9]

The third moment was the export of this vision of warfare and politics under the banner of the French Revolution. Had the revolutionary army collapsed, as it almost did on several occasions, this totalizing moment might have passed. But the army did not collapse, at least not until 1812. As a result, the idea that national armies were larger, more dedicated, and ultimately more powerful than standing armies began to take root soon after Valmy, even outside of France. With the rapid expansion of French power under Napoleon, the export of the nationalist vision and the vision of modern war proceeded inseparably. In Prussia, for example, though significant groundwork for the establishment of a universal service law had been laid even before the revolutionary wars, the defeat at Napoleon's hands at Jena prompted more drastic modifications. The new Military Reorganization Commission declared in 1807 that the new army would be based on the principle that "all men are obliged to defend their fatherland."[10]

The details of this twinned rise of nationalism and universal conscription in continental Europe over the course of the nineteenth century lie beyond our scope here.[11] Despite a significant wave of popular mobilization to repel the invaders in 1812, Russia had the fortune or misfortune to emerge victorious from the Napoleonic Wars without permanent changes in its political and military institutions. As soon as Napoleon's army left Russian soil, popular support for the war effort waned and conservative elites warned of the dangers of mass mobilization.[12] No Prussian-style reforms were launched. Military needs were still filled by recruit levies from serf villages and captive urban communities and the Russian army remained the standing instrument of the great autocrat. Russia continued to be the strong conservative anchor on the eastern edge of Europe. Before long, however, the subversive seeds of the nation were planted at the heart of the autocratic system, not primarily by radicals or dissident intellectuals, but by the most trusted men of the realm: the army high command.

The Early History of the Russian Citizen-Soldier

Readers accustomed to the standard characterization of Russian military men as conservative or "reactionary" will be surprised by this description of leading army officials as subversive. The misreading of the military's role in political change is fully understandable. Most tsarist military men not only looked askance at those political forces in Russia that called themselves "progressive" but also claimed to stand outside of politics altogether. They had sworn loyalty to the tsar and fatherland and stood clear of debates, parties, and elections. When ordered to, they even fired at those who challenged the Romanov regime.

But this apparent unity with the autocratic regime was illusory. The aims of autocratic conservatives and of military men diverged dramatically over the latter half of the nineteenth century. Even in the first half of the century, the legacy of the French Revolution was influential for many important officials. The Decembrist movement was only the most radical of these developments; many others more peacefully sought to convince fellow elites of the dramatic transformation of the military landscape that the Napoleonic Wars had produced. Their efforts were mostly in vain until the Crimean War (1853–1856). Army reform was limited and firmly subordinated to the conservative political direction set by Alexander I and Nicholas I prior to the latter's death in 1855.[13] It was only the devastating loss to the European coalition on the soil of the Russian Empire that allowed military reformers to join the rest of the reform generation in pressing for substantial change in Russia's social, political, and military systems.

The leader of this generation of military reformers was unquestionably Dmitrii Miliutin (minister of war, 1861–1881). From the start of his career, Miliutin had been dissatisfied with the military system of the ancien régime. He argued as early as 1839 that troops were not simply masses of flesh and weapons but were also "a unity of people endowed with minds and hearts." As a result, he insisted that each field commander now had to "lead like a person" and had to strengthen his traditional authority over his soldiers with "moral power."[14] When Miliutin rose to the top spot in the military bureaucracy, he devoted himself to implementing reforms that would correspond to this vision of moral community. In the face of protest from old-style officers and the nobility at large, he convinced Alexander II to decentralize (and thereby eventually democratize) the field command in 1868 and then to implement universal conscription in 1874.[15]

As we have seen, Alexander's 1874 decree represented a decisive shift in Russia's political-military constellation. With his declaration that the state's strength lay not with God or the monarch but mainly in the "moral and intellectual qualities" of soldiers who pledged themselves to unite on a basis of equality in order to defend the fatherland, he undermined the traditional bases of autocratic power. By linking the moral qualities of the "people" with the strength of the state, he proposed a decidedly national and anti-autocratic formulation, for in *ancien régimes* war was the business of rulers and the army was the servant of the monarch.[16] After 1874, the fundamental basis of Russia's military system was a national one.

When politics turned more conservative after Alexander II's death in 1881, the top of the military bureaucracy reflected this conservative shift. Within military intellectual circles and in concrete discussions about training techniques, however, Miliutin's vision held sway under the hegemony of M. I. Dragomirov, who consistently stressed the moral aspect of soldiering and the need to make soldiers autonomous moral actors. Dragomirov had been recognized as the preeminent expert on military training in Russia since the 1860s, when he had argued in an article entitled "The Impact of the Spread of Rifled Weapons on the Training and Tactics of Troops" that rifles had "raised the question of respect for individuality" and were clearly "hostile" to massed troops. As a result, the task of trainers was to lead soldiers so that they not only understood their specialized training but also remained "energetic and sensible people."[17] Straight through to the end of the century, Dragomirov constantly repeated his call to pay attention to the moral strength and individuality of soldiers, publishing his widely used *Textbook on Tactics* in 1879, becoming the strongest voice on training in Russia in the latter half of the nineteenth century, and gaining an international reputation.[18]

By the end of the nineteenth century, no self-respecting military theorist really doubted that Miliutin and Dragomirov were right about the need for a morally autonomous soldier. Nor did anyone dispute that those individuals needed to subordinate themselves to a larger, unified community in order to be effective.[19] E. I. Martynov made this "national" thrust explicit:

> Only a strictly national *(natsional'naia)* policy that pursues exclusively the interests of its people has the right to lead in a struggle of mass armies of whole armed peoples . . . . People's love of honor, the interests of the dynasty, the personal sympathies and antipathies of leaders, all these petty reasons gradually will retreat to the background, replaced by a new powerful force—the public opinion of the country . . . . The difference between the soldier and the peaceful citizen will more and more get smoothed out, and the army, which was earlier a specialized caste, will gradually merge with the people. A complete democratization of the military trade will become obvious when standing troops completely disappear and every citizen will be a soldier at the same time.[20]

Even in 1894, Russian military men were calling for a political community that was national in form, military in content.

The nation that military intellectuals desired throughout the period under discussion was a multiethnic one. At first blush, this long-standing dedication to a multiethnic political community by leading military officials seems a bit odd. Military men, after all, had been among the first people in Russia to adopt the idea of ethnicity as an important factor of behavior and have long carried the stigma of being narrow-minded nationalists at best and chauvinists at worst.[21] But, though Russian nationalists could be found everywhere within the army, their vision of "Russia" was usually expansive for two basic reasons.

The first reason was anthropological. Being involved in the business of transforming individuals, military officials also usually subscribed to a dynamic view of ethnicity. Far from being racially locked in the primordial slime, ethnic traits were the result of environmental and historical factors, sometimes quite recent ones. Thus N. P. Mikhnevich, a leader of the so-called Russian nationalist school of military thought, argued that the reasons for the "greater hardiness" of Russian troops and the "originality" of Russian tactics lay in the conditions of their natural environment and in the "historical age of the people." "Historically young peoples," Mikhnevich argued, "are always distinguished by greater military capabilities than are peoples that have lived through longer historical pasts."[22]

This was not an innovative theory on Mikhnevich's part. The "youth" of the Russian nation as an important factor in its development was quite frequently found in Russian nationalist theory.[23] But the reference to the youth of the nation, along with the appeals to the importance of the natural environment, provided for an "open" national theory. If ethnic traits could change, then assimilation and eventually national unity were possible even in a multiethnic state.

The second reason was mathematical. In the 1897 census, only 44 percent of the population of the empire was Russian according to the standards used by census takers; the total reached only 67 percent when it included Russians, Ukrainians, and Belorussians.[24] Since military officials believed that all their soldiers needed to be equal members of the political community in order to fight with conviction, initiative, and "moral strength," any attempt to limit the draft pool to ethnic Russians would have significantly reduced it and led to fewer manpower resources in time of war and to a physically weaker cadre army. As a result, the military consistently pressed for larger and larger conscript pools.

These anthropological and mathematical considerations did not always lead to the conclusion that an expansive construction of the nation was necessary in the arms and manpower race that dominated military thinking prior to World War I, but it did lead most thinking men within the military establishment to press for a multiethnic Russia. As we will see in chapter 2, when officials within the General Staff asked for input from local military commanders in 1910 and 1911 about the question of conscripting previously exempted ethnic groups on an equal basis with the Russian population, they received near unanimous approval of the idea. The only disagreements concerned the timing of the implementation process.[25]

This desire for a multiethnic nation was based on a belief in the power of assimilation. For military men, however, assimilation had to have a specific content for it to truly strengthen the armed forces of the nation. Merely speaking Russian or reading Pushkin would not be enough. The norm for assimilation was an explicitly militarized one, and military intellectuals clearly understood that ethnic Russians as well as all other groups in the society would need to be militarized if the Russian nation were to survive in the modern era. By militarization, they had in mind a fairly stable set of ideas. First, of course, they intended that the whole male populace should learn military technique. More important, however, was the inculcation of a sense of participation, of belonging, and of loyalty. Through the creation of such affinities, they sought to build up a store of tremendous potential energy that could be unleashed through the kinetic process of mobilization.

By militarization, they also meant that the process of creating citizens and soldiers should take place simultaneously both inside and outside military institutions. Miliutin had been clear on the potential citizen-building role of the military. "General obligatory participation in military service, uniting in the ranks of the army men of all estates and all parts of Russia, presents the best means for the weakening of tribal differences among the people, the correct unification of all the forces of the state, and their direction towards a single, common goal."[26] This principle remained firm right up to the Soviet period, at which point the army became a "school" for Soviet citizens.[27]

The role of civilian institutions and leaders in preparing soldiers was equally obvious. Military men were painfully aware that they were living through an era of "spectacular change," and that new technologies and ideas of war had led to a situation in which "the role of the state and people now equaled the role of the army."[28] Here lay an area of great concern for military planners, many of whom were convinced that Russia's educational system and cultural elite were insufficiently nationalistic and insufficiently martial, and hence a source of great weakness. Just a few days before war broke out with Japan in 1904, Martynov made this charge explicit in a provocative article entitled "What is the Strength of Japan and the Weakness of Russia?" In contrast to Japan (and Germany), where educational institutions were the "hearths of the national spirit," Russia had educators, publicists, and cultural figures who systematically spread the notion that nationalism was "obsolete," that war was a "remnant of barbarism," and that the army was the "main drag on progress." This attitude had not yet "ruined" the Russian soldier (though Martynov was worried about the rise of pacifism in the ranks), but it had crippled the officer corps. As a result, when the "decisive battle" occurred, the Japanese would go into the fight with the "sympathies of all its people from the highest level to the lowest," while "behind the back of the Russian army there will be an indifferent, if not hostile attitude" from the educated classes.[29]

The charge that most members of Russian educated society were effete cosmopolitans who disdained war and sought to undermine the glory of Russia was overstated, but the army was right to believe that it faced significant opposition to its program to militarize Russia's educational system and public sphere. The widespread hostility to the tsarist regime certainly included disaffection with the armed forces, and there were substantive and vocal critics of the military establishment in the cultural world. Count Lev Tolstoi led the way with an unending stream of religiously based condemnation of violence and the modern state. Other writers took delight in skewering the army as well. Most hurtful to military men were Leonid Andreev's "Red Laugh" and Aleksandr Kuprin's novel *The Duel,* a dismal depiction of army life that became the literary sensation of 1905.[30]

It took the Russo-Japanese War and the domestic strife accompanying it to bring these simmering conflicts between military men and their civilian critics to public and political attention. Russia's military efforts during the war were disastrous. Japan destroyed two of Russia's three fleets and won every significant battle of the war, from Port Arthur to Mukden.

One of the major effects of this catastrophe was a broadening of the political base of the militarization movement. Reformers in the General Staff had long struggled to build support within the officer corps, not so much because those officers had resisted the message of Miliutin and his followers but because many of them simply didn't care and didn't bother to study the issues raised by military intellectuals in St. Petersburg. The war served to shake officers out of their somnolence and to convince them that the message of the General Staff was on target. In the midst of the war itself, officers up and down the chain of command made unfavorable comparisons between the patriotic fervor of Japanese soldiers and the "apathy" of the Russian rank and file. In the immediate postwar period, the nearly universal conclusion of military men was that the war had been lost because of the difference in political commitment. This interpretation was offered not only by Russian officers, but by foreign observers as well, whose comments on the war and the lack of Russian nationalism were quickly translated and published in Russian.[31]

The massive publicity given to the long-standing concerns of military intellectuals made a decisive and immediate impact upon the postwar political scene. Military reform became one of the dominant issues of the day. If the Russian army couldn't hold its own against Japan, how could it hope to repel Germany? The loss to Japan was a slap on the wrist; even after the defeat Russia only had to scale back its colonialist pretensions in the Far East. Being defeated by Germany would be far worse; it could entail a destruction of Russia as everyone knew it, with significant border adjustments and an acknowledgment of German hegemony in eastern Europe. Military concerns now focused on national protection rather than on imperial expansion. Reform was in the air.

In order to determine how to reform, policymakers had to identify who was to blame. There was no dearth of candidates. Nicholas II and his government had mishandled foreign and domestic policy so badly that they found themselves in a war they were unprepared for; then they turned relatively peaceful public grievances into a full-blown revolution. The military elite had done little better. Though Russian soldiers fought fairly well, failures of command and coordination had resulted in a string of embarrassing defeats. Finally, the military presented a strong and widely shared explanation for defeat, one that corresponded directly with Martynov's assessment of Russia's "weakness" on the eve of the war. Russia had lost the war because of deep systemic reasons: militarized nations would always defeat fragmented societies. The military's message was clear and consistent in the flurry of political reform that followed the Russo-Japanese War: militarize or perish.

Ideology and Subjectivity

Before examining the political battles surrounding conscription, it is important to outline the theoretical approach taken here to the ideologies that structured these contests. Perhaps the quickest and clearest way to do so is through two short tales. The first is from the Book of Isaiah. At the start of Isaiah's prophecy, God is angry at the rebelliousness of his chosen people, promising woe, destruction, and the emptying of the land because its inhabitants have broken the "everlasting covenant" (Isaiah 24:5). After detailing the horrors that await the Israelites, God steps back for a moment to remind them of that covenant: "But now thus saith the Lord that created thee, O Jacob, and he that formed thee, O Israel. Fear not, for I have redeemed thee. I have called thee by name; thou art mine" (Isaiah 43:1).

If being called like this were enough, the relationship between ideology and belonging would be relatively simple. But, as God shortly makes clear, true incorporation depends on the response of those who are called:

> But thou hast not called upon me, O Jacob; but thou hast been weary of me, O Israel. Thou hast not brought me the small cattle of thy burnt offerings; neither hast thou honoured me with thy sacrifices . . . Put me in remembrance: let us plead together: declare thou, that thou mayest be justified.

The cost for refusing the clarion call of the sovereign was high: "Thy first father hath sinned, and thy teachers have transgressed against me. Therefore I have profaned the princes of the sanctuary, and have given Jacob to the curse, and Israel to reproaches" (Isaiah 43: 22–28).

The second story occurred thousands of years later, in the waning days of socialist Yugoslavia. Here a similar scene is reenacted, this time with the leviathan of the modern state playing the role of the frustrated God.

A few months ago, a Yugoslav student was called to regular military service. In Yugoslavia, at the beginning of military service, there is a certain ritual: every new soldier must solemnly swear that he is willing to serve his country and to defend it even if that means losing his life, and so on—the usual patriotic stuff. After the public ceremony, everybody must sign the solemn document. The young soldier simply refused to sign, saying that an oath depends on free choice, that it is a matter of free decision, and he, from his free choice, did not want to give his signature to the oath. But, he was quick to add, if any of the officers present was prepared to give him a formal order to sign the oath, he would of course be prepared to do so. The perplexed officers explained to him that because the oath depended upon his free decision (an oath obtained by force is valueless), they could not give him such an order, but that, on the other hand, if he still refused to give his signature, he would be prosecuted for refusing to do his duty and condemned to prison. Needless to say, this is exactly what happened; but before going to prison, the student did succeed in obtaining from the military court of law the paradoxical decision, a formal document ordering him to sign a free oath.

Slavoj Zizek, the political philosopher who relates this second tale of a call, a refusal to respond, and a powerful punishment, draws an important conclusion that applies equally to young Yugoslavs and old Israelites. "In the subject's relationship to the community to which he belongs, there is always such a paradoxical point of *choix forcé*—at this point, the community is saying to the subject: you have the freedom to choose, but on the condition that you choose the right thing . . . the subject must freely choose the community to which he already belongs, independent of his choice—*he must choose what is already given to him.*"[32]

There is much more that can be said about this fundamental paradox: the most important choices political subjects make—"with whom will I belong?" or "who is my sovereign?"—are in fact choices rarely available to actual human beings. Isaiah's God reminded the Israelites of this lack of choice no less than five times in the space of one chapter: "I am the Lord, and there is none else" (Isaiah 45:5, 6, 14, 18, 21). Early modern political theorists attempted to resolve the dilemma by positing a binding primal choice taking place in a distant (one should say mythical) state of nature. Modern (and postmodern) psychoanalysts place the primal "choice" in the realm of the "atemporal unconscious." In all of these accounts, actual conscious human subjects do not choose; they are chosen outside of time and outside of human agency.[33]

Despite this illogical, ahistorical kernel at the heart of belonging and identification there is an identifiable process by which actual human beings become incorporated into political communities. In general, that process occurs according to a template in which the call (of the sovereign) and the response (of the subject) are embodied together in a covenant (of ideology). This is a mutually constitutive process; it establishes the legitimacy and power of the sovereign, the identity of the subject, and the content of the ideology that mediates the relationship between sovereign and subject.

The notion that individuals become *subjects* with identities, duties, loyalties, and a defined place in the established order as the result of being "called" by a superior power through the medium of ideology is not new, as the passage from Isaiah suggests.[34] Nor is the idea that identities are formed through unequal dialogue between sovereign and subject new to Russian historians. Indeed, one of the more significant developments in recent Russian historiography has been precisely on this theme.[35] It is worth reiterating, however, that the response, though weaker than the call, is equally necessary for constituting the covenant. Powerful gods and states cannot rule without it. If it were not necessary, why would an almighty God plead with the Israelites to "put me in remembrance?" Why would the Yugoslav state insist that soldiers sign a book declaring that they had voiced the oath?

People like the principled Yugoslav conscript who refuse the call of the needy behemoth that appeals to them are always in a small minority. Most respond within the framework of the ideology through which they are called. Each specific historical ideology is built through this continuing interaction. The content of the ideology changes over time as both subjects and sovereigns misrepresent, manipulate, and misrecognize the signals that are exchanged. This change may be small or large, slow or fast, but the fact that ideology is interactive means that it is a dynamic and vital historical force.

In short, ideology is the covenant between sovereign and subjects regarding the way that power will be organized, the way that reality will be publicly understood, the way that events will become imbued with meaning, and the way that individuals will be able to find their place in the world. This understanding of ideology as living, changing, and participatory is quite different from the understanding most Russian historians exhibit when using the term. For too long, ideology has been a term of opprobrium, designating either a systematic and explicit set of ideas about society and the world found in one or more authoritative sources, or a system of "false consciousness" that hides the truth of "real" social relations. Instead, we would do better to understand ideology as a support for reality that structures rather than masks social and political relations.[36] Ideology enables subjects and sovereigns to speak and behave in a way that masks not material conflict but rather the gaps in the psychological and social fabric of individuals and communities. It produces order and meaning in a chaotic and humbling world.

This ideological function is never fully successful, and it often fails quite spectacularly. Isaiah's Israelites and the Yugoslav conscript are cases in point. They did not choose who called them or the nature of the call, but they could and did refuse to heed the call. The covenant of ideology is always vulnerable to this refusal to engage it, and in instances of refusal sovereign and subject frequently collide. This collision, like the relationship within the covenant itself, is never a match between equals. But the dependence of sovereigns upon ideology does in fact give power even to the powerless—the power to refuse the terms of the ideological contract and to suffer the consequences.[37]

In the chapters that follow, I provide a detailed account of a specific historical iteration of this dialogue of ideology between subject and sovereign. Through an examination of one of the most comprehensive and important ways that the sovereign calls its subjects, military conscription, I intend to flesh out the ways that a "modern" national ideology functioned in the first quarter of Russia's twentieth century. The lack of a hegemonic ideology of any sort in the time period under discussion makes this task more complex. As we will see over the course of the book, competing ideologies functioned throughout the period. This multiplicity of political ideologies was confusing for contemporaries, and it confuses current historians no less. But it also provided a context for complex interrelations between ideas and practices and no small degree of creative hybridization.

The Nation

I approach the question of the nation with this more general understanding of ideology and subjectivity in mind. The nation, in this book, is taken to be a type of ideology rather than a state of consciousness or a social collectivity. As Rogers Brubaker puts it, nationalism "is produced—or better, it is induced—by *political fields* of particular kinds. Its dynamics are governed by the properties of political fields, not by the properties of collectivities."[38]

The nation is indeed a political field of a particular kind, but one that has proven remarkably resistant to classification. Given the multiplicity of scholarly definitions already present in the literature, I hesitate to attempt any specific, concise, and universally applicable definition of the nation. Indeed, the description of ideology formation offered above gives good reason to doubt that any precise definition will ever work. With each separate sovereign and each set of subjects actively and continuously engaged in shaping specific ideologies, no two national ideologies can ever be the same.

Still, even when recognizing this diversity, we must also realize that some ideologies share important commonalities across time and space. Among the features that national ideologies share are the notions that central "national" institutions ought to supersede local power structures, that no members of the nation should possess special rights and privileges, and that a historical, territorialized "people" is the sovereign, legitimizing political force in the country. Finally, the nation incorporates the idea that citizens must be political actors.

This is a broad definition, no doubt too broad for some readers, but I make no excuses for my rather ecumenical approach to the literature on nations and nationalism. Various readers of this manuscript have pointed out parallels between my work and that of other scholars. Recent works by such writers as Brubaker, Benedict Anderson, and Eugen Weber are most frequently mentioned, but others have cited the work of "classic" scholars of the nation like Hans Kohn and Carleton Hayes.[39] These parallels are visible in part because I have been influenced in my own thinking about the question of the nation by all of these writers (and many more), but also in part because there is significantly more agreement between them than disagreement. The works, say, of Hayes and Anderson, sixty years apart, are by no means wholly incompatible. Substantive debates about their relatively minor differences have a place, but that place is not here. I will highlight differences within this literature and assert my place within it only when it seems useful and productive within the context of the book as a whole.

One important difference that should be mentioned at the outset is my disagreement with the many influential scholars who sharply differentiate between "good" civic nations and "bad" ethnic or racial ones.[40] I believe that this distinction between civic and ethnic nationalism often conceals as much as it reveals. In some cases, the attempt to posit a "good" civic nationalism is used to salvage some fundamental liberal tenets from the devastating nationalist outcomes of the twentieth century. In this reading, the horrors of the two world wars, of repeated episodes of mass murder, and of nativist policies of discrimination, exclusion, and persecution are fundamentally the result of the perversion of the national ideal caused by the cancers of racism, ignorance, and "backwardness." The "true" national form, on the other hand, is liberating. It has promised equality, has effected the devolution of sovereignty from the elite to the masses, has helped destroy imperialism and great-power chauvinism, has built social solidarity, and generally has operated as the vehicle through which the highest ideals of humanity were realized.[41]

The national form I describe here, however, complicates this vision. The particular ideology promoted and sustained by Russian state and military intellectuals was closer to a "civic" than an "ethnic" pole on the national register, but it still enabled a great deal of violence, discrimination, impoverishment, and inhumanity. One might be tempted to explain this phenomenon of a "good" civic nation gone bad in terms of Russian peculiarities, as another example of a liberal western idea corrupted by Russian hands or by tragic Russian circumstances. There is some plausibility to the argument for Russian particularism. That it was military men who were most successful in promoting nationalism rather than liberal intellectuals certainly had an impact on the historical outcome of the project. In the same vein, it is difficult to deny that Russia's strategic situation complicated the development of civic ideals to a degree unthinkable for states like Great Britain or the United States. Constantly threatened by powerful neighbors and lacking any natural barriers to invasion, Russian rulers always concerned themselves obsessively with security issues. Finally, Russia lacked what Jürgen Habermas calls "constitutional patriotism," that commitment to certain codified principles and procedures of political life that checks the tendency to excess on the part of political leaders and gives liberal content to many nations near the "civic" pole.[42]

Even given these caveats, however, there is too much consonance between Russia's experience and that of other nations to ignore. This book will outline those areas of commonality in detail. We will see that Russians used the same language of duty, self-sacrifice, and masculine vigor when articulating the proper relationship between individual and community that "civic" and "ethnic" nationalists elsewhere did. We will see that the problem of ethnic diversity faced by nation-builders in an age of scientific racism was one faced by nations as far removed from the Russian experience as the United States.[43] We will see appeals from the state to defend the motherland in terms both understandable and unremarkable across Europe and North America at the time. We will see responses by common Russians that closely approximate those by citizens of countries far to their west.

Classifying this dynamic and this dialogue as national is important not only because it helps us understand nations better but also because it helps us understand twentieth-century Russia better. Although I hope that this book will pose several substantive challenges to the field of Russian history, I want to lay particular stress on two of these challenges at the outset. First, I hope that the evidence presented here will show that rural Russians were not uniformly illiterate, ignorant, and apolitical peasants. To the contrary, there were significant parts of village society in early twentieth-century Russia that were literate, aware, and engaged in the major political issues of the day. On the eve of World War I, at least two-thirds of each incoming class of recruits could read at least a little.[44] The enormous volume of correspondence to and from the village during the Great War showed both that rural Russians could read and write and that they were willing to weigh in on issues of public policy.[45] Recent research has already put in doubt the powerful paradigm of the insulated, parochial, and apolitical Russian peasant held by historians with such otherwise different views as Richard Pipes and Moshe Lewin. Andrew Verner, for instance, has shown that rural Russians were quite knowledgeable about national events by the turn of the century and used the 1905 Revolution as a vehicle for a halting engagement with national politics.[46] I will demonstrate that these Russians fully came into their own as political actors over the course of the war years (1914–1921).

Second, I hope to emphasize the importance of total war for the development of twentieth-century Russia. In particular, I make the argument here that the period of total war proved transformative for the tsarist regime and formative for the Soviet one. It was war that occasioned the nationalizing moment, and it did so in a variety of ways. As we delve into ethnic politics, economic transformation, and public mobilization, however, we should never forget that war is fundamentally about violence, and this fact must be remembered if we are to come to any decent understanding of the changes it brings about.[47] There are many ways to examine the connection between the nationalizing moment and the murderous moment. We will start with a study of the conscription process itself.

CHAPTER ONE

Forming the National Compact

Military conscription, wherever it is introduced, is an institution buzzing with political energy. As the set of policies and practices that regulates the intersection between the civilian and military realms, it is fertile ground both for "high" bureaucratic politics and for the "low" personal politics of individuals seeking to gain some measure of influence in their dealings with state and local communities. This chapter will be concerned with the ways that the high and low politics of conscription worked in Russia in the first quarter of the twentieth century. This is an important story, one told far too infrequently in studies of the military and the nation. One often encounters the theory that mass armies entail mass political participation, but even when this connection is explored as a political project in its own right, the driving forces for change are frequently limited to elite perceptions of politics, society, or external threats.[1] This awakening to the political implications of modern mass armies among an important subset of the Russian political elite did indeed prove extremely important. Using staff academies as organizational bases and an expertise in matters of war as a basis for authoritative claims, military intellectuals became a coherent and influential political pressure group.

But they were not the only such group. The space for mass participation that opened up in the realm of military service in the waning years of the tsarist regime was filled by regular Russians too. At first, lacking a solid institutional base and effective levers of political influence, enlisted men and their families had relatively little impact. Over the course of the long war years of 1914–1921, however, the tactics used by regular soldiers and their families became more and more important. As elites struggled to mobilize millions of men and to prevent their desertion, the demands of soldiers to receive political rights in exchange for the "sacred" duty they were fulfilling in uniform had ever greater influence. The result was a real transformation of political life. By the end of the Civil War in 1921, the lines between high and low politics and between civilian and military spheres had become blurred.

Those lines were significantly more clear in the period before the Great War. The universal service law of 1874 had established a schizophrenic system, setting up dual power between the military and civilian bureaucracies at all levels of conscription administration. Contrary to later Bolshevik (and liberal) rhetoric, which lumped them both together in the "reactionary" camp, the officials of the War Ministry and the Ministry of Internal Affairs (MVD) were constantly at odds with one another. Military men despised the fact that the MVD relied on them for internal pacification, and the two institutions held quite different ideas of the way society and politics should be structured.[2]

Nevertheless, the two feuding partners had to interact on a continuous basis in order to conduct the yearly draft. They met at the central level through constant communication between the two ministries involved and at the local level in district and provincial draft boards. Local draft boards were the linchpin of the conscription system, as all concerned parties knew. Civilian officials dominated, occupying four of the five positions on each of these boards, and they used this power to ensure that the wide range of exemptions and deferrals offered under the law was granted. As a result, military officials seeking strong men for the army felt constantly embattled and suspected that draft boards were prone to grant illegal exemptions to needy families, to paying customers, and to their own friends.[3]

Even legal exemptions proved to be a point of contestation and frustration. In principle, the 1874 law had been passed in order to institute "universal" conscription. In practice, budgetary concerns meant that only about 30 percent of every yearly draft cadre would be enlisted into the army. There were three potential ways to determine which 30 percent would go into the army. Army men thought that battle considerations should take priority. Focusing on the health and strength of the young recruits would result in the medical exam being the primary site of selection. Civilian officials wanted social considerations to take pride of place, so that the elite could get exemptions or deferrals for education and labor-poor families could keep healthy workers on the farm. The third possibility, the one most in the spirit of universality, would have been to randomly choose recruits on the basis of a draft lottery. In the spirit of compromise, the 1874 law incorporated all three methods, which left ample room for political jockeying by interested parties. In the end, however, the law served civilian interests first.[4]

Civilian interests came first because civilian exemptions were granted first. Millions of young men were not required to show up at the draft office. Many ethnic groups, notably the Kirgiz of Central Asia, were exempt from the draft and were not required even to register with local draft boards. Other groups, mostly in the Caucasus and Finland, were exempt in return for the payment of a special military tax. Even after draft lists were drawn up, conscripts were eligible to receive educational, occupational, and family deferrals or exemptions. Students, for instance, could defer their service for a period of three to nine years and then had the right to serve abbreviated tours of duty as short as three months. Educated society had other breaks in the conscription process by occupying many of the positions in professions that were exempted entirely from the draft. Religious officials of all types were not required to serve in the armed forces, nor were a very wide range of academics, professors, and other high-ranking educational professionals. Schoolteachers were enrolled in the reserves but were not required to serve on active duty so long as they retained their jobs.

Finally, a wide range of exemptions were given to men whose family situation made military service especially burdensome. Three family categories existed prior to 1912. Only sons and young men who were the sole support for orphans constituted the first category. The second category was composed of able-bodied "only" sons in a family with an able-bodied father but brothers younger than eighteen years old. The third category consisted of men whose closest sibling was on active duty or who had died in the service.

These categories structured draft day procedure. All men required to appear at the induction point drew lots, but medical exams started (according to lot number) within the group of men who had no entitlements. Only after all men within a certain family entitlement group had been examined would men from the next group be subject to enlistment. Every young man declared healthy by the board and its doctors would be enrolled until the district's quota was met, at which point selection would stop. Even before the significant changes that occurred after the 1912 reform, which made men with family entitlements virtually immune from conscription, a gentile's chance of being drafted dropped precipitously from 52 percent for men with no entitlements, to 36 percent for men with a third-category entitlement, to 9 percent for men with a second-category, to zero percent for a man with a first-category exemption. Chances of being drafted were higher in all categories for Jews.[5] Thus, though the lottery served as the symbolic centerpiece of draft day and great effort was expended to prevent cheating and corruption in the drawing itself, the random and "universal" aspect of the process was of only limited importance.

The peculiarities of "universal" conscription within the old tsarist system also helped to structure an emerging realm of "low" politics surrounding the draft. The first reason that conscription policy became a vibrant realm of political action at the lowest level was ideological. The 1874 law had declared that the fundamental desire of the state was to have an army staffed on the basis of a community of civic equals but had then instituted a system in which certain social groups received disproportionate benefits. This internal contradiction was an irritation not only to military planners but to conscripts as well. Regular Russians had been irritated by state policy before, but they were actually granted a vehicle for expressing dissatisfaction in 1874, if only in an oblique way. The law made provisions for commoners to inform the state of violations of conscription law, and Russians made ample use of this invitation not only to target individuals in their community but also to express their vision of the proper bases of military service and civic duty.

One of the most important themes of the letters addressed to the state regarding conscription was fairness. Citizens proved ready and willing to blow the whistle on fellow citizens who were trying to get out of military service, a fact confirmed by the numerous denunciations relating to military service still preserved in military archives.[6] When common Russians did denounce their neighbors, they almost invariably did so using the language of duty and state interest. In 1910, for instance, a peasant named Anton Orliuk concluded his denunciation of the local postman for having dodged the draft in the following way: "In the interests of the state, I consider it my duty to inform Your Excellency about these facts and request an investigation of them, a verification of his health, and an accounting of guilty persons before the law."[7] Orliuk almost certainly had a personal bone to pick with the postman (he had been told of the draft dodging in a private conversation three years earlier), but in order to effectively appeal to the state, he had to use the language of equality and state interests. He thereby entered into the ideological realm established by the 1874 decree, using it and confirming it by doing so.

The second reason the draft became an active realm of political contestation was because the byzantine system of deferrals, entitlements, and exemptions opened the door wide for regular Russians to practice "low" politics at the individual level by manipulating the exemption and entitlement procedures. At each of the moments of filtration and documentation, from registration until induction, there was an opportunity for clever, connected, or simply contrary young men to avoid serving in the military. Unfortunately, it is impossible to say with any precision how extensive these practices of draft evasion were, since the most effective methods were designed to leave no imprint upon the record-keepers of the state.

There are, however, files on the conscripts who failed in their attempts to make a clean getaway, scattered memoirs of men who attempted evasion, and figures for the ones who did not bother to conceal their attempts to resist the state's call. These records, though incomplete, are sufficient enough to show the wide range of evasion techniques practiced by Russians when faced with the prospect of military service. For those with an education or wealth, obtaining an exemption from the draft was not particularly difficult. Political lobbying efforts had succeeded in creating a whole set of exempt occupations that attracted a great many young men to professions they otherwise would not have pursued, and state officials consciously used draft exemptions as incentives to attract entrants into understaffed professions.[8] If it proved impossible to get a legal exemption, it was not much more difficult for those with deep pockets to bribe officials in the local military commissariat to grant an undeserved entitlement. Throughout the period, corrupt officials and clerical workers could and did run businesses on the side that provided conscripts with forged documents.[9] These tactics were too expensive for most conscripts. It was far cheaper simply not to show up for the draft when called. This option brought with it the risk of arrest and imprisonment, but it remained popular nonetheless. In 1913, 144,271 registered men failed to appear, about 9.4 percent of the total draft pool. Of these men, only 16,994 were later excused for having a valid reason.[10]

The main reason, however, that most young men who wanted to evade did not take these early routes is that the easiest, cheapest, and hardest-to-detect method came a bit later, during the medical exam. Soldiers had three chances to fail their medical exams. They were examined on draft day, on induction day, and upon arrival to their unit, and if at first they did not fail, they could try and try again. Most of those seeking to fail their exams did so at the first opportunity. To take 1909 as an example, only 58 percent of the draftees were unanimously declared fit for line service by their local draft boards during their first medical exam. The other 42 percent were either placed in noncombat positions, exempted, reexamined by the provincial board, or given yearlong deferrals to get healthier. After the conscription reform in 1912 (on which more below), when the military was able to be more picky about the health of its soldiers, the percentage of men declared fit plummeted to 44.9 percent. By the eve of World War I, only a bit more than half of the men on draft lists were taking physical exams, and less than half of those that did were passing them.

There were many reasons why men failed their exams, some having to do with military draft board members insistent on strong soldiers and some having to do with serious natural health defects. But one reason for the high rate of medical exam failure was the varied and ingenious attempts of Russian conscripts to damage themselves. One of the traditional methods of Russian peasants in the nineteenth century had been self-mutilation, often done by cutting off the trigger finger. That method seems to have been used very rarely by soldiers in the twentieth century. Judging by the paltry number of men arrested as self-mutilators, conscripts had moved on to more sophisticated methods. Again, the low rate of discovery makes it impossible to know the extent and practices of self-mutilation, but one wave in Nizhegorod province was marked by men pouring caustic fluids into their eyes or ears in order to fail their hearing or vision exams, a fact that gives reason to note the generally high rates of medical rejection for eye and ear disabilities during medical exams in the late imperial period.[11] Far the most common reason for failing a medical exam was simply "weakness," a condition that, though hard to fake, had the advantage of being temporary. Inducing illness, self-starvation, and other methods to weaken oneself prior to a medical exam were hard to detect. As the chief of the Mobilization Department admitted in 1910, it was "very difficult to distinguish between the really weak by nature and the ones that intentionally exhausted themselves."[12]

The variations on the theme of failing health exams showed a great deal of creativity. In one case, a father hid his son's birth records and took him to the local office to have his age determined. They declared him older than he actually was, and it was estimated at his medical exam a few months later that he was not as developed as he needed to be. He received two deferments and was placed in the second-tier militia before his real birth records were uncovered and the game was up. Others appeared and passed their draft medical exam but sent a cripple to go to their unit for them. When the cripple was rejected, the healthy conscript then received a certificate of exemption. Still others hired professional "fixers" to get them health deferrals or exemptions by damaging their health in covert ways. These men worked efficiently, sometimes even ruthlessly, and were difficult to bring down unless denounced.[13]

The presence of these low-level fixers and the interest and involvement of high-ranking state officials indicate that the draft was important at all levels of the social and state hierarchy. At the top, there were intense struggles to see whether civilian or military institutions should run the draft and determine the social and military priorities for selecting a minority of young men to serve in the army. At the bottom was a political struggle in which the stakes were at least as high, the struggle to determine which young men would leave their villages and towns for a few years or forever. This lower-level struggle, like the upper-level struggle, was articulated in the language of state interest, civic equality, and simple justice, as Orliuk's denunciation shows. But there was a big difference. In central bureaucracies numbers reigned, while the struggles at the local level involved men with first names, families, farms, and sweethearts. It would take some time before central politicians came to terms with the fact that there were multiple levels of conscription politics and that those levels worked in different ways. That process would start in earnest in response to the massive military, social, and political catastrophe of 1905.

Military Reform in the Wake of Disaster, 1905–1914

The Russo-Japanese War had not yet ended when the cycle of recriminations over who or what was to blame began. Three days before the Portsmouth Treaty was signed, the Mobilization Department lashed out at critics who blamed the army command for losing the war to Japan. The real culprit of the war was not the beleaguered military, it claimed. Instead, the blame rested with civilian officials who had failed to prepare young Russian men physically and mentally for the war and who had resisted the army's desire to build a stronger and broader recruit base. The military service law, they argued, was constructed on "peacetime principles," and as a result the "interests of the armed forces" had suffered.[14]

In order to prevent a repeat of the Manchurian debacle, the Mobilization Department recommended sweeping changes to the military service code to strengthen the influence of military men and the military ethic at every step of the conscription process. It was the start of a period of military reform that would dominate high military politics until the outbreak of World War I. The loss to the Japanese had caused many young officers to engage in a period of fruitful self-reflection, and the result was a spirited debate about the future of the Russian army in which the "necessity for reorganization of the army was talked about, written about, shouted about."[15] Many public-spirited politicians who rose to prominence in the brief constitutional period welcomed this debate and actively participated in it.

In the specific context of the military service code, military reformers targeted the great number of social exemptions available to conscripts under the 1874 law, which made the physical fitness of young men a secondary consideration. Reformers were quick to blame the poor physical quality of their soldiers for the loss in the Russo-Japanese War. Worse, in the postwar period, the level of fitness and health among soldiers appeared to be dropping rather than improving.[16] This manifested itself not only in a qualitative decline of the abilities of soldiers, but a quantitative one too. Given that the draft was a one-shot system, any man who was inducted into the army and subsequently died or became so sick that he had to be released was not replaced by a new conscript. As a result military units were chronically under strength. In 1908, over 38,000 men were sent home from their units for health reasons, or a total of 9.2 percent of the contingent of new soldiers.[17]

The second major deficiency revealed by the Russo-Japanese War was the poor quality of Russia's reserve officers. Reports of battle commanders after the war criticized the reserve officers for being morally suspect and technically incompetent. Worse, many reserve officers never even made it to the battlefield, because the rate of officer evasion was disconcertingly high. In the Moscow military district alone, 27 percent of the reserve officer corps failed to appear during mobilization, of which only about half had legitimate excuses.[18] Military reformers concluded that the current system of allowing educated men to go into the officer reserves with little or no military experience, and frequently with a hostile attitude to the army, was not working. Martynov's lament about the military weakness of educated Russia now had statistical support.

During a period in which the army was continuously trying to get its budget raised in order to increase the number of men under arms, and was also working on its officers to provide moral education for young recruits, these problems were embarrassing and unacceptable. Moreover, they were easily blamed on the deficiencies of the 1874 code, which had given such generous entitlements both to labor-poor families and to the educated elite, as well as a final say in the selection of soldiers to civilian officials. In 1908, after a barrage of complaints from throughout the military system about these and other problems, Nicholas II authorized the formation of a special commission to do something about the military service law.[19] Aleksandr Lukomskii, the head of the Mobilization Department, chaired this new commission, which worked virtually up to the eve of World War I.

The military initiative was fairly radical. It attacked the status quo preferred by conservatives in the MVD and forwarded a consistent national line. The Mobilization Department proposed a plan to reform family entitlements, educational and property entitlements, the reserve officer volunteer system, the composition of draft boards, the process by which draft quotas were assigned, the time frame of the draft, and the process by which conscripts were assigned to their units after they were inducted.[20] The family entitlement proposal put forth by Lukomskii to the commission recommended a narrowing of the pool of first-category entitlements, limiting it to men who were the sole working member in a family, and condensing the other entitlements into a single second category.[21] Additional reforms were similarly far-reaching. The General Staff now wanted volunteer reserve officer candidates to serve for eighteen months and teachers to lose their right to immediate enlistment into the reserves, asking instead that they serve two years in the active forces. It also sought to overturn the civilian dominance of local draft boards, asking for an increase in the number of military doctors on those boards, for additional military members to be added to the board, and for the district military commander to be named deputy chair of the board, with the right to veto a draft board's decision to induct a soldier. In addition, the General Staff hoped to change the process of the draft itself. Rather than assign each draft area a fixed number of recruits, it wanted to predetermine the percentage of each entitlement category to be drafted based on statewide averages of physical fitness and to create a system by which understaffing could be eliminated through a supplemental February draft.[22]

Conservative officials in the MVD opposed nearly every one of the War Ministry's nationalizing recommendations. The proposed changes to the family entitlements prompted the MVD representatives in the Lukomskii Commission to "categorically declare" that they would not countenance a complete overhaul of the entitlement system, because "the population has gotten used to the existing structure of entitlements . . . and any sharp alteration, especially a curtailing, of them may on the one hand banefully affect the well-being of the population, and on the other hand elicit serious unhappiness in it." At most, the MVD was willing to accept "some partial adjustments and curtailments." In the face of this opposition, the Mobilization Department backed down, with Lukomskii glumly noting that though his plan was better both for the populace and the army, "purely practical considerations" of political expediency made compromise the wiser choice.[23]

The battle over educational privileges was just as sharp, with nearly every civilian ministry protesting the suggested changes. The Ministry of Justice, the Holy Synod, and the Ministry of Enlightenment all pleaded with the MVD to protect their interests, and the minister of internal affairs, Petr Stolypin, tried to do so. Stolypin found unpersuasive the military's argument that "teachers should not be freed from military service but should be required to pass through the ranks in order to morally train the adolescent generation." He countered that the difficulties faced by educational organs in finding qualified teachers were greater than the military's difficulty in finding reserve officers.[24]

The only point that gave Stolypin pause was the army's argument that the need to have a "militarization of our schools" made a draft of teachers necessary. Here too Stolypin had an answer, claiming that drafting teachers would in fact demilitarize schools. Since the draft exemption was one of the strongest incentives for attracting male teachers, eliminating the exemption would further increase the percentage of women in the profession. This, in turn, would be catastrophic since women were "hopeless from the point of view of instilling a military spirit and military discipline into students."[25] Stolypin left the door open for compromise, though, noting that both the Ministry of Enlightenment and the Holy Synod were prepared to "sacrifice their own interests" for the sake of the army if it were clearly shown that it would result in a better military system. That compromise eventually came about, with an increase in the time that officer volunteers had to spend in the ranks and the lifting of the teacher exemption over the course of a five-year transitional period.

Compromise was also reached in the other aspects of the reform. The military was not able to get additional military doctors on draft boards, but it did gain an extra representative on those boards. More importantly, the district commander acquired veto rights over inducted soldiers. Prior to 1912, a majority ruled, but after the reform either military man on the board had the right to demand a reexamination by the provincial board, thus giving the military another chance to keep weak men out of the army.

The army also proved successful in pushing through a statewide draft quota to replace the previous system of district quotas. This turned out to be the most controversial provision in the reform bill, not only in the Lukomskii Commission and the State Council, but also in the debates on the Duma floor. Opponents argued that introducing a statewide assessment and a supplemental draft would lead to a situation in which regions with higher draft participation and better physical fitness profiles would bear a greater burden than would those areas where such levels were lower. Soldiers had to feel that the process was fair, not that they were drafted because "somewhere, in another place, someone didn't show up." Otherwise, the War Ministry would be guilty of reintroducing the old practice of *"krugovaia poruka"* (mutual responsibility) into dealings between the state and its citizens.[26] The charge of reintroducing *krugovaia poruka* was spurious. What had happened was not the introduction of *poruka* (responsibility for another), but the expansion of the *krug* (circle). When draft quotas were assigned by district, a slot vacated by a draft evader was filled by someone from his own district. Now, that slot would likely be filled from a different district in the supplemental draft. The shift to the statewide assessment was therefore a common nation-building move that reduced still further the relevancy of the local community to the conscription process.

The problem lay in the envisioning of that nation, since most critics were not talking about minor variations in evasion rates between Tula and Moscow provinces, but about discrepancies between Jewish and Russian evasion rates. As will be seen in chapter 3, excluding Jews from the national *krug* was part of another military project, so the War Ministry jumped at the chance to discriminate against Jewish subjects. The empirewide assessment was implemented, but Jews were assessed and drafted as a separate body. Two *krugs* were created out of the hundreds that had existed prior to the 1912 reform.[27]

The political pattern was thus standard throughout the reform process. The army would forward a broad, ambitious national project, which the Ministry of Internal Affairs would attack, citing reasons of tradition and the desire to maintain the status quo. After considerable haggling, the two sides would come to a compromise. The army had the momentum and was able to drive policy consistently closer to its own national ideal, but its victory was far from complete. Nicholas was obviously more comfortable with the conservative political position maintained by the MVD, one that stressed the importance of social position, of local community, and of the traditional hierarchy of power, but he was also nervous about completely thwarting the army's desires. The result was a wavering and often self-contradictory policy.

The 1912 conscription bill was nevertheless a fairly big success for military reformers, who got what they thought they needed in the short term and were optimistic about getting yet more in the near future. The new reforms promised to rapidly increase the physical quality of recruits (and eventually reservists as well), to bring the divided country closer together by forcing the educated elite to serve with peasants and workers, to establish a statewide draft system, and to reduce dramatically the number of each cohort that received an "unconditional" first-category draft exemption.

The points they had compromised on seemed less significant. They had deferred the question of changing the status of certain ethnicities in order to get their primary goals achieved, but the Lukomskii Commission kept working on possible changes to the ethnic exemption provisions. They failed to do away entirely with the family entitlement system, leaving a still large number of recruits not only untrained, but completely convinced that they would never be called up. Finally, though they had made progress, the structures that would sustain massive and lengthy mobilization were not yet in place. They had really only made the adjustments necessary to conduct a short war. That the upcoming war would be short and would come in the near future was the general consensus in Petersburg military circles, so there was every reason to be pleased with the bill that had just passed.[28] Unfortunately, the war lasted far longer than expected. One by one, the problems that had been deferred in 1909–1912: an emergency reserve force that believed itself exempt from military service, a lack of cohesion amongst different sectors of the populace, and a vast pool of unregistered and unwilling recruits of "backward" ethnicities returned to haunt the army and the state.

World War I

The war actually started quite well from the perspective of mobilization officials. Despite never having conducted a general mobilization under the Miliutin system, the best estimate is that about 3,915,000 men were mobilized nearly on schedule.[29] The reforms within the military over the past ten years had clearly borne fruit, and the experience was far more positive than the botched partial mobilizations of men during the Russo-Japanese War. Careful observers would have noticed, however, that success in the administrative realm did not correspond to success in understanding the processes of low politics that became evident in the very first days of the mobilization.

The realm of low politics surrounding mobilization was far more complicated.[30] There were, in fact, many displays of patriotism offered by Russians up and down the social ladder during this period. Many top officials were present at the impressive patriotic demonstration by about a quarter of a million people on Palace Square in St. Petersburg, and this rally was replicated in numerous provincial towns across Russia. Patriots were so excited they began to believe that most Russians supported the war, but in this belief they were, in the main, mistaken: the rallies supported Russian soldiers, not the war. Though the rallies for the departure of troops to the front were marked by a desperate good cheer, the mood in most regions in the preceding days was rather more somber. Few harbored illusions that they would gain any particular benefit from a military victory. War had always meant sacrifice and loss, and not many regular Russians believed that this one would turn out any differently. Small signs of protest were visible in places. In Riga, alongside the portraits of the tsar, workers and reservists flew banners proclaiming "Down with the war!" Less showy resistance began in earnest as well. During the first week of mobilization at one district office, over 200 men went absent without leave out of the approximately 2000 who had appeared.[31]

Large signs of protest were also evident, most impressively in the wave of mobilization riots that washed across Russia in July and August 1914. For reasons that remain unclear, these riots have consistently been ignored or downplayed by later historians, despite the fact that the major riots were mentioned in readily accessible accounts by military men.[32] One reason, perhaps, is that many contemporaries were prone to claim that the uprisings were the result of alcohol, not dissatisfaction, since one of the common activities of rioters was to break open the closed liquor stores and loot them. It stood to reason for some officials, therefore, that "liquor was the source of all misfortune."[33]

The rampages for liquor were predictable. Induction into the active forces had long been an occasion for drunkenness on the part of young Russian men. Some villages even upheld a tradition of paying for the liquor for the young men to consume.[34] Needless to say, this ritual was frowned upon by military officials seeking a quick and efficient mobilization, and they successfully argued that liquor sales should be cut off during the mobilization period. The obvious solution from the perspective of reservists was simply to break open the closed stores, and in locations where local officials failed to provide police protection for the stores, it was a solution that was carried out.[35]

But the lack of liquor, and the effects of its consumption after the stores were looted, cannot be taken as the sole explanation for these widespread riots. In Ekaterinoslav, the riot was not sparked by a run on the liquor store, but by the unfurling of a patriotic flag and an attempt to start a pro-war demonstration. In Belebeevskii district of Ufa province, the riots began with a looting of bread stores. In the city of Birsk, liquor played no part in the riot. Reservists "dispersed the police and destroyed the induction center, thanks to which the work of medical examination and forming units to send to the front had to stop."[36] In Barnaul, rioters seized control of the city for a time, torching houses, stores, and a liquor warehouse, and prompting a full-scale flight by local residents. More than 100 people would die in battles between reservists and police before order was restored.[37]

These rioters were not simply rowdy drunkards. Instead, many were so serious that they were willing to die even before the liquor started flowing. The mobilization riots should therefore be understood as complex phenomena that encompassed a multitude of sins. Some men attacked the police, others stole bread, others got drunk, and many took part in all of the above. Just as importantly, many reservists showed displeasure with the war and did what they could to derail the process of being sent to the front. The events of 1914, patriotic rallies and massive riots alike, showed the capacity and willingness of regular Russians to engage with big political issues regarding the war. "Low" politicians had emerged as a force to be reckoned with, but "high" politicians did not reckon with them until it was too late.

In the meantime, maintaining a constant flow of men into the army to replace casualties proved to be a task that stretched the resources and capabilities of the Russian General Staff. The initially promising offensives into East Prussia and Galicia in 1914 had soured rather quickly, and the amount of Russian casualties (more than 1.4 million by 1 February 1915) surprised even the men whose job it was to consider worst-case scenarios. A serious manpower crisis emerged in late 1914, not in late 1916, as most contemporaries and later scholars believed.[38] The Mobilization Department came to the conclusion that Russia would soon run out of men. New resources had to be located. The first inclination was to conduct a reexamination of men medically exempted, but this pool was not large enough. Officials then turned reluctantly to the idea of drafting forthcoming cadres of soldiers before their time, despite their belief that younger men were likely to be physically immature and despite the fact that most were not yet registered on the draft rolls.[39]

By early 1915, though, all other choices facing planners were worse. Either they had to draft the older contingents of first-tier militia reservists, putting men they believed to be morally and physically weak into the army, or they had to start drafting the only sons in the second-tier militia, a move that everyone knew would cause dissatisfaction. So the drafts of youngsters were declared. Three new age groups were called up by early August 1915, effectively lowering the draft age by two years to nineteen, where it stayed until the end of the war.

Even these fresh young men were not enough, for as bad as 1914 had been in terms of human losses, 1915 was even worse. As elsewhere in

World War I, the basic military tactic was to bash away endlessly at enemy trenches with artillery fire until an infantry attack could proceed. The stalemate produced by this tactic in France resulted from the fact that enough soldiers could survive the bombardment in their maze of deep trenches to man machine guns during the infantry charge and that a rough equivalence in artillery prevented either side from establishing dominance. Different conditions existed in eastern Europe. In early 1915, the Russian army was at a marked disadvantage both in its trenches and in the amount of its shells. The result was unmitigated disaster, as German and Austrian troops broke through first in Galicia, then in Poland, forcing mass death and mass flight. By August, the casualty count had ticked up to over 4 million men captured, killed, or wounded.

General V. A. Sukhomlinov, the head of the War Ministry, took most of the heat for the disaster. He was sacked after one of his subordinates, Colonel Sergei Miasoedov, was convicted of treason and hanged. Sukhomlinov's replacement, A. A. Polivanov, enjoyed popularity among reformist military men and in the Duma, but not with the tsar. The situation at the front was disastrous and promised only to worsen. In one of the darkest moments of the war, Polivanov walked into a meeting of the Council of Ministers on 16 July 1915 and announced with a shaky voice that "the fatherland is in danger." The council sat in an "interminable silence," while Polivanov literally twitched in anguish and anxiety.[40]

It was fortunate for Russia that the man in place to deal with this disaster was the most talented individual to hold the top spot in the military since Dmitrii Miliutin. In a series of bold decisions, Polivanov and other prominent centrists convinced the tsar to rejuvenate the war effort by appealing to broad sectors of the population to get involved not only in the fulfillment of duties but in the decision-making process as well. With the munitions question now in the hands of industrialists, war-industrial committees, and Lukomskii (who had become Polivanov's assistant and the point man regarding supplies), production and distribution improved. The turnaround was dramatic. By 1 January 1917, Russia had not just closed the munitions gap with Germany but had taken the advantage.[41]

The manpower situation proved less tractable to reform, since the army, through its wasteful sacrifice of men in the early months of the war, had used up all the men clearly liable for service according to existing law. The only option was to begin drafting men who had been tacitly promised they would never have to serve. Everyone knew that the popular response to a draft of only sons would be negative. Indeed, top officials had spent much energy in the winter of 1914–1915 putting down rumors that a draft of the second-tier militia was imminent, and the tone of the rumors had left no doubt as to the unhappiness that would be caused by such a draft.[42] Given the unpopularity of the move, Polivanov was fortunate that he had garnered the support and trust of much of the Petersburg and Moscow elite in the prewar period, because in order to change the conscription law he had to get approval both from the Council of Ministers and from the Duma. Getting approval from the first body posed little problem. The ministers knew that radical action had to be taken and trusted Polivanov to chart the correct course.

The Duma was a different matter. The military disaster signaled the end of the temporary truce between the government and the Duma during the first two wartime sittings of the Duma (in July 1914 and January 1915). Liberal newspapers were now publicly deriding Duma members for their previously passive stance, charging that "[t]hough the State Duma has been convened twice since the beginning of the war, it has quite simply neither learned the mood of the country nor understood the nation's activities and ambitions. It has been rhetorical and decorative while the country suffered." Pavel Miliukov, the liberal leader of the Kadet Party, admitted that the people expected Duma members "to brand the culprits for the national catastrophe," and feared that if the Duma remained pliant such anger might be expressed in more damaging ways.[43]

There was little doubt, then, that the military would be in for strident criticism when the minister of war appeared before a closed session of the Duma on 28 July 1915. Polivanov got lectured from both sides of the aisle. A. I. Savenko, a leader of the Nationalist Party who had preached in January that "in time of war there are no parties and no nationalities in Russia, only a single strong, terrible, granite Russian monolith,"[44] now caustically blamed the army and government for their poor leadership. "War is an exam," he fumed, "a great exam, and it must be said that if during this great exam the Russian people and Russian society passed the test of maturity, then the government, and in particular the military administration, has failed."[45] Even right-wing politicians like Savenko were now publicly accusing the military leadership and the tsar's government of splitting the "single Russian monolith." Attacks from the center and the left were even more acidic.[46]

Polivanov refused to reply in detail to the deputies, but he tacitly laid the blame for the disaster on his predecessor by promising a detailed, dispassionate investigation of the events that had led to the current "mess."[47] Polivanov's response was enough to get the Duma's assent to send the bill back to the Military Affairs Committee, where the question was debated once again, but this time with more attention to detail and less to rhetorical flourish. It was in these committee meetings that the full extent of the manpower emergency was made clear. Not only had the number of men killed, wounded, and captured been stunning, but desertion had also become epidemic. The representative of the War Ministry admitted that 500,000 men had deserted in the first year of the war alone.[48] The disaster gave the Duma some leverage in demanding changes, as members raked the military over the coals for failing to keep up with the Germans, not only in shells, but just as importantly in the number of rifles and machine guns.[49]

In demanding a reform of the supply system to Polivanov's ministry, they were preaching to the converted. Indeed, the sharp criticism probably helped Polivanov and reformers within the War Ministry rather than hurt them, as it gave them additional support in their struggle with the tsar and the MVD to mobilize "society" to improve military-industrial efficiency. But the demands of the committee went beyond calls to fix the supply problem. In addition, it asked for an end to exemptions for policemen, for a series of medical reexaminations of men, for shrinking the size of the rear by sending "excess" soldiers in support services to the front lines, and for the draft of ethnic groups previously exempted under the law.[50]

Desperate for men, the army accepted all of these strictures, protesting only the drafting of exempt ethnic groups, which they rightly understood to be too complicated and explosive to deal with in the midst of the war. Five days later, on 19 August, the Duma met in full session to consider the bill, and already the MVD had taken the question of drafting policemen off the table, insisting that a separate bill needed to be vetted and approved. But the other questions remained. Regarding the draft of ethnic groups, A. I. Shingarev, a prominent liberal Kadet and the committee spokesman, rejected the War Ministry's argument that the process would be unpopular and too difficult, saying that "even they [the ethnic groups] themselves cannot reconcile themselves to their exemption. They find it shameful and insulting," before "categorically" demanding the draft of exempted ethnicities.[51] The War Ministry, in the face of these demands, agreed to work for the quickest possible draft of previously exempted groups. After further heated debates about the police exemption (the elimination of which the army supported), the bill was passed.[52] Nicholas approved the measure, and the draft of second-tier militiamen began on 5 September 1915.

Once again, the change to conscription law elicited a reaction from all levels of society. Mass politics was a constant feature of political life during the war, and the response to the draft of the second-tier militia was even more negative than had been anticipated. A flood of letters protesting the removal of the family exemption came into various state and military offices, including a strident letter from workers in the Donbass, who threatened a strike and the declaration of an "internal war" if second-tier militiamen were drafted before policemen.[53] And strikes broke out as a result of the mobilization, including one in Petrograd munitions plants that required threats of immediate retaliation by the local city chief to quell.[54]

Riots exploded again as well. A report by the MVD's Police Department counted no less than 70 incidents relating to the initial 5 September mobilization alone.[55] In Petrograd, a crowd composed mainly of militiamen marched down Nevskii Prospekt, singing and screaming before attacking a policeman. In other locations, policemen were not surprisingly the targets of attacks as well. In Tula, a stone-throwing crowd stomped through the city yelling, "We won't go until they draft the police and reconvene the Duma [which Nicholas had prorogued just days before]." In Astrakhan, militiamen tussled with Persian workers and destroyed more than forty stores before turning upon local officials and wounding the governor, vice governor, police chief and other officials. With liquor stores long closed, there was no blaming these riots on demon rum. Nor were they simply the reflection of other social discontent or unhappiness with the regime. Conscription policy itself was the central cause of the unhappiness.

The tsarist government was not adept at listening to the response of its subjects, however, and the clear political signals from below were ignored as politicians and military officials stumbled together toward 1916. The military tried to keep its promises to the Duma by conducting periodic medical reexaminations and seeking to transfer soldiers from rear units to the front when possible. This shifting of soldiers meant shortages in the support services so crucial for the conduct of total war. The military leadership soon hit upon a way to fulfill all their promises to the Duma by sending soldiers from rear units to the front and replenishing the rear units with newly drafted ethnic groups, in particular the Kirgiz.[56]

The draft of the Kirgiz was strongly protested by military and civilian conscription officials, who asked how they could conduct a draft without registration lists or the parish records kept by Orthodox communities. Their questions were not answered. They asked why a population that had been so hostile to the idea of military service over the past forty years would welcome its introduction, as some Duma representatives had claimed, but again, no reply was given. They warned of possible rebellion and were ignored.

Conscription began on 2 July 1916 and was immediately marked by widespread confusion. No preparatory measures of any sort had been taken.[57] Corruption ran rampant. Having no birth records or registration lists, the tsarist governors were forced to turn to clan elders to submit lists of men, along with their ages. Private scores within Kirgiz society were correspondingly settled. Aleksandr Kerenskii, who had been sent to the region to monitor events for the Duma, found 60-year-old men listed as 30 years old while 25-year-old men were listed as 50 years old.[58] In addition to social paybacks, there were monetary payoffs to both Kirgiz and Russian officials. General A. N. Kuropatkin, who was pulled away from the European war to deal with the rebellion that ensued, estimated these bribes to number in the millions of rubles in the Fergana and Semirechie regions alone.[59]

Popular uprisings, based on dissatisfaction with the draft, with Russian colonizers, and with their own elite, began only two days later, on 4 July. Riots sprang up across Turkestan, many of which had to be put down by force. On 17 July, all of Turkestan was placed under martial law. By August, the revolt had spread to Syr Daria, where detachments of 5,000–8,000 Kirgiz attacked Russian troops on the Tashkent-Orenburg railroad.[60] By September, nearly all the steppe was aflame in revolt, and a special expeditionary force was sent to deal with the uprising. Both sides targeted civilian populations in the ensuing war, and escalating fury led to increasingly brutal massacres until the fighting finally slowed in early 1917.[61]

The draft had been a complete disaster. Although 110,000 Kirgiz were eventually called up, the difficulty of the process and the poor transportation network ensured that only a small percentage of them made it to their workplace before the Provisional Government rescinded Nicholas's order of 25 June. In the meantime, putting down the revolt had required more than 14 battalions of troops and 33 "hundreds" of Cossacks. Some 9,000 Russian homesteads had been destroyed, and 24 Russian officials, 97 soldiers, and 3,588 Russian settlers had been killed. Losses among the Kirgiz probably numbered in the tens of thousands.[62]

Each successive alteration to draft regulations, therefore, brought greater and greater opposition, and that opposition was expressed more stridently and more coherently, but it must be noted that a pervasive unwillingness to fight in the war was present from the very first day of mobilization. When reading patriotic articles from newspapers, soldiers often reacted negatively, saying, "They forcibly drove us into this damned war, torture us here, and they still write, those sons of bitches, that we ourselves want to fight. What bastards!"[63] The same unwillingness can be seen in intensified efforts to evade service during the war. This evasion was not primarily manifested by simply not appearing for the call-up. Again, medical disability was the favored tactic. Some sought the crippled and infirm to take their medical exams for them, while others took advantage of smudged and faded documents to claim exemption.[64]

One eager draft dodger, Aleksandr Dneprovskii, used multiple methods of evasion. Born in 1896, he thought he had until 1916 before he would be drafted, and he tried to gain entry to art school in early 1915, but failed the exam. When it was announced that his age group would be drafted in August 1915, he became frantic, and being already slight in build, decided to starve himself until draft day. He was not alone in his desperation. Some of his fellow draftees "tried to damage their heart, others gave themselves hernias, ruined their eyes or inflicted wounds on their legs . . . and others gave bribes from 300 to 500 rubles to the police chief, doctor of the draft board, and other members of the draft board."[65] Self-starvation did not work, and Dneprovskii was inducted and sent for training to Poltava. There, suffering from the regimen after his long hunger strike, he resolved on another plan. Slipping out of camp with a group of ill soldiers, he made his way to the local library, where he felt sure no one would ask to see his documents. He spent all his days there and his nights hiding until his company moved out, at which point he purchased a false passport and went home.[66] Meanwhile, other more sophisticated measures were being taken all across the empire. Some men enrolled in fire brigades "with the intent of evading military service,"[67] while others used medical knowledge to get excused. One author of an intercepted letter advised a friend to take a "colossal amount" of phenacitin the night before his medical exam, because his heart would work very badly the next day and he would be excused.[68]

The picture painted here of significant dissatisfaction with the war should not be understood as a fundamental split between "state" and "society," or even between laborers and the educated elite. The situation was far more complex. In the first place, the educated classes, state officials included, were not unanimous in their desire to wage war. Indeed, because so many of the positions that received mobilization exemptions were in the state bureaucracy, clever draft dodgers sought to enter state service (including military posts in the rear) whenever possible.[69]

Neither was there unanimity in the lower classes. Many enlisted men claimed to be patriots, and there is no reason to doubt them. Many others had a rather more skeptical view of the war. Their attitudes were not so much marked by traditional peasant fatalism as by "sullen resignation."[70] The war had come, and there was nothing they could do about that, but they remained fiercely engaged with other aspects of military politics, upon which they could (and did) have an effect. Their pragmatism would be revealed in full in 1917, when it became clear that their attitude toward the war *did* have a bearing on whether it would continue. The "soldiers' plebiscite" determined Russia's exit from the war and helped bring the Bolsheviks to power. Though this political activism was most evident in 1917, there were rumblings of it much earlier.

Conscription policy was one of the realms in which many Russians, not just soldiers, were politically active well before the revolution. Literally thousands of letters were written to state and military authorities over the course of the war. Some of these correspondents expressed opposition to government policy, but many sought to uphold a vision of national duty. Whistleblowers were prolific throughout the war. In 1915, a concerned Polivanov wrote Prince B. N. Shcherbatov (the minister of internal affairs), noting that "a significant number" of letters regarding specific instances of abuse or evasion had already come into military offices and that the number was growing with each draft. The number written since the beginning of the war was simply "enormous."[71]

The central theme of nearly all of these letters was neither blind patriotism nor protest against conscription per se. Rather, the main theme was fairness, as it had been before the war. What was most disliked (or at least most complained about) was not the fact that one's son was drafted, but that other members of the population were not. One group of soldiers' wives, for instance, complained to the MVD in 1916 that there were too many exempt occupations and too much bribery:

> At present anyone who doesn't want to serve in the troops serves on the railroad. On the railroads, guards are freed (I don't know what they're guarding), porters are freed (I don't know who they're opening doors for at present), guards for railroad gardens, gardeners, assistants and others (I don't know who can think about gardens at a time like this, and anyway the garden wouldn't die if the gardener left it for a half year or a year). And anyway the "necessary" Russian public is living in clover, and even allows itself to reproach those who went to the war that 'your husbands or brothers are fools, but mine's a good boy, he gave 100 rubles to the bosses and they put him on the list for freeing them and he didn't go.' I want to know whether any mortal could remain

silent when they hear such a conversation between a well-groomed "necessary" person and the shrivelled wives and children of people "not necessary
for anyone" and taken for the war. I can't in my heart blame government circles for this, but I want just to tell this to you, your excellency. All this was un-
noticeable at first, when the male population was large, but the ranks of them
have thinned with every day and now each of them gets thrown in your face
and can lead to bad results.

They asked for a broader application of conscription laws and claimed that
they relied on "his excellency's fairness, as all Russian people do. The
whole Russian *narod* will stand in the ranks of the army, not even excluding cripples, to defend against the enemy, but only when fairness is seen
in everything."[72]

These women were not alone. "We expect fairness," said one recruit who
was upset that the son of the village elder had mysteriously gotten an exemption while he was inducted.[73] Another warned that "the whole *narod* is
unhappy with conscription because it isn't equal and not everyone undergoes it, and there's a lot of grumbling about the minister of war, because he
didn't structure conscription equally and make it obligatory for all."[74]

Was this just traditional peasant envy and peasant egalitarianism rearing its
petty head? One certainly senses the remnants of small-scale social control in
the tattling on and scolding of those who dared to try to make themselves an
exception to the general rule. But this traditional egalitarianism corresponded
rather nicely with the idea of the equality of citizens that lay at the heart of
the national ideology. Indeed, as both the Orliuk denunciation and the complaint written by the wives of reservists show, the frame of reference for complaints about conscription was not the village but the nation. Peasants were
arguing for equality amongst groups within a national context and they
brought the state into the equation even when the object of the denunciation
was not a stratum of the population but an individual within their own local
community. This shift of frames of reference is significant, for it suggests that
peasants and "peasant consciousness" were not nearly so parochial and isolated from the national milieu as has often been claimed.[75] To the contrary, it
seems to be the case that in the final years of the tsarist regime, unbeknownst
to urban intellectuals, peasants had indeed become Russians.

The Revolutionary Army

The last draft of the tsarist army happened on 3 February 1917, when the
1919 cadre (b. 1898) of soldiers was called to the colors. It would be the last
forced conscription of any significance for more than a year. With the February Revolution came a revolution within the army, as the old system of discipline and command was overturned in favor of soldier committees, and Petrograd politicians tried to woo soldiers to their side.[76] The Provisional
Government, nominally in charge of the bureaucracy for staffing the army,

continued with the politically safe medical reexaminations and formed special volunteer units of revolutionary enthusiasts, some of them female, but even these had to get the approval of the military section of the Petrograd soviet. As 1917 dragged on, and the summer offensive on the southwestern front failed, it became increasingly clear that Petrograd officials could no longer staff the army, for rear units refused to go to the front and threatened insurrection if they were ordered to do so. By the beginning of September, General A. P. Verkhovskii, the minister of war, had come to the painful realization that the only way to save the army was to shrink it radically in the midst of the greatest war Russia had ever fought.[77] Thus, the best that the Bolsheviks could hope for when they took nominal power in late October was to limit the destructive forces of soldiers as they demobilized. They understood that the old army was in its death throes and hoped to replace it with a class-based militia.

As novel as the idea of replacing the hallowed Russian army with an untested militia was, it was not a particularly controversial position for the Bolsheviks to take within socialist circles. All European revolutionaries agreed at the outset of the twentieth century that the proper form of armed forces in a socialist state was a militia. Standing armies were the servants of the ruling class, the main reason that the rule of a privileged minority was possible. It seemed obvious to most revolutionaries that arming the entire population, training them in military affairs, and developing in them the consciousness that they were being exploited would result in an end of bourgeois regimes and prevent the reemergence of minority rule. Militias were, as a result, a "fundamental point" in the programs of social democratic parties across the continent.[78]

There was little in the experience of 1917 to shake socialists from their convictions. The seemingly endless Great War had begun to break down the formidable standing armies of the Great Powers. In Russia, that process had been especially obvious, but the morale and staying power of other belligerents had visibly declined as well, most notably in France, where mutinies threatened to destroy the war effort.[79] Meanwhile, the experience of worker militias had been extremely encouraging. The Red Guards that had been formed in major industrial centers throughout Russia had proven successful as urban armed forces, prompting newspaper columnists to claim in September 1917 that the Red Guards had shown the feasibility of abolishing a standing army and replacing it with an "armed people." In October, these urban worker militias were one of the primary sources of armed might that the Bolsheviks used to assume power in Petrograd.[80]

Few were therefore surprised that the Bolsheviks continued along these revolutionary lines in their first months of rule. The new Commissariat of Military Affairs was headed by staunch militia supporters and haters of everything associated with the old army. At their first meeting on 3 November 1917, the leaders of the commissariat agreed that all commanders of the army should be elected. As to the question of what should be done with the professional military men who had been trained by the tsarist regime, Nikolai

Podvoiskii dismissively suggested that "we should let the officers scatter." Five days later they published the "Declaration of the Rights of Soldiers," which officially declared that the army should be fully democratized and command posts made elective throughout the army.[81] Nikolai Krylenko, one of the three commissars of military affairs, was only echoing the military theme of the year when he announced on 13 December that he expected an immediate transition from a "standing army to an armed people."[82]

The first steps in this direction were taken on 15 January 1918, when the Worker-Peasant Red Army was officially formed. It was a class-based force that actively sought out worker participation, guardedly accepted peasants who had proved their revolutionary credentials in the army, and declared its antipathy to everyone else. Soldiers declared in their oath that "by entering the family of the Worker-Peasant Red Army," they were giving their word that they would fight "without betrayal" for "the great cause for which the best sons of the worker and peasant family have given their life, for the cause of the victory of Soviet power and the triumph of socialism."[83] The Bolsheviks had rejected the ideals of the modern army that defended a territorialized state by recruiting an army from a territorialized people. They were instead creating a revolutionary army that was devoted to global upheaval and that recruited its soldiers on a class basis.

The revolutionary Red Army was a failure for two major reasons. In the first place, it depended upon a smooth transfer of local power from the old tsarist/Provisional Government ministry functionaries and zemstvo officials to the soviets. Soviets everywhere were less than a year old and their officials required a great deal of training to make a modern bureaucracy run. It was unrealistic to assume that organizational or political questions would be resolved in time to mobilize even a volunteer force effectively, especially in rural areas, where soviets were sparsely scattered and existed as little more than the old village authority structure with new titles.[84]

The second major problem was that the Bolsheviks were hoping to create a mobile force under the direction of central leaders. On a flow chart, no doubt, this looked feasible. After all, local soviets were formally subordinated to central institutions like the All-Russian Central Executive of Soviets (VTsIK) and the Council of People's Commissars (Sovnarkom). All that was needed was effective leadership and able administration from VTsIK and the Commissariat of Military Affairs, and the locally raised troops could be channeled into the centralized Red Army. Again, though, it proved unrealistic to expect novice bureaucrats to pull off such a challenging task. The Military Section of VTsIK instead decided to try to do what it knew best, and busied itself for the first few months of Bolshevik power with agitational work, focusing its efforts more on raising consciousness than on raising troops.[85]

Even had the Bolsheviks miraculously found the organizational resources to staff an efficient conscription bureaucracy, they would have had trouble finding sufficient numbers of men. Early 1918 was the worst possible time to try to recruit an army. Too many men were now staunchly opposed to fighting and were interested in being around for the renegotiation of power in localities across Russia. The Bolsheviks, though, thought revolutionary enthusiasm would overcome these difficulties and that the proletarian warriors enrolled in Red Guard units would constitute a firm nucleus for the new Red Army.

These high hopes were soon dashed. As it turned out, even the expected mass transfer from Red Guard to Red Army failed to materialize. Older Red Guardists had no desire to leave their homes and factories, while many others of all ages refused to join up after learning of the salary offered to volunteers. Men who had not belonged to the Red Guards were even less willing, and the volunteer drive suffered. Recruitment in Petrograd province went by far the best, but even there, they garnered only 25,796 soldiers by May. In Moscow, there was an initial rush as a result of high unemployment, but the stream dried up quickly and further campaigns drew little response. Elsewhere, the situation was grim. In Tver', hunger and lack of organizers led to "listless" recruitment. In Siberia, volunteers were rare in cities and absent elsewhere, and the population was either "indifferent or ill-disposed" to the Red Army. After two months of recruiting, only 153,678 men had enrolled throughout the country.[86]

The failure of the volunteer system slowly became apparent at the same time that Bolshevik anxieties about survival became more acute. The specter that loomed over their heads was not domestic counterrevolution, the potential strength of which many top Bolsheviks surprisingly tended to underestimate in early 1918, but rather the German army.[87] The German threat had reappeared with a vengeance on 18 February 1918, when the Germans tired of the diplomatic game being played by Trotskii at the Brest-Litovsk peace talks and attacked Soviet Russia. Most of the old army had gone home, and all that remained to face German troops were "screens" of men left over from the old army and scattered Red Guard or Red Army units. They were outnumbered, outgunned, and facing seasoned troops. It was no contest, and the Germans marched swiftly to the east.

The threat to Bolshevik rule was immediately apparent, and a retreat from radical revolutionary ideals was begun. Mikhail Bonch-Bruevich was the man best positioned to witness this shift back toward the ideals of the "modern" army. He was uniquely connected both to the world of tsarist military professionals by virtue of his graduation from the General Staff Academy and to the revolutionary world through his brother Vladimir, who was an Old Bolshevik and a close confidant of Lenin's. When World War I broke out, he was a colonel heading a regiment in Chernigov. By the time of the October Revolution, he was commander in chief of the northern front.

Like all other military professionals in Russia, he was appalled by the army's disintegration in 1917 and blamed it on the revolution and the despised soldier committees, which he held responsible for the breakdown of authority. He had agreed to serve as the commander of General Headquarters (Stavka) for the Bolsheviks in November because he thought that Lenin's party was "the only force capable of saving Russia from collapse and complete destruction." By the end of the year, he was less enthusiastic about his brother's circle.[88] Ordered to close down Stavka, he warned the Bolshevik leadership that the shift in military policy left the border undefended, but his mandate to disband the old headquarters of the army was not reversed.

On the morning of 19 February, Bonch-Bruevich telegrammed Lenin with the news that the headquarters of the old army was officially dissolved and began to pack his bags. The last remaining old officer was about to "scatter." At 6 P.M., though, he received a short telegram from Lenin saying "You are instructed to come to Petrograd at once bringing the remaining GHQ [Stavka] personnel." Bonch-Bruevich guessed correctly that the German offensive had led to a change of heart.[89]

The trip from Mogilev to Petrograd was a miniature revolutionary epic. Delayed by railway men who suspected counterrevolution, the Stavka officers' train eventually made it out of the Mogilev station along railways clogged with deserters and already threatened by German cavalry patrols. The men eventually made it to Petrograd on 22 February, where Bonch-Bruevich called his brother Vladimir from the train station asking for a ride. Upon arrival, the group of gray-haired men in army greatcoats drew "astonished stares" as they proceeded to Lenin's office. Lenin then told Bonch-Bruevich why he had been summoned: "You and your friends shall have to start figuring out immediately measures to defend Petrograd. We haven't any troops. *None at all*. The workers of Petrograd shall have to serve as our armed force."[90] Tsarist military professionals were involved once again in decisions in the main halls of power. The modern vision was making its comeback in the realm of high politics.

This retreat from revolution in military affairs was evident even the day before the generals marched into Lenin's office at the Smolnyi. On 21 February, Sovnarkom issued an appeal to the country over Lenin's signature entitled "The Socialist Fatherland is in Danger!" It would be the mobilization theme for the Bolsheviks for the rest of the Civil War. The focus on defending the endangered territorialized political community was combined with revolutionary class themes in nearly all broadly distributed public appeals from then on. When Trotskii appealed to workers in Kazan' in August 1918, for instance, he told them that "Russian white guardists had sold you to the foreign bourgeoisie."[91]

This increasing focus on territory and nativeness will be explored in greater detail in chapter 3. For now it is important to note that, though the notion of a "socialist fatherland" eventually became a widely accepted component of Soviet propaganda, it was at first an awkward one. After all, had not Marx said that workers had no fatherland? How did a focus on preserving a territory coincide with expanding a nonterritorial world revolution? Lenin explained that the Bolsheviks had "won the right to defend the fatherland," but that "these are not national interests; we affirm that the interests of socialism, the interests of world socialism, are higher than national interests, higher than the interests of state. We are 'defencists' of the socialist fatherland."[92]

The rapid German march soon put this formulation to the test. Most high-ranking members of the party took the crisis to be the moment when they would in fact have to decide between the interests of socialism and the interests of state. As a result, Lenin's call to sign a peace treaty with Germany was stridently opposed, and the question of war and revolution consumed the party for the two weeks between the resumption of hostilities and the signing of the Brest-Litovsk peace. Faced with a German ultimatum, Trotskii joined Lenin in arguing that the first priority was to protect the existence of the socialist state rather than launch immediately into a "revolutionary war" with volunteer proletarians leading the way. Proponents of "revolutionary war" remained powerful, though. It was only when Lenin threatened to resign, claiming that "a revolutionary phrase about revolutionary war might kill our revolution," and that "the 'slogan' of revolutionary war in February 1918 is an empty phrase, behind which there is nothing real, nothing objective,"[93] that men like Mikhail Uritskii and Nikolai Bukharin abandoned their opposition and agreed to end the war. The decision to make peace with Germany and sign the Brest-Litovsk treaty on 3 March 1918 was a crucial moment in the history of the revolution, for it laid the basis for the creation and defense of the territorial state and committed the armed forces to take the defense of Soviet territory as their primary duty.

The peace thus signaled a return to more traditional practices in the military. On 3 March, the same day that Trotskii signed the treaty, the Supreme Military Council was formed to direct military affairs. Podvoiskii, the leading military radical since October, was joined by Mikhail Bonch-Bruevich as head military specialist and Trotskii as chairman. With all the zeal of a new convert, Trotskii argued from then on that military affairs were a (nonideological) "art" rather than a (Marxist) "science."[94] Since the art of defending a bounded territory was what military men knew how to do best, it followed that Bolshevik leaders should respect that expertise. This they did, as Bonch-Bruevich immediately began recruiting his old colleagues to serve the new regime as "military specialists."[95] Authority was returned to military intellectuals who had learned their trade in the late imperial period.

The implication for manpower policy was quite clear. With the option of decentralized guerrilla revolution now discredited, only the militia army and standing army options remained. Both of these scenarios for the creation of a military force entailed the abandonment of volunteer recruitment. At a conference of major military officials at the end of March, Lenin decided to accept the recommendation of Bonch-Bruevich to rebuild the old standing army through the institution of universal conscription. On 8 April, military commissariats were created to conduct registration and to inform the leaders of local soviets that the days of regional control over armed men were over.[96] On 22 April, militia proponents found a home when the Universal Military Training Administration (Vsevobuch) was formed to organize the mandatory military training of every male citizen in his "leisure" hours. Though the first draft would not occur until after the Czech rebellion and the outbreak of full-fledged civil war in May and June 1918, the groundwork for the conscription system was, in theory at least, already laid.

But the Bolsheviks would learn quickly that the minefield of conscription politics was not so easily negotiated. The conflict between military and civilian priorities and interests and between central and local political actors quickly appeared again. During April and early May, Bolshevik leaders exhorted local officials to get the structure working so that preparatory work for a draft in the not too distant future could be accomplished, but those exhortations fell on deaf ears. By mid-May, local military commissariats had been created in just 50 of the 304 military districts in European Russia, and the story was even worse in the east.[97] Exasperated, Lenin sent a radiogram across the country on 18 May reminding officials everywhere of the pressing urgency of creating local military offices and threatened chairmen of soviets at the provincial, district, and county levels that they would be held "directly responsible" if the orders of the center were not met.[98] One week later, a party of Czech prisoners of war travelling eastward on the Trans-Siberian railroad revolted when anxious local officials tried to disarm them, touching off an uprising in the east that would threaten the Bolshevik regime within a matter of months. It was the beginning of massive civil war.

Conscription and Citizenship in the Civil War

Needless to say, one week was not enough time to create the necessary institutions and bureaucratic linkages essential to conduct a traditional draft. There was no real possibility of carrying out a true mobilization, but now the Czech uprising had forced the Bolsheviks to draft the population before the mechanisms that would have allowed them to do so effectively were in place. They would pay the price for this for the rest of the war. The announcement from VTsIK that a "forced levy" (prinuditel'nyi nabor) would take place came on 29 May. The terminology of the decree was strange. State officials did not normally refer to drafting soldiers in terms of coercion and extraction. During the 1912 debate, in fact, objections had been raised to the term used throughout the late imperial period, voinskaia povinnost', because it had the negative connotation of "burden" rather than a positive connotation of "duty."[99] The Bolshevik order for a "forced levy" was a rare acknowledgment of what the actual process would have to be. It was also a signal that the ideological basis for compelling men to serve in the military was shaky and incomplete.

Throughout the dangerous summer of 1918, the Bolsheviks attempted to draft as many men as possible while simultaneously developing an ideological and institutional infrastructure for conscription that would sustain them over the course of a long war. Starting in June, the Bolsheviks attempted to tap all "workers and non-exploiting peasants" between 21 and 25 years of age in 51 districts in the Urals and Siberia. But an orderly call-up on class lines was not to be. With no draft lists or functioning draft organizations, officials pleaded with factory committees, house committees, and village elders to provide lists of "toilers" in that age range. Their pleas were ignored. As one official confessed, "things are very sad in Ekaterinburg. We have no forces upon which we can rely, everyone is running from the front. I fear that within days the city of Ekaterinburg will fall. Workers are very hostile to the soviets. There is no organization. . . . [Nevertheless], there's work going on here to prepare a mobilization."[100] These were the conditions under which the 1918 mobilizations would take place: panic, disorganization, lack of support from the center, lack of cadres in the periphery. Mobilizations happened, but only in the very crudest fashion. They were levies not supported and enforced by a documentary regime or cohesive mechanisms linking state with society, but by coercion alone.

Meanwhile, the ideological and institutional foundations of the conscript army were laid by the Fifth Congress of Soviets on 10 July, which linked citizenship to military service and extended the range of both to peasants as well as workers. "Soviet power," the delegates claimed "always recognized, and the Fifth All-Russian Congress of Soviets once again solemnly reaffirms, that every honorable and healthy citizen aged 18 to 40 has the duty to come to the defense of the Soviet Republic from her internal and external enemies at the first call," and that the citizen's duty to appear belonged to both "workers and working peasants throughout the country."[101]

The sequence of events outlined here is important because it points to the basic fact that the Bolsheviks committed to a worker *and* peasant army (with the latter overwhelmingly dominating in numerical terms) in March 1918, when they decided to have a conscript army.[102] It was at that point they set about building an army of millions of men rather than thousands, and they were not bashful about calling up the rural population. Their reliance on urban centers, factory committees, and party cells to staff the army in 1918 had less to do with their class outlook than with their inability to create local conscription organs. When forced to field an army before they were ready to do so, they of necessity had to turn to other organizations, of which there were some upon which the Bolsheviks could rely in cities, but of which there were almost none in villages.

This situation mandated substantial decentralization in the conscription process. In some cases, this was administrative decentralization: local communities (and in cities, local factories, trade unions, or city districts) were asked to provide a certain number of recruits, preferably volunteers, but few questions were asked. In other locales, especially during 1918, this manifested itself troublingly in the creation of local forces, as well as in local recruitment for the Red Army.[103] The most common manifestation of decentralization, indeed of a splintering of authority during the Civil War, was pure impressment, a legal tactic for Red Army commanders, who had the right under article 12 of the Regulations for Army Commanders to mobilize men within an ill-defined "battle region" on their own authority and by their own procedures. By September 1920, 354,373 such cases were on file at the Mobilization Department.[104] Many more must have gone unreported altogether.

The fragile pane of authority that shattered in 1917 was obviously not restored in 1918. Given the immediate need for armed forces, the Bolsheviks could not wait for it to be put back together again. As a result, accepting decentralization and inefficient performance was the only short-term option, and one that they felt could only be maintained through the application of brute force. In this belief, they were probably right. Citizens across the land were obviously in no mood to go fight yet another war after the bloodbath of 1914–1918. Given the weakness of the forces that tried to compel them to do so and the proliferation of weapons that resulted from the literal creation of a "nation-in-arms" in World War I, armed opposition was almost inevitable, and it erupted everywhere. Reports from army staffs are filled with accounts of peasants gathering together rifles and holding off Red mobilization detachments, then doing the same when the Whites rolled into town. The constant refrain throughout 1918 was that "in the countryside mobilization is proceeding unsuccessfully, peasants are being mobilized by force."[105]

This situation continued during the Civil War, but the Bolsheviks gradually recentralized power both physically and ideologically. This recentralization can be witnessed through the forms of their drafts. From June through August 1918, mobilizations were partial and limited in scope, area, and age groups drafted. On 11 September, though, the Bolsheviks finally felt strong enough to issue a comprehensive, countrywide draft call of all workers and non-exploiting peasants born in 1898.[106] The establishment of a republicwide draft system did not solve all conscription problems overnight. As a later summary of the draft process admitted, though intended to establish a more regularized and fair system of conscription, the 1918 autumn drafts into the army were haphazard. Some regions mobilized soldiers effectively. Officials in other locales did not even feed and house their new conscripts and watched them slip back to their villages.[107] Given the inability of the military administration to conduct mobilizations efficiently and fairly, it was no wonder that regular Russians responded with revolts and an epidemic of evasion throughout 1918.[108]

The year of reckoning for the Bolsheviks was 1919, particularly in regard to manpower. The only positive thing that could really be said on the first of the year was that, bad as the situation was for the Reds, it was at least as bad for the Whites and the foreign powers in Russia. The Civil War and the question of central political leadership in Russia were of course tremendously important to Bolsheviks, White leaders, and foreign politicians. For the soldiers in all the armies involved, however, fighting for the lesser of two evils was simply not worth risking death and/or family impoverishment. The Civil War itself was the main point of detestation among most Russians. They had little preexisting desire to slaughter their co-nationals and blamed the apocalyptic disaster on the parties that continued to insist on war when most men and women wanted peace. How to induce these reluctant men to enter the army and then make them stay once conscripted became the central policy question of the war.

The year started off badly in this respect for the Red Army. Practice had not made perfect in terms of mobilization procedures. The first drafts in 1919 on republicwide principles were greater failures than the autumn drafts in 1918 had been.[109] As a real manpower crisis emerged, the Bolsheviks once more felt compelled to decentralize the conscription process. They had come to realize that centralized universal conscription depended on a set of institutions (among them reliable local bureaucracies and a documentary regime) that simply did not exist. The Mobilization Department therefore tried returning to the system that had predominated in the summer of 1918, in which central authorities would demand a certain number of men and local communities would determine who would go. A set of drafts reflecting this shift were conducted: the 24 April 1919 request for each county in the republic to send 10–15 men to the army, the demand for trade unions and party organizations to send 10 percent of their members to the army, and separate drafts of returned World War I prisoners of war, postal workers, railroad workers, and workers in other specific institutions throughout May and June.[110]

The underlying principle behind all of these drafts was the same. The army wanted a number of soldiers and was willing to sacrifice its control over selection procedures in order to guarantee that the quota would be met. The risk that policymakers decided to take was the pernicious impact of local civilians. Especially in the period of the Civil War, a good man was hard to find, and officials at all levels tried to hold on to them when they could. This danger was understood from the outset. The Mobilization Department telegrammed district chiefs days after the announcement of the county draft pleading with them to "pay the very strictest attention to the fulfillment of the first point of the decree so that elements not suitable for military service and unreliable for the defense of the Soviet Republic are not able to enter the army."[111]

The decentralization of conscription represented a real gamble. Expectant central officials, so eager to know whether the ploy had worked that they asked for updates on its progress every other day, found out the bad news beginning in mid-May. From Tula province came the report that the mobilization was proceeding "with difficulty," and that it "was not a success." From Tambov, the news was even worse, as officials of local soviets proved unwilling to select conscripts on their own authority, "preferring the drafts of entire age groups."[112] Nearly a month after the declaration of the draft, Tambov had gotten 24 recruits, having expected 5,165. Tambov was on the low end of the scale, but not by much. Riazan' province by mid-May had gotten only 288, Tula 173, and Moscow 99.[113] Nationwide, the draft (which was mercifully ended at the beginning of June) only netted 24,364 men, instead of the 140,000 expected.[114]

One of the reasons for the disaster was the unpopularity of local control over the process. The Bolshevik leadership had seriously underestimated the importance of fairness imparted by uniform national rules. A sense of the level of resistance to the county draft is evident in the report of a revolutionary enthusiast (named "Komissarov") who rode out into the countryside to prod villagers into complying.[115] Soon after his arrival in Roslavl' district (near Smolensk), he realized that "we couldn't count on a painless mobilization" in the countryside because peasants viewed the mobilization "as undergoing punishment rather than as the defense of the revolution." The rural administration was no help, as county and village soviets "wavered for a long time," knowing that actually implementing the mobilization would elicit "an explosion of unhappiness, and maybe even worse."

After several lengthy meetings, Komissarov convinced officials at local soviets to announce the central directive, a move that led to unhappiness and anger based not so much on the fact of mobilization as on the unfairness of the method. The conscripts, Komissarov observed, "declare that county officials don't have the right to choose them. Let them choose by year of birth [they say]." Meanwhile, local officials refused to make these life-and-death decisions about their neighbors. "Shoot us, [they said] but we won't choose anyone. Do what you want: burn us or cut off our heads, and upon further strong pressure they pleaded with us to dismiss them."

Soviet officials learned their lesson from Komissarov and others who telegrammed in similar recommendations. Decentralized drafts were enormously unpopular. The notion that universality and equality should be observed in the conscription process was so engrained that neither local elites nor young men wanted to depart from the established way of conscripting soldiers. Bolshevik leaders proved unusually able to understand the way that "low" politics worked and remarkably willing to change policy based on that understanding. Krylenko, who had visited Vladimir province and learned that local officials were conducting lotteries to determine who would "volunteer," correspondingly urged that they "either preserve the volunteer principle or take each year in its turn." Efraim Sklianskii, Trotskii's right-hand man, responded that he should order local officials to abandon the "volunteer-draft" principle and return to drafting age groups.[116]

But Komissarov pointed to another important factor in the failed mobilization as well. "Without a doubt," he claimed, "if the battle against desertion had been conducted sufficiently energetically, then we would not see this type of evasion, and we would only have to deal with grumbling on the part of the conscripts." Combined with the fact that the Bolsheviks had already called up nearly all available age groups by June 1919, it was clear as the summer campaigns developed that stemming desertion would be the key to preserving both the Red Army and the revolution as a whole.

Here again Bolshevik sensitivity to the dynamics of low politics and the capacity to mold their actions in response to it differentiated the Bolsheviks from their political opponents and helps explain their success. White and

Red commanders alike were dealing with the problem of desertion in the summer of 1919, but their different approaches helped to determine the outcome of the Civil War. At heart, all military commanders understood the problem in much the same way: as a deficiency of civic virtue on the part of the Russian peasantry. Desertion in World War I had been epidemic, not just in 1917, but throughout the war. As mentioned above, military officials speaking in closed sessions of the Duma Military Affairs Committee quoted figures of 500,000 deserters in the first year of the war alone, and the total number of Russian deserters probably reached 1,900,000 men.[117] It was therefore not only for Marxist class reasons that military officials had serious doubts about the civic virtue and staying power of Russian peasant soldiers. But Red commanders found a way to overcome their doubt. The Bolsheviks saved the Red Army by fully establishing the citizen-soldier as the paragon of the political community. This maneuver, though in line with the ideas and sympathies of Bolshevik leaders, was made in response to signals "from below." The moment would have lasting influence, not only on Soviet military affairs but also upon the shape of the Soviet civic community.

This interpretation of civil war desertion and the Bolshevik response differs significantly from that of most previous historians, who have tended to argue that desertion was fundamentally rooted in peasant interests and experiences. The most detailed argument that desertion and desertion policy hinged on peasantness has been offered by Orlando Figes, who cited a "tendency of soldiers to desert during the harvest season" before concluding that "[m]ass desertion from the Red Army was a direct expression of general peasant protest against the Bolsheviks."[118] The Bolsheviks ended up mobilizing peasants and winning the war in spite of all this, he claims, because the "threat of a White victory. . . galvanized thousands of peasants, previously registered as deserters, to return to the Red army between July and September 1919."[119]

But Figes's own statistics fail to back up this "peasant" interpretation. His arguments that deserters acted as peasants depends on the harvest season hypothesis, but as he noted in the quote just cited, the story of the harvest season in 1919 was the *return* of deserters to the army. Indeed, in the midst of the 1919 harvest, military officials noted that the number of voluntarily appearing and arrested deserters had risen to such a level that planners were expecting the "source" to dry up soon.[120] In the first two weeks of September, 16,364 men deserted, while 97,420 returned to the army or were captured. Throughout the Civil War, desertion failed to follow an agricultural pattern. The peak times for desertion were in December 1918 and in May–June 1919, and the peak return time was in the midst of the 1919 harvest. Soldiers deserted in December because they were cold and starving and in May-June they departed for these reasons too, as well as for family concerns and a general bottoming out of morale. In other words, desertion patterns were determined by the flow of *soldier* conditions, not *peasant* conditions.

Instead of trying to explain the reasons for desertion by describing a "peasant" cosmology, the Civil War desertion problem is better understood in terms of the relationship between the state and its citizens. On the one hand, the story of the rise and decline of desertion was part of a longer dialogue between young men and the authorities to define the legitimate "contract" between state and soldier that had been taking place throughout the twentieth century. On the other hand, the superior capacity of the Reds to get a handle on desertion reflected the increasing ability of the Bolshevik Party to implement the cardinal features of the total war state: a documentary regime, state-sponsored entitlement programs, and propaganda campaigns to shape public opinion primary among them.

Over the course of 1919, the Bolsheviks, through their pronouncements on military service and their concrete policies toward soldiers and deserters, created a state-sponsored discourse that finally incorporated the idea that soldiers acquired rights when they performed their national duty. In doing so, they validated the long-standing feelings of soldiers who believed they deserved to have their family's welfare protected by the state in their absence, to receive a promise of respect from state authorities, and to be granted privileges in relation to their nonwarrior fellow citizens. In return, soldiers validated the same discourse, which legitimated, among other things, the state's right to pursue, verify, and punish citizens who failed to perform their civic duties. In short, the Bolsheviks mobilized soldiers more effectively than did their enemies because they had reached a workable consensus with the young men of the republic about the "duties and rights" of state and citizen in relationship to military service.

Despite the popularity of the Bolsheviks among soldiers during 1917, this consensus took some time to hammer out. The Red Army struggled to draft and retain its conscripts from the first draft forward. The initial solution Bolshevik leaders hit upon was that evasion and desertion had to be deterred like any other crimes, and that the more severe the threat, the stronger the deterrent. Orders sent along with the first conscription decrees instructed local officials to apply "the harshest measure of punishment" to draft evaders, and this approach remained predominant throughout the rest of the year, most infamously in Trotskii's declaration in November 1918 that he would "put an end" to desertion by employing "merciless measures" of mass execution.[121] Trotskii's directive to shoot all deserters and those who coddled them accurately reflected the willingness of military officials to use capital punishment as a deterrent for the crime of desertion, a willingness further attested to by repeated and ominous demands for more revolvers to be produced and sent to commanders as the Civil War heated up.[122]

But the demand in Trotskii's order to shoot "every soldier" who deserted was unusual. The more general line taken by military commanders was to use a two-pronged approach to the problem of desertion. This stance was reflected in a December 1918 decree signed by Lenin. In it, Lenin denounced desertion as a "heinous and shameful" crime and blamed those "depraved and ignorant elements" that committed the crime for the problem. Targeting both of those elements, he ordered a two-week amnesty of punishment for those (presumably shameful and ignorant) deserters who voluntarily returned to their units and a stepping up of punishment for those (presumably heinous and depraved) ones who stayed at large.[123]

In the spring of 1919, this approach was failing, in large part because it neglected the fact that many of these men saw themselves (and were seen by others) as honored citizens and responsible family men. Military censors reported that soldiers were writing home about the high level of desertion ("There are many deserters, about 30 percent of our regiment has run away"), while their families were writing them the inviting news that "we've got a lot of deserters here and they're all living at home."[124] Desertion shot up as soldiers took to the forests or to their home villages, individuals forged documents or dressed in women's clothing to obtain train tickets away from the front, and desperate men gave themselves over to the enemy *en masse*.[125] The national newspaper *Bednota* reported that throughout the spring of 1919, during which time it received about 60–70 letters a day from Red Army soldiers, desertion and what to do about it was a hot topic in the ranks. The overwhelming majority of all letters concerned the welfare of soldier families, more specifically the welfare of peasant soldier families. Moreover, according to the soldiers writing in to the editorial offices, "90 percent of deserters left the Red Army under the influence of appeals from home. People from home . . . even reproach them: 'Now Vania Mar'in has come back—he wasn't afraid and is feeding his old mother, but you don't think you can.' . . . the influence of these letters on soldiers is very great."[126]

This realization that desertion was linked to the catastrophic conditions in which the families of soldiers were living, and did not simply boil down to "duty" or "consciousness," came late, but it was better late than never. In April 1919, the head of the Central Desertion Commission wrote the party's Central Committee urging that repression be mixed with "proof of concern for the families of Red Army soldiers" in the form of increased pressure on local soviets to provide soldier families the benefits they were due.[127] In addition, deserters whose families had suffered catastrophe were to be given "much lighter punishment," in most cases simply being returned to the front.[128] This focus on the family was the most important aspect of the new desertion policy, and it will be discussed in greater detail in chapter 3.

The final part of the new anti-desertion initiative was to publicize the new measures as widely as possible. The June decree ordered all local commissars to take "personal responsibility" for posting desertion edicts in "all public places."[129] The campaign against desertion was to be brought to every village meeting hall and empty wall in the republic in "big letters."[130] By all accounts, the Bolsheviks came close to doing so. In Tula province alone, over the course of the amnesty week, about 200 agitators distributed 150,000 flyers, or, on average, about 30 for every deserter who voluntarily appeared in the province. The results, Tula agitators claimed, were excellent: "The population became convinced that it was impossible to desert and hide."[131]

The appeals went well beyond a mere publication of decrees (though those certainly were numerous). Some, like the "Open letter to comrade Red Army soldiers" published by the Riazan' provincial military commissariat in 10,000 copies, were designed to put special stress on the family theme, saying that "every politically conscious Red Army soldier stands for the defense of his rights, the rights of his family, the rights of laborers of the whole world." Deserters were traitors who "abandoned their brothers like a coward." Worse, since deserters had to be replaced, they took a "worker from his family, children from their mothers and fathers, husbands and brothers from wives and sisters, and fathers from weak little orphans. He's our enemy, comrade Red Army soldiers."[132]

Other appeals focused less on the class theme and appealed to religious and patriotic sentiments, like this flyer distributed in the Dankovskii district of Moscow province in July 1919 that targeted deserters by claiming that "[y]our crime is no better than the crime of Judas's betrayal, your action is worse than the action of Cain!" before asking "have you finally lost your mind? Don't allow the . . . drunken bandit Denikin and the landowner-admiral Kolchak to get here and drench the Russian land with the blood of workers and peasants!"[133]

The massive coordinated campaign produced almost immediate results. In Volokolamsk, the district was put under martial law and the "struggle with desertion was crowned with success . . . the district was cleansed of the aforementioned element."[134] Trotskii, after going to Riazan' to watch the process in person, was also impressed with the new direction of the struggle with desertion and the results it gave: "The experience of Riazan' province, which is exceedingly backward, shows the possibility to achieve excellent results with the intelligent combination of repression and agitation."[135] Another official summed up that the "reasons for desertion are common knowledge: lack of understanding of class struggle, a desire to help people at home work the fields, the lack of help for their families, war weariness, and so forth."[136] The reasons for desertion had become clear, and an effective method had been found for dealing with the problem, but that method required an intense coordinated effort that incorporated local and central state, party, and military authorities.

A key part of this effort was the tightening up on the documentary controls that constituted one of the primary means of power inherited from the tsarist regime. The effort began soon after Lenin's December 1918 order to crack down on desertion. On 18 January 1919, the Revolutionary Military Council of the Republic (RVSR) issued a decree requiring all men in military service to have their identity papers on them at all times.[137] Next came an edict ordering local house committees to "verify the documents of all males."[138] In February, railroad workers were instructed to conduct document verification procedures at all train stops.[139] The document checks would continue through the rest of the war. At first, there was a lack of consistent documentation from various institutions, but by 1920 detailed rules concerning document checks at railway stations and in all state and party institutions were dispatched and implemented throughout the country.[140]

The Bolsheviks knew what they had to do to keep desertion under control, namely to keep this bargain with their soldiers by providing them and their families with material security and social prestige. To their own great chagrin, they often failed to do so. When, in the autumn of 1920, 60 percent of the reserve troops in Moscow district lacked sufficient clothing and equipment, desertion rose sharply. Officials responded, as they had ever since June 1919, by conducting sweeps, shooting some men, and confiscating property, but they realized as they did so what the root cause was, and that "desertion in reserve units cannot be eliminated through repression alone."[141] In August 1920, a report on the causes for desertion came up with many of the same reasons as those that had been "common knowledge" in 1919: running away to do fieldwork, lack of food or other supplies in the unit, lack of leave time, and lack of support of soldiers' families.[142] The only reason that had disappeared was "understanding of class struggle." In sharp opposition to the position at the beginning of the war, military officials now were convinced that the reasons for desertion lay not in the misunderstandings, lack of consciousness, or the evil intent of the soldiers, but in the mistakes of their own military and civil administration.[143] Military service had become not only an explicit civic duty but also an implicit contract between soldier and state. In short, the Bolsheviks proved able to merge the realms of high politics and low politics in regard to conscription policy.

Even though problems continued, it is clear that the centering of military attention on the problem of desertion,[144] the tightening of the documentary regime, and the urgent attempts to convince every possible deserter and draft evader that escape was impossible were successful. The army that had been melting away in the spring now solidified in the summer and autumn. Over the course of the period from April 1919 to July 1920, deserters fell into the hands of authorities more than four million times.[145] The majority of these cases occurred in the periodic amnesty weeks, during which deserters could appear without fear of punishment, but the number detained by sweep detachments, at railroad stations, and during "verification gatherings" increased as well.

It was the institution of verification gatherings that finally signaled that the Bolsheviks had built a strong enough state apparatus to make a credible claim they could uncover and punish violators of the military service law. The Council of Worker-Peasant Defense announced on 27 August 1919 that all men in the republic would have to appear at a district gathering to determine their military service status.[146] Verification-gathering committees were to determine the identity and military service status of all the 16–45- year-old men in the area, uncover draft evaders and induct them into the army, and find deserters before moving on to register all newly arrived residents in the district.[147] In all, over a period of less than six months, 2,239,604 men showed up to be verified and 272,211 men were enrolled in the armed services.[148] Over the course of the next six months that number almost doubled. By August 1920, 470,106 men were inducted into the Red Army as a result of verification gatherings,[149] for once exceeding expectations, despite the fact that local commissariats were both understaffed and obligated to conduct the gatherings in very short order.[150] The final round of verification gatherings took place in late 1920, during which time officials medically examined over one million more men.

The noose was tightening around those who rejected the consensus between state and citizen-soldier and who continued to try to avoid fighting in the Civil War. The years 1919 and 1920 were marked by repeated propaganda campaigns for deserters to appear, by the frequent appearance of armed detachments searching for deserters and draft evaders, and by the subsequent punishment of whole families and villages for harboring these "traitors." In addition, the state showed its firm will and ability to govern by conducting verification gatherings and document checks on a large scale and displayed its empathy by offering added benefits to soldier families and amnesty weeks for those who deserted or evaded because they were "weak of will" and needed enlightenment. The attitude to dealing with deserters within military tribunals had shifted from one of "merciless punishment" to one that gave the vast majority of deserters a second chance while employing exemplary execution for a small minority.

The fact that a military service consensus had been reached and conscription had been normalized over the course of the second half of 1919 is most evident in the comparison between the draft results of the 1900 cadre in May 1919 and those of the 1901 cadre which took place in December 1919 and January 1920. In Voronezh, Kursk, Orel, and Riazan' provinces draft evasion among young men born in 1900 ranged from 75 to 90 percent.[151] Overall throughout the republic, only 189,302 men were enlisted from this age group.[152] When the call went out for young men born in 1901, though, the evasion rate in Riazan' was down to 15 percent and in Kostroma to a mere 4 percent.[153] In the republic as a whole, the draft netted 310,991 men.[154]

It was therefore the rare soldier indeed who either volunteered or was conscripted, followed the rules, and stayed in the ranks until the end of the war. The policy shift in the spring of 1919 to consistently give men a second chance while simultaneously making it much more difficult to get away with desertion and evasion was crucial. It was an army staffed by "second-chance" men that rolled to victory in late 1919 and 1920. The results of the desperate but successful struggle with desertion were not only felt on the battlefield, though. The increased presence of social controls, of armed detachments, and of a documentary regime throughout the Soviet land was largely the result of this massive struggle to fight desertion and solidify the political community. At the same time, entitlement programs for soldiers and their families, in embryonic form prior to World War I but in rapid development during that war, matured during the manpower crisis of the Civil War and remained a permanent aspect of Soviet life. Many of the defining features of Soviet society were fixed in the kiln of total war.

Demobilization and Reconstruction, 1921–1925

With the military threat from White forces and Polish forces neutralized by the end of 1920, the question of staffing the army took a new turn. Having desperately scrambled to conscript and keep every warm-blooded man it could for the past three years, the Red Army on the eve of 1921 numbered more than 5 million soldiers.[155] With the economy in shambles, these men had to be returned to the workforce in very short order. The only real question was how. The plan resolved upon at the Tenth Party Congress in March 1921 was to shrink the army while simultaneously increasing the percentage of workers and communists in its truncated form. This decision was fully in line with the class framework that shaped Soviet national ideology. Throughout the Soviet era, Soviet planners saw the core of their "people" as urban workers, an understanding that made the content of their ideology quite different from that of other national ideologies and led to policies that would have been unthinkable in other contexts. In this case, the floodgates were opened for peasant soldiers to return home, as the army sent age group after age group into the reserves. Over the course of 1921, 3.7 million men left the army, leaving only the men born between 1899 and 1901.[156] A series of supplemental drafts in newly reconquered areas allowed the Bolsheviks to muster out even these men on schedule and to delay their first peacetime draft until 1924. By that time, they had been able to conduct a thorough registration of the young men of the country and to start the political process of defining the bases of universal conscription in a communist state.

The first peacetime conscription law was promulgated on 29 September 1922 and was, by comparison with the tsarist code, telegraphic.[157] The basic principle was outlined in the first article, which required "all citizens of the RSFSR of the male sex" to bear arms "for the defense of the Republic." The only exception was to be people deprived by courts of their voting rights. Attached to the first article was a note that read: "People, who by their class position or actively expressed hostility to Soviet power cannot be trusted to defend the RSFSR with weapon in hand, will be drafted into military service on a special basis."

As will be seen shortly, the injunctions against class enemies had been issued (but not completely enforced) during the Civil War, and they reflected a redrawing of national boundaries of belonging. What should be noted here, however, is how familiar the first paragraph of this article is. Once again, the state was establishing the principle of service based on the "objective" factors of place of residence and age, but this time without the buildup of exemptions and irregularities that had so frustrated tsarist military officials. Only a couple of deferrals and exemptions remained (for students and only sons, for instance), but even these were much truncated. Men in labor-poor families were exempt from summer service, for instance, but were expected to train with the army during the winter, when they were not doing fieldwork.

Most of the military high politics of the immediate postwar period was concerned with the old question of militias, however. During the war itself the question was, in practice, moot. Men were neither going to the training grounds after work (the ideal of the militia proponents) nor to the barracks (the ideal of standing army proponents), but to the front. In 1921, however, the debate actually meant something. Despite the wartime promises to move to a militia army, the delegates of the Tenth Party Congress took a very conservative position and resolved that an immediate transition to a militia system would be "incorrect and dangerous in practice."[158] Delegates did call for the introduction of militia units in the major industrial centers of the country, setting the stage for a "mixed system" of armed forces comprised of cadre and militia forces.

From 1921 to 1923, however, militia units failed to spring up and flower around the country. For the whole period, the only one was a militia brigade based in Petrograd.[159] In 1923, the situation changed. In January and February ten cadre divisions were converted into "territorial units," and in August the government issued a decree calling for more of them and establishing the principles upon which they should be based.[160] Again, this was a training and fiscal decision. Ideally, Red Army officials would have liked to have brought in all men to the cadre army and trained them in two years. As was the case before the revolution, however, the state could only afford to draft one-third of the men. So, though facing the same number-crunching problem that the tsarist army had confronted, the Red Army acted with much more inventiveness and zeal, creating units on the cheap around the country. By 1 October 1924, the Red Army had 43 territorial rifle divisions in place and launched a concerted effort to supplement them with a number of single-ethnicity, territorially based units within the space of the next few years.[161]

Though no republicwide drafts occurred, 1923 had been a year of transition and reorganization. By 1924, the army was ready to conduct its first peacetime call-up. In an attempt to further cut costs, the military had decided to institute 18-month terms in order to keep conscripts in the barracks for only one winter, but they changed their mind shortly before the spring draft of 1924. In order to prevent confusion, however, they decided to go ahead with the spring draft in 1924, but henceforth to conduct yearly drafts in the fall. The first full peacetime draft in over ten years took place that May, during which time the army was to induct two-thirds of its contingent, with the following one-third to be added in October 1924.[162]

Given the serious morale problems of the interim army of 1921–1924, the disorganization and confusion in military circles after the recent shake-ups, and the poor record of Civil War drafts, the 1924 drafts promised to be dicey at best. After all, the military establishment had had little experience with a peace-time draft, and in those areas where it had conducted supplemental drafts, a general criticism was raised that "[l]ocal military commissariats have still not learned that a draft does not have the same character as a mobilization, and they conduct them with excessive haste and with the same methods that they applied during mobilizations of the Civil War period."[163] Indeed, after the 1924 drafts, Mikhail Frunze, the man soon to replace Trotskii as head of the Red Army, painted a dark picture of what had happened, citing shortfalls in territorial units, peasant discontent, and administrative bungling. Those criticisms have led some scholars to characterize the spring draft as a "near disaster."[164]

Frunze, however, appears to have been playing a complicated political game. In fact, it seems that he was deliberately deceptive in his public characterization of the 1924 drafts as failures, perhaps in order to garner support for his reform proposals by criticizing the status quo. His characterization of the 1924 experience was much different in a secret report to the Revolutionary Military Council of the Soviet Union (RVS SSSR) plenum in November 1924, in which he claimed that peasants "willingly appeared, at up to a 100 percent rate," and that the move to territorial divisions had given "positive results."[165] Another reporter at the same session concurred, saying despite all the reasons why the draft should have been a failure, it had instead been a "complete success," a fact that a Rabkrin (the state inspectorate) investigation had confirmed.[166] Still others concurred with this positive view. Iosif Unshlikht reported privately to Stalin that despite the fact it was the "first experience of a draft in peacetime," it was impossible to characterize it as anything but "an unconditional success." The appearance rate was an impressive 95.5 percent, and rather than having to deal with problems of large numbers of evaders and deserters, one of the main difficulties had been processing the unexpectedly high number of volunteers. Better, the draft had been conducted for the most part with the "friendly assistance of local organizations."[167]

The relative success of the draft into the cadre army was underlined by internal memos within the Political Administration of the Worker-Peasant Red Army (PURKKA, or simply PUR) as well. The lessons of the spring draft were studied and sent to all district political administrations prior to the autumn draft. PUR officials were to conduct an inspection of district barracks, to pay more attention to the class discrimination process during the draft, to observe the physical exams closely to make sure that weak individuals were not being allowed in, to pressure local party committees to send "experienced and prepared" workers to the call-up points, to explain prior to draft day the nationality policy of the Soviet Union and how outdated the old traditions of drunken brawling on draft day were, to take the necessary steps to organize "comradely meetings" of inductees when they arrived in their units, and to inform both local military commissariats and potential draftees of the family entitlement rules.[168]

These were not cosmetic changes: the problems of chauvinism and draft day brawling among conscripts were both serious and long-standing ones, as was the problem of physical weakness. But the list of changes reveals that the spring draft had, for the most part, gone extremely well. Three of the changes were to try to make the conscript's entrance into the army not only painless, but perhaps even pleasant. As far as getting the required number of people, the suggestions were those relating to a surfeit of men rather than a deficit. Warm bodies were no longer enough. Now they could afford to be picky about class origin and physical condition.

Moreover, it was clear that the serious problems that still faced conscription officials were social ones rather than technical ones of military administration. Physical weakness, chauvinism, fighting, and the ignorance of local peasants and party officials were the intended targets. Indeed, the report noted the major problem revealed by the spring draft had been that the "overwhelming majority of peasants (even in specialized units) were at a low cultural and political level," which was expressed in displays of religiosity, national antagonism (especially anti-Semitism), and a high rate of illiteracy (up to 20 percent in the North Caucasian, Moscow, and Transvolga military districts).[169] As was the case before World War I, social concerns once more took pride of place in the conscription and political administrations of the army.

It was in this context that the so-called Frunze reforms of the army took place.[170] The policy decisions that ultimately shaped the army for the next decade had begun in 1923, but a concerted effort to deal with systemic questions in a coordinated way and pass them into law took place in 1924–1925 under Frunze's leadership. Included in this package of reforms was a new military service law, passed on 18 September 1925. It was a detailed law, composed of 229 articles, and it cleared up the remaining ambiguities and confusions of the demobilization period.[171]

There had been movements to reform the law and various projected regulations floating around military circles ever since 1923, but these initiatives had not led to concerted action until the creation of a commission to compose a new service law in December 1924.[172] The commission had fifteen items on its agenda, many of which, like considerations about the terms of service, the system of reserves, the mechanisms of registration, the question of 'backward' ethnic groups, and the number of exemptions and deferrals, were the same ones that had occupied military planners before the revolution. Others represented old problems with new postrevolutionary twists. In giving family entitlements based on the number of working hands in a family, for instance, they wondered whether women should be counted as able workers. There were, finally, new problems altogether. Questions about Civil War regulations regarding conscientious objectors, the rear militia of class enemies, and the mandatory pre-draft training that teenagers performed were all put on the table as well.[173]

Just as revealing as the inclusion of these concrete items, however, was the clear focus on terminology that was present from the very beginning. No less than three of the original fifteen questions dealt directly with which rhetorical formulations to use, and much of the subsequent revision of the law as it went to separate commissariats for vetting was based on disputes over proper phrasing.[174] This focus on terminology was especially apparent in the discussions regarding the crucial first article of the law, which established the basis for military service in the Soviet Union. In the original draft, the statement of purpose was split between two articles:

> Article one: the Red Army and Red Navy are part of the laboring classes, armed for the direct defense and preservation of the political and economic rights of laborers, and also the integrity and inviolability of the territory of the USSR.
> Article two: the defense of the USSR with weapon in hand is the honorable right of all laboring citizens of the USSR, for the realization of which they are trained in military affairs.[175]

This was the commission's first lunge at what would be troublesome questions, namely, was the Red Army primarily to be the arm of (a nonterritorially based) international revolution or of territorial defense? Further, who should have the right (or duty) to serve with weapon in hand? The national answer to these questions is that armies exist to protect the territory inhabited by members of the political community and they should be staffed by all male members of that community. This national answer had been given during the Brest-Litovsk debates in 1918 and again in the 1922 code, which had stressed defense and citizenship in its first article.

In 1923, however, an aborted conscription plan authored by the Mobilization Department had envisioned the role of the army much differently, as an international revolutionary force. The projected law began with the statement that the "preservation and expansion of the conquests of the October Worker-Peasant Revolution lie upon the armed forces of the Soviet Union" and urged, not surprisingly, a strict class filtration for incoming soldiers. This formulation had immediately made at least some readers nervous; on two separate copies, critics crossed out the words "preservation and expansion" (okhrana i rasshirenie) and replaced them with the word "defense" (zashchita), the same word, not coincidentally, which had been in article 1 of the military service law since 1874.[176]

The version written by the commission sponsored by Frunze lay between the national formulation in the 1922 law and the internationalist formulation of the 1923 project. By the time the project had been vetted by various state and military institutions and revisions had been made, the national aspect was given considerably more weight, and a majority of the commission members agreed to word article 1 to read that the "defense of the revolution" was the "responsibility of all citizens of the USSR." The commission, though, could not come to full agreement on the wording, and the projected law went to the RVS along with a rival version supported only by the PUR representative, who suggested that it read

> 1) The defense of the hard-won October Revolution, which established the first Worker-Peasant power in the world, is the responsibility of all laboring citizens of the USSR.

1a) Non-laboring elements are deprived of the right of defense of the USSR with weapon in hand in view of the possibility on their part to use their position and weapon to the detriment of the goal of the laborers. In order not to free these elements from the burden of preparing for the conduct of war, they will be enlisted in another type of duty and monetary taxation both in peace and in wartime.[177]

The major difference between the two positions was noted in the report of the commission. The PUR representative pushed for a stronger formulation than had the majority of the commission, arguing that the defense of the revolution lay only upon the laboring "citizens." Non-laboring "elements" (not "citizens"), were only included so that they would not escape a "burden." Their role was merely "preparing for the conduct of war" and constituted a "different" type of duty. The majority, by contrast, felt that the taxes and trench work performed by non-laborers constituted the fulfillment of a "military" duty, and that the defense of the revolution was the responsibility of "all citizens of the USSR."[178]

The RVS came down on the side of the majority "national" position: "The defense of the hard-won October Revolution, which established the first Worker-Peasant power in the world, is the responsibility of all citizens of the USSR. The defense of the USSR with weapon in hand belongs only to laboring citizens. Non-laboring citizens are deprived of the responsibility to defend the USSR with weapon in hand."[179] By the time the law was passed in September, the wording was more national still: "The defense of the USSR is the responsibility of all citizens of the Union. The defense of the USSR with weapon in hand is granted only to laborers. Non-laboring elements are required to fulfill other military responsibilities."[180]

In 1923, some planners envisioned the "armed forces of the Soviet Union" protecting and expanding the worldwide revolution. By September 1925, all mention of the revolution had disappeared. Now the armed forces of the Soviet Union were to defend the territory of the Soviet Union and would be staffed by the population of the Soviet Union. The only proviso that differentiated this basic principle from those of other national armies (including the prerevolutionary Russian army) was the continuing distrust of class enemies, who, though citizens with military responsibilities, were still prohibited from carrying weapons. This proviso was significant in its own way, as was the ambiguity in the wording referring to non-laborers, calling them "citizens" in the first sentence but "elements" in the second. But the thrust, indeed the explicit decision, of state and military leaders was clear: the Red Army was a national army, not an instrument of global revolution.

The national army, however uncomfortable it may have been for radical communists, was the result of a long period of political negotiation between soldiers, their families, and the state regarding military service. The rhetoric employed in this negotiation was almost always centered around equality and fairness, but this rhetoric was misleading. Instead, armies firmed up and enlistments rose when soldiers were given preference both materially and in terms of social prestige. The high rate of appearance (and volunteering) in the 1924 draft (and beyond) reflected this fact quite well. Mark von Hagen has stressed the degree to which soldiers in the Civil War were treated as a privileged class and has correlated many of the problems experienced by the army during the demobilization period to a loss of this sense of special privilege.[181] That prestige was reestablished in the mid-1920s as the result of a conscious effort to make army service more palatable and honorable and to make army veterans a privileged group throughout the country.

The set of benefits given to soldiers and their families was extensive and it formed the core of low politics in the 1920s. The government offered privileges in acquiring agricultural help, tax breaks, special access to living quarters, first crack at social security benefits, preferential treatment for their children in schools, access to health care, and more.[182] In addition, conscripts fully expected to learn skills in the army that would help them upon their release. The army really was a "school" in quite a literal sense, and soldiers knew it. Reports of the behavior of young conscripts repeatedly mentioned the "great interest" they showed toward educational work and bemoaned their "scornful reaction to combat training."[183]

The opportunities for social mobility went well beyond the ability to move from a low-skill job to a high-skill job, from peasant to commander, or from village to city. Bolshevik leaders were explicit about their desire to use army veterans as a pool of reliable cadres in state and party positions as well. Army veterans had, indeed, taken up these positions in large numbers throughout the early 1920s. Fully 72.8 percent of the chairmen of executive committees of county soviets were Red Army veterans in 1922.[184] But the leadership was not satisfied. An audit of PUR conducted by the party's Central Control Commission in 1923–1924 was sharply critical of PUR's activities and urged them to do even more in this realm. They had to turn the barracks into "a school of communism" and to "sovietize peasant youth," making it a "reserve for the party."[185]

This initiative was confirmed by a circular to all provincial party organizations just before the release of men whose term was up in 1924. It instructed local party organizations, among other things, to "instruct" the veterans about current policy issues, to give them instructional materials and copies of recent legal reforms, to ensure that veterans receive all the entitlements the law provided, to take measures to secure work for all communists just released, and to bring all the recently released men going home to their villages into "social and cultural work in the countryside."[186]

Conclusion

In the late imperial period rank-and-file soldiers occupied the bottom rung of the social ladder. Banned from street transportation and public entertainment, forced to travel in cattle cars when riding on trains, and

shunned by all levels of society, soldiers were not honored citizens. Just before the Great War, Aleksandr Guchkov, a prominent centrist in the Duma,
led a movement to change this situation, but it yielded no concrete
results.[187] No wonder one of the immediate and continuing demands of
soldiers during 1917 was the garnering of equal civil rights. Those rights,
once acquired, were tenaciously defended.

The Bolsheviks, positioning themselves as a soldier's party, supported
such rights both for ideological and practical political reasons in 1917 and
trumpeted their support of equal social status for soldiers immediately after
the October Revolution. Talk, however, is cheap. What differentiated the
Bolsheviks from their tsarist predecessors and from their enemies in the
Civil War was that they proved able to implement and enforce workable
military service laws that resonated with their soldiers and potential soldiers. This insight into the politics of military service came in the late
spring of 1919, when the Reds appeared to be on the verge of defeat. By incorporating soldiers and soldier desires into their political sphere and political ideology, the Bolsheviks won the war and cast the die of the Soviet system in what turned out to be a lasting way.

The conscription law of 1925 confirmed the Bolshevik commitment to a
national army with privileged soldiers. Soldiers had gone from a virtually
"untouchable" caste to a position of entitlement in society in the space of a
mere twenty years, a turnabout that was as unmistakable as it was rapid. It
was a transformation that occurred because of total war, not because of the
revolutions of 1917, the occurrence and content of which were, in any case,
predicated to a large degree on the prior transformations that took place during World War I. Indeed, no socialist thinker prior to World War I envisioned
either the form that the Red Army was to assume or the social status that its
soldiers and veterans would enjoy in the mid-1920s and well beyond.

The reasons for this surprising development are complex and not reducible to purely functional considerations. The Red Army and its soldiers
enjoyed preferential treatment not simply because, as the Bolsheviks liked
to claim about the tsarist system, the "throne rested upon bayonets," or because it provided the only defense against a hostile outside world, though
both of these facts were clearly true. Neither should the widespread desire
of Soviet citizens to serve in the army be viewed as pure careerism or a desire for social mobility, though those factors were undoubtedly powerful as
well. Soldiers loomed large mostly because the military had insinuated itself into the political community, indeed had helped shape it in fundamental ways. This shaping was not done solely by officers and bureaucrats. Soldiers themselves forced officials to reconsider their projects and retool them
to better correspond with soldier and conscript desires. As the rest of the
book will show, the form being taken by the army-influenced political community was national, and it was thoroughly militarized.

CHAPTER TWO

The Nation and the Dilemma of Difference

Military intellectuals forwarded a nationalist program in order to build a more competitive army. Believing that only nations could win modern wars, they ardently desired a unified, homogeneous community of independent men (aided by dependent women) who could both show initiative and submit to hierarchical discipline on the battlefield and in their civic lives. As a result, these men consistently displayed a commitment to an inclusive, multiethnic, multi-class army that would grow more inclusive over time. Russian nationalists failed to build the unified community they so desired. But they succeeded in creating a nation.

There is no inherent contradiction in this result if the nation is viewed as a type of ideology rather than a human community. The problem with making this conceptual leap is that it implicitly assumes that those millions of nationalists or nation-builders in the last two centuries actually did not know what they were doing as they were doing it. Scholarly hubris aside, there is nothing logically wrong with this position. The history of unintended consequences is so rich that one sometimes wonders whether there is any other kind, but it does require a bit of explanation.

The explanation for why nationalists spent so much time trying to create a physical community but ended up creating a metaphysical medium of power is linked to the mechanisms through which they tried to act on large populations. In particular, the rise of the social sciences, statistics, and "population politics" in the nineteenth century allowed officials to work on categories and to believe that they were working on people. Ultimately, of course, this work had very definite repercussions for actual people, but the initial work was that of categorization.[1]

The nationalist method is to define the political community by invoking naturalized population categories to demonstrate the unity within one's own political community and the divisions that separate it from other political communities. It is a powerful method, but there is madness to it. In addition to articulating differences from other nations, it also enshrines categories that divide populations living in the national territory. This is the nationalist's dilemma of difference: the very method that provides coherence to the national form simultaneously undercuts the unity that is desired. Every national project thus involves a scramble to define "natural" population categories and to align those categories with notions of belonging and political power.

But some nations are harder to consolidate than others. All nationalists are faced with preexisting and constantly developing ideas about what constitutes social identity and about those categories that "naturally" structure human behavior. In the Russian Empire, the problem of social identity was especially acute. Notions about possible categorizations of human beings were not simply in a state of flux. They were, for most officials, hopelessly muddled. Earnest attempts by recent historians to find consistency within the worldview of late imperial officials have run into tremendous trouble, and the most proficient scholars of social identity in late imperial Russia have stressed the indeterminate, indeed even contradictory, nature of ideas about social location.[2]

As if categorical confusion were not enough, the physical mobility of people living in Russia further complicated matters. Millions of European peasants migrated to Siberia, Central Asia, and the Caucasus in the years leading up to World War I, and millions more left rural communities to go to the rapidly expanding Russian cities on a part-time or full-time basis, a mobility that became even more pronounced (and two-way) during the seven years of war.[3] When this massive uprooting took place, the worldviews of both the wanderers and those who stayed at home underwent a significant change, but that change almost never occurred the way tsarist and Soviet observers thought it would.

It was in the midst of this conceptual and physical indeterminacy that military nationalists tried to articulate a vision of political community that stressed rootedness, natural and indisputed categorizations of humanity, and the essential solidarity of a diverse population. To make matters even more complicated, nationalists did not stand outside the discourses that helped to structure understanding of the world and of humanity. They were not puppeteers who pulled the strings of population marionettes in ways purely and rationally optimal for their eventual national goals.

A few words are therefore in order about some of the beliefs on population categories and human differences that were commonly held in Russia in the first years of the twentieth century. First, most educated Russians in both the tsarist and Soviet regimes generally subscribed to an overall vision of human difference and history that was structured by the stadial progress of civilizations. Like many Europeans, they believed that civilizations progressed at different rates but passed through the same stages.[4] M. A. Slavinskii expressed this view clearly in 1915 when he argued that many ethnic groups living in Russia were "nothing more than ethnic material [*etnicheskii material]*, the plasticity of which is almost limitless," while others were at the European level of development. As a result it was the role of the Russian people to preserve the "enormous laboratory" of the Russian Empire, where "one may observe all the forms and types of national flowering, all the stages of their birth and development: from the very first national shoot to their lush blooming."[5] The question for Slavinskii and many of his contemporaries was not *whether* "backward" civilizations would become like their "advanced" neighbors, but *when* they would. On a practical level, the question was whether the "preserver of the laboratory" could speed the process of progress along, and if so, how. The central problem was one of time.[6]

The second broadly applicable tenet to stress is that, as the powerful "modern" ideas of the French Revolution, German Romanticism, Marx, and Darwin became progressively more ingrained in Russian thinking, particularly among elites, the structuring principles of the old regime began to give way to new principles. More specifically in the Russian case, ideas of estate and religion as population markers progressively declined as ideas of ethnicity and class as determinants in human behavior increased in power.[7]

Ethnicity and Class under the Old Regime

The universal conscription law of 1874 was intended to increase both military capability and social solidarity. Dmitrii Miliutin and his compatriots focused their efforts on destroying the accretion of old-regime obstacles to that solidarity. They took selection authority away from local communes, erased as many privileges based upon estate position and religion as they could, and focused their attention on creating a system of civic inclusiveness. That inclusive desire extended to those members of the polity who were not ethnically Russian. Miliutin insisted that the army was both a reflection of the broader political community and a transformative agent within it. As a result, he consistently pushed for more ethnic groups to be covered under the new law, saying that military service presented the best means for "weakening tribal differences among the people."[8]

This did not mean, however, that immediately bringing all previously exempted ethnic groups under the conscription law was necessarily the best way to reach that final goal. The question of timing was crucial, even for the most ardent reformers. Though some members of the commission that drafted the 1874 law pressed for casting the net widely and bringing even the many nomadic groups of recently conquered Central Asia under the law in the very near future, the committee decided to defer the draft of "backward" ethnic groups. Among those arguing against a broad draft principle was A. P. Suprenenko, a State Councilor who wondered aloud whether it was in the state's best interest to inculcate a "martial spirit" among steppe peoples while the Russian presence was still so weak there and while fellow tribesmen lived within the borders of other states or remained unpacified within Russia's own borders.[9] He and others argued that the best approach was to wait patiently until imperially sponsored economic development worked its assimilative magic and prepared Russia's various "tribes" mentally, socially, and physically for the demands of military service.

This imperial belief in the possibility of assimilation began to fade as the century progressed, however. As Darwinism, social Darwinism, and ethnically based theories of social organization and social behavior infected all of Europe in the last quarter of the nineteenth century, so too did they catch on in Russia.[10] Qualities like "martial spirit," bravery, and courage began to be ascribed to specific ethnic groups, which were now increasingly understood in terms of a weakly defined notion of "race." The question of the relationship between ethnicity and military ability was posed directly by Mikhail Dragomirov, who claimed that the unusual staunchness of the Russian soldier was "the result of the racial [rasovye] peculiarities of the simple Russian man and the stern position in which mother nature placed him. His father's helper in difficult peasant work from his childhood . . . in slush, in wind, in cold, in heat reaching 30 degrees [Celsius], sometimes more, the Russian boy little by little . . . gets used to calmly looking death in the eye."[11] This excerpt shows how the idea of "race" was penetrating intellectual and government circles in late imperial Russia, but the idea that "blood" was significant, though perhaps implicit, was still largely unarticulated. More pertinent to human behavior was the cultural and physical environment in which children were raised.

Also present in this passage from Dragomirov is recognition of the importance of "class" to military performance. Class, for military officials, was both more and less than it was for ideologists of economic production in early twentieth-century Russia. Military professionals tended to agree with Dragomirov that a particular relationship to nature and the experience of living in a commune defined the "peasant" more than the official estate system did. Likewise, army men in the early Soviet period were less fixated on their soldiers' relationship to the means of production than their orthodox Marxist colleagues were.[12] The concern of these men both before and after the revolution hinged on the difference between rural and urban conscripts; they had little use for the fine class distinctions within rural and urban society.

At first, military planners were unanimous in their preference for peasant soldiers. Indeed, from the beginning of debates on universal service in the 1870s, conservatives argued against the plan because they thought it would lead to a shift in the balance between peasants and workers, both in society and in the army. They feared (just as many others hoped) that conscription would expose peasants to the wider world, lead them to move out of their villages, and create a "large rootless population, itself unhappy and in its own time dangerous to the state."[13]

Reformist military men agreed. The young peasant, according to one progressive trainer, was the heart of the army and the joy of the company commander. He had a "simplicity, testifying to a complete lack of falseness, the goodhearted tone of his voice, a certain naiveté in his answers, and finally, the colorful physical appearance of these people—all this produces an exceedingly pleasant impression on you." The young factory worker, on the other hand, had "sunken, shifty eyes" and belonged to the stratum of society "where work alternates with debauchery and drunkenness." As a result, this trainer claimed, he had never seen "even a slightly moral man from this social group." [14]

Given that Russian society and the Russian army were overwhelmingly composed of rural men, one would have thought the army could have found protection from the urban threat in numbers. Instead, army officials feared contagion of their "simple" and "naïve" charges.[15] In 1912, when disorder erupted in several territorially based units in Vladimir province, there was unanimity among military officials as to the reasons. There had been a noted decline in the moral level of peasant youth in the units, which manifested itself as "debauchery and an inclination for abusing alcohol." In the same breath, they noted that social democrats were happy with the proposed transition to territorially based units, since local boys would not shoot at them.[16] No direct connection was made in this letter, but the Ministry of Internal Affairs (MVD) did not refrain from linking moral decline with worker influence in its follow-up examination.[17] The solution to the worker problem in this case was to order local military officials to station conscripts "from the city and factory population, as well as people with a depraved nature" far from their home province.[18] Class was a very real factor in military manpower decisions well before 1917.

If there was little ambiguity in the way that military planners and conscript trainers looked at the relative moral qualities of peasants and workers, there was a great deal more when they looked at the role of ethnicity in social behavior. Nikolai Butovskii, one of these trainers, commented that most of his peers looked at non-Russian speakers as the "most thankless material in the business of morally training soldiers." This was a mistake in his view. For him, nationality (natsional'nost') had meaning "only in the area of receptivity, which depends on special character traits and on a greater or lesser knowledge of the Russian language." In virtually the same breath, however, he made note of ethnic differences. "Chukhontsy" (Estonians) were marked by honor, religiosity, accuracy, and efficiency. Tatars, because of their "national peculiarities," worked best as grooms. Jews, whom he excepted from his claim that nationality had little meaning, were to be placed in the regimental band, since they were morally unfit for combat duty.[19]

Butovskii's main thrust in regard to ethnicity, though, was an attempt to get his peers to change their outlook toward non-Russians in the army, and realize that, with the exception of Jews, all were capable of being good soldiers with the proper treatment and training. His repeated exhortations to his colleagues suggest, in addition, that there was a great deal of variance in the way that ethnic minorities were treated after they had been conscripted. Officers (and NCOs) had quite different ideas about assimilation, ethnicity, and culture.

The changes of outlook that occurred during the nineteenth century, though showing up with increasing regularity in military writings, did not bring about a sea change in the laws regarding non-Russians until the twentieth century. As with the rest of conscription policy, it took the shattering loss in the Russo-Japanese War and the mortal fright of the 1905 Revolution to reopen debate on ethnic policy within the army. The events of 1904–1906 were a shock to military officials; one of the outcomes of this shock was that ethnicity came to play a much larger role in the way army leaders interpreted events. Smug beliefs in the natural superiority of Europeans to Asians had come unceremoniously crashing down. Japanese soldiers were admired for their martial qualities, while those same qualities had proved conspicuously missing among many of the tsar's soldiers. Not only had the legendary "staunchness" of the Russian peasant failed on several occasions in Manchuria, but those same peasants then refused to display their legendary submissiveness to fate, rising in hundreds of mutinies over the course of the revolution.[20]

The ethnic question was also ascribed new importance as a result of the conflicts that erupted in the Transcaucasus and the western provinces of the empire during the revolution. Most of these revolts were directed at the imperial government, but they quickly assumed an ethnic frame as local nationalists articulated their dissatisfaction in terms of Russian oppression and as a destructive war in the Transcaucasus between Armenians and Azerbaidzhanis made the question of ethnic identity nearly impossible to ignore.[21]

The ethnic scare was a serious one that was evident throughout the military and state apparatus. In June 1905, the tsar decreed that all conscripts who were natives of Transcaucasia (regardless of religion) should be assigned to units outside of the Caucasus. In this status, the Transcaucasians joined conscripts of the Baltic region, who for many years had been systematically assigned to units outside of their home region.[22] But peacetime deployment far from their ethnic brethren was not enough. The viceroy of the Caucasus wished also to let the Mobilization Department know that deployment of Caucasian natives in the Caucasus was unacceptable even in wartime.[23]

As the importance of ethnicity increased, the notion that religious affiliation was the primary social category in the empire increasingly wore thin.[24] For some time, many officials had been using religions as code words for population groups they understood to be ethnic in nature (the most obvious being that "Catholic" meant "Polish"). Now open calls were made to do away with the religious veneer. In a memo to the General Staff, the Main Staff commented that it had no objections to removing all service limitations currently enforced against certain religious groups so that military policy would better correspond with the tsar's new policy of religious tolerance.[25] The army was particularly concerned about two religious groups, Catholics and Jews. Catholics were barred from entering the General Staff Academy, while Jews were prohibited both from entering the academy and from becoming officers. The prohibition against Catholics was the result of the recurring rebellions in Poland dating from Russia's annexation of large parts of the country in the last quarter of the eighteenth century. Given the likelihood that Russian troops would be asked to march again into Poland, it seemed politically wise to make sure that the general leading the march was not Polish.

In 1906, this prohibition still seemed wise, but the removal of religious barriers, far from being a problem, presented an opportunity for better inoculating the army against political disloyalty. Now, claimed one military official, "nationality [natsional'nost'], and not religious faith, should determine the right to enter the [General Staff] Academy. In practice, the conversion of Poles to Orthodoxy or Lutheranism eliminated all limitations. . . . But a change of religion can hardly be linked to a change of political convictions."[26] This straightforward claim is remarkable in two respects. First, it contradicted the traditional notion that loyalty to the tsar was, in fact, linked to religion. Converting to the state religion was for centuries accepted as a signal of political loyalty in official parlance. Second, it demonstrated that nationality was increasingly perceived to be the determining factor in political loyalty.

Though the shift to discriminating against Poles on the basis of ethnicity rather than religious affiliation was never made, army policy did officially shift in regard to Jews. In a secret order from the Main Administration of the General Staff in 1910, it was made clear that, when implementing discriminatory policies, "Jews should be understood in the tribal sense, regardless of their religious affiliation."[27] Ideas about the bases of social behavior and political loyalty were visibly shifting from the category of religion to the category of ethnicity among military officials.

A great many factors therefore coalesced in the turmoil of 1905 to open the door for ethnic nationalism as a component of policy making in the years leading up to World War I. The rise of ethnicity as a marker of population groups, outbursts in the name of ethnicity during the 1905 Revolution, the gnawing fear that the loss to the Japanese had signaled national decline and racial inferiority, and even sops of religious freedom thrown to liberals by a besieged autocracy all led to a situation in which nationalism and loyalty were increasingly viewed in ethnic terms.

That said, the period from 1905–1914 was also marked by the fastest arms race and most profound international anxiety that the "national" world had yet seen.[28] The military and conscription corollary to this acceleration of industrial war machines has already been traced: state planners believed that more men were needed. It stood to reason, not only for military planners but for political officials as well, that it was necessary for the "population currently freed from military service to be brought into it gradually, but by means of decisive and urgent measures . . . in conditions appropriate to the peculiarities of their lifestyles, religion, climate, and so forth."[29] The numbers game simply could not allow for a restrictively ethnic army without endangering the existence of the state and the ethnic nation for which that army would fight. So the tension between the ethnic nation and the multiethnic nation remained, but with the added urgency of humiliating defeat and looming war.

One obvious answer to the dilemma between the increased need for large numbers of soldiers and the increased attention to ethnicity as a determining factor of behavior was the creation of ethnic units. There were only a handful of ethnic units in the Russian army prior to the turn of the century, all of which could usefully be understood as units of 'martial races.' They were not units of national integration, in other words, but provided forces of useful 'outsiders,' characterized by marginality and dependency, who had special skills that the central elite could use.[30] The first call to consider the creation of ethnic units as a technique of solidarity rather than separateness came from Prince I. I. Vorontsov-Dashkov, the viceroy of the Caucasus, who suggested forming special Muslim units in a letter to the tsar in 1907. His goal, ultimately, was assimilation, his target the pan-Islamic movement, and his tool the army. He reiterated his original position in a 1911 letter to Stolypin, in which he argued that the "danger of meeting our own battle-trained Muslims in the Turkish or Persian armies" was not really that serious because "spending time in the ranks of our army would undoubtedly assist the development of a feeling of devotion to tsar and fatherland among Caucasian Muslims, while simultaneously weakening Muslim religious ties. Meanwhile, we would have in the Muslims people imbued by nature with a martial spirit, courageous horsemen, and excellent shooters."[31] As with the authors of the War Ministry memos cited above, Vorontsov-Dashkov assumed that ethnicity, not religion, was the primary determinant of social and individual behavior, including political loyalty. Indeed, though the state clearly played a role in the assimilation process, the process itself was passive and naturalized. Dangers would pass, the mere fact of being present in the army would speed up assimilation, and martial spirits would be imbued by nature. The state's role was merely to provide the opportunity for these natural processes of assimilation and identification to take place.

In response to this call for assimilation, the General Staff expressed exactly the fear that Vorontsov-Dashkov had tried to head off, that religious loyalty would prove stronger than political loyalty. It objected that forming ethnic units not only posed a danger to the domestic order, but also was untenable in strategic terms. Vorontsov-Dashkov's belief that Muslims would be reliable in a war with the Ottoman Empire was far from universally accepted, and the army wanted to preserve flexibility in terms of troop deployment. Sending a fully Muslim unit into battle with other Muslims was not an idea that appealed to many members of the General Staff.[32] The General Staff decided that if the government found it necessary to accept only volunteers, then they must be stationed outside of the Caucasus and Turkestan, and that if the government found it acceptable to bring them under the general conscription law, then again, they should be stationed outside of the Caucasus and Turkestan. In short, Caucasian natives should be drafted, but also should be given "even more onerous conditions for an initial trial period."[33] The army's leaders followed the same principles they had since 1874: they preached (and believed in) the long-term goal of the multiethnic nation while practicing short-term imperial policies of ethnic discrimination. The key, as always, was temporal. Caucasian Muslims would be held in a discriminatory position only for the near future.

The larger question of how to deal with ethnic difference had to wait for the debate surrounding comprehensive military reform. The question of dealing with ethnic exemptions was officially deferred until the second round of reforms, and work did not start on composing legislation until late 1910.[34] The first and supposedly quicker set of reforms was not passed until 1912. World War I broke out before the second set could make it through the labyrinth of the late imperial legislative process. Nevertheless, the discussions within the commission and the reports from around the empire on the question reveal a great deal about the difficulties faced by military planners. Despite having a lengthy agenda, Lukomskii acknowledged that the most pressing task of the commission was the question of drafting ethnic minorities in general and the Kirgiz in particular.[35] The populations exempted from conscription totaled about 13,700,000 of the 128,300,000 in the empire in the 1897 census, of which nearly half were the "non-Russian population of Turkestan and Kirgiziia."[36] Given this mandate, the commission asked for input from military officials in Siberia and Turkestan as well as the Caucasus.

The appeals for information themselves are instructive. Typical of the genre was the following, in which General Ia. G. Zhilinskii, the chief of the General Staff, reminded the Priamurskii governor-general of the urgency of the ethnic question and added that

> The core population of the empire, taking upon itself the main burden of state obligations, has been required on top of that to bear the sacred duty of defending the motherland for the population of the frontier. Such an abnormal state of affairs leads to a gradual impoverishment of the center of the empire while the frontier, free from military service, develops at its expense. The government and State Duma have turned their attention to this fact several times. . . . it also has a broader state significance, since military service, bringing non-Russians into close contact with the Russian population, undoubtedly will have an exceedingly positive influence on their existence, spiritual and cultural development, and consequently will assist in the gradual Russification [obruseniiu] of the non-Russians.[37]

Zhilinskii's position was a quite common one in the period between the Russo-Japanese War and World War I, and it revealed one of the major weaknesses of the tsarist empire. Empires often build domestic support by privileging a certain portion of their population, what Russians called their "core" population. But the tsarist government usually proved unwilling to do this, preferring to act in the interests of the state rather than the interests of their core population. In particular, the intense desire to assimilate "backward" peoples on the frontier led to a string of policies that sought to invest resources in the frontier and create favorable conditions for cultural assimilation.[38]

As a result, an increasing number of Russian chauvinists were viewing the imperial structure as a disadvantage for Russians. According to them, both the socioeconomic and the civilizing burdens lay on the dominant nationality; Russians were being forced to pay for the economic development of the frontier and the material improvement of non-Russians, and in addition were taking on the major state obligations, in particular military service. Thus the call for equality of ethnicities was made by many Russian chauvinists in the center in order to avoid footing the bill for underdevelopment on the frontier.

The opposite position was taken by many of the European settlers who had moved east in the great migration at the turn of the century. Their arrival in Siberia and Central Asia had forever changed the character of ethnic relations on the frontier. Europeans moved onto nomadic pastures, fought with local populations, and generally adopted a combative attitude toward natives that contradicted the general thrust of state policy.[39] This faction called for the establishment of a more consistent imperial relationship in which Russians were favored, and that position was supported by imperialists in central Russia as well. One author breathlessly claimed that the "decline of the core Russian population" due to the seizure of their possessions by "non-Russians and foreigners" was taking place both on the frontier and in central Russia. "Battling this sad, parasitical occurrence is possible only by strengthening the core Russian population, strengthening our villages," he argued, and added that the army, "that great school of the people, can and should help the motherland in this respect."[40] But, as Theodore Weeks has ably pointed out, the tsarist state proved unwilling to consistently implement an imperial policy that favored its core population, and as a result drifted from one unpopular position to the next.[41] The mixture between empire and nation pleased no one and antagonized everyone.

Thus, most Russian nationalists in the army itself gave little serious thought to creating a single-ethnicity army of Russians alone. They tended to agree more with Zhilinskii that drafting non-Russians killed two birds with one stone by lessening the burden on Russians while Russifying the non-Russians. The popular principle of equality before the draft board was therefore adopted even by Russian chauvinists in the military bureaucracy. At the same time, officials with a more expansive view of political community continued to use the Miliutin principle, and seemed genuinely overjoyed that the question of incorporating non-Russians had been raised again. The commander of the Turkmen cavalry division commented:

I welcome the decision to introduce universal military duty everywhere, in particular with it being based on its characteristic features—obligatory and personal for everyone. The decision is wise in all respects; first of all, the most heavy obligation will be equally distributed amongst the whole population of the empire, and secondly the whole population will be magnanimously offered the great honor and right to defend the fatherland. It is magnanimous because the very idea of "non-Russian" will decline, since through the act of introducing universal military duty, Russia will recognize all its tribes not as non-Russian children but as its native children.[42]

Stressing universality for this commander was not inconsistent with stressing ethnic differences, however. Quite the contrary, he attributed all kinds of special ethical and physical qualities to his Turkmen charges.[43] These differences, however, did not prevent their effective incorporation into the larger imperial army.

Thus, even though their views were radically different, a certain section of the narrow "ethnic" nationalist groups and a section of the expansive "civic" nationalist groups were able to find common ground in the debate. The response of local commanders at a series of military conferences in 1910 and 1911 to the question of whether non-Russians should be drafted was virtually unanimous. Siberian commanders meeting in Tomsk declared that the proper course was to draft all non-Russians, but only after land reform and judicial reforms among nomadic peoples. In Tobol'sk there was hesitation about drafting certain ethnic groups, but again only because of concerns that assimilation had not proceeded far enough. Groups like the Samoeds, they claimed, were at the "very lowest level of culture," indeed were still "primitive tribes," and drafting them would be premature. These concerns were absent in the Transcaucasus, where the main worry was that previously exempted groups would flee abroad if threatened with conscription. This worry was not sufficient, however, as military commanders and Vorontsov-Dashkov alike declared that the time had come to conscript Muslims in the Caucasus, a recommendation accepted by the Lukomskii Commission and formally included in the draft legislation. In all of these recommendations, military commanders agreed in principle with drafting non-Russians and making them a constitutive part of the Russian army. The only disagreements revolved around the timing of the draft.[44]

Though the second military reform bill and the recommendations regarding drafting non-Russians never made it to the Duma floor, tsarist legislators were so involved in the ethnicity question that they raised it during the debates surrounding the first bill, which had studiously avoided the problem of non-Russians and the even more touchy "Jewish question." Muslim deputies were among the first to speak about the conscription bill. Deputy Khakh-Mamedov, for instance, argued that the principle of military service as a civic duty should be upheld for all. Forcing Muslims to pay a tax rather than serve in the army was "an undeserved, bitter offence." Military service was not only a "high obligation," but also a "natural right." The exclusion of young Muslims reinforced the idea that they were "not sons of a common motherland, but stepsons."[45] Duma members expressed strong support for drafting Muslims. When Khakh-Mamedov finished his speech, he was greeted by applause from the center, the left, and the right wings of the Duma.[46] Religion was notably absent from the discussion. Ethnicity was clearly the crucial factor that determined "martial spirit" as well as political loyalty. Another Duma member made even clearer how far the idea that religion was a political marker had fallen, saying that "the feeling of love and devotion to the motherland always comes out on top over feelings of abstract religious sympathies."[47]

In the Duma debate, as in the War Ministry debates, those more concerned with protecting Russian interests than with the ideal of an inclusive political community per se argued along the same lines as non-Russians seeking equal treatment before the law. As one Russian deputy argued, "If you really consider that the army should serve the state, defend it, then [you must argue] that the military burden should be fulfilled by everyone in an equal measure," and asked "who will bear the burden that we take from Muslims and Jews? Well, it will lie on the peasantry. . . . You talk about equality, well then put equality into the law."[48] Within the sphere of military service, at least, there was broad-based support for a policy of multiethnic civic equality.

Thus, on the eve of the Great War two trends were clearly visible. First, there was a growing coalition seeking for greater numbers of non-Russians to be drafted. Second, there was a hardening belief that the assimilation of non-Russians should take place in integrated units rather than in ethnic units. The problem of ethnic units, though, in contrast to that of broader application of military service obligations, was primarily one of political danger rather than social assimilation. Military officials had come to take it as a general law that once an ethnicity proceeded past a certain stage in its historical development, ethnic army units automatically began to display greater loyalty to their ethnicity than to the multiethnic nation. As Lukomskii reported in 1910, "historical experience has shown, that the formation . . . of native troops has usually resulted in the necessity of disbanding them upon the development of national self-consciousness [natsional'noe samosoznanie] and centrifugal yearnings among the separate ethnic groups [narodnosti]."[49] Thus, even those ethnic units that had been formed and survived the 1905 Revolution untainted were falling into disfavor. A formal call for the disbanding of the Dagestan cavalry regiment, one of the oldest of the ethnic units, was made less than two months prior to the outbreak of war.[50]

The Great War and the Apogee of Ethnicity

World War I had an immediate impact upon the development of the ethnic question in the armed forces, accelerating the first trend of seeking to conscript more non-Russian ethnic groups and reversing the second trend of dissolving ethnic units into integrated ones. In both cases it was public pressure that accounted for the changing relationship between ethnicity and conscription. Two factors played an especially large role in the dramatic development regarding ethnic units. First, of course, was that the War Ministry became very concerned with turning nearly every healthy man into a loyal soldier, rather than just 30 percent of them. The demand for warm bodies was large in 1914 and critical from the summer of 1915 on. This demand overrode objections on the grounds of domestic stability or long-range planning.

Second, the propaganda campaign launched by the tsarist government leaned heavily on the theme of ethnicity, especially early in the war. Literally overnight, the tsarist government moved from a policy of containing ethnic nationalist feelings to mobilizing them.[51] Top officials consciously raised expectations that the Romanov dynasty would recognize ethnic nationalist aspirations after the successful conclusion of the war. Nicholas II, visiting the Caucasus, proclaimed that "Armenians can expect a shining future."[52] Grand Duke Nikolai Nikolaevich, the supreme commander of the Russian army, was even more explicit. On 1 August 1914, he published an appeal to Poles:

> The hour has come when the sacred dream of your fathers and grandfathers can be realized. One hundred and fifty years ago, the living body of Poland was ripped into pieces. But her soul did not die; it lived in the hope that the hour would strike for the resurrection of the Polish people and the fraternal reconciliation of the people with great Russia. Russian troops bring you the good news of this reconciliation. . . . Under the scepter [of the Russian tsar] Poland will be reborn, free in its faith, language, and self-government. . . . Russia believes that the sword that struck down the enemy at Grünwald has not rusted.[53]

This was bold talk from an army and government that had gleefully participated in ripping the "living body" of Poland into pieces, had brutally suppressed Polish uprisings in 1830, 1863, and 1905, and continued to forbid the entrance of Poles into the General Staff Academy. One would have been hard pressed a month earlier to find a military or government official who genuinely believed that the Grünwald sword was not rusted beyond repair. But the "truth" of this broadsheet is not important in this context. What is important was that this appeal, and others like it, opened up political space for ethnic nationalists to press for separate and autonomous institutions within the Russian Empire. Almost immediately this discursive and institutional space was filled with the creation of single-ethnicity units.

On 28 October 1914, an obscure noble landowner from Warsaw province named Vitol'd Gorchinskii approached General N. N. Ianushkevich, then Grand Duke Nikolai Nikolaevich's chief of staff, with a simple request, to form a Polish detachment that would join in the war effort against Germany. The request was approved "as an exception and only as an experiment."[54] The project quickly snowballed from plans for a "detachment" to a full "Polish Legion" that would tap not only Poles in Poland but those in the diaspora as well; reports from Chicago suggested that the Polish community there was willing to provide up to 30,000 men.[55] By December, Gorchinskii was in the midst of training his initial 400 men, and the Polish Legion was sent to the front on 7 March 1915.[56] The army now had 400 new soldiers that it would otherwise not have tapped, the possibility for adding thousands more from the United States, and a concrete model of Slavic unity upon which it could make further appeals.[57] It also had a precedent. Over the next several months the Stavka approved requests for a Latvian brigade and a Russian brigade in Galicia.[58]

Meanwhile, in the Transcaucasus, the outbreak of war allowed Vorontsov-Dashkov to forward his plan for ethnic units once again, this time with immediate success. Already by the middle of August 1914, the formation of a Chechen cavalry regiment, a Circassian cavalry regiment, a Kabardin cavalry regiment, a Tatar cavalry regiment, another Dagestan cavalry regiment, and an Adjarian infantry batallion were approved. In January 1915, Nikolai Nikolaevich approved the formation of six Armenian, two Georgian, and one Muslim brigade in the Caucasus. By June, ethnic soldiers had begun training in these units.[59] Vorontsov-Dashkov no longer pushed for "Muslim" units, but split the peoples of the Caucasus up by ethnic group. The General Staff quoted Vorontsov-Dashkov as saying that the time had come to "use the martial peoples of the Caucasus," and he divided them into "tribes."[60] The idea that ethnicity was increasingly differentiated from and more important than religion had grown even over the past seven years.

As a result, ethnicity was seen as perhaps even more dangerous than it had been before, and creating ethnic units an even bigger gamble. Some gambles were never made; a call for Finnish ethnic units upon the outbreak of the war was rejected, for instance.[61] Some gambles begun were not carried through; the Adjarian infantry battalion approved in 1914 was quickly scuttled in 1915 when government officials became convinced that Adjars had collaborated, as an ethnic group, with Ottoman occupying forces in December 1914.[62] And the Polish gamble was seen as precisely that. There was precious little talk about Grünwald swords in internal military memos.

The move toward greater inclusivity for non-Russians in the army likewise got a big boost from popular sentiment. Though the War Ministry wanted greater inclusivity, it decided to postpone the question of exempt ethnic groups and the submission of the Lukomskii Commission legislation until after the declaration of war because it considered the question too complicated to deal with in a wartime situation.[63] But as the war dragged on and the country entered the summer of 1915, increasing casualties and rumors that the second-tier militia would be called up led citizens across the country to voice their dissatisfaction with the exemptions for ethnic groups. One letter begged, "For God's sake, for the sake of greater fairness . . . call up the Muslims . . . and reinforce the ranks of the defenders of our motherland."[64] Non-Russians in Siberia were also targeted by concerned citizens, who urged the government to give those ethnic groups the chance "to be of some use to the suffering fatherland by fulfilling the high duty of a citizen."[65] A group of peasants in Tobol'sk province made a similar claim and then added that the government should "take the Russian population into consideration, which has only sons and providers for their fathers and mothers drafted while they [non-Russians] remain completely free observers of current events."[66]

This public frustration was bound to manifest itself in the Duma, where members were not only aware of the broad-based appeal of drafting exempted ethnic groups, but also had been calling for legislation on the issue since 1908. The situation was compounded by the increasing hostility between the Duma and the War Ministry. It was no surprise, then, that when Polivanov came to the Duma with hat in hand asking for more men through a draft of the second-tier militia, the Duma responded angrily that they wanted to see a draft of non-Russians as well.

Most Duma members, though still cognizant of the civilizational framework that was to structure liability for military service, were in 1915 far more interested in stressing the theme of protecting Russians from unfair burdens than stressing the theme of long-term assimilation. Deputy Tregubov made it clear that though the Russian people were bearing their cross in the "great war of peoples (narodov)," it was also necessary to place the same demands" on those subjects who have not to this point borne this burden," even if they did not understand what was at stake in the war.[67]

The theme of assimilation was not absent from these discussions, but the time frame was radically shortened due to the pressures of war. Rather than think in terms of decades, they thought in terms of months. A. I. Shingarev, in his official report of the Military Affairs Committee to the full Duma on 19 August, declared that though training these new conscripts would be difficult for linguistic reasons, the difficulties were not insurmountable. "There are many elements in our nation [natsii]," Shingarev claimed, "which is rich with separate peoples and ethnicities [narodami i narodnostiami], many elements do not sufficiently know Russian, however, upon entering the army, they gradually learn it, if the period of instruction for these elements is extended to four or five months, they will be in a position to learn Russian."[68]

Again, there is a clear difference in vision here. Where Tregubov saw a Russian people in pitched battle with other peoples and needing the help of colonized peoples that enjoyed imperial protection, Shingarev saw a multiethnic nation in which the Russian people did not enjoy an explicitly privileged position.[69] Their demands, however, were identical. They both wanted the end of ethnic exemptions. The requests of the Duma in 1908 had been turned into "categorical demands" by 1915. The Duma approved the draft of the second-tier militia as the army begged, but the War Ministry was forced to deal with the question of non-Russians immediately rather than delay it until the end of the war. The representative of the War Ministry at the Duma session discussing the manpower problem humbly promised to work for the "fastest possible" draft of non-Russians.[70]

Goaded on by popular demands and severe pressure from the Duma, the military bureaucracy had agreed to draft non-Russians, despite the fact that they were not registered by any state organ, despite the fact that they had no draft bureaucracy on the ground, and despite the fact that officials knowledgable about the situation were well aware of its possible dangers. From the beginning, disaster was written on the wall. A report from the Pension and Service Department of the Main Staff on 19 September 1915 noted that the governor-general of Turkestan feared a "powerful ferment" if natives were drafted, which could well result in Afghanistan and Persia appealing to those natives on the basis of religion. The Steppe governor-general urged "caution on this touchy question."[71]

The Ministry of Internal Affairs was even more alarmed. A. A. Khvostov disputed the assertion that the Kirgiz were military material, saying that they were "by nature cowards and slow-witted" as the result of the nomadic way of life. "I think," he concluded, "that risking a ferment on the huge territory of the Central Asian steppe region for barely useful military material is not worth it."[72] Khvostov's position was bolstered by a similar report from the head of the MVD's Conscription Administration, who warned the War Ministry that the state lacked both police and army troops on the steppe. "This impotence of ours," he warned, "could bring about a rebellion even among the naturally cowardly Kirgiz. Risking that during a difficult war, and even after the conclusion of the war, for useless military material, is groundless."[73]

For the War Ministry, the question of drafting the Kirgiz had always been one of timing, and the ambivalence evident in the project they submitted to the Council of Ministers in November 1915 suggests that the War Ministry understood how badly timed the Duma's demands were. In the end, though, they fulfilled their end of the bargain with the Duma. They repeated their desire for eventual inclusion, noting that they supported the 1874 principle that "every Russian subject has the sacred duty to defend Throne and Fatherland," that the army could act as a civilizing influence, and that presently the burden of the draft fell disproportionately on the population "in the center."[74]

The report also argued, however, that "in these conditions, we can expect that introducing conscription for the Kirgiz will not come about without uprisings and outbursts of unhappiness. . . . The question arises of the expediency and timing of introducing conscription among them."[75] This was hardly a ringing endorsement of a Kirgiz draft. Indeed, in the same report, they officially recommended that the Kirgiz not be drafted and proposed that they be drafted.[76] During the meeting of the Council of Ministers itself, Polivanov submitted the Lukomskii Commission reports, which endorsed eventual conscription of the Kirgiz and other non-Russians but recommended a gradual approach. Senator Stefan Beletskii, of the MVD, was more straightforward and repeated the constant concerns of that ministry: they had no family registers, much less draft lists, the effort would result in uprisings across the steppe, and the Kirgiz were unsuited for military action. The council duly noted that both ministries felt that the situation should be resolved after the war.[77]

Forced to draft the Kirgiz but unwilling to put them in uniform, the military and government officials took the middle road, proposing in 1916 to draft them in labor brigades, thus freeing up more men for the front. Over the spring of 1916, the Council of Ministers approved the measure for officially bringing non-Russians under military service laws and then stationing the units for work rather than battle.[78] On 25 June 1916, the tsar and General D. S. Shuvaev, the war minister, officially declared the labor draft of male non-Russians from 19 to 43 years old from nearly all the remaining major unconscripted groups.[79]

As described in the previous chapter, the draft was a complete disaster, resulting in tens of thousands of casualties and the necessity to send thousands of troops into Central Asia in the midst of the war. Daniel Brower has recently suggested that the explosion on the steppe was bound to occur "as one of the desperate rebellions thrown up against the alien colonial intruders and against the decay of hallowed, native ways," and that "the likelihood of an uprising among the Kyrgyz was in these conditions very great regardless of tsarist wartime policy."[80] To be sure, there was more to the steppe rebellion than dissatisfaction over conscription. Colonial relations in Central Asia were tense and getting worse as the twentieth century progressed. Nomadic lands were being appropriated by a large influx of Russian settlers, and ethnic relations had deteriorated significantly as a result of economic conflict.

But neither is the rebellion purely reducible to the economic aspect of ethnic tension. Conscription had been for decades one of the hot-button issues for natives of the steppe in their relationship with the tsarist regime. All reports suggest that the draft was avoided like the plague throughout the late imperial era. Discussions about getting nomads to settle down frequently centered around conscription. It was clear to officials on the scene that there were instances in which some groups thought it economically advantageous to give up their nomadic lifestyle, but refused to settle down because they feared conscription if they did.[81]

Steppe dwellers wanted to join the army even less than their Russian counterparts did. Some, like Kalmyks in the Don region, were included on Cossack rolls and conscripted in that fashion. O. I. Gorodovikov (who would later become commander of the 2nd Cavalry Army in the Civil War and the deputy commander of cavalry during World War II) remembered what soldiering meant for him in the late imperial period. News that he had to show up for service came to him "unexpectedly and unhappily." On induction day, he and seventeen other Kalmyk boys went to the draft board accompanied by their families to the mournful sounds of harmonicas and drunken singing. He did not get happier as time went on. They were sent to Poland, where they were met by an older soldier (their *diad'ka*) who took their money and forbade them to leave the base without him. The horror stories of army life, he soon realized, were all true. In addition to bearing the abuse that Russian soldiers did, the young Kalmyks were singled out as "heathens," made the butt of Cossack jokes, and constantly denigrated. While the Cossacks rested, the Kalmyks were forced to do "all the dirty work." The whole time, according to Gorodovikov, the Kalmyks pined for home, for the steppe, "where they feel free." Believing desertion to be futile, 13 of the 18 decided to make themselves sick in order to get sent home. For 25 rubles, they bribed an orderly in the division for a medicine that would make them sick. All 13 were released. All 13 died upon their return home from the poison they had drunk. Gorodovikov was left with little choice; he stayed in the army. He did not return home until his term expired four and a half years later.[82]

Needless to say, the stories of army life that spread across the steppe were not positive, and steppe dwellers preserved their exemptions with all of their strength. It was not surprising, then, that conscription turned out to be the issue that lit the powderkeg in the steppe. Officials in the know had warned of the dangers of drafting non-Russians, and their dire predictions were proven correct. The sudden draft of previously exempt ethnic groups after years of pursuing a path of cautious and gradual incorporation into the army and civic communities proved to be too much, too late. The steppe rebellion was brought under control only days before the collapse of the old regime.

That collapse led to a further intensification of ethnic policies in the army, driven by two primary factors. First, the center-left parties that came to power in Petrograd as a result of the February Revolution were profound believers in the importance of ethnic nationalism as a social, cultural, and political force and were equally strong proponents of a "civic" nationalist ideal of equality before the nation and state. As a result, they viewed a proper political community as one in which nationalities were in a separate but equal relationship with one another.

This relationship was articulated quite clearly in the army. A. I. Guchkov, the new minister of war, addressed the "equal" part of the equation by signing a terse order on 16 March 1917 that ended all official restrictions promulgated on the basis of religion or nationality.[83] The "separate" part found expression in the revival of interest in ethnic units. The tide toward structuring the army through ethnic units, which had ebbed somewhat over the last year of war when Polish units proved more prone to desertion than did integrated ones and the army was forced to disband many of its Transcaucasian units, rose again with the adoption of a nationality policy formulated along proto-Leninist lines.

The second factor contributing to the intensification of the ethnic vision was that the men who had come to power in Petrograd had far less of that power than their predecessors had. All over the empire, local ethnic nationalists were filling the power vacuum left by the collapse of the autocracy, and those nationalists took an intense interest in military affairs. The popularity of ethnic units rose sharply. On 19 April 1917, the Muslim Bureau in

Novonikolaevsk (present-day Novosibirsk) asked Guchkov for permission to form a Muslim unit with Muslim commanders.[84] Despite some initial wavering on the issue, the General Staff eventually argued that there was no indication that Islam was serving as a unifying political force and that the government should support the Muslim plan because it was distinguished by a transethnic national character *(obshchenatsional'nyi kharakter)*. The plan was approved by the war minister, though it outlived his tenure.[85] Most other nationalities had more immediate success. Over the course of 1917, officials approved a new Georgian cavalry regiment, two Armenian rifle brigades, a Finnish rifle brigade, a Lithuanian reserve battalion, and the wholesale Ukrainization of units on the southwestern front.[86]

The impetus for Ukrainization seems to have come from soldiers themselves, or at least their nationalist representatives.[87] On 11 May 1917, the staff of the Kiev military district wrote the duty general of the southwestern front reporting that 300 Ukrainian soldiers at a distribution point had submitted a petition to be stationed in the same regiment, and asking what to do.[88] The response was fairly quick. The duty general ordered that the Ukrainian troops waiting in reserve echelons be transferred to the 23rd Reserve Regiment and then sent into a single division of the 41st Army Corps.[89] From the principle of new, volunteer single-nationality units something quite different had emerged, the forced ethnicization of entire divisions in order to create ethnic units out of formerly integrated units.

After the February Revolution, ethnic units must have made perfect sense to military planners now fully used to looking at the world in ethnic terms. Military authorities received already cohesive units (with ethnicity forming the bond) and still benefited from large numbers since separate ethnicities were fighting separately but for the same goal, and yet were directed by a single high command. As it turned out, however, forced ethnic units were much more problematic. Less than two weeks after the Ukrainization process began in the 41st Army Corps, General Mel'gunov, the commander of the corps, begged the duty general to stop the process, saying that Ukrainization was proceeding "painfully."[90] Mel'gunov was not specific about how the process was painful, but General Muzhilov, the main commander of the 7th Army, was. He argued that if commanders viewed Ukrainization of a corps simply as raising the percentage of Ukrainians within it, then nothing other than trouble would result: "Ukrainians under the leadership of any corporal will begin to forward all possible demands, the core population will oppose this, not considering its own small numbers; the leadership, beginning with the head of the divisions, who are not Ukrainian, will support the minority—you get rubbish.[91]

Sergeant Baturin of the 34th Army Corps had a different, but similarly negative view of Ukrainization. He claimed that soldiers, both Ukrainian and Russian, were "depressed" and did not understand why the major shakeups were occurring. Prior to Ukrainization, about 25 percent of the corps had been Ukrainian, and the Ukrainians in the corps had enjoyed "solidarity with their comrade Russians, that is, no one had anything against serving together." Indeed, there were even instances when Ukrainians left the newly Ukrainized corps to be with the purged Russians, "with whom they were linked by friendship and long service in the regiment." Rather than unity, severe strife resulted as bitter Russians left the regiment.[92]

Thus, instead of solving the problem of ethnic nationalism and harnessing its power, the leaders of the southwestern front had just made their situation twice as bad. Their mistake was twofold. First, they appear to have believed that the political power of ethnic nationalism was essentially benevolent, despite years of concern in military circles regarding ethnic units. They did not foresee the advantages Ukrainization gave to some over others and the ruthless ways that these advantages would be used. Second, they believed that ethnicity was a naturally solidifying force, completely ignoring the fact that many of their soldiers had more allegiance to their "primary" combat group than to their putative nationality. Primary group solidarity was strong in all armies, and it was no less so in the Russian army.[93] The Ukrainian Rada was happy, as were other Ukrainian nationalists, but the effect on many of the men in uniform seems to have been depression and demoralization.

Class and Ethnicity under the New Regime

The questions of ethnic exemptions and ethnic units played almost no role during the short volunteer period of the Red Army. Explicit prohibitions against accepting non-Russians were not made. Indeed, volunteers were never asked to state their ethnicity, a fact that has led some Soviet historians to trumpet the institution of the volunteer Red Army as the end of the "tsarist policy of distrust toward non-Russians."[94] Perhaps this was true, but it was also irrelevant. Most soldiers came from the overwhelmingly Russian industrial centers of the country, and as a result the number of non-Russians in the army was small, even by the meager standards of the volunteer army.[95] Thus, though non-Russians were accepted in the army and ethnic units were formed, demonstrating some amount of trust, non-Russians themselves did not waver in their distaste for state recruitment policies.

In addition, the focus on class membership in the volunteer army inevitably stacked the deck in favor of Russians, who dominated the ranks of the industrial working class far out of proportion to their representation in the empire as a whole. Class, which had been a significant but secondary measure of differentiation for tsarist military planners became, with the workers' revolution, the primary category by which military capability, morality, and civilizational progress were measured.

Indeed, even non-Marxist observers would have been hard pressed to attribute either the fall of the monarchy or the fall of the Provisional Government to ethnic determinants. As already noted, the tsarist regime survived an ethnic rebellion in 1916 and smaller revolts elsewhere that took on ethnic nationalist overtones.[96] Events in the metropoles of Petrograd and Moscow were disproportionately important, and class in the metropoles figured far larger than ethnicity. Given the fact that Marxists took power in October, the sudden rise in prominence of class as the primary explanatory category of social behavior seems overdetermined. Concomitant with class attaining categorical preeminence was the sudden reversal of normative valences within the category itself. Almost instantaneously, workers were transformed from pockmarked, fawning drunkards into manly ascetic warriors. Peasants were no longer the rock of the nation, the repository of military virtues. They turned from loyal, obedient, and self-sacrificing soldiers into malingerers who were necessary but inclined to disloyalty, disobedience, and selfishness.

One thing, however, had not changed. Peasants, both before and after the revolution, were thought to be unusually susceptible to influence of all kinds. Peasant moral codes and political beliefs were seen to be fragile. Prior to the revolution, given the fact that it was precisely this peasant morality that was the wellspring of the nation, such fragility was a source of great concern to populists and nationalists of all stripes.[97] What was troubling for tsarist officials became a tremendous opportunity for Bolshevik planners. Workers could act as role models and teachers of their benighted little brothers. Class difference could eventually be erased, along with the "petit-bourgeois" morality that was thought to predominate in rural areas. The army was to play a role in this moral transformation of backward peasants, just as it was in the transformation of backward ethnicities, though it also faced the same dilemma regarding the timing of this transformation.

Once again, planners believed that having a heterogeneous force (mixed with peasants and workers) would lower the battle capabilities of units in the field. Class membership, they thought, provided automatic cohesion and reliability, attributes notably missing not only in the Russian army in 1917, but indeed in other armies around the world as well after the French army mutinies in 1917.[98] As the standing armies of Europe proved both their inability to achieve decisive victory and their capacity for mutiny, the Bolsheviks' positive experience with forming Red Guards seemed to affirm the socialist position that class-based militias were superior to standing armies in both the social and military sense. But, as seen in the previous chapter, though the Bolshevik leadership held no illusions that they had come to power with solid and loyal peasant backing, the perception that they needed a large army meant that they had to draft peasants nevertheless.

Thus died the idea of a proletarian army. But class did not disappear. Instead, Bolshevik planners declared that they were forming an army of "laborers" *(trudiashchikhsia)*. As a result, Marxist class analysis, with its division between "poor," "middle," and "rich" peasants, its fine distinction between various types of industrial workers, and its urban schema of the proletariat, white-collar workers, and the bourgeoisie, gave way to a much more simplistic categorization for military planners. Four basic groups emerged around the axes of urban/rural and exploiting/non-exploiting. Even this simplification of categories did not succeed in clarifying class in the Red Army. A mechanism for precisely determining class position eluded mobilization officials for the whole Civil War. In one of the few drafts that sought to conscript urban laborers while leaving rural laborers untouched—in Moscow province in the summer of 1918—officials found it impossible to make even the basic distinction between urban and rural because of the fact that even city dwellers had been forced to work part-time in factories and part-time on peasant plots just to get by.[99] After these summer 1918 drafts, draft boards ceased for all practical purposes to try to make distinctions between urban and rural laborers, a necessary move given the massive demographic changes of the Civil War, when millions of urban dwellers returned to villages to wait out the storm.[100] By October 1918, Moscow conscription officials had given up even the pretense of differentiating. When draft statistics were compiled, workers and peasants were lumped into a single category.[101]

Trying to make distinctions within urban and rural communities proved even more difficult. The Bolshevik belief that poor and middle peasants had different levels of class consciousness was literally irrelevant for conscription officials, while the crucial differentiation that Marxists made between blue-collar workers and white-collar workers was likewise ignored. The two were lumped together in statistics on Red Army soldiers.[102] The distinction between "exploiting" and "non-exploiting" rural and urban inhabitants was much more salient; the question of what to do with kulaks and the bourgeoisie will be discussed later. Even here, though, class discrimination was of secondary importance to gaining men. By August 1920, less than one half of one percent of all draftees had been labeled class enemies and placed in work brigades by draft boards.[103]

Though the differentiation between workers and peasants was weak in conscription practice, it remained strong in military ideology. The peasant problem nagged at officials from the top to the bottom of the army command structure. Nikolai Podvoiskii was optimistic about the problem, sharing Trotskii's belief that peasant weakness could be overcome by making sure peasants had enough worker role models to serve as a "communist point of cohesion with the peasant masses."[104] Podvoiskii's faith that there would be cohesion in integrated units was not universally shared, though. Heterogeneity was seen as a disability in the army by many committed Bolsheviks, who thought universal conscription "would in essence lead to the arming and organization of petty bourgeois counter-revolutionary forces."[105] Continued pressure for more soldiers, though, combined with consistent support for national military ideas over revolutionary ones on the part of Trotskii and Lenin, meant in the end that the army would be multi-class.

Just as the institution of conscription forced certain decisions about categorical differentiation in regard to class, so too did it force the Red Army to take a stand on the question of ethnicity. The principle established from Moscow was the culmination of the trends that accelerated during World War I. Bolshevik leaders made it quite clear that all ethnic groups should be drafted on an equal basis with Russians and that ethnic units, where desired, should be formed. This principle was laid down even prior to the announcement of the first draft in a 24 May 1918 order from the Commissariat of Military Affairs, which established that ethnic units were to be allowed, but not in any greater size than a company.[106]

The question of drafting previously exempt ethnicities likewise came up almost immediately. The Central Executive Committee of Soviets (TsIK) for the Republic of Turkestan wrote the Commissariat of Military Affairs in September 1918, asking for direction regarding two natives living in Tashkent who claimed that they were not liable for the draft by virtue of being natives of Turkestan. The Turkestan TsIK noted that no explicit mention of non-Russians had been made in the conscription decrees and therefore they were following the established policy of adhering to tsarist law wherever it was not explicitly contradicted by Soviet decree. Pavel Lebedev wrote them a terse note in reply saying that "Natives of Turkestan, being Russian subjects, are liable for conscription equally with all other citizens of the Russian Republic."[107] The principles were clear.

The practice during the Civil War was not clear. The period between 1917 and 1920 was marked by the decentralization of state power. Local officials made decisions, and those decisions were often far removed from central directives. Taking the Kirgiz as a case study of this process, one finds much more confusion than execution of straightforward principles. In the summer of 1918, the Commissariat for Kirgiz Affairs officially requested the formation of a special department located in Saratov to form Kirgiz ethnic units, a request that was granted by Trotskii. Almost immediately, this department realized how big a task preparing a draft was, in particular amongst people whose only conscription experience had been the disaster of 1916. By August, the department had significantly reduced its ambitions, saying that drafting Kirgiz immediately would be "impossible," but that it was creating a small department to conduct agitational and voluntary recruitment work.[108]

Elsewhere, the Kirgiz question was worked out differently. In the Steppe Kirgiz region in 1919, a special commissar reported that over the course of eight months only three squadrons of Kirgiz had been formed, and these were completely unfit for battle. In Semipalatinsk, the Kirgiz were first drafted, then exempted because the lack of registration data made it impossible to figure out who was supposed to appear. Worse, when the Kirgiz had been drafted, they proved unreliable. Through it all, central officials knew not only that events in the borderland were out of their direct control, but also that they were not informed of most of those events even after the fact. In 1919, the Registration Department noted that "very few reports" were coming from Turkestan and that registration there was "in embryo." One hapless circular telegrammed to all district military commissariats in 1920 complained that "there is reason to think that not all mobilizations of former non-Russians are known to the center. As a result, please telegraph whether these mobilizations are taking place presently or not."[109]

The failure of the Bolsheviks to compose and implement a nationality policy in the army was apparent, but both local and central officials were groping toward a common understanding of how ethnic difference affected politics and how ethnic tension might eventually be erased. At the basis of this shared understanding was the idea that ethnicities (more precisely in this context, nationalities) were temporary manifestations of the late capitalist system. They were real, in other words, but they were neither essential nor permanent. Eventually, assimiliation was not only desirable but also inevitable. The big question was how to effect this assimilation and how to effect it in the shortest possible time. The answer given by Stalin and Lenin was to create political units that were "national in form and socialist in content" and thereby prevent bourgeois nationalists from using ethnicity as a wedge to slow down the assimilative process and threaten state power.[110] Though focused on developing national differences in the short term, this policy was grounded in the belief that people would assimilate in the long term. People would eventually outgrow their national forms and merge.

There was also a current of essentialized ethnicity present in the worldview of many leaders, and this current gained in strength through the 1930s, got a huge boost during World War II, and was canonized in Stalin's famous *Pravda* article on linguistics in 1950.[111] This progression has led some to see the move toward essentialism as initiated by Stalin in some way and to link it with his battle for "socialism in one country."[112] The current was, however, also present in the mindset of the main opponent of Stalin's program of "socialism in one country," Leon Trotskii, who shared a great many of the ethnic assumptions of his Bolshevik colleagues. The starkest example of these assumptions occurred in late 1922 and early 1923, when "Comrade McKee," a black American communist, approached the Soviet leadership with a proposal to create a black American unit of the Red Army. McKee was supposed to meet with Vladimir Antonov-Ovseenko, the chief of staff of the Red Army, but Antonov-Ovseenko was unexpectedly unable to make the meeting. He nevertheless telegrammed Trotskii recommending against the unit on the basis that "negroes are in the highest degree unadapted to our climate."[113] Trotskii, by his own admission, accepted this argument and sought to explain it to McKee.

Trotskii did not go into detail about his meeting with McKee or McKee's specific response to the attribution of the inability of blacks to live in the cold, as McKee met with Trotskii in Moscow in late January. The upshot was clear, however, in a repentant telegram Trotskii sent to Antonov-Ovseenko following that meeting:

> Comrade McKee, a negro, brought up the idea of including a small number of young negroes in the Red Army. I supported this idea. But we decided that negroes could not withstand the northern climate. I believed this at first, forgetting that in America negroes live and function at different latitudes. McKee categorically refuted these climatic reasons. I think that it would be very desirable to train several young negro-revolutionaries, for example in the Kremlin school.[114]

Even in discussions of direct cross-cultural interaction and training, ethnic assumptions lurked behind assimilationist decisions, though men like Trotskii conscientiously changed their minds when they realized that those assumptions were misplaced.

Trotskii's conscientiousness and ethnic open-mindedness were less evident lower down in the military bureaucracy. One report in 1920 on conducting the draft in eastern Siberia resulted in a laundry list of reasons why Civil War drafts of non-Russians were going so poorly. The list combined environmental and racial factors, including the "wildness of non-Russians, ignorance of the Russian language, infectious diseases, habituation to their climate, and inertness to the teaching of socialism."[115] The recommendations were strikingly reminiscent of tsarist recommendations: go slow, begin with a labor draft rather than military draft, and by all means "station them along parallels, but not along meridians, since this mortally affects their health."[116]

In many ways, then, Bolshevik and tsarist approaches to nationality policy in the army, though they used different strategies, rested on similar inconsistent bases of racialist, essentialist assumptions and universalist, assimilationist ones. Military planners in the 1870s, in 1908, and in 1923 all feared that steppe dwellers would succumb to tuberculosis as a matter of course if they were moved north of their home latitude, and Trotskii shared the same fears (at least initially) in regard to black Americans. At the same time, the thrust of policy had, if anything, become even more strident in the desire for inclusion of different ethnicities in a single army and the desire for their eventual assimilation into a single multiethnic nation.

This conflict was perhaps clearest in the only real attempt by the Bolshevik leadership to enunciate its position on drafting non-Russians during the Civil War. On 10 May 1920, the Council of Labor and Defense decreed that all non-Russians were liable for the draft while simultaneously giving the right to local officials of all stripes to exempt any ethnicity from the measure, so long as they defended their reasons in a report to the council.[117] This decree was less a policy statement than a plea for more information about the process. It merely legalized the existing practice of making decisions regarding non-Russians on the local level and defined the ambivalence felt toward them by the army and the state. By 1920, there was a growing movement to start exempting non-Russians once again, given the problems encountered during the Civil War and the need to conduct more preparatory work, and the government was giving little guidance about how to proceed.[118]

It would be a full year before more detailed instructions on how to decide which "local circumstances and peculiarites" might qualify an ethnicity for exemption were sent out to the frontier. The Mobilization Department came up with four applicable categories: (1) "political considerations, in light of which the militarization of one or another group of undesirable non-Russian populations could be dangerous for the state," (2) geographic conditions that made the draft too difficult, (3) the "physical and cultural qualities of the population, in light of which one or another tribe, due to its wildness and physical weakness, could turn out to be completely useless for staffing the army," and (4) local conditions that made a temporary exemption expedient. In addition to these considerations, the Mobilization Administration asked for detailed reports regarding ethnicities, including lists of those unable to serve. The administration also made clear that any such exemptions would be temporary.[119]

Soviet military officials, in other words, had come to much the same conclusions that tsarist officials had come to regarding the inclusion of non-Russians. Two principal dangers existed. The first danger, though never absent in discussions about "backward" nationalities, was primarily articulated in regard to more "developed" nationalities, like Ukrainians or Georgians. The danger was political in that these groups might use the training and the weapons provided by the state to threaten the existence of the regime. The second danger voiced by officials related to "backward" nationalities, who, being unprepared "civilizationally" for military service, brought down battle efficiency, presented a threat to morale and discipline, and were physically weaker than their Russian counterparts.

Military officials under both regimes relied on the same understandings of civilization and culture, or rather subscribed to the same jumbled combination of these two quite different concepts.[120] On the one hand, most military officials in both periods seem to have subscribed to a rather Lamarckian understanding of ethnicity when considering domestic policy. They thought explicitly in terms of ethnicities that had their own peculiar "physical and cultural qualities," but believed those qualities had been determined environmentally over time. It stood to reason that changing the environment in which "savages" lived would also lead to a growing convergence of ethnicities as backward nationalities assimilated physically as well as mentally.

On the other hand, the officials were rather more Darwinian in foreign policy, believing that the world order was defined by the competition of nations (which were glibly assumed to be analogous to different species), in which ethnicities, classes, and nations engaged in wars to determine who was fittest; thus who would survive. Anthropology and ethnography were the fields in which the "naturalness" of categories was determined, and military officials were deeply engaged in both of them from the beginning. Throughout the period under study, the military was a primary location for the major project that linked "scientific" thoughts about ethnicity with "social" ones: anthropometry. Military doctors under both regimes were obsessive about measuring the bodies of their conscripts and relating those ethnophysical traits to social behavior. Anthropometric measurements were diligently conducted on nearly every single incoming conscript.[121]

Given the continuity of anthropological understandings of ethnicity among military men, it was no surprise that in response to the 1921 request of the Mobilization Administration quoted above, the Military Commissariat of the Georgian Republic thought it advisable to draft "only those non-Russians who were drafted in the old era."[122] The abundance of ethnic units that had sprung up during World War I and the Civil War had likewise disappeared during the demobilization period. By the beginning of 1923, only five remained.[123]

It was in this context of army officials slipping back into the comfortable pattern of the pre-World War I era that the party reinvigorated the debate surrounding ethnic (in Soviet parlance now "national") minorities in the spring of 1923. There were two crucial moments in this shift within the Red Army.[124] The first was a secret letter from Trotskii to Antonov-Ovseenko and the rest of the Revolutionary Military Council on 20 March 1923 outlining his plan for a new approach to the national question in the army.[125] The second was the Twelfth Party Congress, which spent considerable time hashing out the national question in general and set the tone for nationality policy in the 1920s.[126]

Trotskii was straightforward in his appraisal of the situation, noting that the national question was tremendously important. He feared not nearly enough attention had been paid to the question of ethnic tension in the army, despite the fact that "the smallest bit of a lack of attention, the slightest false tone in this question threatens the most serious consequences," even if the question only concerned the battle readiness of the army.[127] He continued that "in the eyes of the most backward ethnic [narodnymi] masses, the army most obviously and imposingly represents the state, its centralized connection, its force."[128] As a result, the army, from lowest soldier to highest commander, had to go the extra yard to make sure that there was no cause for dissatisfaction on the part of native populations. When the inevitable happened and there were violations of national solidarity and "national fraternity," Trotskii ordered the guilty parties to be tried at "painstakingly prepared public trials."[129]

Trotskii's circular was clearly linked to forthcoming discussion of the "national question" at the Twelfth Party Congress, which brought the question of ethnicity back to the forefront of army concerns and made it once again a hot-button issue for policy planners in the military. The general decision to pursue "affirmative action" in the realm of nationality policy was explicitly declared to be the policy for the armed forces as well, despite the fact that Stalin did not mention the army either in his original theses or his keynote speech, except to refer vaguely to a "military" aspect to the question.[130] Other delegates were more forthright in their criticism of ethnic relations in the army than Stalin had been, accusing the army both of chauvinism and of failing to take steps to correct the "factual inequality" that existed between Russians and non-Russians. Mykola Skrypnik accused the army of being a tool of "Russification,"[131] a sentiment shared by the Georgian Sergei Ordzhonikidze, who proclaimed that "objectively, the Red Army is not simply an apparatus for training peasants in a proletarian spirit—it is also an apparatus of Russification."[132]

According to Skrypnik and Ordzhonikidze, the army was failing in what Trotskii had just labelled its "mission" to act as a representative and agent of change and to create a fraternity of nations. Slipping by inertia into old chauvinist habits, the army had become an agent of oppression. No one stood up to contest these criticisms.

Though Stalin had not mentioned military reforms in particular, after the attacks on the army a quick addition was made to the resolutions of the congress. The new resolution was completely in line with the idea expressed in the general party line that progress and assimilation would occur most quickly if conducted in native languages and in ethnically separated groups. The congress resolved that "training in the Red Army be strengthened in the spirit of spreading the idea of fraternity and the solidarity of peoples of the union and that practical preparatory measures for organizing national military units be taken."[133] Ethnic units were once again officially ordained the vehicles of progress, the magic bullet to solve the army's eternal ethnic problem.

The sudden focus on the national question took many commanders by surprise, and not everyone responded with enthusiasm. Some military workers did not ascribe to the national question the importance that it now commanded, and they dragged their feet.[134] But, if many party members, state workers, and military workers were cool to the idea of the new nationality policy, they made little impact with the policymakers within the military bureaucracy, who were eager to hitch their fortunes to this policy initiative. Both past and future military leaders weighed in on the question, including Shaposhnikov, Tukhachevskii, and Frunze. All agreed that the process would not occur overnight. As Stalin had pointed out, backward nations would take a while to catch up. In military terms this meant that their usefulness in battle would be only of secondary importance for the time being. The main short-term task was to bring different cultures closer together *(sblizhenie),* to create "a common language with those masses of laborers alongside which one or another military unit is stationed."[135]

Among other things this meant not rushing headlong into drafting non-Russians. As Moisei Rafes reminded his colleagues, "Tsarism was not successful in using masses of Kirgiz, Uzbeks, and so forth for their imperial goals. Its attempt during the war to mobilize part of the native population in Turkestan was foiled by massive uprisings." Thus, he urged caution and learning from tsarist mistakes. But Rafes urged a shorter time frame than either his tsarist predecessors or the immediate postwar military planners had envisaged. Where his forebears had preferred to let socioeconomic change lead to a change in attitude to the military, Rafes sought to institute the opposite. For him, the Red Army was the "only living incarnation of the 'Union'" and bore the burden of assimilative work. Since the order of the day was the creation of native elites, who could then bring their fellow nationals up to a higher level of civilization by teaching them in their native languages while being aware of native "peculiarities," the corresponding step in the army was clear: the creation of national military academies that would train those elites.[136]

The Soviet military structure, as it worked out the problems of the "national question" over the course of 1923 and 1924, followed the path blazed by its tsarist predecessor as it tried to come to terms with the fact of ethnic diversity, the desire to promote civilizational progress, and the necessity to preserve battle readiness. By the end of 1924, the Revolutionary Military Council had adopted a five-year plan for creating an army that reflected the ethnic diversity of the country.[137]

At the heart of the solution to the ethnic problem in the military was a division of non-Russians into two different categories. The first category consisted of nationalities that had performed military service before (such as Ukrainians, Belorussians, Tatars, Bashkirs, and Transcaucasian peoples). The second was made up of peoples whom the army's Political Administration (PUR) considered not to have served (such as Kirgiz, Uzbeks, peoples of the northern Caucasus region, Iakuts, and so forth).[138] The first category posed little problem. In addition to forming national military academies to train larger numbers of officers, the regime decided to draft ethnicities in this category and immediately place them in ethnic units. The only limit to their numbers would be related to how many of their fellow nationals were already prepared to become officers.

The second category was a bit trickier, for military planners were aware of the dangers posed by prematurely drafting "backward" non-Russians. Rafes had already raised the specter of 1916, and the lesson was clear. Forcing these non-Russians to serve helped neither in purely military terms nor in speeding along civilizational progress. Without some kind of willingness to serve on the part of its conscripts, any draft would be dangerous and counterproductive.

Army leaders were also stuck in terms of practical measures, even had the political dangers been absent. Given the edicts of the Twelfth Party Congress, all work in ethnic units had to be done in native languages, thus requiring native elites with military expertise or military experts with intimate knowledge of native languages and customs. There were precious few of either category. Among non-Russians, there was still no system of registration in place in many frontier areas, much less reliable records. These were all familiar problems to twentieth-century mobilization experts in Russia.

The answer was a clearly designated process by which these national minorities could be brought into the army as quickly as possible. The immediate steps were to open national military academies and to offer admission to the Red Army for volunteers of these nationalities. At the same time, a massive propaganda campaign began on the frontier to popularize the idea of military service and conduct preparatory work such as draft registration and pre-draft military training.[139] Prospects for including even the most backward nationalities were thought of in years rather than decades.

In some cases, these ideals were met. In the northern Caucasus region and in Turkestan, the directives to accept volunteers into units that would eventually become ethnic units had begun as early as the autumn of 1923, when Sklianskii ordered officials in the North Caucasus military district and the Turkestan front to create units with 10 and 15 percent components of volunteer national minorities respectively.[140] Within five years, the status of the mountaineers of the northern Caucasus region and the natives of Turkestan had "progressed" to the point that they were brought under the military service code.[141]

The key to success, as it had been for ethnic Russians in the Civil War, was the promise of entitlements and social mobility for soldiers. PUR's Information Department reported in 1926 that a substantial improvement in the mood of non-Russians had been noted. The reason was the increased desire of young people to serve. Komsomol (Communist Youth Union) members were especially eager, forming 50 to 70 percent of the volunteers in Tadzhik units and 50 to 60 percent in Kirgiz units. More showed up, in fact, than could be accepted. The reason, according to PUR, was the "unexpected growth among young people of the yearning for enlightenment," especially in Russian. These were kids who wanted up and out of the *kishliak* and knew how to do so—army service and the ability to speak Russian.[142]

Steppe nomads had successfully resisted military service (with brief exceptions during the war) for the past fifty years through a combination of their own perspicacity in avoiding registration and resisting state incursions and the Russian elite's views of them as physically unfit and culturally backward. In the space of a couple of years that situation had been decisively changed. Nomads had been enticed to join the army by promises of a better life, and army officials were beginning to assert there was "no basis to assert that Kazakh cavalry units, in the near future, with a correct, gradual . . . [approach] will lag in a battle sense behind other units of the Red Army."[143]

It would be foolish to believe that this sea change in views toward ethnicity, culture, and military service took place across the board, especially given the contradictions that were always present in the discourse about ethnicity in Russia. Some believed that ethnicity could be transcended, others that ethnicity was the basic social fact from which all others flowed. Most held some kind of combination of these two contradictory positions. In the military, the belief that ethnicity could be transcended, that a greater political community (and therefore a greater army) could be created along other lines was usually at the fore. But it was always tempered by the nagging feeling that, despite desires for unity and homogeneity, ethnic difference existed and that it mattered.

Throughout the period of the New Economic Policy (NEP), though, class difference mattered even more than ethnic difference. The relationship between peasants and workers was the crux around which NEP politics revolved, and that relationship, central in 1921 when NEP was instituted, became even more crucial as the 1920s went on and the paths of the peasant revolution and the worker revolution increasingly diverged.[144] Building the *smychka* (union) between peasants and the proletariat was the most important task facing the NEP army.

In even more explicit terms than those used with "backward" nationalities, the substance of the *smychka* was to be peasant assimilation to worker norms. Again, class heterogeneity was seen as a tremendous military weakness. Peasants, for influential leaders like Sergei Gusev, were prone to "particularistic strivings" that weakened both the Red Army and the republic. It was therefore the self-described mission of political workers to "clear up his [the peasant's] petit bourgeois psychology and lay firm foundations for a Communist world view."[145] Other authors were just as clear as their tsarist predecessors had been about the assimilative function of the army. M. I. Kalinin gushed in 1924 that

> The Red Army is the tangible *smychka* of workers and peasants. All young peasants and workers in peacetime are fulfilling for the first time one of the most serious state responsibilities . . . and by this makes himself a full-fledged citizen of the Soviet republic. . . . Peasants from the most godforsaken villages, workers from the largest factories are united in companies, battalions, and regiments for a common goal—defense of the Soviet state, living in the same barracks, rising at the same hour, learning military art together in the barracks . . . all this unites and links *[smychkaet]* workers and peasants drafted into the army into an invincible military cohort. The task of the working city dweller is to bring the culture of the city to the peasant.[146]

Even in these essentially benevolent representations of worker-peasant interaction, then, the *smychka* in the army was far from any kind of alliance of equals, much less a structure that favored peasants.[147] Rather, the Bolsheviks, like their tsarist predecessors, employed short-term practices of categorical discrimination in order to further the long-term goal of nation building, but the discrimination practiced by the Bolsheviks was structured primarily around an urban/rural nexus rather than a center/periphery one.

The point, again, is not merely about unequal power relations, but also about the ascribed categories that structured those relations. The peasant/worker split was one of the central understandings of difference in the NEP period. Workers were understood to be superior fighters, superior leaders, and morale boosters in the army, a perception that led military officials to fight with other institutions to retain a high worker percentage in the armed forces.[148] Peasants, on the other hand, were perpetual disappointments, who displayed "low cultural and political levels."[149] Other reports were even more tangibly supercilious. One political worker smirked in 1922 that many conscripts had never been out of their native villages and, upon arrival in the big city, were dumbfounded by such modern contraptions as trams and automobiles.[150]

Indeed, by 1924, the ascribed differences between workers and peasants in intellectual capacity were so great that political training officials in the Komsomol (which by that time had responsibility for conducting political training both for pre-draft-age boys and for conscripts while they were at the call-up point awaiting stationing elsewhere) began to differentiate the types of materials they gave to peasants and the ones they gave to workers. Stating baldly that there were two separate contingents of readers, the Komsomol Central Committee told its charges to produce two types of literature. They were to give teenagers with peasant parents posters and broadsheets with illustrated poems or stories, little "joke-sketches," or one-act plays, while teenagers with worker parents qualified for popular works of military science and military history.[151] It was not hard to see which of these groups was on the fast track for command school.

Rural inhabitants were fully aware of their second-class status. In some cases, the awareness that being a peasant was a disability spurred young village hotshots to leave their peasant days behind. As early as 1922, great numbers of men showed a fervent interest in moving up through the ranks and into the city. The same Ukrainian peasants who were stunned by trams also displayed a "general desire to enter commander courses, schools, and to become commanders and wear a handsome uniform. They relate well to communists and Soviet power, but are unhappy with local power. They want to serve in Piter [Petrograd]."[152]

In other cases, this awareness spurred a sense of "revolution betrayed." When peasants were taught in the army about the proletarian nature of Soviet power, they often reacted unhappily, since pre-draft propaganda usually stressed the dual nature of this power. One peasant was reported by the Political Administration to have said that "the heart aches when you hear that the state is only a workers' state, after all, in the village they say 'and peasant.'" Another angrily declared: "If the state is a workers' state, and the party a workers' party, then don't put us (peasants) in the army." Prior to entering the army, this political worker noted, "Peasants imagined the union of workers and peasants as an equal union," and the Bolshevik call for peasants to transform into workers was turned on its head. Why should workers lead the union of peasants and workers, some of these soldiers asked, when peasants represented the majority? "The basic question," as the Political Administration would later report to Kliment Voroshilov, "that unites the peasant masses is the question of the relationship between city and village—it is jealousy toward workers."[153] By the end of NEP, then, "worker" and "peasant" were categories of difference that meant something both to state officials and to the population at large.

Conclusion

Over the course of the nineteenth century, the problem of how to understand and address the question of difference within the Russian Empire was by no means always clear. The ambiguity and confusion regarding ways to understand and organize the population had certain positive effects for the old regime. Lack of categorical clarity and a corresponding organizational structure served to hinder social and political mobilization at the substate level and helped preserve monarchical rule. By the start of the twentieth century, however, Russia found itself in a situation of intense industrial and military competition with mobilized societies both in Europe and in Asia. The Romanov tsars tried to have it both ways, to have mobilized soldiers and economic actors without the accompanying ferment of modern politics and modern social behavior. They found that they could not have it so. As a result of the demands of war mobilization, ethnicity became firmly ensconced as a basic tool of social categorization. Revolutionary movements and then revolutionary rule solidified class as an important category of difference. By 1925, the young Soviet state had built a structure of mobilization and governance that relied heavily on both.

These military and revolutionary demands for categorization prompted state actors to articulate their power and their vision of social order categorically. This maneuver enabled successful political and social mobilization, but it also served to thwart their own initial desires and the stated political principles of their regimes. Thus, though neither officials in 1873 nor officials in 1923 wanted to see ethnicity become a basis for political power, both sets of officials instituted policies that helped to structure the country on ethnic bases. Notions of science and civilization played no small role in the formulation of these policies. Anthropology and ethnology were respected sciences, and the Bolsheviks certainly considered themselves social scientists. Communists measured skulls with as much gusto as did their liberal counterparts in Britain and America. They constructed policy within the discursive limits of late nineteenth- and early twentieth-century anthropology and ethnology.

The deployment of social science produced an understanding of difference within Russia that cannot be glibly glossed over as the construction of the "Other." Rather, questions of political belonging and cultural identity were understood within a complex matrix of difference and similarity. Military officials did not look at a world simply defined by "Russians" and "non-Russians," but one in which Turkmen and Ossetians merited their own military units because of their "martial spirit," while Kirgiz remained undrafted because they were nomadic, "cowardly," and living on the Chinese border, and while Tatars and Finns paid military taxes because the tsarist government feared a courageous nationalist rebellion. Urban and rural stereotypes further complicated the picture. Both regimes, as Shingarev pointed out, governed a "nation" composed of different peoples and ethnicities.

This diversity ran counter to yet another current dominant within nationalism, a current that demands homogeneity, demands discursive and physical border guards who try to ensure that all articulation of difference takes place at the political cusp. There is a tremendous amount of power at this cusp, a fact that nation-builders have been quick to understand. But the very moment of articulating that difference and exercising nationalist power opens up fissures within the heterogeneous populations that always occupy the territory controlled by particular states. This is nationalism's dilemma of difference, a dilemma due to the basic contradictions of nationalism itself, which demands the articulation of difference while simultaneously demanding the articulation of unity.

CHAPTER THREE

The Nation and the Challenge of Unity

Why did the "dilemma of difference" outlined in the previous chapter so trouble both military and political leaders in the late imperial period? After all, the old regime had an ideology that laid out certain naturalized justifications for differences within the population while providing a basis for unity among that population at the same time. Some men were born to rule, others were born to trade, others still to till the land. This essential difference between peoples justified the intricate structure of discrimination that lay at the basis of the imperial regime. At the same time, though, all of the empire's subjects were supposed to be united by loyalty to their tsar and by incorporation into a statist historical tradition. The Bolsheviks, likewise, easily explained existing differences and the need for discriminatory policies by referring to a continuing class struggle while they appealed for loyalty and unity on the basis of a feeling of solidarity with one's class and loyalty to the revolution. Antinational old-regime conservatism and explictly internationalist communism were powerful ideologies, and they competed directly with the national ideology dominant in military circles. The argument of progressive military men that it was a "law" of military science that the nation was the most effective bundle of mobilizational concepts available to military propagandists and legislators was continually challenged by proponents of these non-national ideologies.

Prior to 1917, the resistance came primarily from the MVD and the Romanov family. Their reluctance to accede to military desires for a society mobilized around the ideal of a nation was understandable. Mobilization as a regular feature of political and social life was the last thing that the besieged autocracy wanted. By definition, autocracy does not rest upon a base of popular support, much less active public participation in politics, and the attempts of the last tsars to appropriate the beneficial aspects of the mobilized public societies in the West while trying to prevent what they saw as negative aspects of the West's "dual revolution" from affecting Russian public life failed miserably.[1] Mobilized groups of men, in the tense, revolutionary atmosphere that dominated Nicholas II's reign, were assumed to be dangerous by officials in the MVD. Even after the tide had clearly shifted in favor of a mobilized society during World War I, as youngsters were mobilized in Boy Scout troops and sport programs, and "society" rallied behind a range of mobilized institutions supporting the war effort, agents of the MVD conducted surveillance not only on clearly subversive revolutionary groups and potentially subversive liberal political groupings, but also upon staunchly monarchist associations.[2]

Nevertheless, the military case was compelling, all the more so since its challenge to the status quo corresponded directly with similar challenges in a number of policy fields; those who thought political problems should be solved by "enlisting" members of society in the political process frequently clashed with those who favored a "gubernatorial," top-down solution to state dilemmas.[3] This attack on the conservative model was not easily dismissed. The result was that the autocracy hemmed and hawed about pursuing a nation and ended up creating an ultimately untenable hybrid, with a military system (since 1874) based on the premise that the army would be composed of mobilized citizen-soldiers fulfilling a duty to state and nation, while attempting, through the activities of the MVD, to stem the tide of actual public mobilization itself.

The problem became acute after 1905, as the military struggled with the aftermath of its defeat by a fully mobilized Japanese army and the MVD dealt with the aftermath of the revolution. The lessons each bureaucracy learned were quite different. The military came to believe that it had lost the war because it had failed to mobilize (in both the broad and the narrow sense) as well as its Japanese opponent had.[4] The lesson drawn by the MVD was that political mobilization had almost toppled the autocracy and had to be hindered by any means possible.

World War I gave the final answer to this dilemma, and for that reason should legitimately be seen as a central turning point in Russian political history. From 1914 on, the state engaged in mass politics in order to achieve mass mobilization, and the Bolsheviks continued this trend.[5] The tsarist government discovered, however, that even the latitude offered leaders in a wartime state of emergency proved insufficient to keep the volatile combination of mass politics and minority rule stable. Within three years, the regime was dead. The Provisional Government encountered similar difficulties in keeping the proliferation of mobilized movements under control and was discredited and ruined in a mere eight months. It was ultimately the Bolsheviks who found the ingenious solution to the dilemma posed by the necessity of mass mobilization and the centrifugal tendencies of mass politics: the creation of a monopoly over mobilizational resources.[6] This monopoly on mobilization was enforced through coercion, but it was legitimated via the nation. Both sets of elites hoped to utilize the natural and historical feelings of devotion to a broader, eternal community and to appropriate those feelings by making the strongest claim to be the particular mortal representatives of it. Both eventually came to believe that they had to manufacture those feelings of devotion, at least in part, before they could utilize them.

Their task was severely complicated by the "dilemma of difference." Russian elites believed that factors such as ethnicity, culture, language, and class were "natural" cohesive mechanisms, and that for various ideological and practical reasons, none of those mechanisms could be consistently and reliably used to develop feelings of affinity between all co-nationals. Non-national mobilization schemes were equally problematic. Just as the tsarist government had discovered that the Romanov dynasty was a poor mobilizational theme, so too did the Bolsheviks come to the realization that it was difficult to mobilize soldiers for the international proletariat. As a result, national ideals of fraternity, family, and the connection of a unified political community to a vaguely defined piece of real estate were used extensively by tsarist and Bolshevik mobilization workers alike. What was desired above all was unity; the categories around which this national unity would be built varied over time.

The instinctive approach taken by conservatives in the tsarist government to the problem of how to create unity was to appeal to a statist historical tradition that transcended ethnic difference and to the figure of the tsar. In one revealing article published in the army's daily newspaper in 1911, a General Betrishev argued (like Martynov had) that unpatriotic teachers had undermined the war effort against Japan. To combat the pernicious effect of those teachers, he suggested creating a government monopoly on textbooks, which "all should be imbued with a hot, passionate love for the fatherland." Not only ethnic Russians, but other school children as well would be incorporated into this statist tradition, as he would "teach Poles and Estonians only about mighty Russia . . . I will tell them that they are children of a glorious and powerful Russian state."[7] Nicholas II underlined this passage and sent it to the commission charged with developing training programs for adolescents. Nicholas also made a concerted effort throughout his reign to promote himself as a popular and unifying figure, one in touch with the masses and in touch with the tradition established by his predecessors.[8]

This notion that the state, gravitationally centered around the celestial body of the tsar, could provide all the force necessary to unite the multiethnic political community was a powerful one throughout the late imperial era. Even men who disparaged the person of Nicholas II and were hostile to the autocratic system were forced to argue in times of crisis for the continuation of the monarchy precisely because they feared the centrifugal consequences of doing away with the dynasty that had served as the focal point for political loyalty for so long.[9]

In the end, though, the center did not hold, and mobilizational officials were compelled to turn to other unifying themes. They did not have very far to look. As already noted, the idea that the center of political gravity should be the territorialized people rather than the dynasty was prominent in political and military thought throughout the late imperial period. Thus, officers and soldiers working at Stavka proclaimed to the country soon after the February Revolution:

> Citizen officers and soldiers! Mighty Russia has become free . . . and is on the path toward creating a new life on the basis of justice and equality of all people populating our fatherland. Preserving that great blessing demands at the present time the all-out support from all sides of all free citizens of free Russia, for which it is necessary above all to conquer our primordial enemy—the German, who stands threateningly on our land.[10]

These appeals based on the unity of "all people populating the fatherland" had existed in tandem with the statist approach throughout the late imperial period, in particular during World War I. The February Revolution simply gave it center stage.

As 1917 progressed, though, the ideal of a basic unity of "all people populating the fatherland" was increasingly challenged by a class discourse that stressed essential conflicts within the territorialized community rather than its essential unity. This development was looked upon with horror by military officials, and indeed by many soldiers as well, who felt that inciting discord during a war waged between whole "peoples" was treasonous and that it sold the lives of Russian soldiers down the river for sectarian political goals. It is significant that the Bolsheviks did not quarrel with this equation. Rather, they called for an immediate end to the war, placing the onus for the conjunction of war and revolution upon those who continued the war, not those who continued the revolution. Throughout 1917, moderates who refused either the (Kornilovist) solution of squashing domestic conflict in order to successfully conduct the war or the (Leninist) solution of ending the war in order to continue the domestic transformation found themselves caught in a buzz saw. One by one, talented politicians like Miliukov and Kerenskii were cut up and spit out.

As reported in the first chapter, Bolshevik leaders almost succumbed to the same fate. Where Kerenskii had run into the sharp edge of the saw on the domestic front, Lenin encountered it on the foreign front. What differentiated the two was Lenin's capacity to turn away from the blade at the last moment. Virtually overnight after the beginning of the German offensive in February 1918, the unity of the territorialized people took priority over their essential differences. More precisely, territory was emphasized more strongly, while the "people" who formed the basis of the political community were more broadly defined as all non-exploiting laborers rather than all urban workers. Unity again returned to center stage, as this 1918 mobilizational pamphlet made clear:

> The hammer and sickle is the symbol of the unity [edinenie] of the urban worker and the rural plowman, who have entered into a union [soiuz], in order to defend to the last drop of blood their land and freedom, worker-peasant

Soviet power, and the socialist fatherland from the enemies and hangmen of the laboring people [trudovoi narod], from the capitalists, noble landowners, kulaks, foreign [inozemnye] robbers, and other counterrevolutionary bastards.[11]

The slogan of "defending the socialist fatherland," introduced in February 1918, served as the device that linked the interests of the territorialized people and the interests of the laboring classes and "unified" this people in order to defend them against "enemies of the people."

In sum, the national position, which placed the territorialized people at the center of the political community, successfully contested the purely statist conservative position and then fought off the revolutionary challenge that threatened to deterritorialize this community by centering it solely around class. But, despite the importance of land in the envisioning of this modern community and the envisioning of political identity, the formulation was never completely territorially based. The structuring categories of political community, ethnicity, and class extended beyond the boundaries of the state. Conversely, not all people living on the territory of the state were members of the political community. Throughout the period, there was a notion of "domestic and foreign enemies" that soldiers were sworn to oppose and domestic and foreign friends for whom they would fight. Thus, the construction of a unified political community was not as neat as a pure definition of that community by territorial or categorical markers. Instead, it took place through explicit definitions of bases of belonging as state officials mobilized public sentiment around domestic and foreign non-nationals and tried to unify the population who belonged in the community around the concepts of territory, family, and fraternity.

Positive Nation Building: Land

One of the most powerful tools in the nationalist's kit is analogy. National affinities are not created out of thin air. Instead, nationalists ask citizens to extend local feelings of identity, belonging, and affection to a broader community. They try to make the case that the love of one's own plot of land is inextricably tied to the national land, that the national family deserves the same respect and devotion as one's own family, and that of these kinship bonds, the fraternal link is the strongest and the most salient for imagining the national community. Whether most Russians actually extended their affinities in response to this appeal is less important, as we shall see, than the fact that the tropes of land, family, and fraternity were quickly found to be the ones that carried political weight.

The appeal to land as a source of loyalty and identity is one of the most common and effective appeals that nationalists make. In Russia the struggle to utilize the powerful emotions that linked people with their physical environments revolved around attempts to give meaning to the word *rodina*. *Rodina*, which is usually translated as "motherland," is an extremely elastic word that loses none of its emotional resonance for that elasticity. In many ways, it is better translated as "homeland," and historically has been used to describe a rather circumscribed (but always ambiguously defined) territory. When soldiers had a "yearning for the *rodina*," this meant not that they wanted to cross the state border and return to Russia, but that they wanted to go home. When military officials suggested that demobilized soldiers occupy important roles *"na rodine,"* they meant that the soldiers should go back to their home towns.[12]

The task of Russian nationalists was to transform this sense of a "home" place from a local one to a national one.[13] Making *rodina* interchangeable with *strana* (country) was the goal. And, despite much post hoc handwringing by influential Russian émigrés, who claimed that Russian peasants lacked the ability to take a broad national view of world events and only saw themselves as residents of a particular province or village, the goal was quite often met. Take the members of the 6th Siberian Rifle Regiment, for instance, who declared their support of the Provisional Government in the following way: "The 6th Siberian Rifle Regiment, discussing in their committees the questions connected with the revolutionary events in our *rodina,* considers that only a single, firm power in the *strana* can lead to the final triumph of freedom . . . Any dual power will only turn out to be fatal for the *rodina*."[14] The linkage between land and loyalty was so strong during World War I that there were several proposals before the Council of Ministers in 1915 to promise land to veterans as a reward for their service. This land would be taken not only from the peasant land bank, but also from the land confiscated from German colonists and from subjects of enemy countries, as well as from the families of deserters. Use of the land, in other words, would depend not upon tradition, much less upon notions of the inviolability of private property, but upon national belonging. As Eric Lohr has argued, this new conception and set of policies toward land was both revolutionary and widespread.[15]

Surprisingly, given the internationalist and anti-rural proclivities of the Bolsheviks, they too sought to use the *rodina* and connections to land as a mobilizing force. During the Civil War, mobilization officials tried to make the link between the fate of one's own parcel of land and the fate of the motherland. In one 1919 appeal issued to mobilize forces for the defense of Petrograd, they made clear the multiple levels on which armed defense worked:

> Workers in Petrograd have taken up positions at the approaches to their city. But Petrograd is not just their city. It is the first city of all Soviet Russia. It is the first city of the laborers of the whole world. . . . In defending Petrograd, you defend your own land, which the big landowners want to take away from you. Your mills and factories. Your homes. Your freedom. In defending Petrograd, you defend all the victories of the worker-peasant revolution. You defend all of Soviet Russia. You defend the laborers of all countries. All to the defense of Red Petrograd![16]

In this selection, mobilization officials combined appeals to locality ("your own land"), to Russia, and, even more broadly, to the world revolution in the "defend the socialist fatherland" mode that dominated Civil War mobilizational literature. The key, again, was to make local interests national, and in some cases even international, in scope. It was a tried and true technique that training officials would use throughout the 1920s. In 1922, the Political Administration of the Petrograd military district sent out a circular informing its charges that it was crucial to teach every young peasant the "link between his plot of land and the fate of the international workers movement."[17] In 1923, in response to the report of a subordinate that rejected in principle any appeal to Russian nationalism even in wartime, the chief of the Agitprop Department of the Political Administration of the Red Army (PUR), Moisei Rafes, wrote:

> The ideological formulation is incorrect. The Russian peasant, trained in the traditions of the former command staff (especially junior command), will fight the war. The basic task is not to get carried away with the communist moment . . . but to build everything on the interests of the peasant. In all agitation, pay attention to the issue of the countryside, link the war with land and bread. As concerns the use of national outlooks . . . there's nothing to fear from it.[18]

As the reference to "national outlooks" makes clear, the appeal to land that propaganda workers were to make to peasants in the next war would not be strictly economic, but would involve the linkage between land and identity as well.

In addition to making a discursive link between national belonging and land, the Soviet state formulated specific policies that made this connection more concrete. The most obvious move they made was to confiscate land from people they labeled traitors. As early as January 1918, the Second All-Russian Congress of Soviets decided to "deprive the right of the use of land" to deserters and to exile them if they tried to claim land in their home area upon their return.[19] These land confiscations eventually extended to the families of deserters and occasionally even to entire villages suspected of harboring deserters as well as the deserters themselves, and truly vast amounts of land were confiscated during the Civil War and in its immediate aftermath. In the month of January 1921 alone, 22,993 cases of property being confiscated from deserters or those who harbored them were recorded.[20] It was a punishment and a justification that quickly became known among the population, as is clear from the blanket denunciation written by "Red Army combat soldier N. Nosov" of the village of Pokrovskii in Tula province, where deserters, in his opinion, abounded. "It's time to take away those who don't want to defend freedom," he proclaimed, "and deprive them of land, since they are our enemies and traitors of the whole republic."[21] As if this linkage between belonging, loyalty, and land were not clear enough, the land taken from those who avoided service was supposed to be targeted not for general state use, but for the upkeep and support of the families of loyal soldiers away at the front.[22]

Positive Nation Building: Family

The land theme, though powerful, was far from the most prominent national image. That honor belonged to the theme of the family. The use of familial affinities as the prototype for national affinities was common in Russia throughout the period. It was intended to inspire feelings of loyalty, closeness, and above all, unity. When Mikhail Rodzianko welcomed Duma members in January 1915, he noted that the tsar had convened them at an unusual time in order to be in complete unity with the common people (narod). "The Russian tsar," he proclaimed to thunderous applause, "with his sensitive heart, divined the feelings of the narod and he has heard here the response of a united, harmonious, Russian family . . . Russia stands . . . indivisible, firm in will, and strong in spirit."[23] When the tsar abdicated, the national family remained, indeed it was rejuvenated. V. A. Zam'sov joyously penned his vision of political community in the verses of a new national anthem he submitted to the Duma for consideration in early 1917: "God bless those courageous brothers/Elected by the narod to the Duma/In 1917 their joyous embraces/United us into a single family."[24]

The Bolsheviks also liked the family metaphor, and they used it frequently. In the very first oath given to Red Army volunteers, men promised before their "brothers-in-arms" and the laboring masses that they would fight for the great cause of Soviet power and the triumph of socialism, "for which the best children of the worker-peasant family have given their lives."[25] In 1925, family images still dominated. In a textbook for military schools, future commanders and soldiers learned that "the leader is required to show respect to his subordinates, because they are both equal citizens of a united republic, because they are comrades serving in a united army, because both of them, finally, are members of a united worker-peasant family, as a result of which respect cannot fail to be mutual."[26] As this passage suggests, officials used the family metaphor not only to build affinitive bonds between co-nationals (in the "united, harmonious, Russian family" appealed to by Rodzianko or the "worker-peasant family" to which the Soviets appealed), but between soldiers as well. The nation was like a family, as was the army, as indeed was the primary battle group to which the soldier belonged. This attempt to utilize kinship bonds as a model for new social relations was intentional and was part of the military's repertoire throughout the twentieth century.

One opponent of a newly instituted (and quickly abandoned) territorial recruitment system in 1912 made the theme of the military family explicit. Under the previous system, he argued, soldiers had served far from home and family, and as a result each soldier was forced to look at his company as "his new family." It was joyful to see units "where a feeling of love and belonging to the unit, to the regiment, is firmly established among the enlisted men, where military men are united from all the corners of mighty Russia *(Rossiia)*."[27] For this author, the key to developing familial feeling in units was transference. In order to properly develop kinship bonds, young soldiers had to leave their "hearth and home," because soldiers stationed near their homes only "strengthen their feeling of belonging to their own family and love for it, and never develop a feeling of belonging to their company or regiment."[28]

Most leaders, however, did not see the need to even temporarily submerge blood-kinship ties. In fact, the stronger those were, the better, since the line given to young soldiers was that their units and the nation were *like* their family, not that they would *replace* their family.[29] The imagery stuck. Even when conditions in the Red Army were worsening, soldiers and commanders tried to keep faith in their new family. "Almost all the guys are barefoot. There are very few bullets for revolvers, and there are no binoculars," one soldier wrote, "[but] the relationship between the command staff is comradely, like a single family."[30]

The crucial task was to build upon familial affections rather than replace them. One of the key recruiting maneuvers during both World War I and the Civil War was to convince potential soldiers (or potential deserters) that regardless of their feelings for the particular regime that was appealing to them, the defense of the country was first and foremost the defense of their blood family. The very first draft of the Civil War was explained in this fashion by the Mobilization Department, which justified its targeting of peasants as well as workers by arguing that peasants "no less than workers" were "interested in the defense of the republic and their own familial hearths from enemy attack."[31] In addition, Bolshevik leaders tried to sell their ultimate goal of a militia system as a family-friendly one, as a system that "doesn't take workers away from family and hearth."[32] The ability to link the danger to the republic to the direct threat to a man's family was crucial, and enlistments went up when the case could be effectively made that one's "family and hearth" were in danger.[33]

Thus the family became a central component of the national political form. Since political frameworks mediate the interaction between citizens and the state, both parties were forced to engage in family rhetoric. In the first place, as already seen, the use of a resonant category like the family made mobilization easier (and in some cases made it possible) for state officials. But citizens too could use the family in negotiations with the state. In particular, soldiers made clear that the discursive use of families on the part of the state had to have a corollary in state welfare policies. If military service was justified because it protected families, then it was incumbent upon the state not to build up the army at the expense of the family.

This push "from below" was resisted for some time by military officials, largely because they still saw Dmitrii Miliutin's political agenda as the crucial one for creating a nation-in-arms. Miliutin's program was intended to destroy the social and political barriers of the ancien régime empire, which thwarted nation building. In particular, Miliutin sought to remove the differential conscription rules that existed for various social estates and ethnicities and to establish an immediate relationship between the state and the citizen in the institution of military service. The family-based entitlements instituted in the 1874 universal conscription law seemed to flaunt both of these principles. As a result reform-minded military planners throughout the late imperial period railed against those entitlements.

In 1900, for instance, future minister of war A. I. Rediger wrote critically about family entitlements that the law gave "the broadest possible entitlements based on family position, which is . . . *in complete opposition to the situation in western Europe, where they worry almost exclusively about their physical fitness when selecting recruits.*"[34] When the loss of the Russo-Japanese War brought concerns about the physical fitness of Russian soldiers to the forefront, the War Ministry pressed again to remove or drastically restrict the family exemptions, an initiative that was strenuously, and ultimately successfully, blocked by the MVD.

The War Ministry lost the battle not because conservative state leaders saw the utility of making the national link between the issue of family protection and that of state protection, but because top leaders in the Council of Ministers, the State Duma, and the State Council agreed with the MVD's assessment that the population had already gotten used to the system of family entitlements. Changing that system would lead to tremendous unhappiness and unrest among the "overwhelming majority of the population."[35] It was fear of public activism rather than any nation-building project that thwarted the military's desires. As it turned out, the warnings of the MVD regarding the danger of revoking family exemptions were on target. By far the largest explosion of draft riots empirewide (the steppe rebellion of 1916 excluded) came in September 1915, when these entitlements were in essence revoked and only sons were called up.

What was missed by officials in the MVD and the War Ministry was why the riots had occurred. The population liked the family entitlements not out of thoughtless inertia but because they corresponded with popular notions of what the political community was and how it should be structured. The major theme of the complaints regarding the 1915 draft of men with family entitlements was that the government had chosen to do away with the "fair" system of family entitlements before it had gotten rid of the "unfair" ones like the draft exemptions given to local police officers. The system of family entitlements was seen by most of the population as one of the fairest parts of the military service system.

This whole system collapsed along with the rest of the old army in 1917, and when the Bolsheviks abandoned their volunteer army in the face of mortal danger the last thing they intended to do was restrict their own ability to mobilize soldiers, especially since the manpower crisis promised to be at least as acute as the one that had prompted the tsarist government to abandon family-based draft entitlements in 1915. At a meeting in Moscow of top military men in June 1918 on the eve of the first drafts, the question of family entitlements was raised. At the urging of Pavel Lebedev, a former mobilization expert in the tsarist army, most members of the commission, including Trotskii and the head of the Moscow military district Emel'ian Iaroslavskii, rejected the idea of family entitlements.[36]

The reasons given by the commission for rejecting family entitlements was that they were "random" in character and that it was preferable to stick to the principle of making the terms of service "identical for everyone."[37] Lebedev underlined these points again in December 1918 in an official report and also made the theoretical justification more clear. "Entitlements for family position," he argued, "cannot be considered fair from an ideological standpoint, since the duty to defend the *rodina* is a duty of blood and cannot be equated with other civic responsibilities." Conscience and fairness would not permit demanding life from one citizen and not from another simply because the latter's family lacked workers.[38] The national focus on equality and immediacy between state and citizen obscured the nation-building potential of a strong pro-family conscription policy.

Again, soldiers and their families forcefully articulated their own vision of the nation. In late 1918, a crisis emerged as commanders close to their troops began to lodge protests against the decision of central mobilization officials to refuse family entitlements. N. I. Muralov, the commander of the Moscow military district, called the removal of all entitlements "excessive" and thought it desirable to reinstate the family entitlement for only sons.[39] Two other high-ranking officials were more forthright about the displeasure of the troops—saying it was due to lack of instruction on the question and the fact that many men being drafted were responsible for feeding large families—and felt it was leading to "undesirable occurrences," including a rise of anti-Soviet agitation.[40] The state refused to budge, believing the need for every warm body overrode the desire to improve morale, but it did increase the welfare benefits given to families of soldiers in December 1918. Further requests to be released from service (of which there were many) because of family situation were denied.[41]

The ideological basis for denying family-based exemptions therefore held firm both during the manpower emergency and after it went away. As the Civil War drew to a close, one commander asked central military officials whether only sons would be demobilized after the conclusion of hostilities and whether future peacetime drafts would exempt them. "No," came the reply, "they won't be demobilized, since there are no entitlements for family position in the Red Army. Nor is it anticipated that any entitlements for family position will be given in future drafts."[42]

That anticipation was incorrect. Beginning in 1923, family entitlements were not only awarded but also brazenly touted in pre-draft agitational campaigns.[43] The full set of family categories was recodified in the 1925 law, and though the military had certainly gained some ground in being able to select the best men regardless of family situation, the number of men who were granted exemptions was again counted in the hundreds of thousands. The military's dream of establishing a purely unmediated relationship between conscript and state had disappeared.

There were two major reasons why top officials reinstituted family entitlements. First, the problem of physical fitness was being addressed in a much different way in 1925 than it had been in 1913. The increased attention paid to schoolboys and schoolgirls and the eventual introduction of a militia-type system for many new conscripts in the 1920s meant that the state could have its military cake (trained, fit soldiers) and eat it too (by not taking men away from their work and families to train them). Just as importantly, though, during the Civil War both military officials and state officials had learned an important lesson regarding families in their life-and-death struggle with desertion. As already noted, the state's decision to devote resources and energy to protecting the families of their soldiers paid dividends and transformed the way that officials looked at the relationship between the state and its soldiers. The real family question of the Civil War was not draft exemption, but support of soldier families.

The law establishing the payment of the *paika* (ration) for soldiers' wives and children out of the state treasury in wartime was passed in 1912.[44] It was the beginning of a real shift in the concept of state-citizen relations from one under which the state demanded that its citizens fulfill certain obligations—as a matter of tradition or duty—to one of reciprocity in which citizens had the right to make demands upon the state. It is not surprising that a program for the families of those who were fulfilling the "highest" obligation to the state should have been the first implemented.

This bargain between state and soldier became more obvious and explicit over time, even though no self-respecting military or government official would have been caught dead suggesting that military service was some kind of contract. Soldiering was a "sacred duty." Anything that hinted of a contract would have raised fears of mercenary motives genuinely distasteful to tsarist and Soviet officials alike.[45] Nevertheless, given the national mobilization tactics used by both states, there was a logic to supporting soldiers' families that went beyond the obvious *Realpolitik* realization that states have to take care of the citizens with guns in their hands before they take care of those who don't have guns. If soldiers were to defend the state in order to defend their blood families, then the state had a moral obligation to "protect" the families of those men who were away. Because the state expected soldiers to treasure kinship feelings and asked soldiers to extend those affinities to co-nationals, it also expected that family misfortunes would tempt men to forgo their duty to their national family when their duty to their blood family became obvious and pressing.

On the flip side, the constant battle military authorities waged against manifestations of self-interest could benefit from these strong family bonds. More concretely, both the tsarist state and the Soviet state threatened punishment of families for the disloyalty, cowardice, or treason of war-weary soldiers. All of these equations depended upon the ability of the state to provide for families of soldiers, a fact that slowly became evident in

World War I. The straightforward connection that Bolshevik leaders eventually made between the problem of desertion and the problem of impoverished soldier families was the key to victory in the Civil War.

The policy of linking family welfare with military service in a negative fashion saw its initial expression during World War I, when officials decided that in order to stem the tide of desertion (of which the most popular form was surrendering to the enemy), they would cut off support payments to the family of any soldier suspected of giving himself up voluntarily. At the beginning of the war, only one article in the disciplinary code touched upon voluntary surrender, and that article mandated the death penalty, a difficult punishment to enact when the soldier in question was in an enemy POW camp and when the crime was so ubiquitous.[46] Over the first couple months of the war, several commanders noted their frustration with the situation, but the best solution they could come up with was to threaten Siberian exile after the war for soldiers who surrendered, thus avoiding the Scylla of letting traitors escape unscathed and the Charybdis of mass executions of returning POWs.[47]

The first person to hit upon the idea of punishing families instead of soldiers appears to have been the commander of the 1st Army. He was enraged by an officer and several soldiers going over to the German trenches during a Christmas fraternization episode in 1914 and ending up captured, and he decided that in addition to sentencing the officer (but not the soldiers) to death in absentia, he would at the same time announce the names of deserters to their home villages "so they can cease issuing the *paika* to their families in their villages at once."[48] It was a policy that was immediately welcomed at the highest reaches of government. On 27 March 1915, the Council of Ministers approved cutting off the *paika* to the families of soldiers who voluntarily surrendered to the enemy or who deserted, and Nicholas II agreed on 15 April of the same year.[49] For the rest of the war, commanders dutifully notified local officials of the names of deserters and requested that their families be taken off the welfare rolls.[50] These requests, judging by the volume of petitions from soldiers' wives who claimed they had been unfairly deprived of sustenance, were conscientiously fulfilled.[51]

The Red Army also recognized the value of the *paika* and acknowledged the need to provide for the families of its soldiers.[52] During the brief volunteer period in 1918, though the state assumed no formal responsibilities for soldiers' families, army organizers were told to inform potential volunteers that their families would receive preferential treatment.[53] Families of Red Army soldiers were to receive apartments, clothing, and food. They were to receive free medical treatment, and in the event that the soldier died, were to receive cash from the state.[54] With each successive crisis, the state responded with an increased profession of concern for families. In August 1918, one of the dark months of the Civil War for the Bolsheviks, the government raised not only soldier salaries, but also the welfare benefits given to families of soldiers, especially those with "large families." They were to be awarded cash in addition to privileged access.[55] In December 1918, the state acted again, this time to forestall having to give family exemptions to soldiers, by declaring once more its intention to provide for the families of soldiers, a declaration that pointed out both the continued commitment of the center to support soldier families and its inability to do so.

The failure to direct resources to the places where they were needed nearly cost the Bolsheviks the revolution. As families starved, soldiers deserted, which in turn forced the state to target families in a nuanced carrot-and-stick approach. On the one hand, in cases where citizen-soldiers failed to fulfill their duty to the state, their families were punished. The kin of deserters were subject to punishments ranging from fines to being struck from the rolls of the local labor exchange, not to mention the now well-established practice of cutting off the *paika*.[56] On the other hand, in the frequent cases where the state failed to fulfill its duty toward the families of citizen-soldiers, deserters were treated with much greater compassion. Indeed, the single greatest factor in determining whether a deserter was declared a deserter with a "weak will" or a deserter with "evil intent," a distinction that often meant the difference between life and death, was the condition in which the deserter's family was living. This was official policy, for the desertion commissions were charged with finding out whether the deserter had been motivated by family circumstances before ordering punishment.[57] Family problems were both the most acceptable and the most common reason for desertion in the eyes of Bolshevik officials. This meant that family policy was the key to stemming the tide of desertion and, as was patently clear in 1919, to winning the Civil War.[58]

The Bolsheviks, as a result, took family welfare very seriously, not only in their propaganda, where their claims of being more family-friendly than the Whites were important both for raising Red morale and for lowering White morale,[59] but in practice as well. Even the hated "sweep" detachments that surrounded villages, threatened civilians, and drove away livestock in a desperate attempts to flush out deserters, were specifically ordered to determine whether the families of deserters had been getting the payments and privileges the state had promised them. This information would then help determine the way those deserters were treated.[60]

Even more significantly, the Bolshevik shift in policy toward deserters in June 1919 was based on linking family policy with military service and on doing so in a very concrete way. The new rules called for increasing the size of the carrot and the size of the stick in desertion policy. On the one hand, the Bolsheviks called for an intensive campaign to confiscate both moveable and immovable property from the families of deserters and those who concealed them. On the other hand, the money and property taken from deserters was to be given to the families of "honorably serving" soldiers. Such transfers were assiduously implemented.[61] The dynamic created was powerful: it allowed for economic redistribution within villages on a massive scale from families of deserters to families of soldiers still in the Red Army. In the month of January 1921 alone, property was confiscated from 20,739 deserter families and 2,254 concealers. In addition, families and concealers paid 217,414,918 rubles in fines.[62]

Neither the attention to families nor the fact that the rhetoric of family protection the state used so liberally in its own propaganda could be used by soldiers in their dealings with the state was lost on conscripts themselves. Given the policy and practice of the regime, the claim that one's family was in dire trouble was often used by soldiers as an excuse for desertion. Sob stories about family circumstances were ubiquitous. Iosif Drozhzhin was one such soldier, whose last-ditch effort to save his life— including an appeal to family values—came after he was sentenced to death for desertion with evil intent by a provincial military tribunal in October 1919:

> I lived as a deserter . . . for seven months, and all that time I did agricultural work, since I'm the only worker at home, and there are seven mouths to feed. I showed up voluntarily, although I deserted because of extreme necessity, but this doesn't justify me, I realize my guilt, but I didn't expect such severe punishment. I beg the Appeals Court to lessen my punishment for the sake of my little children . . . and send me to the front.[63]

Family values were encoded into the relationship between the citizen, the army, and the state.

The broader implications of this linkage between family and military service have rarely been addressed. Mark von Hagen, one of the few scholars to have taken the trope of family seriously in the context of the army, makes two crucial points on this issue, however. The first is one alluded to above, that the appeal to family and the belief that kinship affinities were strong and important came naturally to army leaders who had long argued that soldiers should feel the same kind of bonds toward their unit that they felt toward their family at home. The family motif was a strong one, and it provided the underpinning of the welfare programs for soldiers and their families that were in place throughout the 1920s. Those programs were explained to soldiers in familial terms, saying that just as families looked out for their members, so too did the army look out for its members.

The second point von Hagen makes is equally important, that the program of entitlements for soldiers' families "further reinforced the soldiers' perceptions of themselves and their families as a new privileged stratum in the postrevolutionary social order."[64] This commitment to showering scarce economic, political, and social resources upon soldiers and their families ended up not only slowing desertion rates in the Civil War but also providing a significant incentive for military service in the postwar period.

Positive Nation Building: Fraternity

A major shift in political symbolism occurred in the early twentieth century. The familial imagery of the old regime prior to this period had been fully patriarchal, and political power was legitimated in this way. As one traditional author explained to young recruits, "a family can live happily only when all its members subordinate themselves to the eldest [man] in the house. Russia is the same kind of family, the eldest is the emperor."[65] This patriarchal imagery extended to the familial rhetoric within the army. Officers were the patriarchs of the family, NCOs were the older brothers, and the enlisted men were younger brothers. M. I. Dragomirov gave new recruits the following advice: "Look at the unit as your family, at the commander as your father, at your comrades as your blood brothers, and at subordinates as your little brothers; then everybody will be happy and friendly."[66]

During the last years of tsarist rule, military reformers became increasingly concerned about the younger brothers. No longer did military victory depend on the wisdom, courage, and brilliance of the elders, because modern warfare had made common soldiers relatively more important. Reformers wanted to increase cohesion, to raise the level of enlisted men, and to create a real esprit de corps. The obvious way to do this was to stress the need for junior officers and NCOs to spend more and more time with enlisted men, teaching them, training them, and inspiring them. The model for this interaction was familial. More specifically, it was fraternal. Army reformers set out to form a "band of brothers."[67]

This was the explicit goal of most of the generation of military men who emerged as a powerful force after the Russo-Japanese War, rose to high positions within the military bureaucracy and the General Staff Academy, and then joined the Red Army as military specialists, providing the organizational and theoretical foundation for future Soviet armed forces.[68] One of the men who set a consistent tone in this regard was A. A. Neznamov, who advised officers in the widely read army newspaper *Russkii invalid* in 1906 that

> Earlier, when a soldier served for almost his whole life, questions of [moral] training *[vospitanie]* were solved by themselves: the military family itself, in the person of the veteran soldier . . . trained the young ones, absorbed them. Now training has become the job of the officer; now the latter had been transformed from an exacting commander into a strict father, an elder brother. Life demanded from the commander, as a substitute for the earlier fear. . . that the commander and his subordinates become linked through mutual trust and love; punishment remains. . . as in the family, only for stupid children. The army is strong through the consciousness of a duty to the *rodina*, respect for the law and devotion to the emperor, as the representative of the *rodina* and the law.[69]

In 1906, Neznamov was straddling the line, telling commanders to be a strict father *and* an elder brother, but as he was to make clear later in the same article, the primary task of the officer was to be an "elder comrade"[70] who was essentially equal before the nation (here described as a combination of the *rodina* and the law), which was represented by the tsar. That is, he was to try to build fraternal relations with his soldiers.

Other officers were insistent on retaining patriarchal systems of authority. In 1906, A. N. Kuropatkin told officers under his command: "The relations between officers and men have always been of the closest. Like fathers to the men, our officers have won that affectionate respect. Remember that to our soldiers the word 'father-commander' is not merely an empty phrase; they believe in it. Remember also, that a commander only wins the heart of his soldiers when he is their father-commander. It is quite possible to be strict and at the same time look after the men's welfare. . . ."[71]

By the time of World War I, the ambiguity within mass mobilization tracts had disappeared, as a plea to stop deserting written by a general on the northern front made clear, saying that "you all swore an oath to be loyal to tsar and *rodina*," and that breaking that oath meant becoming "unworthy to your fellow brothers and sons of Russia and to our heroic army."[72] Russia was the mother, and all officers and soldiers were "fellow brothers." The idea propagandized by the military leadership that fellow soldiers were brothers caught on. Well before the February Revolution put the word fraternity on everyone's lips, men across the empire used the concept when speaking about affinitive ties between fellow soldiers or fellow nationals. Reservists in the wilds of the Priamur district told military officials in 1915 that "each of us . . . willingly showed up when we were mobilized, being sure that we were going to help our brothers smash the enemy."[73] Another letter "from below" complaining about the draft exemption local policemen received recommended sending all 300,000 of them into "the ranks of our fighting brothers."[74] The image extended even to men who had never served in the army. When Kirgiz representatives petitioned the Duma for a deferral of their labor draft in 1916, they also stressed that they felt the eventual imposition of conscription among the Kirgiz was not only just but was their "civic duty" as well. "We Kirgiz," they proudly proclaimed, "consider ourselves the equal sons of a unified Russia and sincerely hope that the victorious war will serve as a stimulus for the introduction of a rule of law for our *rodina*, for the passage of reforms necessary for the good of the fatherland, and for the establishment of fraternity between the sons of the fatherland who come from different tribes.[75]

This widespread use of fraternity as a metaphor in the late imperial period is not only surprising, given the overwhelmingly patriarchal imagery usually propagandized by the autocratic regime, but it is also indicative of the beginnings of a basic shift in the structure of the political community. Fraternal political communities are radically different from patriarchal ones. First, traditional hierarchies are disrupted. The unquestioned authority of father over son disappears, and authority between brothers must be renegotiated. It is no accident that fraternity appears on banners alongside equality. Second, it signals a change in the glue that holds society together. Rather than fear, affinity must provide cohesiveness.

The result of the undermining of vertical authority and affinitive ties and their replacement with horizontal power structures and cohesive bonds, if not immediately obvious to the very military men and state officials who championed fraternity in the waning years of the tsarist regime, became so after the "father" abdicated in March 1917, leaving the brothers to fight it out. Ironically, given the embrace of fraternity by many army ideologues, it was in the military where the most immediate disruption was felt. The basic reason for the crisis of authority in the army was that, despite the vocal support of reformers for the idea of building fraternal bonds between officers and soldiers, many officers simply had not bothered to establish authority on any other basis than the traditional patriarchal, unquestioning command-obedience model. In those units where reform-minded officers had sought to create a fraternal bond and had succeeded (reform-minded officers were often shunned by soldiers who distrusted their intentions), the shift of models of authority was less traumatic than it was elsewhere in the army. Where officers proved willing to engage in "mutual understanding and respect," they fared relatively well.[76]

The Provisional Government, to its great detriment, chose the wrong side of this issue and found itself in opposition to one of the great slogans of the February Revolution. Preempted by the Petrograd Soviet's explicitly fraternal Order No. 1—which gave power to the "band of brothers" by instituting soldier committees—and predisposed to seeing a change in authority relations in the army as a breakdown in authority itself, the Provisional Government soon found itself associated with patriarchal officers, a political liability that neither new proposals for fraternity-based "revolutionary-volunteer" units nor Kerenskii's rise to power proved able to overcome.[77]

The loss of the Provisional Government was the gain of the Petrograd Soviet and, increasingly, the Bolshevik Party.[78] Given the long history of fraternal metaphors in the European socialist movement, it was therefore hardly surprising that the Bolsheviks reaffirmed their support of fraternity when they took power. Again, the keys were the institutionalization both of "equality" and of the creation of mutual affinitive bonds. Hence the initial reaffirmation of the soldier committees, which would determine the "general will" that the unit would be bound to follow, and the repeated assertions of equality in the army, including the prohibiiton against wearing any decorations or medals save St. George Crosses (which were for battlefield achievements). Discipline, as with the Provisional Government's limited attempt to institute fraternal relations, was to be based on "comradely influence, the authority of committees, and comrade's courts," that is, on the decisions of the band of brothers.[79]

Soldier committees died with the old army as part of the conscious strategy by the Bolshevik leadership to step back from unfettered revolutionary idealism in military affairs. The institutional form of fraternity therefore changed, but the ideals and functions of brotherhood did not disappear. To the contrary, the aspect of equality inherent in fraternity remained prominent. In early 1918, as the Red Army was being formed, the soldiers in the 136th Infantry Division complained to the Commissariat of Military Affairs that the "defense of the *rodina* and the revolution" should be "mandatory in an identical fashion both for command staff and for soldiers," and added that protests of some revolutionary soldiers were explained by the fact that "we are achieving fraternity and equality, but nevertheless, we see a distinction in salaries, and there should be no difference in the salaries between command staff and rank-and-file soldiers."[80]

So too was the theme of brotherhood providing solidarity visible in the Soviet era. Commanders and soldiers, being from the same "family" of laborers and being equal citizens, were bound by moral ties, political workers argued, in sharp contrast to the bonds of fear instituted under the tsars. "Now the Red Army is composed of workers and peasants," these political workers crowed. "The Red Army soldier and the commander come from the same family of laborers—they are blood brothers." The discipline of "the stick and punches in the mouth" had been replaced by "conscious revolutionary discipline."[81]

Solidarity, equality, loyalty—these were the bases of fraternity. No wonder, then, that fraternity was the model chosen very early on to describe not only the kind of interaction that separate individuals in the nation should have, but also the type of interaction that ethnic groups should have within the nation. State actors during the Civil War regularly referred to different ethnic groups as "brother peoples."[82] By late 1918, the idea that ethnic relations would be understood in fraternal terms had percolated down to regular soldiers. "Long live the World Revolution!" cheered the soldiers of one regiment, "Long live the fraternity of peoples!"[83] The use of the fraternal metaphor continued, even multiplied, as the 1920s wore on.[84]

Fraternity was a wonderfully useful concept, incorporating all the aspects of nation that state officials desired (affinitive solidarity in particular) and reinforcing the popular slogan of equality without significantly lessening maneuvers of power and domination. After all, as Ukrainian nationalists (and Russian peasants) would soon grow tired of hearing, within any fraternal system there is room for older brothers and younger brothers, leaders and followers. It was not until the 1930s that the fraternal revolution "retreated" under Stalin's paternalistic pressure. It is a sign of just how pervasive the fraternal rhetoric was that as late as 1927 a group of Pioneers wrote: "Dear brother I. V. Stalin, we send you [tebe] our fraternal Pioneer greeting and wish you success in your work."[85]

I have stressed the affinitive and equalizing aspects of fraternity so strongly because they are crucial for understanding the nation-building process in Russia. Unable to use purely ethnic or class identities as "natural" cohesive mechanisms when forming military and political communities, army ideologues instead relied upon the images of family and fraternity as their major "natural" cohesive force, and as a result they committed themselves to family, in their actions as well as in their rhetoric.

Negative Nation Building: Pariahs

If positive nation building relies on the extension of warm local affinities to an intangible broader community, negative nation building relies on the mobilization of deep personal anxiety and anger through national channels. The task of nation-builders becomes easier the more obviously they can make the case that gnawing feelings of insecurity and injustice are the result of the work of non-nationals and that the dividing line between safety and terror, between prosperity and ruin, is the national boundary. This boundary need not run solely along state borders. Russian nation-builders pointed out, exploited, and believed in the existence of domestic non-nationals and foreign non-nationals.

"Domestic non-national" is perhaps too analytic a term for what was in essence a visceral phenomenon. It would be more accurate to describe these domestic non-nationals as "national pariahs." These pariahs played a crucial role in the formation of Russian national identity for two reasons. First, like all marginal groups, they helped define the contours of what "Russian-ness" or "Sovietness" were in the early twentieth century. Pariahs were defined by the primary population categorization. Thus, Jews were religiously defined in the nineteenth century and became ethnically defined when religion gave way to ethnicity as the primary population marker in the first years of the twentieth century. After 1917, when class became the primary population category, so too did class enemies take center stage as pariahs. The presence of religious, ethnic, and class "enemies" helped to define the nation's religious, ethnic, and class identity.

Second, national pariahs functioned as scapegoats. This function was central in the early twentieth century, because the events of that period were catastrophic not just in human terms, but in national terms as well. Social and communal disintegration defined the age, and what can only be called a profound identity crisis occurred throughout the country. Dealing with the implications of this long national catastrophe was difficult, because nationalism is an ideology quite unprepared for explaining catastrophe. Centuries earlier, times of trouble were explicable as signs of divine wrath against the people and were indeed explained that way. But when the "people" themselves assume the immortality and infallibility of a deity another means for explaining national failure must be found.[86]

One of the primary means for explaining such failure in Russia (both then and today) was by more sensitively defining "national character" and how this character compared with that of other nations. When faced with national defeat, a common nationalist practice is to admit inferiority in one sphere of human activity while maintaining a deeper sense of superiority. It is this maneuver that Partha Chatterjee has described as an endemic feature of nationalism in the colonial world. In India, he argues, the objective superiority of Western technology and military technique did not give rise to a "derivative" nationalism that simply mimicked the Western models in toto but led to a separation in the national ideology between the spiritual and material spheres of life. The West had proven superiority in material matters, but nationalist politicians argued that Indians were superior in the (more important) spiritual sphere of national life.[87] Colonization is not necessary to bring this national mindset about, as a long strand of Russia's intellectual tradition shows. Part of the ineffable "Russian soul," which intellectuals ranging from Slavophiles to populists to Solzhenitsyn tried to define, was an essence that was not only nonmaterial, but antimaterial.[88]

The second means for explaining national catastrophe derived directly from the first. Because Russians were good-hearted and antimaterial, the argument went, they were unusually susceptible to chicanery and craftiness. Those who would save the simple Russians from the almost limitless trickery of their enemies, therefore, trained themselves to be on the lookout for "spies and hidden enemies" everywhere. Without the presence of these crafty enemies of the *narod,* whether they be foreign enemies who enjoyed a material superiority or domestic ones who lived to dupe and trick the gullible *muzhik* (peasant), national failure would be much harder to swallow, for it would imply absolute national inferiority.

The national pariahs in the tsarist period were Jews. There is not space enough in this context to analyze the full phenomenon of Russian anti-Semitism, or even the full dimensions of anti-Semitism in the army. The focus here will be on just two crucial aspects of the "Jewish question" as it related to the army: 1) how marking Jews as pariahs helped to set the boundaries of the nation, and 2) how the persecution of Jews served to preserve the image of the *narod.* In many respects, Jews were seen as the polar opposite of the Russian *narod,* cunning where the Russians were simple, "cosmopolitan" rather than "core." They were, as Laura Engelstein has pointed out, the "prime culprits in the symbolic drama of imagined national peril."[89] They posed all the threats to the simple folk that urban residents did and more, since they were assumed to have connections and links outside of the country, especially with Germans. They were also assumed to have more money and more business savvy than native Russians. It was this last set of assumptions that justified the panoply of laws that relegated Jews to second-class status, as Russian chauvinists feared that with a level playing field Jews would dominate Russian economic life and become masters of the Russian people.

The army may not suffer from *all* the ills of society at a higher temperature, but it certainly was more feverishly anti-Semitic than the rest of the population. Anti-Semitism in the army had a different dynamic than that in the civilian sphere, however. Completely missing was any sense that the Jews would exert military dominance in the way civilians feared Jews would exert economic dominance. To the contrary, officers were convinced that Jews were an unmartial and unpatriotic "tribe," whose only useful function in the army was to be musicians or orderlies. In the words of Lukomskii, Jews lacked the moral prerequisites for honorable soldiering because of their "racial characteristics."[90] That they posed no physical threat did not mean they were not dangerous, however. Army officials were convinced that Jews posed a tremendous moral liability. They feared that Jews would start panicked retreats that impressionable young Russians might join, that they would lead soldiers to desert en masse, or that they would sell sensitive information to the enemy.[91]

Jews, therefore, were made the object of official discrimination as soldiers. Fearing mass surrender of Jews in moments of crisis, army leaders in the interwar period categorically forbade the stationing of Jews in the key military fortresses that were supposed to protect the Russian heartland from German aggression, and these leaders even went so far as to prevent the entrance of Jews into such fortresses for training sessions.[92] Of more import for most Jews in the army was the iron ceiling that they faced in regard to promotion within the army. The goal of many privates in the Russian army was to be promoted to noncommissioned officer status, since NCOs ordered disciplinary measures rather than suffered them. Jews, who certainly were the object of more than their fair share of beatings and other punishments, undoubtedly wished the same.

In the period between 1905 and 1914, however, the chance that a Jew would get promoted, slim before the Russo-Japanese War, virtually disappeared. The central military establishment made it very clear that promoting a Jew to the position of noncommissioned officer was to be an exception only (Jews were formally forbidden from rising any higher than NCO). In 1910, even the loopholes for decorated Jewish veterans were closed, when Lukomskii forbade the promotion of any Jews to an NCO position in a combat unit and strictly controlled their promotion to musical and noncombat posts.[93]

This officially sanctioned anti-Semitism made a Jew's army experience a miserable one, and it was predictable that attempts by Jews to avoid military service would be more fervent and more numerous than those of their gentile counterparts. This evasion, in turn, led to suspicions that Jews had no commitment to the nation, which led to even greater anti-Semitism. Thus the state and military were centrally implicated in the problem of Jewish draft evasion.

But military officials continued to blame Jews alone, and the more that young Jews avoided the draft, the more strident officials became. The accusation that Jews, as a "tribe," were shirking the primary national duty of military service was a serious one, and it was strenuously refuted by influential Jewish politicians like Jacob Frumkin and later historians like Salo Baron.[94] Despite these protestations, though, it is clear that Jews did attempt to avoid service en masse. In 1912, for instance, 4.55 percent of Orthodox subjects failed to appear for the draft when called, but fully 33.02 percent of Jewish conscripts were no-shows.[95] The actual level of evasion among Orthodox conscripts was certainly higher than the statistics showed, because Russians found it easier to get away with the variety of tricks (both legal and illegal) that got one out of military service than Jews did, but even after taking these hidden Orthodox evaders into account, the Jewish level was significantly higher than the level of Orthodox evasion.

Even politicians sympathetic to Jews were convinced that Jewish draft dodging was a serious problem. Most military men throughout the late tsarist period felt that Jews were nonmartial and that they avoided military service whenever possible. This belief, in turn, became the basis for a series of administrative regulations that made Jews in the army the object of yet greater discrimination and official suspicion. Jews were subject to different and punitive draft laws, ranging from a special 300-ruble fine levied upon Jewish families if their sons failed to appear for the draft to the photographing of Jewish conscripts to prevent them from paying sickly neighbors to take and fail their follow-up physical exams for them.[96] None of these procedures were applied to evasion-minded non-Jewish citizens.

The presence of second-class citizens in the army was uncomfortable for military theorists. As already noted, the dominant trend in army thinking was that only armies composed of equal citizen-soldiers were capable of victory in wars with other nations of the same type. The political battle on the "Jewish question" in the army was thus waged by three political groups. Two were strong supporters of the national position that all citizens had to be soldiers and vice-versa. One side, the exclusionists, urged that Jews be excised from the army and the polity, while the other argued that Jews should obtain full standing in each. The third position was the antinational conservative one, which wanted to maintain the status quo.

The exclusionists dominated in army circles throughout the late imperial period but proved unable to realize their dream of an army without Jews. Official attempts to prohibit Jews from the army took place in 1903, 1904, and again in 1907, when the Council of State Defense preserved the status quo only with great reservations, saying that "the council, recognizing that Jews are exceedingly harmful to the army, nevertheless unanimously came out in favor of preserving natural military duty for Jews and pointed to the necessity of taking measures within the army itself to reduce this evil."[97]

The army's politicking did not stop. In 1908 the most forceful call to date was made by the War Ministry and the Duma's Defense Committee to prohibit Jews from the army as a group "that corrupts the army in the time of peace and is extremely unreliable in the time of war."[98] Prime Minister Petr Stolypin killed the bill in committee.[99] The question, though, would not and could not go away. After another call to deal with the "Jewish question" in 1909, the Duma's Defense Committee took up the issue once more in 1911, when it called for a bill to be passed that would bar Jews from the army. This time, the exclusionists in the armed forces sought ammunition for their political battle and sent out questionnaires to senior troop commanders that asked them to relate the physical, moral, and combat qualities of Jews, as well as their political reliability.[100] Stolypin again killed the project, but his subsequent assassination led the new head of the Mobilization Department, Sergei Dobrorol'skii, to test the waters for yet another try with the exclusionary bill.[101]

The final movement was one that was intended to come to fruition after the end of the war. It was launched by Stavka chief of staff General N. N. Ianushkevich, the man most responsible for the wholesale persecution of Jews during World War I. In 1915, he sent questionnaires to military commanders with the explicit purpose of collecting material for later legislative use. This intent was passed down the chain of command along with the questionnaires. One chief of an evacuation point was told by his superiors that the material was being gathered so that when the "Jewish question" was decided after the war there would be "systematized material . . . which would prove all the harm that Jews posed [in the army]."[102] The February Revolution ended all these exclusionary dreams by bringing the very politicians who had most vociferously argued for the liberal position of Jewish equality to positions of power. The "Jewish question" in the army was thereby "solved" by lifting all previous restrictions on Jews and declaring an amnesty for Jewish draft dodgers provided they now showed up to fight for the Provisional Government.[103]

The explicit subtext of all these discussions regarding the place of Jews in the army was the place of Jews in the political community. Military service was directly linked with citizenship rights, as one member of the Duma stated during the service law debate in 1911: "a citizen of the Russian Empire who evades the performance of his sacred duty before the motherland should not have all the rights of a Russian citizen," a statement that elicited a positive response from the right side of the chamber, not least because it was directed at Jews.[104]

The peculiar relationship of Jews to the army therefore signaled a peculiar relationship to the larger political community. Unlike Latvians, Georgians, and Kirgiz, for instance, Jews were seen as being outside of the expansive community imagined by most military nationalists. Instead of assimilation, the answer to the Jewish problem seemed to be exclusion. One young officer who participated in the public debate surrounding the Jewish military service issue in 1911 went so far as to suggest that "if Jews are living badly in Russia, then let them go wherever they want, like to . . . Manchuria," and that "we can only greet that great hour when Jews leave," adding sarcastically that "somehow the Russian army will get along without Jews."[105]

When World War I broke out, the volatile mix of entrenched anti-Semitism in the army, ethnicized politics, and the army's assumption of civil governance in zones near the front led to a catastrophic explosion that affected the lives of hundreds of thousands of Jews.[106] Tsarist officials prior to the war had, in Hans Rogger's view, been "immobilized . . . in an incongruous and contradictory position which they lacked the humanity, the courage, the wisdom or the single-minded fanaticism and determination to change decisively either for better or for worse,"[107] but now the civilian government in much of the Pale of Settlement had been subordinated to the Stavka and its single-minded chief of staff Ianushkevich. Ianushkevich immediately began to change affairs quite decisively for the worse.

In no small part due to the Stavka's influence, the tsarist government embraced ethnic "population politics" as a necessary component of the war effort.[108] Many influential officials began to see ethnicity as the sole determinant of political behavior. The main targets of this population politics were Germans and Jews. On the home front, livelihoods were at stake. For residents in the war zone the stakes were even higher, and the tragedy yet greater. Jews, for reasons to be addressed shortly, were labeled as politically unreliable and quickly became the target of brutal persecution by the military. The main goal of army officials was to get Jews out of the war zone by any means possible. To that end, hundreds of thousands of Jews were forced to become refugees, sent eastward for intended relocation to provinces thousands of miles away, east of the Volga river.[109] The ones driven east were lucky. Some groups of Jews were literally prodded across no-man's land into Austrian or German territory by Russian troops.[110]

The Jews who managed to avoid forced relocation often fared little better. They were openly treated as the enemy by occupying Russian troops, were dragooned into labor brigades to sweep snow in local towns, had their shops looted with the explicit or implicit permission of military commanders, or were simply robbed at gunpoint in their homes and told that any protest would result in their arrest and execution for some trumped-up charge.[111] Worse, the military leadership adopted the official policy of taking "hostages from rabbis and rich Jews while warning that in the case of treason on the part of the Jewish population the hostages will be hanged."[112] This practice of taking hostages both reflected and reinforced the idea that Jews were loyal only to other Jews and hence could not be expected to have loyalty to Russia.

The main charge leveled against the Jewish population was that they were at best sympathetic to the Germans and Austrians, and at worst spies and traitors. Their supposed susceptibility to treason stemmed, in the eyes of the military officials, from racial traits like love of money, their "cunning" nature, and from the historical "fact" that Jews were a people without a homeland. "The Jewish race," one anti-Semite argued prior to the war, lacked a "yearning for a motherland," and hence could simply not be patriotic. Jews were loyal only to fellow Jews.[113] During the war, the tsarist government did its best to make this myth a reality, just as it had by taking Jews hostages.

The irony of the situation was lost on most of the gentiles in the area, especially among the young recruits from outside of the Pale. These young men often had their first encounter with Jews when they ran into Jewish refugees departing the front. L. Voitolovskii remembered that when his unit encountered its first group of refugees, both officers and soldiers spat that they were spies and that "[t]he Polacks and Hymies ran away!"[114] This group of refugees was multiethnic, as most were. Jews made up only a portion of the millions of refugees who flowed away from the front during the war. But the Jews were singled out by Voitolovskii's unit. When a soldier seeing another group of refugees made fun of the Jews he was greeted with laughter from his comrades. When a second soldier tried to join in on the fun by saying that Poles were no better, no one laughed, and he was quickly corrected. "Poles are a necessary people," he was told "a Pole is a peasant, he's tied tightly to the land."[115]

Given the importance of a tie to land in the national ideology, the belief that Jews were uniquely unable to form an attachment to land was a crucial factor in their pariah status. The lack of attachment to land meant, in the national mindset, a lack of loyalty, despite the fact that Jews were explicitly forbidden to reside in rural areas or acquire real estate after 1864.[116] Jewish politicians in Petrograd actively tried to counteract the assumption that this enforced "rootlessness" meant a deficiency of patriotism. N. M. Friedman, a Duma deputy, argued in August 1914 that Jews had always "thought of ourselves as Russian citizens and have indeed at all times remained loyal to our country." "Nothing," he continued, "could ever alienate the Jews from Russia, their native land, to which they feel bound by centuries-old ties."[117] The protestations of Friedman and others of a similar mindset fell on deaf ears. The belief that Jews lacked a spiritual and material bond to the land and hence to the country prevailed.

Accusations of disloyalty quickly became accusations of spying. All civilians in the war zone were in danger of summary execution by frightened troops,[118] but the campaign by Ianushkevich to tar Jews broadly with the charge of spying especially endangered Jews. It was made abundantly clear to soldiers that Jews were spies. Trains of deported Jews left stations with "spies" painted on the wagons that held the human cargo.[119] An untold number paid with their lives. The sight of lynched Jews in small towns in the west of the empire was not uncommon.[120] Worse, the more that hysterical (and occasionally cynically manipulative) soldiers hanged Jews accused of spying, the more prevalent the belief that Jews were prone to spying became. Jews dangling at the ends of ropes were object reminders of where the otherwise murky national boundary lay and the consequences of being left on the wrong side of that line.

In addition to marking the line between citizen and pariah, though, Jews served another largely subconscious function, that of scapegoat. The scapegoating was heartfelt, not manufactured. Hans Rogger has justly criticized scholars who have seen anti-Semitic policies as a cynical and officially inspired attempt to deflect criticism from the regime. As he notes, anti-Semitism was "no cold-blooded, hypocritical toying with popular instincts and passions by men who knew better." Jews were perceived as a real threat, not a convenient target.[121]

The figure of the Jew enabled nationalists to preserve their idealistic image of the pure *narod*. Failures were assumed to be the fault of the pariah. The well-publicized Kuzhi incident during World War I shows this quite clearly. Kuzhi was the site of a German massacre of Russian soldiers that was initially blamed on local Jewish residents. The assumption was that Kuzhi Jews had hid the German soldiers in their potato cellars and then informed them when the Russian soldiers had gone to sleep. It was only later, as the result of a Duma investigation, that it was discovered the potato cellars were too small to fit human beings and that the blame lay with the commanding officer, who had failed to secure his perimeter.[122] Kuzhi was not an isolated incident. When a colonel commanding an artillery battery was killed by shrapnel while at an observation post, hardly an unusual occurrence in World War I, the search was on for traitors and spies. His unit rounded up a Jew and a half-German "for signaling," and "of course we finished them off right away."[123] When the Russian army sought the reasons why their soldiers were surrendering en masse to the Germans to avoid fighting any longer, the conclusion reached by military intelligence and reported up the line all the way to the minister of war was not that their soldiers were fed up with deficits in food, weapons, and competent leadership; nor was the explanation that Russian soldiers lacked the will to continue. Instead, they argued, it was due to "special agitators, the majority of whom are Jewish," who spread propaganda amongst the troops.[124]

In all these cases, that which was not immediately understandable within a particular mindset became explicable when it was possible to blame a pariah. Given the belief that war was understood to be the test of national character, the failure of Russian soldiers to pass that test upon occasion was a puzzle that few Russians wanted to pursue to its conclusion.[125] When faced with overwhelming evidence of the scope of desertions by ethnic Russians, Mikhail Rodzianko, the chairman of the Duma, literally could not bring himself to accept that the reports were true. "I just got a letter from General [A. N.] Kuropatkin," he wrote General M. V. Alekseev in 1915,

> maybe it's apocryphal, I don't know, but in it he bitterly complains about the ease with which our enlisted men, and even, to my great sorrow, our officers surrender. When my acquaintances tell me about this, I indignantly repudiate these stories and my face flushes with shame. I just cannot believe that Russian people, no matter how small their numbers, don't have sufficient valor in the battle against the Germans.[126]

It was far easier to blame Jewish cunning and Russian simplicity than to admit that Russians too could be "cowards" and "shirkers."

This trope of cunning enemies of the people, masked, and waiting for the opportunity to betray the gullible *narod* is familiar to students of the first decades of Soviet power. Indeed, the function was much the same, despite a similar tendency among scholars to see the state's use of scapegoats as a cynical manipulation.[127] And, while it is no doubt true that manipulation was involved in all Soviet campaigns against "enemies of the people," it is by no means clear that the fear of these enemies was wholly cynical. There is, indeed, some recent evidence that may suggest that these persecutions were rooted in heartfelt fears among top officials, even as the political uses of "enemies of the people" became more clear.[128]

Those enemies were not the same, of course. With the shift of emphasis from ethnicity to class, national pariahs were officially defined in class terms after the Bolshevik revolution. Broadly speaking, the state-sanctioned national pariahs were exploiters of other people's labor or social parasites.[129] The "bourgeoisie," "kulaks," and priests were the main representatives of these ostracized categories. Like Jews in the tsarist period, these groups were formally discriminated against in the armed forces. Indeed, the dilemma regarding the Soviet pariahs was similar, though it mixed the repulsion for the outcast typical of policy toward Jews with the fear of military effectiveness of the outcast typical of policy toward Germans or Poles. The problem lay in the fact that, with universal conscription, each pariah not drafted constituted a "burden" on the "core population."

The Bolsheviks were more straightforward than their predecessors had been. Rather than pretend that pariahs were part of the army and then limit their actions and persecute them under provisions of classified directives, they came right out and proclaimed their distrust and their unwillingness to hand weapons to the enemies of the people. The solution to the dilemma was the creation in July 1918 of the "rear militia," a body of conscripted pariahs who performed noncombat tasks such as trench digging, road building, and repairing boots.[130]

Pariahs enrolled in the rear militia were there exclusively because of class position or previous occupation, a fact that is clear from the very registration forms they had to fill out upon enlistment.[131] No information on the ethnicity of the members of this militia was requested, even for demographic purposes. The number of people enrolled in the rear militia was exceedingly low and remained a sore spot for class warriors for some time. From 1918–1920, only 19,318 men were conscripted into the rear militia, or less than one half of one percent of all men drafted.[132] Given the fact that the major instruments used to identify potential pariahs for this purpose were overwhelmingly urban (house committees and soviets), the majority of those eventually tagged for the militia must have been urban as well. A very large number of people who had used wage labor (in particular in the countryside) were given guns and placed in the Red Army.

A great number of pariahs probably avoided service altogether. The lack of clear rules and the inability to sufficiently account for the population in the early stages of the Civil War made evasion particularly easy. One local draft board head wrote helplessly to the Moscow district chief that mobilizing rear militiamen was "proceeding listlessly." Only fifteen people showed up over four days, most of whom were simply arriving late for the previous mobilization into the regular army. The only exception was truly exceptional, a "religious worker who declared himself to be a revolutionary and a communist, but who is refusing service in the Red Army because he is an enemy of blood."[133] Pariahs proved devilishly hard to find, both because they were intent on evading and because the state was so weak.

This marking of pariahs to define the national community was of great significance, particularly during a time when the boundaries of that community were unclear or unfamiliar. Indeed, much of the handwringing regarding the question of military specialists was due to this identity crisis. "Building a unified, powerful Red Army—this is the goal of everyone who holds the interests of the proletariat dear," one official wrote in 1918, "[b]ut that army will come about only when 'Red officers' stand at its head. There is, however, no common language between the 'former officers' and the political commissars. They don't understand each other and can't find the necessary, suitable tone for joint work."[134] Unity and power went hand in hand as a matter of course, and the charge that military specialists hurt the army stemmed, for him, not so much out of the fear that they would betray the revolution as that they reduced military cohesion. Though this particular author left out a discussion of masking and treason by national pariahs, these themes dominated the military specialist question. When a spy ring in Petrograd was uncovered in 1919, the immediate blame was laid on military specialists, as *Izvestiia* reported: "Just how spies work is shown by the excerpts below. Above all, they have agents among the command staff." Even Trotskii, the major spokesman for the military specialists, admitted his own personal belief as early as 1918 that "[m]any of them commit acts of treachery."[135]

Being former "exploiters" and henchmen of the tsarist regime, military specialists were, by state definition, national pariahs. The proper place for them, in the Bolshevik framework, would have been in the rear militia, bearing burdens without bearing arms. Unfortunately, giving them power and guns was a necessity, and a policy decision came from the very highest reaches of government supporting this position. But the fact that protection from Lenin and Trotskii often failed to save them and that successive party congresses registered their distress about the situation is an indication of the power of the image of the pariah.[136]

Take, for instance, the case of M. D. Bonch-Bruevich, the prominent military specialist encountered in chapter 1. Despite the explicit and powerful support of both Lenin and Trotskii, Bonch-Bruevich was plagued throughout his short tenure by sharp criticisms from outraged Bolshevik purists. A letter to Lenin at Sovnarkom in November 1917 from party faithful accused Bonch-Bruevich of being a member of the Black Hundreds (a far-right organization of thugs) and vehemently protested his appointment as chief of staff.[137] The accusation was baseless, but continued attacks led Bonch-Bruevich to tender his resignation, purportedly for health reasons, in August 1918. Lenin did not accept the resignation right away, but telegrammed Trotskii about the letter. Trotskii was shocked, saying "we can't replace him" and fuming that "it's possible they've been nipping at him in my absence."[138] On the same day, Trotskii telegrammed Bonch-Bruevich begging him to stay, but the pleas went unheeded. Bonch-Bruevich was gone.[139]

The continuing struggle regarding military specialists need not take space here. Suffice it to say that if even the most crucial military specialists with the highest political protection, family connections, and proven loyalty were the objects of persecution and were successfully brought down, something deeper than a mere cost-benefit analysis of risk and gain was at play. Among those deeper factors were a real, visceral fear of the pariah and a desire to destroy the most visible symbols of the larger crisis of national identity. The need to draw a clear dividing line between national and non-national was profound and was profoundly disturbed by the use of pariahs in crucial positions.

Just as pariahs marked boundary lines in the Soviet era, so too did they serve as scapegoats. Those marked as non-nationals by the regulations defining membership in the rear militia were blamed for nearly all the misfortune of the Civil War. One high-ranking official in southern Russia, searching for reasons for the failures of the 10th Army in the region, pointed to the fact that the army was "exceedingly motley in its class and territorial composition," and that because of the unpredictable nature of the war a large percentage of his army was made up of "kulak or half-kulak elements."[140] These kulaks, because of the "political ignorance of the mass of soldiers," were able to act as disintegrating forces and led to the misfortunes of the army.[141] The report went further, delineating again the line between national and enemy, claiming that the percentage of kulaks in one region was so high that they were literally "conducting war in enemy country."[142]

The Moscow District Commissariat described the importance of its agitation section in similar terms, arguing that prior to its intervention "both the army and the civilian masses, being politically undeveloped, and as a result being unable to understand events at crucial times, frequently followed kulaks and other enemies of Bolshevism."[143] When the Red Army tried to draft peasants in Sunsk county, it found that the peasants reacted with hostility. The reason, according to the Political Department of the 3rd Army, was clearly that "kulaks and priests were conducting anti-Soviet propaganda."[144] Again, this was a mobilizable difference. In one Civil War flyer, the army's Political Administration (PUR) maintained that the people unhappy with Soviet power were: "generals, colonels, engineers, merchants, students—and not a single worker, not a single peasant." They explained the uncomfortable fact of worker and peasant resistance to Soviet power by saying that "enemies" were trying to split the people and that "for this purpose, they unleashed their spies into the people [narod] and Red Army, and the spies began to incite the politically naïve against Soviet Power."[145] The theme of a politically naïve narod being particularly susceptible to the cunning influence of the enemy had obviously persisted across the revolutionary divide.

This fear of the pariah took on such dimensions during the Civil War that nearly all instances of unrest were pinned upon them. When Bolshevik officials tried to undertake a draft in Riazan' and Tambov provinces in November 1918 without conducting an agitation campaign, a series of draft riots resulted during which a "White guardist" named Guliaev purportedly spread rumors that Soviet power had been overthrown in the center. This complex uprising was simplified and classified as a "kulak rebellion," a phrase that would be endlessly repeated throughout the Civil War.[146] Just as Jews made it possible to absolve the Russian people from "sins" in the eyes of the elite, so too did kulaks, priests, and the bourgeoisie make it possible to absolve the Soviet people of its own heretical actions. The formula allowed elites to believe that they expressed the general will—even when popular support was clearly lacking, and it legitimized their separation of the ideal nation, which they genuinely wished to represent, from the actual population under their control. Though this scapegoating was cynical from time to time (blaming kulaks for one's own mistakes was undoubtedly common), and despite signals that designating rebellions "kulak rebellions" was becoming a rhetorical habit, the belief that kulaks really were a harmful element in the army and that they were behind most civilian unrest was widely held. As late as 1924, in completely classified documents, military officials wrung their hands over how exactly to locate and expunge pariahs.[147]

Pariahs were therefore tremendously important and served similar functions under both regimes. Just as the tsarist regime practiced "population politics" in regard to its pariahs, so too did the Soviet regime. Substitute "Jews" for "former officers" in the following Soviet document and one gets a document that could just as easily have been produced in World War I: "On the basis of Trotskii's . . . order, the families of former officers who went over to the Whites should be arrested as hostages and their property confiscated." Making a similar substition of "Jews" for "kulaks" in the following document produces the same result: "With the goal of preventing banditism and rebellions . . . you must take hostages from among kulaks, from influential people or from suspicious people, or those who sympathize with bandits. . . . "[148]

And, in fact, substituting "Jews" for the pariahs defined by the Soviet regime was exactly what much of the population did, to the dismay of leading Bolsheviks. Despite prolonged and serious attention to the problem of anti-Semitism by the Soviet and Red Army leadership, anti-Semitism ran rampant in the Soviet Union and in the Red Army. When the 1st Cavalry Army rode to Warsaw (and back) in 1920, it conducted pogroms along the way. Shouting the age-old rallying cry of "beat the yids *[bei zhidov]*," they rampaged through towns and villages ransacking stores and even killing Jewish officials of local soviets. Pogroms continued well into the 1920s.[149]

Each entering draft cohort displayed anti-Semitic behavior soon after joining the colors, beating up Jewish soldiers and ransacking Jewish stores just as their forefathers had. In 1925, in Gomel' province, a group of soldiers went to a Jewish farming collective and demanded 25 rubles. When the farmers refused, they were beaten. In the city of Smolensk, draftees waylaid Jews passing by on the streets, yelling "beat the yids" and then clubbing them senseless.[150] Just as anti-Semitic activity continued in the same way, so too was it justified in pariah terms. Young soldiers grumbled that Jews were draft dodgers and that they profited at the expense of simple Russians. As PUR admitted in 1926, "[a]nti-Semitism exists in all regions . . . [and] revolves around old motives: 'There aren't any Jews in the army' and 'yids have all the power' and so forth." Not even the fact that Jews were now allowed to become farmers helped their situation. They were still thought to be just as rootless and shifty as before, but the accusations changed. Now peasants (especially in Ukraine) blamed the Jewish farmers for "hindering" their farming efforts and scoffed ominously that "Jews don't know how to work the land and have to turn to wage labor."[151]

The commonalities between Jews and class pariahs went beyond the mere fact that the population could not simply discard its old prejudices and develop brand new ones. The very fact that Jews had been prohibited from agricultural areas and confined to small provincial towns in the west virtually ensured that the kinds of occupations (like small trader) they had traditionally pursued were the ones that were proscribed by the Bolsheviks. "Jew" and "speculator" had meant virtually the same thing to many gentiles before the revolution, and the shift of terminology under the Bolsheviks was not particularly significant for them. In some regions, local military commanders filled their rear militia units exclusively with Jews, even unemployed Jews or white-collar workers who were supposed to be drafted into combat units. Elsewhere, a group of older soldiers complained that Jews were sitting at home while Russians fought and bitterly commented that "this is how we're achieving fraternity and equality: one suffers a whole year in the Civil War, and another stuffs his pockets through speculation." After the war, soldiers still grumbled that "the yids, those bastards, keep raising prices," and wondered aloud "if the army consists of workers and peasants, how did Jews end up in it?"[152]

Others made the connection between Jews and class enemies clearer still. A group of draftees in Krivyi Rog smashed a row of stores in 1922, and upon being confronted explained that it was out of "disagreement with NEP." But, as one PUR official noted, when one took account of the fact that all the storeowners were Jews "a different picture emerged." Another soldier was more straightforward. "Beat the yids!" he yelled, "they're all speculators!" Exasperated PUR workers who dealt with anti-Semitic outbursts noted dismally that these displays were the result of "cultural backwardness."[153]

National pariahs existed throughout the early twentieth century, and their features were similar. They were cunning, treasonous, and lacked a real tie to the land on which they lived. As such they were the polar opposite of the *narod*, which was honest, true, and rooted to the land. The boundary between the national and the non-national was thus sharply drawn and was institutionalized in the army.

Negative Nation Building: Foreigners

Rallying against the "outside" enemy was also an important way of marking the national boundary. It was suspected that, like national pariahs, foreigners were aware of the fatal weakness of the Russian people (their openhearted and gullible nature), and had saturated the country with spies in an effort to exploit this weakness. As a result, the naïve *narod* had to be taught to always be suspicious and on guard. As young conscripts were told in 1913, defending Russia from the "encroachments of neighboring states" was the job of the army, and that job could only be fulfilled if soldiers both pledged to heroically battle the "enemies of the Fatherland" on the battlefield and to remain tight-lipped. "The enemy," young men were told, "always tries to uncover our plans . . . For this purpose they send their scouts and people in disguise—spies, who try to observe our configuration, find out the number and type of our troops, and to eavesdrop on our conversations."[154]

This warning to young soldiers was repeated throughout the period, whether during war or peace. The Soviets were even more obsessed by spying than their tsarist predecessors had been. Trotskii, for instance, was convinced in 1922 that "imperialist agents" were making intensive efforts to infiltrate the Red Army and that naïve young soldiers were not displaying "the necessary caution in relations with foreigners and their Russian counterrevolutionary agents." As a result, he ordered that servicemen be forbidden not only to do any kind of work in "foreign, diplomatic, philanthropic, or other institutions," but also to come into "any kind of contact" at all with foreigners without notifying their commissar.[155] The prohibition of contact with foreigners remained in place throughout the rest of the Soviet era, and the list of Soviet citizens forbidden to mix with foreigners expanded to include not only soldiers, but military-industrial workers and others as well. This was no cynical maneuver, but a fear of foreign infiltration genuinely felt. Spy mania slipped effortlessly into xenophobia, even for a devoted internationalist like Trotskii.

Both of the examples above relate to officially sanctioned spy mania and xenophobia in periods of peace. Needless to say, both increased when the country was at war.[156] Mobilization against spies and foreigners was a popular tactic for state and military officials. Aleksandr Guchkov, fearful of defeatism in the capital, exhorted "citizens and soldiers" in 1917 to fight German spies and traitors. Echoing the nearly daily warnings about spies that had saturated the Russian public sphere during the war years, Guchkov cautioned that spies hid everywhere. "There is no title that the spy might not assume, no occupation behind which he might not try to hide his vile activity; he assumes every kind of disguise and, hiding in the crowd, stirs up and disturbs the timid and the weak."[157]

Despite the fact that the Bolshevik Party was one of the most prominent victims of this xenophobic mobilization campaign in 1917,[158] Bolshevik officials desperately trying to stabilize the northern front a bit more than a year later against the incursion of Allied troops played the "spy and foreigner" card themselves. They began by arguing that class divisions were the real ones but quickly appealed to citizens on a quite different basis, warning that the invading Englishmen, Frenchmen, and Americans, accompanied by the defeated Russian bourgeoisie, "will buy you and drive you as hired killers not against the Germans and Turks, but against your own native [rodnykh] brothers." "Let everyone," they continued, "whose heart has not gone stale do everything in order to smash the foreign oppressors."[159] The "bourgeoisie" had once used xenophobia and spy mania to discredit the Bolsheviks, but now the tables were turned.

This was a conscious decision to mobilize the population on the basis of repelling foreign foes rather than on the basis of fighting for the revolution, and it was a decision that was supported at the very top. As Stalin explained in a closed session of the Eighth Party Congress in 1919, since peasants would not (and did not) fight for socialism, much less for proletarians, it followed "that our task . . . is to make them fight against imperialism, and in this way achieve the merging of the armed peasantry with the proletariat."[160] Throughout the Civil War, the battle to define "natives" and "foreigners" was of tremendous importance.[161]

The question of who made the best case that the enemy was "foreign" during the Civil War was crucial, because it was clear to all involved that this mobilization of emotion around the fear of foreigners (and spies) struck a popular chord. Soldiers and citizens responded eagerly to mobilizational rhetoric about pariahs, and the response to xenophobic mobilization was similar. In 1914, for instance, one concerned citizen wrote anonymously to the Council of Ministers asking it to advise the tsar to "save the army from spies, masked Germans and Jews, from the lowest soldier to General Boron."[162] Eduard Dune found much the same fear expressed by an old man fishing on a river in southern Russia during the Civil War. The "ancient" man asked Dune "who were the Communists, the Latvians, and the Chinese who would come after the Bolsheviks?"[163]

Spies were lurking everywhere, and not just during the Civil War. In 1925, a guard of an aviation storehouse in Voronezh saw two figures who disappeared into the darkness when he told them to "freeze." Later the same evening, a vision of figures in the darkness peering through windows prompted more shouting, and even shooting, but without result, the figures having vanished again into the night. The shadowy apparitions were enough to prompt the declaration of an immediate security alert in all Air Force units in the Moscow military district.[164]

Fear of foreign espionage permeated the military establishment. This fear not just of foreign spying but of foreigners themselves was transmitted to every incoming soldier. Throughout the early Soviet period, lectures and discussions on the topic of "who are our enemies?" were conducted by political workers.[165] The answer was clear: not only the domestic, counterrevolutionary pariahs, but foreigners as well. Soviet soldiers no less than tsarist ones were sworn to defend the fatherland against "foreign and domestic enemies." Every young soldier, on the slight chance he had not been inundated with the fact before, had the image of "encirclement" and the "Soviet fortress" etched into his consciousness.

But again, despite this upsurge in mobilized xenophobia, it was clear that neither the tsarist nor the Soviet state was uniform in its anti-foreign rhetoric, much less that a simple dichotomy of "us" and "the Other" emerged. As always, identity, pathos, and mobilizational methods were far more complex. For not only did the tsarist state and the Soviet state include subjects who were not ethnically Russian or proletarian by class position in their armies, but they accepted foreign subjects as well. As early as 1914, citizens of Allied powers who happened to be in Russia were allowed to join the Russian army, just as Russians stranded in France fought for the French army. In 1916, this dispensation was given even to prisoners of war of foreign powers, so long as they were Slavic (excluding Bulgarians, who were allied with the Central Powers). The tradition continued under the Bolsheviks, who built entire units of foreign volunteers dedicated to the revolution and threw them into battle in Siberia.[166]

These foreign units showed again the complex ways that competing ideologies produced institutional formations unlike those in other national contexts. It is undeniably true that the competing tradition of internationalist ideology made Russia a special case throughout the modern era. Russian intellectuals prior to the revolution were often attacked by nationalists for their excessive "cosmopolitanism." After the revolution, the internationalist strand got yet stronger. Even as the state and society grew increasingly xenophobic, a commitment remained to international organizations (most notably the Comintern), and the rhetoric of world revolution never completely disappeared. This commitment to internationalism was real and it produced real differences both in ideology and in practice.

One of the results of the clash between nationalism and internationalism was an imprecise and therefore dangerous ideological relationship to the figure of the foreigner. Even citizens with a low level of political awareness knew that there was a distinct normative and legal difference between French citizens and Austrian citizens before 1917 and between a German worker and a German baron afterward. But injunctions from those concerned with security to be cautious with any stranger played an important role as well. Few were so rash as to gamble that a foreigner was a "good" foreigner when the penalties for contact with "bad" foreigners were, in Trotskii's words, "inevitable and merciless."[167]

Conclusion

If, as noted American politico Tip O'Neill once remarked, "all politics is local," so too is all political imagination based on local forms. Not only nonethnic or multiethnic nations use land, family, and fraternity as supportive structures, but ethnic nations do so also. Indeed, ethnicities themselves are unthinkable without the foundational myth of common descent, "blood," or race and virtually as unthinkable without a homeland. It was a savvy decision, therefore, to try to reappropriate those powerful local emotions and transfer them to the multiethnic nation rather than to a single ethnicity. The decision to do so was both conscious and fruitful.

Not only did the strongest and most consistent efforts to build the multiethnic nation come from the military, but it was also the military that identified land, family, and fraternity as effective mobilization themes. Well before the Great War, even well before the Great Reforms, the army had trained its men to envision an obviously "constructed" community (the agglomeration of strangers that composed a regiment or platoon) in terms of family and fraternity, had incorporated the mortal recruits into an immortal community narrative (regimental histories were quite popular and constitutive parts of basic training in both periods), and had tied those communities to particular parcels of land (regiments were frequently named after a region of the country). When army intellectuals became convinced that a much broader community had to be constructed, therefore, they had the experience, the language, and the methods ready at hand.

This particular stance toward the nation often clashed with ethnically based national stances, but the result was not total victory for the ethnic vision. Indeed, despite the fact that the multinational affinities propagated by military intellectuals were not always fully adopted by the individuals they were trying to mobilize, one thing seems clear: however weak the expansive national identity was, ethnic national identity was weaker still.

The problem of much subsequent, narrowly ethnic, nationalist historiography is that it assumes the battle was between "true" nations and the bastardized regimes that were either "Russifying" or "breakers of nations."[168] Actually, the main struggle was between local and personal concerns and those of the broader political community. Hence the importance of the creation of entitlements by the militaries under both regimes. Rather than framing the problem in terms of nation versus family, they framed it as nation and family versus foreigners and pariahs. Nationalists used preexisting local affinities and fears and shaped them not only with word, but with deed as well, to align them with national affinities and fears. This meant that the state, in order to mobilize through the nation, had to protect the local interests of its soldiers, which indeed it did.

CHAPTER FOUR

The Nationalization of Masculinity

One of the insights provided by the study of universal conscription is that the nation, seemingly centered on the ideal of community, actually shifts the locus of political operations away from the local community and establishes it at the level of the individual. This political shift was obvious when Russia began discussing the introduction of universal conscription. The commission charged with drafting the new military service law in 1871 was called the "Commission for Drafting Regulations Establishing Military Duty on an Individual Basis." When the manifesto establishing that law was issued in 1874, the title announced the establishment of military duty on a "universal" basis instead. It is that simultaneous appeal to the individual and the universal, couched in the language of particularistic community, that makes the nation such an enigmatic and powerful political form.

One of the reasons the national form is able to operate on so many levels is because it insinuates itself into other powerful discourses and transforms them in a "national" way. This transformation is especially noticeable in discourses on gender. Though much has been written about gender politics in the first quarter of the twentieth century, relatively little attention has been paid to the transformation of masculinity in the same period. One of the most important "national" and "modernizing" identity shifts occurred precisely in this realm. Masculinity was "nationalized" in the period of total war, as the "production" of masculine ideals was taken out of private or local hands and put in the hands of the state and as masculine attributes took on "national" qualities.

The key to both processes of nationalization was the creation of mass institutions to propagate a consistent image and ethic of manliness. Without those institutions, the project of wresting the authority to define masculinity from the local communities in which it traditionally was vested would have been impossible. The most familiar mass "nationalizing" institutions are those of "print-capitalism" and mass education. These institutions were also present in the Russian case, of course, and both dramatically extended their reach in the late imperial period.[1] But independent publishers and educational professionals did not act alone in their endeavors. As will be seen below, in some aspects of cultural and social nationalization, the military was intimately involved. The production and propagation of masculine ideals was one such area where military men were involved in every step of the project. In addition to helping to frame and mold the output of the materials produced by nonmilitary organizations, military professionals played a key role in creating new mass organizations in which boys could be taught how to be a specific kind of man. This process of nationalization focused on two areas in particular: the male body and the masculine ethic. The two were distinct, but closely related.

Forming the Military Body

Of the many problems revealed by the Russo-Japanese War, few were more pressing for policymakers than the poor physical shape of the troops. It was this anxiety about bodily capacities that was the decisive prompt for army planners and military men to get involved in militarizing young citizens of the Russian Empire in the period between 1905 and 1914.[2] The army needed strong and healthy men to be successful and became increasingly strident on the importance of having well-formed conscripts. Though long ignored in draft policy in Russia, this priority came to center stage even before the Russo-Japanese War was over.

The major recommendation of mobilization officials called for a significant change in the draft process to ensure that military needs were filled before civilian ones. In particular, these officials wanted a system in which only strong men able to withstand the physical privations of the soldier on the march would be inducted into the army.[3] Army reformers in the Lukomskii Commission stressed over and over again that the empire's conscription laws needed to be much more concerned with the physical shape of its draftees than it had been before, even though this clearly implied a lessening of the importance of social factors (such as family situation and education level) in the recruiting process.

Military officials were also determined to improve the health of soldiers after they had been inducted. Reformers urged improvements in both living conditions and travel conditions for soldiers going to their units and sought to institute hygiene-awareness programs.[4] By 1912, even the training camps for reserve militia men became arenas for health consciousness. The physical fitness of these older men was closely observed and the program of activities on Saturdays and holidays throughout the realm included gymnastics programs and doctors lecturing on hygiene.[5]

The main target of military reform after 1905 lay outside of military institutions. According to reformers, the primary reason for the bad physical shape of their contingent was the "conditions in which commoners live, it lies in the fact that the mass of our population degenerates as a result of poor nutrition, of the unfavorable hygenic condition of [their] life and work and so forth."[6] In this respect, as in others, military reformers quickly expanded the realm of their interest beyond that of their own institutions, moving from the transformation of conscript bodies to the formation of adolescent bodies. This focus on the young reached its apogee under the Bolsheviks, but the movement itself predated the revolution. It grew out of nationalism and total war; only later did it become a hallmark of totalitarianism.[7]

One of the main locations for military involvement with youngsters was in primary and secondary schools. From 1874 on, the military had been indirectly influencing primary education both in the halls of power and on the ground, a fact confirmed by teachers in Moscow province in the 1890s, who noted that army needs shaped the content of their courses.[8] After the Russo-Japanese War, military men looked for ways to have direct contact with their future conscripts. Starting in 1909, for instance, lower and middle school students in the Caucasus spent part of their summer learning gymnastics under the watchful eyes of army officials.[9] Teenagers in Central Asia were introduced to military education in 1910. Most of these boys (the few girls in school on the steppe appear to have been excused) were Slavs, but boys in "native schools" also appear to have received some military instruction.[10]

By 1911, enthusiasm for militarizing youngsters was reaching a fevered pitch. An interministerial commission (the Lesh Commission) was established to work out a plan for introducing all teenagers to physical education and military affairs.[11] In Odessa, in the same year, the First Congress on Physical Development and Sport proclaimed that the great significance of physical education and sport was becoming clearer to Russian "society" with each passing year and that immediate and serious measures needed to be taken to popularize and organize the physical "upbringing" *(vospitanie)* of adolescents.[12]

There appears to have been little resistance to these programs. Russian "society" responded with enthusiasm, and even bickering bureaucracies like the Holy Synod, the Ministry of Popular Enlightenment, and the War Ministry were able to agree that physical education was needed in every school.[13] In all the discussions, the armed forces played a crucial role, from participating in commission debates to authoring manuals for village teachers to use when teaching physical education to their charges.[14]

The most striking change, however, came not from initiatives to expand the militarizing capacity of previously existing schools but from the movement to create additional institutions outside of the schools to increase physical fitness and teach military affairs. Two institutions arose at roughly the same time in 1908 and 1909 to take up the task of physically developing the younger generation. One of these institutions was a direct borrowing from Britain; Russian officers created Boy Scout troops on Robert Baden-Powell's model almost immediately after Baden-Powell himself formed the first troops in England in 1908.[15]

But, since the ideals of nationalism had already taken root by 1908, it was not surprising that a separate formation, based in Russia's revered past, should also have arisen. A host of "play companies" *(poteshnye roty)* sprung up around the country. The name was borrowed from a much different phenomenon, the mock units that Peter the Great created as a young boy in the late seventeenth century to experience military life and to play at being a soldier.[16] These new companies were a specific response to the growing perception that Russian adolescents were physically inferior to their western counterparts and that they lacked the patriotic fervor and sense of duty that the teens of Russia's threatening enemies possessed. Significantly, the men who formed play companies and Scout troops sought to remedy the situation through mass organizations outside of formal state institutions.

Play companies originated in Ekaterinoslav province some time in 1908 or 1909, and within two years they had spread across the empire. The army leadership and the government remained largely reactive while enthusiastic citizens (the majority of whom were either retired military men or officers working on their own time) formed these new groups. The increased attention toward adolescents was welcome to military officials, but conservatives were plagued by anxieties that the new "spontaneous" mass organizations would spin out of control and lead to disorder.

Quickly, then, and largely as a result of those fears of anarchy, officials in St. Petersburg pushed for the center to take control of the process and thereby displace the local initiatives that had founded the movement. On two occasions, the tsar himself stepped into the fray to try to instill some order into the process. The order he envisioned was to have active military troops take over primary responsibility for ensuring that the children learned military affairs in a "correct" and "solid" way by offering "exhaustive" assistance to the local play companies.[17]

Even this attempt to standardize the training of teenagers was not explicit enough, for local officials feared that armed bands of youths could easily be turned to the side of the revolution. The St. Petersburg governor warned that

> the mob is always impressionable, it easily changes mood and still more easily falls under the charm of leaders. The same people who raised red flags in our time of troubles now enthusiastically are prepared to participate in expressions of loyal feeling. . . . Introducing, therefore, organization into a mob of children, of young people, is acceptable only with exceeding caution. Unfortunately, this caution is not apparent.[18]

For this governor, militarizing youngsters was only a positive move if their loyalty could be counted upon. Conservative tsarist officials once more resisted the inexorable pressures of mass politics in an era of modern war. As with the question of arming minority nationalities, the question of arming bands of youths was a step not taken lightly.

The state's response to this particular dilemma was to try to harness the forces that sought the creation of a nation-in-arms by allowing the play companies to be formed while seeking ever greater control. As the numbers of these units multiplied, so too did government concern. Finally, in July 1911, the tsar and the War Ministry came out with a statute regulating the companies, requiring all units to inculcate the same values, follow the same regulations, and be subject to the watchful eye of the army. The right to form these troops was also strictly limited to high-ranking officers on active duty or in the reserves, sporting societies approved by the state, fire brigades, special military training societies, and "trustworthy people."[19] Play companies had become serious business.

The goals of the play companies were straightforward from the beginning of the experiment: "a) spiritual instruction and physical development; b) the preparation of the younger generation [sic], as a future citizen [grazhdanin] of Russia and a future soldier [voin] in particular."[20] Play companies, which had begun as an exercise in local initiative to increase the preparedness of the Russian army by militarizing teenage boys, were centralized and "nationalized" within the space of three years.

As in so many other areas of Russian life and state policy, the outbreak of World War I proved to be a watershed moment in the nationalization of masculinity. The first noticeable change was that the commitment to mobilization led to a dramatic increase in the tempo and scope of the physical fitness project. The Temporary Council on Physical Development and Sport urged the army and government in September 1915 to "mobilize youth and sport" by requiring all educational institutions to conduct courses of military training and by subsidizing sport clubs and organizations.[21]

These somewhat limited measures were soon sharpened into a stronger proposal. By November 1915, physical education specialists were asking for all sport organizations and primary and middle schools to conduct predraft training (doprizyvnaia podgotovka) for every student aged 16 or above according to a single curriculum developed in the center, and promising 20 rubles for every normal graduate and 50 rubles for every graduate who qualified to be a future instructor.[22]

The reasons for the new project were obvious and familiar. General V. N. Voeikov, the Head Observer of the Physical Development of the Population of the Russian Empire, noted that the war had made necessary the directing of all possible forces and resources of the state toward achieving victory. The army's primary need at present was a cadre of new men capable of battling the Germans. However, that need was unfulfilled because "the men we are drafting, in most cases, do not meet the demands presented by the modern conditions of war either in their general physical development or in their hardiness and discipline."[23] The Council of Ministers and the tsar quickly agreed that the output of expenditures for "mobilizing youth and sport" was well worth the estimated cost of 13 million rubles, and they approved the measures in late 1915.[24] As with ethnic units, the Great War swept away remaining political objections to the idea of a nation-in-arms.

Over time, but with increasing rapidity following the Russo-Japanese War, the tsarist government moved away from an old-regime indifference to the physical fitness of its subjects to a nationalist interest in shaping human bodies to serve the nation and state. The Bolsheviks turned the interest into obsession. If tsarist officials had resisted too long the realization that total war demanded a regime totally involved in the physical development of its citizens and had paid the price in the Great War, Bolshevik officials, learning their trade during their own total war and acknowledging the lessons of World War I, consistently strove to shape the bodies of their citizens.

Two institutions dominated military-physical education during the first decade of Bolshevik rule: Vsevobuch (the Universal Military Training Administration) and the Komsomol (the Communist Youth Union). Vsevobuch was of primary importance during the Civil War years but declined in importance afterward, giving way to the increasing power of the Komsomol before its functions were finally transferred to the staff of the Red Army and the Komsomol in 1923. The history of Vsevobuch has generally (and properly) been related to the major struggle between the supporters of a militia army and the supporters of a standing army within the Bolshevik Party. What is important in this context, however, is less the conflict between these factions than their working compromise during the Civil War. Supporters of standing armies were given wide latitude in conducting the war and in controlling soldiers, while supporters of a militia system were given predominance in preparing civilians for military tasks.

The principal task of Vsevobuch was the creation of citizen-soldiers. As one Vsevobuch official explained, being a "citizen of Soviet Russia" meant preparing oneself "in a political, cultural, and physical manner, so that one is in a position to give oneself up . . . for the defense of one's proletarian fatherland." The main task of Vsevobuch, therefore, was the "transformation of the working class and the peasantry into a militarily organized and armed people."[25] As this passage (and dozens of others like it) made clear, citizenship implied political consciousness and physical fitness. One's relationship to one's own body was a statement of political belonging and loyalty. A Vsevobuch slogan in the Moscow military district made the relation between bodies and politics quite explicit: "You're still not a sportsman? That means that you still don't know how valuable your health is to the Proletarian Republic!"[26]

Needless to say, the earlier the state could involve itself in transforming bodies, the better. One early report from Vsevobuch suggested inculcating military morality and stressing physical fitness even earlier than school age by ensuring that childrens' games lauded heroism and self-sacrifice and that they prepared both the souls and bodies of youngsters so that they would turn out to be "dextrous, brave, ingenious, and resourceful leaders of our future army."[27] Military officials also envisioned their entry into the lives of children through sports. By the beginning of 1919, sports programs aimed at children were blossoming around the republic.[28] "Energetic work on the organization of sport" was being conducted even in places where formal military training had ceased due to typhus and a lack of rifles.[29] Tactical exercises for adolescents on the verge of being drafted were to take on a "sporting character," so that they would learn "personal initiative, resourcefulness, and enterprise." Gymnastics was also to be "established in a way that will develop in the trainee an interest and a love for it."[30] Many of the organizations that conducted Vsevobuch's programs were the same sporting clubs and shooting societies that had been "mobilized" in 1915 by the tsarist government.[31] The link between sport and military preparedness was obvious to all and concerned both the "sporting spirit" and the young body.

The desire to make military-physical education fun was not new. Tsarist trainers had also been aware of the need to utilize sport more often and of the fact that soldiers enjoyed playing sports far more than drilling on the parade ground. They had also been quite alert to the role that competition for prizes could play in increasing technical expertise. Prizes for the best shooter in each company were commonly awarded. Again the difference for the Soviet military was in degree rather than kind.

Like the tsarist government, the Bolshevik government sought to institute strict central control over military-physical organizations. The fate of the Boy Scouts is a case in point. In 1918, Vsevobuch was quite willing to use existing Scouting organizations to prepare children and adolescents. Indeed, they consciously modeled their programs on the Boy Scouts, assigning their instructors to read three books on Scouting and officially stating that Scouting programs fulfilled the basic moral and physical-training tasks that were necessary in pre-draft training.[32] No mention was made about the obvious imperial provenance of the Scouting movement.

This initial stance also revealed the early belief among revolutionary idealists in Vsevobuch that the "decentralization of initiative" was a positive thing.[33] Directives from the center stressed that one of the major principles to guide the work of Vsevobuch should be to give local organs "the widest possible autonomy."[34] Local Vsevobuch officials could only conclude from the fact of conscious modeling on Boy Scouts and the desire for decentralization that existing units should be preserved, perhaps even encouraged.

The Boy Scouts, who were disparaged from the start by officials in the Commissariat of Enlightenment and the Komsomol for their "bourgeois" and "imperialist" connections, also suffered from the change of heart regarding local initiative in Vsevobuch circles that occurred when local organs themselves begged for direction. The Boy Scouts were firmly denounced at a 1919 Komsomol Congress, at which delegates demanded that all Boy Scout organizations be disbanded immediately and that the Komsomol itself take control of the physical development and upbringing of Soviet Russia's youth.[35] This attack was followed a month later by a similar initiative from the head of Vsevobuch, Podvoiskii, to the Central Committee of the Bolshevik Party.[36]

Shortly thereafter, however, Podvoiskii modified his complete opposition to the Boy Scouts, telling a conference of party workers in rural areas that the question of what to do about Scouting organizations had become a difficult one. The solution was no longer to disband them, but to take them over and use everything possible from the system while excluding "only that which contradicts our principles." The reason for the turnaround was simple: "It's very important for us to take advantage of the system of bringing up youth peculiar to the bourgeois order since our system of pre-draft training has not yet fully crystallized."[37] That system crystallized soon after the end of the Civil War. Scouting organizations were, as a result, quickly transformed and "taken over" by central authorities.[38]

The restructuring meant greater central control, at first jointly administered by Vsevobuch and the Komsomol and later simply by the Komsomol. By 1922, the Boy Scouts had all but disappeared in Soviet Russia.[39] This development was cheered by revolutionaries like Nadezhda Krupskaia, who had long seen the Boy Scouts as an organization that engendered chauvinism, served the interests of the bourgeoisie by "training" youngsters to be "the slaves of capital," and was antithetical to Soviet norms.[40]

The disappearance of troops called "Boy Scouts" did not, however, mean that the military ideals of Baden-Powell's system had declined in importance. Rather, it meant that those ideals had been sucked out and institutionalized under a different name. It was no coincidence that the Pioneers, groups for adolescents run by the Komsomol, were formed precisely when the Boy Scouts were being forced to disband. The first Pioneer organization (not even the name fell far from the "Scouting" tree) appeared in Moscow in February 1922 and was approved by the Komsomol in May 1922. At the Fifth Komsomol Congress in October 1922, central officials homogenized the physical-training components, the organizational structure, and ethical "laws and habits" that would be taught to all Pioneers in the country.[41] Even the slight heterogeneity of organizations and physical ideals that existed during the Civil War was washed away. Unified curricula and the watchful eye of the Komsomol laid the foundation for the propagation of a single bodily ideal for adolescents in the Soviet Union.

That ideal physical type had changed little during the previous sixty years of social turmoil and revolution. The core qualities remained the same: health (zdorov'e), strength (sil), hardiness (vynoslivost'), and dexterity (lovkost'). Virtually all texts relating to physical education drew from this short list of attributes. In 1861, M. I. Dragomirov urged the introduction of gymnastics into all units to develop "dexterity and strength" and to train those in the units to be "hardy."[42] Fifty years later, the same ideals were evident in a questionnaire, sent out by the General Staff, intended to gather materials to support its drive to exclude Jews from the army. The first question of that survey asked officers to comment on the "physical qualities of Jews: health, weakness [slabosilie], hardiness."[43]

After the revolution, "health, strength, hardiness, and dexterity" became something of a catechism. Vsevobuch frequently grouped them all together in its literature, and one term rarely appeared without at least one of the others. In 1918, a directive sent to all instructors stated clearly that the "final goal and task" of physical education in schools was "to physically transform the weak child into a healthy, developed, and hardy citizen-soldier through methodical training."[44] Slogans published in the Moscow military district during the Soviet-Polish War in 1920 also exhorted youngsters to work on their health, strength, hardiness, and dexterity, telling them that "you only live in peace when you are strong, dextrous, and healthy."[45] After the Civil War ended, strength, hardiness, and dexterity were mentioned less often as the task of improving the health of the civilian population (*ozdorovlenie*) took on greater dimensions, but the bodily standards propagated during the Civil War remained virtually constant during the NEP period.

These standards were rigorously taught to the Pioneers. Listed in the "laws and habits of young Pioneers" was the law that "[t]he Pioneer is healthy, hardy, and never lets his spirits fall."[46] His habits were to make him the model of strength: each day he was to rise early, wash his hands, neck and ears, brush his teeth, sponge off his body, and do gymnastics. He was to refrain from smoking, drinking, and spitting on the floor. He was always to be ready.[47] The catechism he learned was the same one his successors would learn. His leader would shout out, "Be prepared!" and he would reply, "I'm always prepared!"[48]

Not only were the capacities of adolescent bodies monitored, but their appearance was too. Again this was a development that predated the revolution. The military was an extremely visually oriented institution. The common thread in all Russian and Soviet training literature was the desirability of showing rather than telling. Whether the lesson dealt with shooting a rifle or proving loyalty to the state, military pedagogues stressed the need to visually train young men.[49] Morality was pictorial as well. No less than 57 paintings had to be removed from barracks and military buildings and given to the magistrate in the town of Plotsk after the conclusion of mobilization in July 1914. Among them were the standard portraits of the imperial family, but there were also paintings depicting the storming of Kars (in the Russo-Turkish War), the Battle of Borodino (the War of 1812), and the "Heroic Deed of Riabov" (Russo-Japanese War).[50]

Show troops were another manifestation of this visual aspect of the military ideal. In addition to the well-known predilection of Russian monarchs for seeing their sharply dressed troops marching on Mars Field, the play companies also gathered from around the country to strut their stuff in front of the tsar in the summer of 1911, an occasion that elicited much enthusiasm from the press. The newspaper *Rossiia* noted with great satisfaction that the Petersburg reporter of the German *Täglische Rundschau*, in commenting on the parade of the *poteshnye roty,* had shown that the traditionally "nonmartial" Russian people were undergoing a "retraining of their character,"[51] which was precisely the image the parade was supposed to give to its domestic audience as well. The Bolsheviks, of course, were always aware of the educational value of the visual, and used show-gymnastics troops to popularize physical education from as early as the Civil War.[52] One of these troops performed three shows in Petrograd in 1921 to rave reviews from Vsevobuch officials and the audience. The evenings were conceived in the spirit of "conducting physical education and sportification *[sportizatsiia]* of the adolescent population," and began with young boys and girls appearing on the stage in smart gymnastics costumes, which "immediately garnered them the sympathy of the public."[53]

Given the importance of the visual, then, it is not surprising the military should have had a bodily aesthetic that it sought to instill in all its charges. One newspaper published by Vsevobuch in Siberia was clear on this point. On the upper corner of its front page, it printed a flag with the inscription: "A free people must be powerful, strong, and beautiful."[54] That aesthetic, the authors in Siberia argued, was not derived from the Russian people itself, for in the population at large, the "uncultured nature" and darkness of the population and the mistaken and false understanding in general about the law regulating the health of a person reigns." Even socialist transformation had been unable to rid simple Russians of their "dread of appearing silly," which acted as a curb on their natural urges to exercise.[55]

The model these provincial officials pointed to instead was that of ancient Greece. Vsevobuch, by "physically reviving the proletariat of our republic," was the "resurrector" of ancient, democratic Greece, "where they valued physical exercise." With time, Vsevobuch would create a "cult of the body and the mind."[56] Physical exercise would become as necessary for "our flowering young men and women" as the air itself.[57] The theme of "New Hellenism" was popular among Vsevobuch activists. Hellenism played a role in many historical sketches on the development and importance of sport in history produced by Vsevobuch.[58] As early as 1918, a proponent of "communist militarism" was suggesting that the young people of Russia should be brought up in a fully militarized atmosphere evocative of the classical period. The examples of ancient Athens, Sparta, and Rome would be "supplemented" and "deepened" with communist content.[59] The efforts that Vsevobuch made during the Civil War to form young Russians into Hellenic images were not in vain. Al'bert Kiram, the secretary of the Hungarian Council of Trade Unions witnessed a display of Soviet sportsmen and sportswomen on Sparrow Hills in 1921 and gushed: "It was a picture out of Greek times. [They are] Spartans of the twentieth century."[60] Show troops, at least, were getting the desired results.

The attempts of Bolshevik leaders to get youngsters to emulate this militarized bodily ideal went from the subtle measures described above, of showing them heroes in pictorial form, to more heavy-handed approaches. In Kursk, Vsevobuch put out a poster depicting two boys, one a "puny boy" and one a "physically developed boy." The slogan read: "Who do you like better? If it's this one, then sign up at your sport square and you'll soon be just like him."[61] In the same campaign, they produced a poster with the slogan, "The spirit is lofty, but the flesh is weak." The illustration showed a naked figure with "a well-developed intelligent head in glasses, but with worn-out, muscleless, crooked arms and legs, tousled hair, a sunken chest, and a big stomach." The poster warned: "Young men, this is your future, if you don't devote a few minutes to physical development."[62]

Reports of how youths responded to physical education and the state-propagated bodily ideal are spotty. Some conscripts seem to have responded with genuine enthusiasm, especially when the physical program revolved around sport.[63] Anton Denikin, of humble origins himself, remembered that he "loved gymnastics and thrived on the military regime that was introduced into school programs in 1889."[64] Indeed, he blamed the Bolshevik victory in the Civil War at least partially on the haughtiness of the elite class, claiming that the intelligentsia scorned sport and the military regimen and hence was "not capable of bearing arms to defend its national ideal in the epoch of civil war."[65]

When these programs were launched in the vast recesses of rural Russia, however, the initial reception seems to have been cautious and cool. One commentator reporting from Shokino, a state farm in the Western military district, noted in 1920 that inspectors had painted an unhappy picture of the state of affairs. Local inhabitants had appropriated Vsevobuch property and were using the new sport-gymnastics hall for other purposes. No one was attending meetings or paying any attention to Vsevobuch: "On the ground, Vsevobuch doesn't enjoy recognition or popularity. They don't know it and don't understand it, they dismiss it as something intrusive and bothersome."[66]

Even as provincial peasants and townspeople flocked to other enlightenment programs instituted by the Bolsheviks, they remained indifferent to physical culture, at least in some areas. In the Urals, for instance, the Council on Physical Culture noted that this general "thirst for knowledge" in the region did not translate into greater interest in physical fitness. On the ground, physical education programs were still marked by a lack of materials, indifference of local society to the activities of the council, and a deficiency of sport workers. The growth, both in quality and quantity, of physical education was proceeding "with great twists and turns, with an uneven tempo, and has led to varying results."[67] The struggle to control the image and substance of the citizen's body had just begun.

Developing Military Morals

The military was interested in more than bodily transformation. It wanted to impact the moral structure of conscripts and potential conscripts as well. In fact, the two aspects of the transformation were understood to be inseparable. Both were folded into the program of moral training (vospitanie) pursued by the tsarist army leadership. The problem with schools, military men argued, was that there was too much book learning and too little moral education going on. That moral education required physical training as well. Exercise was necessary because gymnastics "facilitated the moral education of children; by developing in young boys dexterity and courage, it exerts a beneficial influence on the formation of character and the spiritual strength of the students in general."[68]

This relationship between body and soul remained strong after the revolution as well; indeed "New Hellenism" supposed that human development progressed precisely to the degree that body and soul worked together to create a "harmonious whole." Officials never tired of repeating the classical phrase, "a healthy spirit in a healthy body."[69] The idea was transformation and ascendance to a higher plane of existence. The "new man" under construction in Russia, one author wrote in 1921, "will be a physically and spiritually harmonious man" whose "emblem is the great word labor."[70] The Hellenistic ideal was infused with communist content.

In addition, military officials made their case on the basis of Darwinist science and nature. One author claimed that the separation between bodily and spiritual development was a "glaring mistake" peculiar to the human species. In the animal kingdom, by contrast, each individual being was endowed with equal rights and equal strength, since, "by means of natural selection, only the best types and the types better adapted over the centuries are preserved."[71] Two factors had derailed the "natural" development of the human species: Christian asceticism and the division of labor. Clearly, the revolution had gotten Russia back onto the right historical track by discrediting both of those social phenomena; what was now needed was to bring about a "psycho-physical renaissance."[72]

Belief in the deep connection between physical and moral development was ingrained in military men throughout the early twentieth century. Officials frequently linked the two together, as the Petersburg governor did in his 1909 report to the tsar. In this report the governor made clear his desire to eliminate military exemptions for schoolteachers: "If I may be so bold, this measure [military exemptions for teachers] brings into the ranks of future teachers a considerable number of young people who are *morally and physically cowardly,* running from discipline and from any kind of subordination."[73]

Military trainers were more explicit. V. Raikovskii was quite frank about the fact that *vospitanie* took place simultaneously in the physical and spiritual realms. He claimed that by training the soldier physically, officers had the "opportunity to impact his soul and his heart at the same time, by cultivating and drilling into him hardiness, patience, and individual and mass discipline." This training would improve his "health, strength, and dexterity." All these qualities together, he opined, were "the true guarantee of success in the service in war or in peace, in the reserves, and in their private life."[74]

Immense importance was accorded to the spiritual/moral side of the soldier by the reigning military theories of the day. For many tsarist and Soviet military thinkers, moral strength was *the* crucial variable in military success, not technological or even rough numerical superiority. The moral qualities that were desired can be put on a list just a bit longer than the list of physical qualities: honor, discipline, a feeling of duty, self-sacrifice, a "hard" will, attentiveness, courage, boldness, initiative, and obedience. As with the physical qualities, these were moral qualities desired for soldiers long before the time period under discussion. The army journal *Voennyi sbornik* was claiming as early as the 1860s that soldiers should be taught "initiative" and "bravery."[75]

These were civic as well as military qualities. As Mikhail Galkin put it in 1906, "devotion to the motherland to the point of selflessness" was the "cornerstone for the building of a modern citizen-soldier," a remarkable claim at a time when devotion to the *tsar* was generally taken to be the foundation for proper civic behavior. The army, as the most competent teacher of "proper" masculine virtues like selflessness and discipline, thus took on the burden of training Russians to be citizens. Without this nationalized masculinity, neither the army nor the society could be strong. "Woe to them," Galkin continued, "who think that discipline is needed only in military service, and unfortunate is that people in which it does not arise! The difference between civilian and military discipline is in the strength of its application, not in its spirit or basis."[76]

These concepts and ideals were not confined to the halls of the General Staff Academy. Even given the recalcitrance of many officers, the increasing literacy of conscripts made it possible for military intellectuals to target soldiers directly. In 1912, the number of illiterate conscripts dropped below one-third for the first time. Fully 55.6 percent of inductees could both read and write, and 11.6 percent could read but not write. The number of illiterate inductees had dropped by 1 percent in each of the past four years.[77] Military reformers eagerly reached out to these readers. From the 1880s forward, publications for soldiers became a big industry, and the literary output continually reinforced these ethical lessons.[78]

As part of this surge of literature for soldiers, the army published explicit texts about the meaning of military service and the military ethic for young men about to be drafted into the army. One such text began with an explanation of why military service was necessary, detailing the history of invasions from the steppe and blaming Russia's vulnerability to the Pechenegs and the Tatars on lack of military training among men. The evil invader "killed him, took what he wanted, drove away the livestock, took away his wife if he liked her, and if he didn't, he raped, tortured, and killed her; he broke the heads of the children on the rocks." Only when "intelligent people came along" did Russia raise troops to protect itself.[79]

The lesson was clear—only a man unconcerned about the honor of his daughters and his wife would oppose the army or refuse to enter it. Lest there be any confusion, the author went on to add that the reason for the Mongol invasion was that Russians "began to forget about enemies" and stopped learning military affairs, stopped listening to their elders. Why did the Mongols leave? "After three hundred years of slavery, the people understood that without soldiers it was impossible to live in peace for a single day, and began to maintain a permanent army."[80] The young readers of this short tract were taught that the only thing that preserved their own well-being and the sexual purity of their women was a strong army, and that an army was only strong when it was composed of men infused with the military ethic.

Nor was this standardized ethic taught only to young soldiers or young men about to be drafted. It was also a constitutive part of the history that primary school students learned. One textbook detailed the career of the much lauded eighteenth-century general Aleksandr Suvorov and explained his success by pointing to his close relationship with soldiers and his loyalty, bravery, and capacity for self-sacrifice.[81] In addition, the programs of physical improvement that were propagated and institutionalized in the pre-war period were suffused with an ethical content: there was no duality between body and soul.

The ethical content of these programs was identical to the military ethic. In Kiev, the instructions to primary school teachers regarding the teaching of military affairs and gymnastics advised that schools "should develop character, harden energy and spiritual staunchness, develop national pride, inculcate a martial spirit and courage and admiration for military prowess." A new generation "healthy in body and soul" would give to the future "not only physically and spiritually strong citizens, but also a completely prepared and reliable element for the army and worthy defenders of our fatherland."[82]

We should not be surprised that the contours of military morality remained the same across the revolutionary divide. Military commissars on the eastern front in 1919 were told explicitly that they had to be a "clear example of revolutionary discipline" by displaying revolutionary consciousness and vigilance, moral purity, boldness, bravery, and the capacity for self-sacrifice.[83] Again, as in the tsarist period, leadership was to be visual, exemplary, and suffused with a moral content. Boldness, bravery, and self-sacrifice were key traits that were to be modeled. The differences (revolutionary vigilance and consciousness, for example) were a matter of degree rather than kind. Vigilance and consciousness had been important factors in the tsarist soldier's ethical code as well, though of course *what* to be vigilant about and which identity to be conscious of changed dramatically in 1917.[84]

Courage and cowardice, already central in the tsarist period, became a crucial axis of revolutionary behavior, and as with the body, the display of one or the other was intimately linked with belonging to or exclusion from the political community. When the Reds were forced to abandon Kazan' in 1918, Trotskii moaned that "[d]uring the attack on Kazan' several units behaved unworthily, as cowardly mercenaries, and not as revolutionary soldiers of the Worker-Peasant Red Army."[85] When the city was retaken, he attributed the success largely to the fact that "our units fought with incomparable courage."[86] The same civic-military ethic was applied in cases of desertion. Trotskii raged, in a widely distributed 1918 order, that "[a]t the same time as regiments of the Red Army are honorably fighting at the front, preserving workers and peasants from Krasnov's robber bands, several cowards, shirkers, and traitors are abandoning their unit and hiding in their villages." Those deserters could redeem themselves by returning to their units and promising to fight "honorably" from that time forward.[87]

The key again is the link between cowardice and treason: during the Civil War the two were identical. One agitational leaflet from Smolensk asked the rhetorical question of who were the traitors in the midst of the people and answered, "DESERTERS!" who betrayed their "wives, sisters, and mothers." The solution was "purge our ranks of these dishonorable people." The ignorant deserter was to go to the front to "place his breast in the ranks of the firm, courageous warriors for the general cause and expunge his guilt," while the deserter with evil intent would be struck by the "heavy punishing hand of Soviet power."[88]

The ethic of courageous and honorable warriors defending women through armed struggle, which figured so prominently in the late tsarist era, thus did not disappear from public view in the Soviet period. Indeed, this vision of soldiers protecting women was propagated by the Central Committee's Women's Department *(Zhenotdel)* as well. The local Zhenotdel produced a slogan for Kaluga province that urged the wives, mothers, and sisters of deserters to understand that "the deserter, in betraying the revolution, also betrays you, for he refuses to defend you from the enemy."[89] The Soviet government spent a great deal of effort convincing its soldiers and their families that not only was the revolution at stake in the Civil War, but that the sexual purity of women at home was at stake as well. Of course, this ethic was propagated to youngsters as well. Vsevobuch made explicit the need to teach adolescents the "lofty moral qualities of the military man" and enumerated several to teach right away: "aggressiveness *[aktivnost']* (the meaning and nature of war is the attack), decisiveness—there is nothing more important . . . hardiness . . . valor . . . and the development of a feeling of duty to his motherland."[90] The Pioneers also inculcated the military ethic, listing among the laws of the young Pioneer the need to be "bold, honorable, and truthful" as well as loyal and self-sacrificing.[91]

As these propaganda campaigns demonstrate, the military's bodily and ethical ideals were both explicitly and implicitly masculine. In addition to the explicit charge to protect the nation's women from foreign men, the army also taught its soldiers that the proper exercise of virtue was best conducted in wholly male institutions. This earnest struggle to insulate the military from feminine contamination had profound effects, not only upon the make-up of the army but on the constitution of the political community as well. The curious story of female participation in Russia's armed forces therefore deserves close attention.

Women and the Military

To my knowledge, no woman was ever conscripted into either the prerevolutionary or the Red Army in a combat position.[92] This is not to say that women were not involved in the production of organized violence. Some women were drafted into the army in noncombat positions, a small number volunteered for combat positions, and a fairly substantial number volunteered for noncombat positions.

The two groups of women liable for forced conscription into noncombat positions were doctors and members of the Communist Party. The first draft of women doctors took place under the Provisional Government, on the basis of a 30 April 1917 decree. Still, the primary civic duty of these women was motherhood: any pregnant woman or woman with a child under three years of age was exempted from the draft, and any woman with children between three and sixteen was only to be stationed in her place of residence.[93] The practice of conscripting doctors was continued by the Bolsheviks, though the number of drafted women was statistically smaller than their representation in the profession. Of the first 467 doctors listed by the Moscow military district, only five were women, far below the 10 percent of the doctor corps that women comprised in 1913.[94] Communist women were also liable for assignment to military positions, but only in the OON or "detachments of special designation" that were staffed entirely by communists. If the rules in place during the time when those detachments were putting down rebellions in Kronstadt and elsewhere in 1921 are any indication of earlier directives, however, communist women were to be placed on combat duty only when they clearly "expressed a desire" to do so.[95]

It was far more common for women to volunteer for noncombat positions. Women were part of the military bureaucracy under both regimes, in varying numbers, but their largest role as noncombatants was as military nurses. These women, whose position and activities are crucial for a full understanding of Russian patriotism and nationalism, unfortunately still await their historian.[96] The position of Russian nurses was an especially difficult one, both physically and discursively. As Hubertus Jahn has noted, during World War I, military nurses (or "Sisters of Mercy") were almost universally portrayed as a "symbol of patriotic virtue." They were to be clean, pure, and bloodless.[97] Their dress, which included a white headdress, viscerally evoked the Virgin Mary. The connection was rarely missed by soldiers. Fedor Stepun, arriving in a military hospital in Pskov after being wounded, wrote in his first letter home that his nurse was "very sweet, simple, businesslike, and level-headed. . . . In all aspects of her appearance, there is, it seems, something Madonna-like."[98]

That Mary's shoes were impossible for mere mortals to fill was never completely comprehended, though. Intercepted letters reveal outrage on the part of soldiers and civilians that the Sisters were occasionally seen out on the street with soldiers and that they got romantically involved with doctors and orderlies.[99] Even high-ranking officials took the time to concern themselves with the off-duty behavior of nurses, trying to prohibit them from appearing in public in uniform, where they had been seen in the presence of "noisy groups" in restaurants and movie theaters. This kind of behavior, the commander of the western front asserted, "deeply injures the highly honored occupation of Sisters of Mercy."[100]

General Beliaev was equally concerned with the behavior of Sisters of Mercy, and he wrote a letter to the chief of the Petrograd military district accusing Sisters not only of walking on the streets with soldiers, but also of leading those men to "personal apartments, the moral and political trustworthiness of the owners of which no one has inquired about." He feared not only sexual contamination, but political contamination as well. Several Sisters had been caught spreading revolutionary literature among the captive and crucial audience of wounded soldiers (many of whom would eventually return to the front).[101]

The control of the Sisters' sexual, public, and political morality was a problem dealt with by the highest officials of the tsarist military. In order to better control that morality, Sisters were recruited and accepted almost completely from the elite strata of society. For the Red Cross, the pre-war standard was that only "educated" women were to be admitted to the courses that allowed one to become a Sister of Mercy. After the war broke out and a surge of volunteers came forth, the Petrograd Mobilization Committee for the Red Cross admitted literate women without education (or with only primary education) as well, but "only very literate ones."[102]

The centrality of the control of morality is perhaps best seen in the case of Paulina Paul'son, a Sister of Mercy who was dismissed for distributing religious literature to soldiers:

> Being an evangelical Lutheran, she is barely literate and only with difficulty deals with the Russian language, she *energetically tries to* propagate her own religious-moral convictions among the enlisted men and, without consulting the [Orthodox] priest, distributes brochures of religious content, and even the Bible, to enlisted men, without any permission to do so. Among her things were found from 10–200 copies of excerpts from the gospels in German, Polish, and French.[103]

This incident can be understood in two ways. First, there is a clear Russian chauvinist tinge. By noting her name (Paul'son), her little knowledge of Russian, her German literature, and her Lutheran faith, the doctor who wrote the report did everything but claim she was the Kaiser's sister.

But the gender aspect should also be examined. As a woman, and particularly as a Sister of Mercy, Paul'son held a strong position of moral authority. Her "crime" was not even in the content of the literature. The content was not "sectarian" in nature; instead, it was the Bible and other acceptable religious tracts. The problem lay in the fact that Paul'son was conducting her activity without the explicit sanction and control of the established religious authorities. Intended to be present for moral support, Sisters of Mercy had the potential to be morally disruptive as well and therefore had to be controlled quite carefully.

The specific moral qualities that Sisters of Mercy were supposed to possess also help to pin down what was specifically masculine about military morality and what part of the ethic was accessible to both genders. An examination of news releases about Sisters of Mercy who received military decorations reveals that women were fully capable of "heroic deeds" *(podvigi)* in the eyes of both state and society, but that the behavior that merited such awards for women was different from that which was expected of men. Women's courage was passive courage rather than active courage (which was inculcated in men through the ideas of "boldness," "initiative," and *"aktivnost'"*). For example, Nina Luchsheva and Ekaterina Muzreleva were awarded the St. George's Medal 4th degree for "coming under the heavy fire of the enemy . . . at great danger to themselves" and "giving aid to the wounded at forward positions." Similarly, Olga Matveeva and Lidiia Iuzefovicha were given the same award for administering first aid and moving five wounded enlisted men and one woman from a city street to a safe location while the city was under unceasing enemy artillery fire.[104]

That it was passive courage rather than active courage that was desired by state officials can be seen in the awkwardness with which they handled a situation in which a woman took it upon herself to exercise active courage. On 17 September 1915, a Sister of Mercy named Rimma Ivanovna was put in a difficult position. While in the trenches caring for the wounded, she realized that all the male officers of the company had been killed by enemy fire. She gathered the remaining soldiers around her, led them "over the top," and successfully seized the enemy position, suffering a mortal wound in the process. A man would have received a posthumous decoration as a matter of course for this type of action in battle, but the army command did nothing. It was not until the Germans complained to the Red Cross about an aid worker taking a combat role that the Russian press even learned of Ivanovna's story. In January, the government, embarrassed by its reticence, decorated Ivanovna with a St. George's Medal fourth degree, the same award granted to women who were heroes in a noncombat role.[105]

The key trait, then, that was shared by both women and men who were recognized for fulfilling the military ethic was "selflessness" *(samootverzhenie)*. Women were offered opportunities for fulfilling this crucial national duty but were usually blocked when they tried to perform active republican *virtù*. They were encouraged to die for the motherland, but very rarely were they allowed to kill for it.[106] Women were to "comfort" or "offer help" on the battlefield. As the experience of women soldiers was to show, allowing women to fight was a step that was greatly feared and resorted to only in times of extreme desperation.

Knowingly accepting women as combat soldiers was first practiced in Russia in World War I.[107] When the war broke out, dozens of women became convinced that their proper wartime role was to be a combat soldier. They rejected suggestions that they adhere to the gendered division of military service and become a Sister of Mercy, and they petitioned the army and the tsar to be allowed to serve as soldiers. Their petitions and experiences reveal the deep connection between soldiering and masculinity. The visceral reaction of nearly all their acquaintances to their requests showed how very destabilizing the idea of women soldiers was. But, both the women petitioners and the state officials who granted their requests took this potentially subversive phenomenon and turned it into a tool for reinforcing and making explicit the link between soldiers and men.

The most famous of these fighting women was a young Siberian named Maria Bochkareva. Her decision to try to enlist was met with immediate mockery. The recruitment clerk chortled to his co-workers: "Here is a *baba* [peasant woman] who wants to enlist!" and dismissed her. Undeterred, she went to the district commander, who, though kinder, was no better disposed to her idea, telling her: "It is very noble of you to have such a desire. But women are not allowed in the army. They are too weak. What could you, for instance, do in the front line? Women are not made for war." He suggested she join the Red Cross (as a Sister of Mercy).[108]

This was a common suggestion to young women who wanted adventure and the thrill of violence and appealed to military and state leaders to allow them to serve on the front lines. Military leaders generally agreed with the Siberian commander that the front line was no place for a woman. General Ianushkevich of the Stavka ordered in 1914 that even Sisters of Mercy be forbidden from medical units in the trenches, citing their "weakness" as Bochkareva's commander did.[109] Bochkareva, however, brushed away the suggestion to serve as a medical nurse, having heard unspecified "rumors" about the Sisters of Mercy. The commander finally relented and advised her that she would have to petition the tsar in order to be enlisted as a soldier, since military regulations forbade the enlistment of women in the army.[110]

Maria's mother was horrified when she learned of her daughter's desire to be a soldier, screaming "[w]ho ever knew of a *baba* going to war?" and promising to bury herself alive if Maria followed through on her plan. Maria's father, though less vocal, was firmly on his wife's side. In a moment of patriotism, Maria ignored her mother's objections, declaring that "the call of the country took precedence over the call of my mother," and telegrammed the tsar. The tsar, surprisingly, assented, sending Maria's mother into a fury. "What kind of tsar is he?" she asked, "if he takes women to war? He must have lost his senses. Who ever heard of a tsar calling women to arms? Hasn't he enough men?" She concluded her tirade by ripping Nicholas's portrait from the wall and vowing never to pray to him again. Local villagers also joined the movement to dissuade Maria, telling her, "they'll make a prostitute of you. They will kill you secretly, and nobody will ever find a trace of you. Only the other day they found the body of a woman along the railroad track, thrown out of a troop-train."[111]

Bochkareva's experience is enlightening. The immediate visceral response was one of amusement or horror; both Maria's mother and the clerk were simply shocked by Maria's suggesting, in her mother's words, an "unheard-of, impossible thing." The commander, on the other hand, was a bit more reflective and attributed her request to misguided patriotism. He lauded her "noble" desire and tried to steer her into the appropriate institution in which women could fulfill their patriotic yearnings. Finally, the villagers touched upon one of the many live wires that lay beneath the whole Bochkareva question. Not only were gender roles shuffled in terms of civic duty and soldiering, but in terms of the relationship between sexuality and soldiering as well.[112] Women and soldiers could only mean one thing: disruptive and violent sexual activity. The great anxiety about the sexual practices of Sisters of Mercy, an anxiety shared by both Bochkareva and government officials, was concerned with the question of sex on the battlefield.

Sex plays a large role in Bochkareva's story. As she progressed through basic training, she came to see male heterosexuality as an integral part of being a soldier. Just before being sent to the front, she joined a group of her comrades in a trip to a brothel, in order to "learn the soldier's life, so that I will understand his soul better."[113] The display of female sexuality, though, was out of the question. In 1917, when Bochkareva took control of the famous "Women's Battalion of Death," she was consumed with concerns about sex. Nor was she alone in her anxiety about this question. The first objection raised in the meeting with Duma chairman Mikhail Rodzianko and unspecified "soldiers' delegates," in which Bochkareva suggested the idea of a Women's Battalion, was that the men doubted they could find other women as "decent" as she. The second objection was from a soldier who asked: "[w]ho can guarantee that the presence of women soldiers at the front will not yield there little soldiers?" When, some time later, Kerenskii approved her plan, he made clear to her that the morals of all of her charges had to be high.[114] The climax of the sexual subplot of her memoirs came during the Kerenskii offensive of 1917, when she discovered one of her women having sex with a man during battle. She raced to them and bayoneted the woman soldier to death but failed to catch the fleeing male.[115]

Bochkareva's presence in the army was disruptive to the gender order only at first blush, for she took as her project not only to transfer herself into a soldier, but to transform herself into a man as well. Her moment of greatest pride was when, after being put through trials and tests by the men in her unit, she was "found to be a comrade, and not a woman, by the men."[116] When she formed the Women's Battalion of Death, again the intent was not to bring women into the masculine project of displaying active *virtù* and carrying weapons but was instead to "shame" the men of Russia.[117]

The intent of this shaming was clearly understood. Viktor Shklovsky, a soldier at the front in 1917, was convinced that the Women's Battalion was thought up on the home front expressly as an "insult" to the men in the trenches.[118] The idea was to get men to behave according to the military-masculine ethic, not to create a gender-free army. The women who joined became "men." They dressed in male uniforms and had their heads shaved bald upon induction.[119] The rationale of top state officials and the women volunteers themselves reveals how exclusive the relationship between soldiering and masculinity was. Women could not be allowed to be soldiers unless they agreed to be masculine, and even then the major reason for their presence in the army was to force *men* to be masculine.

Understandably, it was a woman faced with this gender dilemma, Elena Iost, who laid bare the relationship between masculinity and the military ethic in her remarkable request to be allowed to serve in the army:

> Your Imperial Majesty, my request is strange and unnatural, but it's not because I, like many others, seek adventure, no Your Imperial Majesty, I'm appealing to You for a completely different reason. . . .
>
> I pray to Your Imperial Majesty to allow me to join the ranks of the troops with the same kind of noble and radiant outburst for the MOTHERLAND, with which . . . my soul, filled with courage and fearlessness and unwomanly boldness, burns.
>
> There is of course another way, easier for women, which is to serve the motherland as a Sister of Mercy, but I can't devote myself to that quiet, sacred business, for due to unforeseen circumstances (the death of my mother) I received a completely masculine upbringing [vospitanie].
>
> My father is a naval captain, who brought me up [vospityval] in the midst of my four brothers in a spartan manner. In general, he didn't like girls and with all his strength he tried to give me an upbringing identical to my brothers.
>
> In sports, which we spent much time playing, and especially in hiking, I always surpassed even my brothers, which made my father unspeakably happy. When I got bigger, the method of my upbringing was always according to the same words of my father, "be like a man," and thus I grew up with a soul, the outlook, and the strivings of a man.
>
> I graduated from the gymnasium and now I find myself at rest, I'm not finding anything suitable for myself, and my soul is yearning to do anything possible to help the Motherland in the ranks of its soldiers.
>
> I know several men, who upon being drafted into military service, cried like babies from fear and grief, even to the point of getting sick, and you would not believe, Your Imperial Majesty, how ashamed, ashamed and offended, I was on account of their lack of spirit and their weakness. I scorned them. They were taken and they were unwilling, and I am prepared for sacrifice with my whole soul, even to spill my blood for the Motherland without fear, and unfortunately they don't take me. Why? Why humiliate me?
>
> When I hear soldiers' songs or see troops (the cavalry, I so, so love horses), I am transformed, everything inside brightens and rejoices, and at the sight of dashing soldiers my soul wants to leap out of my body, and I want to be among them and also to be a defender of the Motherland, the sacred, dear, and unceasingly loved Motherland.
>
> My father gave his assent for me to devote myself to the business of serving the Fatherland.[120]

Iost captured the essence of military morality and was cognizant of its link with masculinity. Sacrifice, duty, courage, strength, and, of course, an "unwomanly boldness" all came through as military and masculine. Every one of these qualities could be equated with Iost's *vospitanie,* which made her, in her own eyes, a man rather than a woman. Most striking was her prescient realization of the nature of her request. Iost was clear that she was not asking for "adventure" or an outlet for her patriotic spirit (though those desires were also evident), but that she was making a "strange and unnatural request." She was asking the tsar to allow her to be a man. She, like Maria Bochkareva when she visited the brothel, was not seeking to change the gendered order as it related to the military, but was offering to change her own gender. For a brief moment, the offer was taken up by state officials (in some cases), but only to chastise men for failing to be masculine.

The moment passed quickly. The final units of women volunteers were disbanded in November 1917, not only because the Petrograd Women's Battalion had sided with the Provisional Government and lost in October, but also because, as one official put it, the "moral significance" of the women's military movement had disappeared.[121] As the old army died, so too did this particular manifestation of women soldiers as object reminders of the failed virtue of Russian men.

The official position of political leaders in regard to women in the army changed in 1917. The Bolsheviks came to power with an explicitly emancipatory message for women that, in principle, opened up military service to both sexes. Many Red Guard units in 1917 had been open to women as well as men, and the Red Army never forbade the voluntary enlistment of women.[122] In popular representations as well, women were portrayed as going off to war alongside men. The most famous novel of the Civil War was Dmitrii Furmanov's *Chapaev,* which began with a scene describing a worker's detachment that included women departing for the front.[123] As described earlier, women communists were also expected to go to the front when necessary. Women were a part of the military establishment throughout the Civil War.

The answer to the question of what role those women played and how many women joined the military remains murky, however. A small but statistically significant percentage of women appeared at the various calls for volunteers that occurred throughout the war. Between 17 May and 19 June 1920, 33 women appeared at the Novonikolaevsk commissariat, 17 of whom volunteered to be a Sister of Mercy. In all, during this month, 701 workers, peasants, partisans, communists, trade unionists, and foreign subjects appeared to volunteer in Novonikolaevsk, making the percentage of women appearing a respectable 4.7 percent of all volunteers from the city (2.3 percent even if the Sisters of Mercy are excluded).[124]

Many women joined to fulfill the feminized military role of Sister of Mercy, but nearly half of the Novonikolaevsk sample did not. Most of them probably ended up working at various levels of military bureaucracies. In July 1918, those women who had joined the Riazan' infantry division were all working as clerks in the chancellery, though their commander had plans to use them as mechanics, telephone operators, and in provisioning organs.[125] Both of the women working with Eduard Dune's Red Army division in southern Russia were clerical workers as well.[126] By the end of 1918, women had become indispensable for local and central military chancelleries alike, prompting one district chief to note that not only were women "completely capable" of desk work, but that replacing them with male clerks would result in a "weakening" of unit chancelleries.[127] By 1919, these women chancellery workers, originally volunteers, were considered to be conscripts and were forbidden to leave their posts voluntarily.[128] Women continued to be hired by chronically understaffed chancelleries throughout the Civil War.[129]

Women, then, were welcome in medical units and in the rear, but there remained a tremendous resistance in military circles on the question of whether to allow women to be present at the front, much less to be a front-line soldier.[130] The Main Staff consistently forbade women to be in any unit that might conceivably end up in battle. "In order to avoid the introduction into the army of principles that contradict the demands of military service and discipline," it explained to Tver' officials, "the admittance of women into service in troop units is undesirable; it is also undesirable to take them in those institutions and establishments that come into direct contact with troop units."[131] Again, though unstated here, the concern seems to be sexual, as the Main Staff stressed its uneasiness with "discipline" and "contact" with the male troops. This vision extended to lower officials as well. The telegram cited above had been in response not to a request for women to serve as soldiers but for them to serve in supply organs as clerks. The reason the Tver' detachment had wanted women clerks was the "greater accuracy and productivity of women on the one hand and the difficulty of finding suitable men for the positions on the other at the present time."[132]

The question of what to do with women in military service was answered by Vseroglavshtab (the All-Russian Main Staff of the Red Army) in August of 1918. All requests to have women serve in any "field" units or even in any provision and supply units were to be denied, according not only to Vseroglavshtab but also to Trotskii himself, who "agreed with its opinion" on the matter. On the other hand, no one saw any "serious difficulties" in allowing women to serve in military commissariats or in the upper administration of the military bureaucracy. The only exceptions to the rule of keeping women off the battlefield and in the office were to be Sisters of Mercy.[133]

But this was the Civil War, when armed forces proliferated and were far from being under the control of central organs. It is certain that women were present on Civil War battlefields, though mostly in auxiliary capacities. The female clerks in Dune's regiment, for instance, traveled with the front-line soldiers and were gang-raped by White forces when they were captured along with their fellow Red Army compatriots.[134] In addition, the possibility remains that women served in a combat capacity in the OON. Material on OON is hard to come by, but the 1921 regulations seem to imply that communist women could choose whether to be a combat soldier. The other major military organization, of course, was Vsevobuch, and that organization was remarkable for its contrast to the "regular" army. In Vsevobuch, the doors were thrown open to women, and significant energy was spent trying to get women to become a part of the "armed people." The experience of Vsevobuch showed that the desire to be in the military was limited to a small number of women.

During the Civil War, a typical split of opinion and jurisdiction in the armed forces meant that at the same time women were being forbidden from combat positions in the army, Vsevobuch was encouraging women to devote their time and energy to train for those very positions. One enthusiastic local commander in Moscow province wrote to Lenin a week after the decree on obligatory military training was issued, crowing that he had organized machine-gun courses for "all workers and peasants of both sexes" and vowing to move his organizational efforts from the city into the surrounding countryside.[135] Again, though, this was from an obvious supporter of a militia system in the new republic, who desired an "armed people" ready to put down their hammers and pick up rifles if invaders arrived. In 1920 the role of trained women was made explicit by Vsevobuch, when it told the Zhenotdel that "[t]he woman worker should know how to use a rifle, a revolver, and a machine gun, in order to know how to defend her proletarian fatherland, her city, her village, her children, and herself during White guard raids."[136] And, just as ideals and institutions representing both militia and regular army systems could coexist well into the 1930s, so could the dichotomy of training women for combat while not allowing them to fight.

The ultimate goal for the radical revolutionaries in Vsevobuch and elsewhere was a system of armed forces in which women would be present. As one Vsevobuch worker maintained, the Soviet republic had been the first to declare equal rights for women, and as a result women were to share "all labor and military obligations" as well. In previous wars, women had taken part not only as Sisters of Mercy, a calling to which they were more suited than men according to this worker, but had also "courageously died with rifles in their hands." He cited as examples the Boer War, the Women's Battalion of the Provisional Government, and women in the Red Army, thus undermining the idea that women were "weak and defenseless." With the passage of time, as military ideologies changed, "detachments of women will be almost as valuable as detachments of men." For the present, though, their significance would be primarily "moral" in nature.

Even for this Vsevobuch worker, though, gender difference was present and important. Women, because of the "physiological peculiarities of their organism," were less able to perform strenuous physical activities and should be given lighter tasks in more appropriate "hygienic and sanitary conditions." Cleaning and mending were among the tasks the author had in mind for women who volunteered for the Red Army.[137] When the process of conscription was finally normalized in 1925, military planners felt it necessary to "indicate in the fundamental law [of military service] the acceptability of citizens of the female sex in military service" and resolved to allow women to enlist voluntarily while refraining from drafting them in peacetime.[138] Shortly after the publication of the law, however, internal correpondence made clear that military planners were envisioning women primarily in the roles of "nurses, dentists, and others."[139]

This ambivalence about the role of women in the production of violence was pervasive. Given the ideological commitment to equal civil rights for women, it stood to reason, as for the author above, that women should be soldiers as well. The figure of the citizen-soldier loomed large. But at the same time the Bolsheviks had incorporated an ideology of organized violence that was more in line with the fully masculinized military systems elsewhere in the world. The tension was palpable and the gender politics complex.

Even radical feminist revolutionaries like Alexandra Kollontai did not advocate immediate equality of men and women in the army; the labor of the army was to be divided along gendered lines. She agreed with officials in Vsevobuch that women had a large and important role to play in the war effort. The front was the "nerve center" of Soviet Russia, and women not only could be useful for the front, but indeed had an obligation to devote themselves to the front just as men did, "to give it [the front] their strength, energy, and all that selflessness with which a woman's heart is rich."[140] She also agreed that a woman's primary place was not with rifle in hand. Women best served the republic as agitators among benighted locals in the battle zone, where they could try to win the hearts of the women over to the Red side. If a given woman was less inclined to want to "raise up the people against the evil and unfairness that rules the world" she could join medical units. There, women who were temperamentally suited "to comfort, heal, and care for all those who suffer" could become a "Red Sister." They could reassure their "dying brother" that he was a hero of the people, dying for the "great cause of the freedom of his class."[141]

Kollontai recognized that there would be a few women who would reject these passive jobs because they were "all auxiliary, not the main business" and because they were "soldiers and citizens just as much as [their] male comrades." For those women who would "prefer a rifle on the shoulder . . . fulfilling this cherished desire is not forbidden." Of course, fulfilling this desire *was* forbidden, a fact that Kollontai tacitly acknowledged by admitting there were some "comrades" who feared allowing women into the army. But these comrades were not correct "because they still look at a woman not as a citizen, bearing responsibility to the state, but as a woman in the narrow sense of the word. It seems to them that where there is a mingling between men and women, there will also be thoughts of courting and love."[142]

Thus, even for Kollontai, who explicitly linked the exclusion of women from the army with the continued exclusion of women from political activity and the continued "slavery and dependence of women," there was a need for restraint when discussing the role of women in the production of violence.[143] Not only did she place soldiering third on the list of suitable wartime jobs for women, but she also failed to mention the question of equalizing conscription law so that women would be liable to the draft along with men. Finally, the quality valued by the military that she appealed to among women readers was one already incorporated into the feminine ideal: self-sacrifice. Even the most radical Bolshevik feminists were not calling for a complete destruction of the gendered structures of the military. Regional conferences of women workers were yet more conservative, focusing their attention and efforts on making sure that local families of Red Army soldiers were taken care of so that the soldiers' spirit would not lag.[144]

What, then, was to be done in practice regarding women in the armed forces? This was a question addressed most completely by Vsevobuch and the Zhenotdel. In 1919, the Conference of Women Workers approved a plan authored by Podvoiskii under which it would focus on the training of teenage girls, much as the state had previously focused militarization efforts on teenage and school-age boys. The women workers hoped they could begin Vsevobuch programs of military training and sport activities in industrial regions and eventually move into the countryside, being particularly careful to make sure that all women communists got training.[145] It was a program intended not only (perhaps not even primarily) to raise the military strength of the republic, but to raise women up to the level of citizen. As Kollontai noted, getting the vote and equal rights did not mean getting citizenship. Citizens were soldiers, and until the time when women were soldiers, their claims to citizenship were necessarily incomplete.[146]

Given the explicit linkage of the male body with soldiering outlined above, how were women to join the community of citizen-soldiers? This was a tricky, and largely unstated, problem. Male bodies were normalized. As the Vsevobuch author quoted above said, women had "physiologically peculiar organisms," and this peculiarity justified second-class (or "auxiliary") status in the army and by extension the citizenry. Women either had to try to subvert the normalized masculine ideal of the soldier's body, to assimilate to this masculine ideal (as their tsarist counterparts did by dressing in uniforms and cutting their hair, all the while stressing, as Elena Iost did, that they were actually the physical equals of their male comrades), or to seek an alternate bodily claim to citizenship.

Not even radicals in the armed forces sought to overturn the masculine bodily norm. Kollontai was explicit about citizenship and the capability of women to fight, but she also felt it politically prudent to urge women to fulfill more traditional feminine roles on the battlefield. Furmanov's Marfa, who was aggressive, dressed completely in a masculine uniform, and readily challenged hecklers at the train station with her peaked hat tipped rakishly back on her head, typified the women who sought to make a claim for citizenship on the basis of soldiering and were willing to masculinize their bodies to do so. These were the women, presumably, who served in the OON and other detachments that allowed women to bear arms.

The second process was institutionalized in Vsevobuch, where the desire to include women in physical culture programs was combined with a belief in radically different types of organisms to produce a bifurcated system of training in physical culture. In 1921, Podvoiskii, in a generally distributed set of directions, made clear to all Vsevobuch officials that the "program and plan of physical education *[fizicheskoe vospitanie]* of young women is special [i.e. different]."[147] Pictures from the period confirm the reports of sport officials that women were incorporated into "light athletics" when they were in Vsevobuch programs. One typical pair of photographs shows a demonstration on Red Square of young men and women in physical culture programs. The men are doing gymnastics on the parallel bars. They are bare-chested and showing well-defined biceps, while the women appear to be stretching in ballerina-type movements in unison.[148]

So, if women were being "tracked" away from the physical model of the combat soldier, why was the Soviet state so concerned with militarizing their bodies? The answer will not be surprising to students of nationalism and the body: women's health and their bodies were of crucial importance because they were to *produce* soldiers, not become them.[149] In the words of Dr. A. Laptev, a Vsevobuch author writing in 1921, the question of women and physical culture focused on their maternal function. From the moment of the joining of sperm and egg, the mother "exerts immediate influence on the fetus . . . he acquires all the qualities of his mother's blood." Maternal influence was not limited to the womb, as Laptev pointed out by using that most national of theories of cultural transmission: "The . . . link is not lost at birth, for the newborn drinks the living milk of his mother, with either its protective or baneful qualities." He went on to make a blanket statement that would justify state intervention:

> Both the moral and physical physiognomy of the tribe is determined not by the strength of the man, but by the influence of the mother. . . . Therefore, he who is interested in the culture of a human is interested most directly in the culture of the mother. Physical culture workers should turn their attention above all to the woman question precisely on this plane. A mother should be healthy both physically and morally, and to this end all efforts should be directed toward the creation of suitable conditions.[150]

Lest his readers still be unclear about the focus of the state's activity, Dr. Laptev added that the "concern over the woman-mother should begin from her childhood and should not end until she has lost the ability to give birth."[151] A similar rationale was offered by Podvoiskii, who argued to the Zhenotdel that "adolescent girls, as future citizens and mothers, should be physically strong."[152] Women's bodies were important to the state insofar as they had a role in creating male (soldiers') bodies.

Nor was this focus on the maternal/military function of women limited to Vsevobuch. In 1919, Mikhail Kalinin urged women to "become impregnated with the spirit of those Roman women, who, accompanying their husbands and brothers to the field of combat, told them that victory must be theirs."[153] After the Civil War, the Agitprop Department of the Central Committee issued instructional theses on the theme of "The Woman Worker and the Red Army," based on the writings of Kollontai and Bukharin, that did not mention the possible role of women as soldiers at all. Indeed, the material explicitly stated: "There is plenty of work for a woman: work in sanitary detachments, in a supply unit." More importantly, the theses stressed maternity and children over and over again in a work explicitly devoted to the relationship women should have to the army. After going through twelve theses on the superiority of Soviet maternity and child-care benefits, the final thesis made clear that the maternal and child-rearing functions were ethically equivalent to soldiering: "Long live the politically conscious woman worker . . . capable of placing the interests of all laborers above her personal interests and above the interests of her family."[154] This was the ideal role for the woman: the Spartan wife who let her men go off to battle (and turned them in if they deserted) and placed state planning above family planning. Her occupational role was to be a "helper," her moral role to strengthen the resolve of men, and her physical role to bear and raise children.

The majority of all women reacted coolly to the attempts by state officials to get involved in their physical development, whether the end was strengthening them to be prepared to fight off predator White guards or to be healthy mothers. Even in the Moscow military district, one of the most heavily urban (and hence heavily targeted) areas of the country, only a handful of women participated in Vsevobuch programs. These volunteers were located mainly in places where urban woman workers were likely to be. In Riazan', a fairly rural province, literally no women took Vsevobuch's 96-hour program in 1920.[155]

The level of interest varied widely from place to place, but nowhere was it overwhelming. In the city of Tambov in 1924, fully 37 percent of the participants in sport circles were women, but in the countryside surrounding the city that percentage dropped to 24 percent. In Armenia, only 15 percent of city sport participants were women, a figure that dropped to 4 percent in the countryside. Both male and female sportsmen were disproportionately party and Komsomol members and as such subject to even greater pressure to join sporting groups.[156] In the Urals region in 1926, officials were forced to admit that women, a small presence to begin with, were even declining in relative numbers in their physical education organizations (from 29.5 percent to 17.6 percent). Only 4,224 women in the entire region were sportswomen after eight years of agitation.[157] Republic-wide, however, the number of women joining sport and physical culture institutions appears to have been growing, particularly among urban women.

Women were gradually being enmeshed in the web of militarization that the state had been weaving for men over the last fifteen years.

Finally, it should be noted that the military ethic (with the exception of self-sacrifice) was articulated not only as different from the female ethic, but also as opposite to it. Misogyny was strong in both popular and elite army circles. As in many armies, pornographic curses were a constitutive part of the training process. Not many of these diatribes were published, of course, but the ubiquity of misogynistic comments in the tsarist period is attested to by Vladimir Littauer, who remembered Grand Duke Nikolai Nikolaevich screaming at a group of poorly performing cadets: "What is this? A boarding school for noble girls?" and later saying that they looked like "rows of pregnant women." In addition, the choral repertoire of army units was largely composed of songs with obscene lyrics: when Littauer's unit would march through a town, his commander would say "Now cut this one out, we're almost in the village and there will be girls." When soldiers had difficulties remembering signal codes, their helpful commanders would give them pornographic acronyms to help their memories along. The prevalence and popularity of pornographic soldier songs was made especially evident during the initial mobilizations in 1914, for reservists wandering district and provincial centers often struck up their favorite tunes, embarrassing many of the civilian residents.[158]

Dirty jokes were just part of the misogynistic soldier culture. Perhaps more influential was the idea that separation from women was necessary to achieve the proper military mindset. In one short book produced for popular consumption by soldiers in 1897, a young soldier nearly allows prisoners under his watch to escape (and hence nearly brings disgrace on his unit), when he begins to daydream about his wife and family back home and stops patrolling. Only the intervention of God himself saves the soldier, when the sounds of prisoners chipping out the wall cut through the wind and rain and alert him to the plot.[159] In 1924, a one-time newspaper distributed to young men about to be conscripted included a poem by Dmitrii Kudrin, which advised men that it was necessary to break free from local peasant women in order to enjoy the "honey" of urban life.[160] Separation from women was a constitutive part of draft day and a defining moment of military service.

This separation was strengthened by the assumption held by all armies in Russia during this period that women were especially prone to some of the worst violations of military morality: rumor-mongering and treachery. Some tsarist commanders, for instance, were convinced that the problem of voluntary surrender in World War I was linked to prostitutes, since brothels were "hotbeds of propaganda" and infiltrated by German spies. As a result, they argued, prostitutes tried to "implant ideas of desertion" into the heads of unwary soldiers.[161] A bit later on, an appeal from "Russian Mothers" printed by White forces warned White officers and soldiers to be especially careful in "conversations with WOMEN, both familiar and unfamiliar. Among them are many spies."[162] The Cheka was no less convinced of the propensity of women to be unreliable, noting that in the Tiumen' district the "Black Hundred element" was spreading rumors that advised local residents not to accept Soviet money because the Whites were returning soon. "In the majority of cases," the Cheka warned, "these rumors are repeated by women."[163]

This ambiguity of the relationship between women and the production of organized violence had an impact on notions of political belonging as well. The question of the role of women in the national community was especially vexing. No nationalist imagined a nation devoid of women. In World War I, women were not simply applauded for their patriotic activities but were expected to perform them. Women too had a duty to the nation. At the same time, however, the idea that women would fulfill that duty in the same way as men was unacceptable. A woman displaying active *virtù* was, as in the case of Rimma Ivanovna, unsettling.

The "woman question," of course, took on a whole new dynamic with the accession of the Bolsheviks to power. Women were formally accepted into the army and were allowed, indeed encouraged, to join the major militarizing institutions of Vsevobuch, the Komsomol, and the Bolshevik Party itself. There was therefore a qualitiative and significant difference between, for instance, the single-sex Boy Scouts and the mixed Pioneers. But the troubling position of women in the political community was not overcome by a statement of equal political rights and formal inclusion into major civic institutions. Uneasiness remained, not only among military officers who prohibited women on the front lines, but also even among women like Alexandra Kollontai, who supported in principle the idea of women performing combat duty, but felt safer recognizing other, more traditional avenues in which women could fulfill their national duty.

By the end of the Civil War, then, seven years of total war had led to a general consensus that women were capable of possessing one national virtue: self-sacrifice. Nations also, as discussed above, can appropriate bodies and make them sites of belonging and loyalty. Here too women were given a particular avenue to fulfill their national duty: childbirth. Women could become members of the political community, but on different, separate terms from men.

Conclusion

Between the Revolution of 1905 and the Stalin revolution, a massive gender revolution occurred. This revolution, however, was not primarily about the emancipation of women but rather about the emancipation of young men from the restrictive constraints of patriarchy. It was begun in anticipation of total war and matured during the years of war, when the masculine model of power ceased being the portly elder of the community and became the muscular, bold, but restrained, young man.

These developments were part and parcel of the shift to the national political form, and they were driven throughout by the armed forces. Military men wrote the physical education texts for schools to use and urged them to include lessons of military morality within their general curriculum. Military men began the Boy Scouts, quickly came to dominate the *poteshnye roty,* and served as virtually the only source of instructors for those institutions. The military, of course, was also in charge of the basic training of conscripts in a country where universal conscription was the law of the land. They exercised strict control over the activities of nonmilitary organs (such as the Komsomol and tsarist sport societies) that from time to time had responsibility for pre-draft training. Beginning in the 1880s, when military training became a part of school curriculums, continuing in 1908 with the formation of *poteshnye roty* and Boy Scouts, and then dramatically expanding during World War I and the formative years of Bolshevik power with the strengthening of sport societies and the Pioneers, youngsters living under the tsarist and Soviet states were exposed to a powerful masculine ideal.

This ideal was strikingly similar to the one developed in western Europe in the nineteenth century, and it served the same political purpose by underpinning the nation. As George Mosse has argued, nations became resonant in modern Europe in part because they were able to appeal to an idealized stable past and in part because they could simultaneously look forward to a glorious active future. The new masculine ideal "was supposed to safeguard the existing order against the perils of modernity, but it was also regarded as an indispensable attribute of those who wanted change."[164]

Sexuality played a large role in this process. Unrestrained sexuality was "both unmanly and inherently antisocial" for it took the vital life force and wasted it on personal self-satisfaction. Real men took this force and used it for the nation, whether by procreating or by redirecting it to the "higher purpose" of the nation. Out of this came the visual models of men as harmonious and self-restrained, yet aggressive, and there followed condemnations of homosexuals and masturbators as "abnormal" and dangerous to society. Notions of manliness and sexuality were co-opted by nationalists to give the nation the simultaneous attributes of stability (self-restraint) and progress (virility). The two, in this conjuncture, could work together rather than at cross purposes.[165]

The same forces can be seen in Russia in the obsession of military men (and women) with sex. Maria Bochkareva, when she bayoneted the libidinous soldier, and the high-ranking officials of the Red Army, when they attempted to keep women out of units that could possibly come into "contact" with men at the front, both feared that undisciplined sex would fatally undermine the disciplined citizen-soldier.

In order to maintain this masculine ideal as a stabilizing and progressive one, it had to be contrasted in some respect with the feminine ideal, otherwise it would not have been masculine. Particularly important in this respect was the distinction that was made between the active virtue of males and the passive virtue of females. This distinction too found a parallel in western Europe, where female symbols of the nationalist imagination, soon after the French Revolution, were made into passive symbols.[166] As noted above, this passivity and the Marian image were staples of the national virtue that the emblematic woman at the front, the Sister of Mercy, was supposed to display.

Sexual separation was also important, though the desire to keep women separate from men while men were exercising their national virtue was not solely linked to the disruptive effects of sexual contact. It was linked as well to the belief that women simply did not and could not share military virtues. They were believed to be rumor-mongering, untrustworthy, and prone to tempt men to think about personal interest before the national interest. The soldier in Tkhvorzhevskii's morality play who nearly let prisoners escape because he was thinking of his wife and the women whom Red Army men were to avoid at all costs are only two examples of how these modern Russian regimes inculcated the idea that gender separation was necessary for men to exercise proper civic virtue.

The separation also helped build a new basis for solidarity. Chapter 2 described how Russia's heterogeneity proved to be a distressing dilemma for nationalists. The homogenization of masculinity gave them their most powerful and ultimately most successful means of making appeals for solidarity. All men within the multiethnic and multi-class nation could aspire to a single masculine ideal. This ideal was powerful and functional. It was precisely through the notions of aggressiveness and self-sacrifice that soldiers combined individualism and acts of communal belonging. More practically for military commanders, the masculine ideal inspired men to combine initiative with subordination.

The efforts to nationalize masculinity, in the end, succeeded in linking gender identity with membership in the political community. The discursive constructions of political community were backed up by the discursive constructions of gender. Even if a soldier did not accept the political claims of the Bolsheviks, he might nevertheless fight in the Red Army because he bought the claims that deserters were cowards and cowards were not real men.

The reverse was also true. Men who sought membership in the political community soon learned that membership and mobility entailed becoming hard, courageous, and strong. They had to become masculine to become citizens. It is significant in this respect that the national pariahs identified by the state, first Jews and then the bourgeoisie, were explicitly denied the capability to achieve the physical and moral stature necessary to be a man, a soldier, and a citizen. Either flabby or emaciated, they were "soft" where citizens and soldiers needed to be "hard," in will and in body.

The situation was a bit more confusing for women. They had two equally difficult paths to "choose" from. One path, certainly, was masculinization. This was the path taken by Bochkareva, by Elena Iost, and by the women commissars like Marfa, dressed in leather jackets with a revolver at the hip (or in a Red Army uniform), ready to tussle with the first man who challenged their presence. The other was to take a separate path from men, to accept membership on the basis of self-sacrifice and the duty to produce young soldiers. This was a legitimate separate path to citizenship, but separate did not mean equal. It meant acceptance of a passive role, of being the "backdrop" to the actions of men.

Gender identity and political identity were therefore co-produced, as they were all across Europe and in the United States, and they were co-produced in a national fashion. The process of instilling both masculinity and feelings of political belonging into a young man, which in 1900 was only attempted at the age of 21, was by 1926 taking place as early as the teenage years. Moving this process to the formative years of sexual and political development proved highly successful. More than one young Russian went to war to protect his manhood more than to protect his country.[167]

CHAPTER FIVE

Violence and the Nation

National belonging depends on more than simple ascription to a particular population category. The active participation of citizens in the polity is equally important. As already noted, one of the central tasks of the military and civilian proponents of a modern regime in Russia throughout the first decades of the twentieth century was "mobilizing" citizens, making them active participants in national affairs. Modernizing reformers attempted to channel the resulting kinetic political energy in national ways, both by focusing the attention of citizens upon pariahs defined by their alienation from the otherwise inclusive national categories of ethnicity and class and by making an explicit analogy between native and national in their constructions of family and land. They also sponsored a reenvisioning of the familial model of "natural" power relations by stressing the slogan of fraternity and proceeded to "nationalize" masculinity in order to build a solid civic and military foundation for the future polity.

This chapter will examine acts of civic belonging rather than the categories that (not always successfully) channeled those acts. There are many sorts of civic acts that serve to link citizens, states, and nations. Voting, for instance, is an important civic act in many national frameworks. Like the performance of violence, voting is not understandable within an individualistic rational choice model. Most citizens live their whole lives without having their individual vote decide the outcome of an election, just as most soldiers go through war without having their bullet or bayonet decide the outcome of a battle. What is important in both activities is the creation of a certain type of civic *sobornost'* (feeling of community) in which conflicts between groups are visibly resolved by large numbers of people acting both as part of a group and as autonomous individuals.

These acts, as surely as the discourses described in earlier chapters, served to mediate power as well as express it. This chapter will focus attention upon the most central and most enigmatic of these civic acts: the performance of violence.

Neither the prevalence of violence in twentieth- century Russia nor its impact on regular citizens can be disputed.[1] Nevertheless, violence has remained surprisingly unproblematized and consequently undertheorized within the historiography of modern Russia.

Training For Violence

At the center of the nation stands the sociable killer. By definition, every citizen-soldier must have the capacity to perform both peaceful and violent civic duties. In this ideal political system, violence is both constitutive and productive. But violence is also understood to be the main threat to every such system. Foreign armies, domestic revolutionaries, and street thugs all threaten the integrity of the polity and indeed of "order" itself. The question of how to enable productive violence while preventing destructive violence is central for any state, but it is constitutive for nation-states, which rely on violence as a cohesive social mechanism to a degree that old-regime states, for instance, did not.

Military trainers play a crucial role in any such polity, for it is their task to produce the orderly killers that form the basis of the nation. The primary strategy used by trainers throughout modern Europe in this regard has been to smother any atavistic desire that may arise during the contemplation or performance of the act of killing another human being. According to John Keegan, they have done so by consciously "desensitizing" their charges to the act of violence itself. Their aim has been "to reduce the conduct of war to a set of rules and a system of procedures—and thereby to make orderly and rational what is essentially chaotic and instinctive."[2] Formal Russian training was little different from the western models that Keegan described. There too they tried to create specialists in violence without focusing strictly on violence as such. They used the same techniques to desensitize their officers and soldiers, talking both below violence at the purely technical level ("aim four meters above your target from four hundred meters away") and above it at the purely symbolic level ("for the fatherland"). The instrumentalization of violence in this fashion made the violent act itself disappear ("aim four meters above for the fatherland").[3]

Thus, when soldiers were called up from the reserves in World War I, their training course focused on basic information, military technique, and the overarching meaning of military service. The first week of training camp consisted of, among other things, teaching soldiers the name of the unit to which they belonged, the names of their officers, the parts of the rifle, how to shoot while lying down, how to shoot from a rifle stand, "why they were drafted," and "the basic responsibilities of the soldier." As the training camp proceeded, lectures became more detailed, touching in the second week on "who our enemies are and why we are fighting them" and the responsibilities of platoon leaders. In the third week, reservists learned "who our allies are" and how to dig a trench.[4] Throughout the training program, soldiers were taught the "set of rules" and the "system of procedures" that purported to make war orderly, at the same time that they were given lofty reasons why those rules had meaning.

This cloaking of the central act of warfare was normally quite effective. Fedor Stepun, writing to his mother from training camp in Irkutsk in September 1914, noted this fact with some surprise:

> Natasha [Stepun's wife] sits and laughs, saying that we're like little boys playing with horses—we also laugh splendidly that we are learning to kill and hide from death. There are, of course, minutes when the horrible meaning of what I just wrote becomes truly understood, but those minutes are very rare. Usually that final goal and essence of war is obstructed and pushed aside by a whole series of penultimate thoughts, actions, events, and measures.[5]

Keeping soldiers preoccupied with the details of daily life and the mechanized techniques of modern warfare helped keep direct thoughts of violence at bay.

But military thinkers knew perfectly well that the act of violence itself could not be completely ignored. For, though violence was an instrumental act for most soldiers most of the time, trainers understood that nearly every soldier meditated on killing and his own death. The dominant voice in training circles throughout the late imperial period, M. I. Dragomirov, warned officers to remember that soldiers were human beings and that they should "never imagine that a serviceman has superhuman qualities." The fear of death and the "instinct for self-preservation" were both natural and powerful.[6]

Dragomirov also believed, though, that there was an equally natural instinct to fight, since "all life is an unceasing and merciless fight to the death." He thus described an internal battle within each soldier between the "moral" will to kill and the "intellectual" instinct to stay alive at the critical moment of each battle. The outcome of the battle depended, in the end, on whether moral strength could overcome the instinct of self-preservation in each individual soldier. The type of moral education described in the previous chapter was therefore of "capital importance," because "only he fights who does not fear to perish; for a man educated in this fashion, there are no surprises."[7] It was the task of trainers to minimize the soldier's fear and to "desensitize" soldiers to the act of violence while simultaneously moralizing the act.

This was why trainers who followed Dragomirov were so convinced that modern warfare was, in its essence, a battle of national will more than it was a battle of artillery shells and rifle bullets. Real victory was achieved only by destroying the will of the other side to fight. In practical terms, most military officials believed that final victory could only be achieved in a major set battle in which the main forces of one side defeated the main forces of the other with an attack that culminated in a successful bayonet charge. That moment of victory was the pinnacle of human experience, as men put their courage "to the sticking point" and achieved physical and moral superiority over another group of men.[8] At this stage, the remainder of enemy forces inevitably crumbled; their wills broken, they fled or surrendered, and total victory was won.[9]

Ignore for now how badly this conception of war corresponded to the actual nature of war in the twentieth century. The point is that all training prior to World War I was geared toward that ultimate moment of victory, when virtue and violence became one in the thrust of a bayonet. That linkage of virtue and violence further helps to explain the overwhelming amount of attention paid to the training of virtue in the Russian armed forces. What appears, then, is a sophisticated model of the training of violence, in which training takes place *above* the act in references to grand symbols, *below* it in the mechanics of movement that produce violent results, *before* it in the preparation for death, *after* it in terms of the glory that accrues to the victorious soldier, and *during* it in terms of virtue. The act of violence itself is absent unless it is there to reflect upon virtue.

The reason for this absence is really quite simple: the army (in particular a short-term conscript army) was given the task of training men who would commit extreme violence in certain highly circumscribed situations, but who could easily reintegrate back into civilian life when they stepped out of uniform. It was (and remains) quite a brilliant strategy. First, teach the proper relationship between violence and virtue (men display virtue by committing violence for the sake of the community). Then, train virtuous men and talented technicians and put them in situations where the dictates of virtue compelled them to fight and their technical aptitude allowed them to win. If violence did not play by its own rules, it might even have been a foolproof strategy.

But violence does play by its own rules. Violent behavior feeds upon itself and continually oversteps the structural boundaries that social or state institutions place upon it. The parallels between the production of violent criminal behavior and the production of violent military behavior are striking. The key to both processes of what Lonnie Athens has termed "violentization" is "brutalizing" the individual.[10] Part of this brutalization is the desensitization to violence Keegan described above, but there is much more to it than that.

In Russia, as throughout Europe, both at the beginning and the end of this century, military training has been structured to "break down" the new recruit before "building him back up" in the proper military way. This process of breaking and building correlates directly to the phases of brutalization.[11] First, individuals experience violent subjugation, through personally becoming the victim of a recognized authority figure who shows them that hierarchy and power are maintained through violent acts. Second, they witness a similar act of violent subjugation upon another member of their "primary group." Finally, their "brutalization" is completed via "violent coaching," during which novices are taught that violence is a "personal responsibility which they cannot evade."[12] That responsibility is underlined by the portrayal of violent actions against enemies as "glorious acts" and the violent actors as "heroes, or at least anti-heroes." These portrayals are almost always achieved by the telling and retelling of personal narratives of the violent acts of relatives or close friends.[13]

The same processes of violent subjugation, personal horrification, and violent coaching were mainstays of army training in Russia. From the very first days in military school in fin-de-siècle Russia, officer trainees were left with no doubt about the authority structure within the army or the methods by which it was maintained. In Junker schools, second-year students subjugated the first-year students (who were called 'beasts') with near continuous hazing, "for which bullying is not an adequate translation."[14] Many of the trainees dropped out under the pressure within the space of a month. In the eyes of the trainers themselves, the outcome was positive and not unlike that described as the goal of violent subjugators: "[I]ts beneficial result for the army was the development of respect for any superior— even for one only a year above you. Consequently, although hazing was illegal, the officers of the school, all of whom had experienced it in their own days, closed their eyes to it."[15]

These men went straight from their military schools to positions as junior officers, where, not surprisingly, they replicated their own training experience when training new conscripts. That training was unrepentantly violent. Not only were soldiers beaten by officers or NCOs on a regular basis for violations of regulations but they also suffered violent acts at the hands of their fellow soldiers, who were forced to participate in the subjugation when men were ordered to "run the gauntlet."[16]

Violent coaching was also omnipresent. The narrative of the glorious and violent exploits of the regimental "family" in previous conflicts was a constitutive part of basic training, and lest soldiers forget over time, their barracks were filled with pictorial reminders of what constituted glory. Barracks walls were covered with paintings of heroic scenes of Russian martial exploits.[17] The themes of personal responsibility for committing violence and the reasons for doing so, stressed by Athens, were also emphasized by military trainers. In the first place, the entire institution of universal conscription was based on the establishment of a personal relationship between the state and the citizen around the nexus of military service. This theme of individual responsibility was strongly emphasized during training sessions through numerous invocations of the notion of duty. World War I reservists were reminded of "why they were drafted" and the "responsibilities of a soldier," and those lessons were followed up by discussions about the evils and shame of self-mutilation, desertion, and the "duties of the honorable soldier after being captured."[18]

Thus, the training process used in the Russian army in the hope of producing orderly violence replicated the process by which individuals learn to produce disorderly violence. The similarity between the two processes is not coincidental. Military trainers, as the result of years of experience, had hit upon the most effective means for preparing men for extreme violence. These trainers intentionally eroded the desire for self-preservation and lessened the importance of death, purposely portrayed the performance of violence as a virtuous and effective act for dealing with important problems, and linked that virtue to ideals of manliness and political belonging. Then they taught young men how to use weapons effectively, how to work together in groups, and how those groups could and should be self-reliant. This was an intentional recipe for producing violence on a massive scale, and it was tremendously effective.

Performing Violence

Brutalization is just the first stage in the violentization process, and in itself is normally insufficient to make a subject dangerously violent. The next stage, according to Athens, is the belligerency stage, when the individual contemplates his situation and his relationship to violence, asking how he can avoid further victimization. Many of these subjects decide that violence is a legitimate and effective course of action in certain circumstances. Though prepared to resort to [often lethal] violence, the subject at this stage has decided to limit his actions to those in which it is both "absolutely necessary for the well-being of his body and mind" and those in which "he has at least some chance of success."[19]

The belligerency phase of the soldier's personal transformation is not well documented in the historical literature, since the Russian peasant soldier, under the old model of the Russian peasantry that stressed the "primitive nature" of the peasant mind, could hardly have been expected to ruminate extensively about the role of violence in his life.[20] Yet, in the few records of conscript thoughts still extant, there seems to have been precisely the kind of thinking about the experience of brutalization and the role of violence that Athens identified. Iakov Dragunovskii remembered his military experience this way:

> I was taught discipline, taught to 'march,' to be not an independent rational man but a humble servant in the hands of the authorities, at whose command I must defend 'the Faith, the Tsar, and the Fatherland from all enemies foreign and domestic.' Those enemies greatly frightened me. What if I was ordered not just in words but in fact to kill? What could I do then, when I was horrified at the very thought?. . . The severity of service increased my aversion to it. Discipline. Fear for one's life. Bitterness.[21]

Even Dragunovskii, though, who was later to adopt nonviolence as a basic moral tenet, took a long time to resolve the nettlesome problem of violence, realizing over the course of World War I that he was "becoming brutalized. When I shot at the Germans from a trench, I did not feel any pity for them. . . . Our compassion for human beings disappeared. . . . I still thought this situation was necessary and willed by God. We had enemies and we had to kill them."[22]

Dragunovskii was probably quite typical of most soldiers. He followed orders and accepted the necessity for killing, but nevertheless gave the question of his role in the war and the reasons for war a good deal of thought. Several authors who spent time in the armed forces agitating for peace noted both the extreme interest in the topic of the necessity and morality of war to soldiers (large crowds would gather around to debate) and the varied opinions that the soldiers had.[23] In the end, after the shouting was done, most of the soldiers, having thought about their own belligerency, apparently decided that when the time came, they would have to commit violence and do it well. The dialogue regarding violence that soldiers conducted with themselves impacted not only the production of violence but the production of their identities as well. As several influential social theorists in the twentieth century have argued, individuals construct the self precisely through this sort of soliloquy, in which the internalized voices of large communities, smaller primary groups, and influential individuals shape the actions and attitudes of every human being as he or she proceeds through life.[24]

The conditions of World War I both transformed Russian identities and rapidly desensitized young conscripts to violence and death, much as their trainers had hoped. Stepun, after only a few days at the front, commented in wonder that

> What's strange, what I still don't understand is this: the impression [of the battlefield] was, of course, great, but by no means as great as I had expected. But the scenes were exceedingly painful. Corpses lay around left and right, both ours and the enemy's, fresh corpses and ones that had been there for many days, whole corpses and mutilated ones. . . . From place to place legs that had been insufficiently buried stuck up out of the ground. The heavy wheels of my artillery ran over these legs protruding from the ground more than once. One Austrian had obviously been buried alive; coming to, he had succeeded in freeing his head and hands and died that way with his head and hands sticking out of the ground. . . . In the name of God, tell me, is it really possible to see all of this and not go out of your mind? It turns out that it is possible, and not only is it possible not to go out of your mind, but much more, it is possible to eat, drink, and sleep on the very same day, and possible even not to dream about it afterward.[25]

Thus did Russian soldiers complete their transformation into violent and volatile men.

Military officials could not fully contain the explosion. Even at the very beginning of the war, soldiers were prone to violent outbreaks toward nonmilitary targets. In August 1914, the 24th Army Corps was upbraided by its commander for its recent activities in Galicia. The corps had destroyed postal stations, cut telephone wires, sacked the estates of landowners and set numerous fires, "as the result of which whole cities have burned." Furious, the commander reminded his men that the supreme commander had ordered men to take "an especially solicitious attitude toward the property of the population of Galicia" and warned that he would use the death penalty to punish those who committed acts of robbery or arson in the future.[26] The problem of violent looting was not limited to foreign regions occupied by Russian troops, for Russian subjects also complained that Russian soldiers were "treating them badly" when they passed through.[27]

As the war rumbled on, year after year, acts of violence increasingly began to take place outside of the sanctioned areas of violent behavior. Armed robberies of civilians (especially Jews) in the front-line zones became commonplace, as did attacks upon whole villages. Civilian massacres were reported on both sides of the pre-war border.[28] Individual acts of terror also mushroomed, as men robbed women clerks at gunpoint, attacked unarmed individuals, and committed sexual assaults. Soldiers themselves, not to mention civilians, admitted that they had become "wild beasts."[29]

Many (though by no means all) of these attacks upon civilians took place against national pariahs. The full extent of the barbarism directed against Jews by Russian soldiers and officers during the war remains unclear, but it is certain that violent assaults were a regular occurrence.[30] Nearly every single memoirist of the war, whether anti-Semitic or not, noted the phenomenon. Fedor Stepun, for one, was appalled by the lack of human respect that his fellow soldiers showed to Jewish civilians. He himself witnessed a Cossack who, while riding in a carriage, was whipping not the horse, but the Jewish driver, who in turn was expected to beat the horse. In addition, Stepun was present when an officer related an incident in which a soldier encountered a Cossack and complained that he had no boots and nowhere to go to get some. At first the Cossack suggested that the soldier search the trenches for boots to take off a corpse, but then they came across a Jew on the road. The Cossack came up "with the magnanimous idea to give the soldier 'yid' boots." When the Jew protested, the Cossack suggested a yet more "humorous idea." He told the soldier to drop his pants and ordered the Jew to "kiss his ass and thank him for letting you live," an order that was obeyed. "It was horrible," Stepun wrote home, "that all of this could happen. . . . But it was more horrible that the narrator, telling the story over cognac, got such a tremendous response from his listeners."[31]

The fact that the violence toward civilians was directed mainly against pariahs suggests two things. On the one hand, the countervailing official and social forces that normally kept violence within prescribed limits were weakened by the outbreak of war. On the other hand, these forces were still in evidence in sufficient strength to keep soldier-civilian relations from completely disintegrating.

The shocks of 1917 proved fatal to those weakened forces, and brutalized soldiers began a rampage that would take five years to bring under control. One soldier wrote privately that "[i]t's hard to live when all around all you see is disorder and only disorder. For so long everyone was ruled by the stick and the majority of Russians are people with no idea of the Motherland, honor, or duty."[32] Another wrote, "Something horrible is reigning: train stations are blown up, supply stations are burned down . . . soldiers in the rear are hopping trains to Kiev and then stealing along the way, forming teams of runaways, which are then caught and sent back to their unit."[33]

Those "teams of runaways" brought trouble wherever they went, forming armed bands that attacked civilian and military targets alike, stealing livestock, raiding distilleries, and taking hunting weapons before heading back to the woods. Local authorities were helpless, unable "to take measures to halt this anarchy."[34] In big cities, deserters, usually well armed, took control of burgeoning gangs and routed police and militia alike, terrorizing even the capital for days on end during the summer of 1917 (there were perhaps 50,000–60,000 deserters there in July 1917). The result, as Tsuyoshi Hasegawa has noted, was that "the means to settle political differences were rapidly shifting from persuasion and compromise to physical violence."[35]

In the summer and autumn of 1917, as the world focused on the momentous developments in Petrograd, vast zones of the western part of the empire were being overrun by these armed bands of men, who robbed local inhabitants and then with their help attacked and looted the estates of local landlords. In July, bands of deserters up to 6,000 strong were roaming the countryside around the southwestern front and "terrorizing" the population.[36] Local officials pleaded with military authorities not to let trains stop in their region and to send cavalry units to restore order, all to no avail.[37] By the time of the October Revolution the situation had deteriorated completely. In Proskurov district "a wave of destruction" washed over the population as members of the 22nd and 34th Army Corps stole livestock, grain reserves, and other food supplies, burned houses, and destroyed forests. No measures to "oppose anarchy" had been taken, because of a lack of reliable forces. None would be found.[38] It was not simply the "peasant revolution" that was ripping through the empire in 1917, but an outbreak of violence emanating largely from the brutalized men deserting the ranks of the army, an outbreak that was as indiscriminate in its targets as it was excessive.

The violence of the autumn of 1917 continued apace as the year came to a close. Telegrams complaining of continued "violence and robbery against peaceful inhabitants" continued to come to central organs, along with the now universal notation that nothing was being done to stop the depredations.[39] The return home of most soldiers over the winter led to an easing of the situation along the major transportation corridors and in front-line areas, but this largely meant that the violence had been displaced to the final destinations of the soldiers, where the indiscriminate looting was now increasingly chalked up to the October Revolution and the Bolsheviks. Observers in areas that had not been front regions during World War I often did not distinguish between the two connected, but still distinguishable, events: the massive return of armed men to civilian centers and the Bolshevik seizure of power.[40]

The soldiers who had returned to the front or who had stayed there during the volunteer period of the Red Army proved little better than their demobilized or deserter counterparts. The routing of the Bolshevik "screens" by German forces in the early spring of 1918 led to a renewal of violence against civilians, for the "demoralized troops . . . during their flight terrorize the population, robbing and committing violence against peaceful inhabitants, and shamelessly requisitioning everything in their path, which is raising up the population not only against them, but also against Soviet power."[41] By the end of April, soldiers had taken to attacking even the hospital trains that contained wounded Red Army soldiers, robbing the men inside the trains of their possessions and food stocks.[42] In Moscow province at the same time, the situation was just as bad, for army detachments were "conducting robberies, taking contributions, and engaging in open hooliganism."[43] Thus the cycle of violence that had developed over the course of World War I continued to gather steam as 1918 progressed, even before the outbreak of the major hostilities of the Civil War. Pitched battles between soldier bands and armed bands from the civilian population were common even before the Czech mutiny. Those battles would last throughout the war and would become one of the Civil War's defining features.[44]

After the penetration of Bolshevik views of violence and the actual experience of fighting the Whites and "Greens" during the remainder of 1918, the problem of violence intensified. Bands of armed men swept across Russia, fighting each other and resorting to simple highway robbery when formal battles were not taking place, sparing no one, waylaying women walking alone to market and engaging in orgies of raping and pillaging after taking cities in battle.[45]

To argue that the brutalization that occurred during World War I is the primary factor in explaining Civil War atrocities is not to absolve the Bolsheviks. For, though the Bolsheviks inherited (indeed rode to power) the wave of violence that the combination of soldier brutalization and the collapse of authority had produced in 1917, the Bolshevik leadership greatly exacerbated the situation by unleashing the Red Terror.[46] States can exert significant, though certainly incomplete, power by being able to set a certain tone regarding violence, its functions and its utilities. This ideology of violence plays the same role as other ideologies. It mediates the relationship between state and citizen that produces both meaning and political power. Just as citizens can impede state initiatives justified through ideology, so too can states, however imperfectly, obstruct cycles of violence that are fed from below and justified through ideology. Unfortunately, the Bolsheviks instead deployed an ideology of violence that was conducive to the further escalation of uncontrolled carnage.

To take one example, terroristic violence in the early years of the Civil War was portrayed as a laudable moral act. Trotskii, even as he tried hard to argue that the terror was instrumental (the instrument of the proletariat to destroy bourgeois resistance), could not help but hint that it went beyond immediate class goals. He repeatedly disparaged Karl Kautsky, a German Marxist critical of Bolshevik extremism, for being a weak-willed, vacillating man of the pen rather than a man of violent action. After excoriating Kautsky for believing that "tearful pamphlets" could change anything, he fulminated that the proletariat would have to pay "with blood" to gain and consolidate power. The proletariat, Trotskii opined, "will have not only to be killed, but also to kill— of this no serious revolutionary ever had any doubt."[47]

This glorification of blood took on ever widening parameters. The reserve with which military and political leaders in the prerevolutionary era had normally discussed explicit violence with their armed forces largely disappeared, and with it disappeared one of the restraining forces on indiscriminate violence. In the "Handbook of the Red Army Soldier," given to all incoming soldiers in 1918, men learned that "our army is called the Red Army because it spills its blood under the red flag . . .and therefore the color of our banner is the color of blood.[48] The literature of the Cheka was also explicit. One article in 1919 proudly trumpeted the fact that "when the weak and nervous confusedly grow pale," the Cheka did not. Instead, "knowing how to burn in anger," Chekists battled counterrevolution "not for life, but to the death. There can be no half measures and halfway policies."[49]

The shift in official attitudes toward violence was marked. Whereas leaders in the late imperial period struggled to keep violence under control, within prescribed bounds, and constitutive rather than destructive of order, Bolshevik dispatches to their armed forces in the Red Army and the Cheka gave a quite different message. Readers of the article in the Cheka newspaper cited above learned that "everything is permissible for us, for we are the first in the world to raise the sword not in the name of enslaving or oppressing someone, but in the name of the emancipation from the anger and slavery of all."[50] Podvoiskii instructed soldiers in 1919 to remember that

> your defender is your rifle, and not the trench. Having killed the enemy with your rifle, you destroy danger . . . Victorious is the side that launches into the attack swiftly and in unison, without stopping, without a hitch. Stab the enemy with your bayonet. Beat him with the butt of your rifle, and he won't withstand the blows, you will be victorious.[51]

M. N. Tukhachevskii would add in 1920 that the Civil War, "by its very nature demands decisive, brave, and attacking actions. Revolutionary energy and bravery dominate everything else."[52] Images of a cleansing, sweeping, overturning violence were ubiquitous.

This message arrived, as already seen, at a moment when violent acts had been rising dramatically around the country, especially during 1917.

Together, the effect was explosive, as violent men fought each other, raided and burned civilian centers, and committed unspeakable acts of violence throughout the land. A White desire to annihilate Bolshevism and eliminate party members contributed to the orgy, but in the end political factionalism played a secondary role. No one side in the war, no matter their color, had a monopoly on cruelty or bloodthirstiness. Virulent violence had become a national epidemic.

Given this situation, much of the population saw the political battles of the Civil War as secondary to the explosion of violence. The main war aim of most people was for the violence to stop as soon as possible. One Bolshevik commented along these lines to the Central Committee that "the population, whether because of the Russian capacity for lengthy patience, or because they have been terrorized, simply groan silently from shame and long for 'any kind of end [to the war].' The majority of the population is unconditionally neutral in the present war."[53] Elsewhere, that capacity for patience ran out, as in Sarapul, where peasants, tired of army bands and food-requisition brigades, revolted. "The food army men," complained the local peasants, "offend our women, making them cook *bliny,* and if they don't like the *bliny,* then they slap the women in the face with them." Incidents like these finally pushed the local residents over the edge, and a rebellion ensued in which peasants called for an end to communism, to requisitions, and raised banners with the slogan "Down with the Civil War." Not surprisingly, the peasants themselves, in the midst of their rebellion, were prone to excessive violence as well: "The rebellion, as is usual, was accompanied by a great deal of brutality, torture was applied, and there were instances of defiling corpses."[54]

The problem of violence was omnipresent in the Civil War, and the Bolsheviks were far more ambivalent about it than so far portrayed. To be sure, there was a strong current of revolutionary glorification of violence, but there was also a simultaneous desire to contain violence in rather traditional ways. The Bolsheviks were not able to overcome the basic contradiction of the modern nation, in which violence is both constitutive and destructive of order. Discipline was not foresworn by the Bolsheviks, and party and military leaders alike struggled to draw the line between acceptable violence and unacceptable violence. They found it very hard to do so consistently, and their efforts to contain violence bore little fruit.

Top Bolsheviks were uncomfortably aware of the fine line they trod when training men for violence. Podvoiskii told the members of the Komsomol's Central Committee that the key to training was the "freeing of the will from personal interests," so that they might be prepared for suffering and inflicting violence. But he noted that this training to kill almost inevitably led to "direct vices that are developed to one degree or another among men with military training, as a group devoted to military activities that are linked with the destruction of people."[55] He suggested a two-pronged approach: first, to pay "close and immediate attention to the development of the intense ideas about the well-being of the republic, consciousness, control over one's passions," and second, to remove the "soil in which vices grow." That soil, he argued, was the "separation of militarized groups from directly useful labor and from the class that performs that labor."[56]

The problem that Podvoiskii addressed with both of these maneuvers was one familiar to prerevolutionary military trainers: how to circumscribe the violent acts of their soldiers. Podvoiskii assumed that violence could be effectively controlled by reframing its meaning. Instead of a direct focus on violence as such, he instead wanted to stress the great symbolic tenets of nation ("well-being of the republic"), masculinity ("control over passions"), and class ("need to conduct labor") during military training.

Military trainers, for their part, focused directly on the technical aspects of warfare in much the same way that the tsarist regime had. "The basis for military training," Vsevobuch trainers learned, "is to teach mainly that which has a direct or indirect relationship to battle."[57] More specifically, the 96-hour program of training affirmed by Vsevobuch in 1919 mandated the following course of study for the first three days: "Day 1, hours 1–2: Conversations: The purpose of universal military training. Understanding military revolutionary discipline. Day 2, hour 1 (2 hours in each day): The rifle and its purpose (shooting, stabbing, beating with the butt). Major parts of the rifle. Day 2, hour 2: Cleaning the rifle. Day 3: Individual training. Standing, turning, and moving with weapons. . . . "[58]

Thus, much in the same way that prerevolutionary trainers had, Bolshevik military trainers sought to instrumentalize violence, including sections on "shooting, stabbing, and beating" only in a lesson on the functions of the rifle, discussing the "purpose of universal military training," and stressing in political lessons the larger goals that would be achieved through victory.

Bolshevik military leaders also stressed discipline in a similar way. To be sure, they repeatedly claimed that "revolutionary" or "comradely" discipline was of a radically different type from the old "tsarist" or "stick" (palochnaia) discipline, and there was something to this claim. But there were also important commonalities. The functions of discipline, for instance, remained the same: to enforce structures of hierarchy through threats and application of power and to demarcate the line between acceptable and unacceptable violence.

Lenin was quite clear about the necessity for discipline, telling one main military commander in 1918 to "[i]ntroduce strict discipline! Indiscipline leads to defeat. Press for the execution of orders, mercilessly punish offenders, hand over disobedient men to the tribunals. . . . Without discipline, no army can exist."[59] Part of that discipline, Lenin stressed, was that a soldier should not kill indiscriminately, but should be a "conscious warrior with initiative. He deliberates, and commanders and commissars must help him, morally train him, and teach him to discriminate."[60] In these views Lenin was numbingly traditional, paraphrasing almost word for word the need for strict discipline and soldier initiative stressed for decades by nearly all European military intellectuals, and making explicit the link between authority, subjugation, and violence.

The two currents of thinking on violence did not coexist easily. The revolutionary glorification of killing and destroying contrasted sharply with the military tradition of containing violence. The Bolsheviks tried to solve the conflict between these two positions by channeling violent activity against enemies of the state's choosing. A manichean view of the world was propagated to soldiers during the Civil War. Not only did they attend political lectures (as they had during World War I) devoted to the theme of "who are our friends and who are our enemies," but their entire education was structured along this bipolar axis. The biology lessons taught to young soldiers in the Red Army included a lesson on "animals that are friends and animals that are enemies of humans."[61]

Soldiers were consistently encouraged to look at the population in this fashion as well, distinguishing between friends whom they were to protect and enemies whom they were to destroy (with pride and perhaps even glee). The problem was that, unlike in the animal kingdom, one could not tell a zebra by his stripes in Civil War Russia. Worse, given the splintering of authority and the need to exercise power continuously through a barrel of a gun, soldiers were forced into self-reliance. One could not depend on a sophisticated and reliable system of authority to investigate, punish, and deter. One's own protection depended on the reliability and trustworthiness of one's unit. This tendency of soldiers to fall back and assume that anyone not in their unit could be an enemy in a time of chaos is widespread and well documented.[62] It was particularly true for Russian soldiers in all participating armies during the Civil War. As a result, the line between friend and enemy was blurry, and when push came to shove, it came down to the line between members of one's unit and nonmembers. If peasants, workers, or even party officials got in the way of a group of soldiers and violence resulted, then one could be sure that political loyalty and class-consciousness played little role in the "construction" of the enemy.

Given the fact of blurred lines between friends and enemies and the nature of violence itself, the attempt to keep violence contained by directing it solely at state-defined enemies was doomed to failure. This is not to say that the Bolshevik and military leadership did not try to use discipline to delimit authorized violence. To the contrary, most leaders shared Lenin's strong views on the necessity for discipline and the extreme danger to the revolution posed by marauding soldiers and indiscriminate agents of terror.[63] Soldiers were, in fact, court-martialed for violations of discipline ranging from conducting pogroms to robbery. Soldiers like Nikolai Redchenko were executed for acts of destruction and robbery because they had "defamed the honorable title of Red Army soldier and are . . . enemies of the people."[64]

Perhaps the clearest expression of Bolshevik ambivalence about violence, however, had to do with arming the population. The ideal of the "armed people" that had been supported by socialists across the spectrum prior to

World War I remained the centerpiece of the militia movement in the early years of the Soviet Union, in particular within Vsevobuch. The stated goal was to give arms to every laborer, as well as training in their use, so that in moments of crisis workers could flow effortlessly from their workbenches into the street to battle manifestations of capitalism and the international bourgeoisie. Indeed, Bolsheviks had reason to believe that revolution was impossible in the absence of this development; Trotskii in any case thought that the success of the February Revolution was contingent upon regular people being armed in their struggle against the tsarist regime.[65]

But the events of 1917, when soldiers deserted en masse with their weapons, leading to the outbursts of violence described above, gave the Bolsheviks, with their new and tenuous hold on the country, significant pause. An "armed people" was not nearly so attractive in practice as it was in principle. In addition, given the Bolsheviks' strong belief that power was obtained and preserved through violence, at least in the transitory stage of the "dictatorship of the proletariat," gun control seemed to be a reasonable policy.

Gun control was a constant struggle throughout the early Soviet period, and it was pursued from the very beginning of Soviet rule. Railroad troops in November 1917 and sailors in March 1918 complained loudly about the Bolshevik policy of taking guns away from servicemen who were being mustered out. The railroad troops used embarrassingly familiar rhetoric, reminding Lenin that the bourgeois press had criticized the Bolsheviks for overthrowing the government with force and maintaining it at bayonet point. They echoed the Bolshevik response: "But who holds those bayonets? We do! Soldiers of the Revolutionary Army. We do! The whole laboring people [narod]!" The troops warned that the reaction to the revolution was impending and therefore "we won't let weapons out of our hands. That way the enemies of the people know that the strength is with us, that power is behind us, but without weapons we can't embody force, and without force we can't hold onto power."[66] The sailors, for their part, complained bitterly that their weapons had been taken away when they were released from service, saying they had been the first to support Soviet power and they continued to support it.[67]

As persuasive as these appeals might have been, they could not overcome the justifiable (and daily justified) fear of armed men beyond the reach of army control. Villagers with weapons inflicted serious casualties upon Red Army units, and bands of deserters armed with their service weapons constituted a continuous threat to military effectiveness and civilian security.[68] Small wonder, then, that the Bolshevik authorities set up a system of "Committees for the Collection of Weapons" with the purported goal of gathering weapons to better defeat the "capitalists," but with the clear aim of trying to do something about the epidemic of guns that had swept across the country. All weapons were to be confiscated, with the exception of hunting weapons, but an exemption for members of the Communist Party allowed them to have one revolver and one rifle. Those who refused to turn in their weapons were to be punished with the "very harshest measures . . . up to and including shooting."[69]

Thus, at the same time that the Vsevobuch propaganda machine was saturating the country with positive comments about an "armed people," and supporting the same in party congresses and in the hallways of power, another campaign to "Give up your weapons!" was being conducted. This campaign was waged not only in select districts or against deserters (for whom possession of a weapon automatically meant being labelled a deserter of "evil intent" subject to the death penalty), but nationwide, as the lead article by Trotskii in *Izvestiia* on 26 December 1918 made clear: "all [weapons] should presently be concentrated in the hands of military authorities. The task is to disarm the population, and by doing this to arm the army, which is growing bigger, surpassing in its growth the work of supply organs."[70]

These disarmament campaigns were ultimately fruitless. Nothing could have been clearer to civilians and military men alike, whether on duty or deserters, than the fact that power belonged to men with guns. This fact, combined with the cumulative effect of years of sanctioned and unsanctioned violence, meant that there was no real hope for reducing the level of violence during the years of struggle with White forces. When the formal fighting ceased at the end of 1920, however, there was hope that violence would die out with the war. That hope was unrealized, and the violence continued into 1921, most famously at Kronstadt and in Tambov province, prompting the Bolshevik leadership to seek to pacify the country. As good Marxists, they turned naturally to the field of economics to solve their problems and introduced NEP at the Tenth Party Congress to satisfy peasant discontent with the economic regime of War Communism.

But NEP did not stop the violence. Indeed, as Vladimir Shishkin has most exhaustively shown, the Russian countryside remained an arena of brutal struggle, for violence remained the favored response of state authorities and civilians alike to a wide range of situations. In Siberia, the phenomenon of "Red banditism," in which party and state authorities attacked civilian populations for real or imagined, past or present offenses, developed so widely that it threatened to undermine Soviet power itself. And, though political and economic motives undoubtedly played a role in the development of Red banditism, so too did the cycle of violence that had been established during the Civil War. Even worse, Red banditism set the tone for the 1920s as a whole, confirming the "atmosphere of violence in society, a feeling of fear in the heads and hearts of people. 'The man with a gun'—the *militsioner, chekist,* or *chonovets*—long remained the herald of approaching misfortune."[71]

This "atmosphere of violence" persisted not just in Siberia,[72] where the Civil War had been particularly brutal, and in Central Asia, where the Basmachi continued to fight against the Bolsheviks well into the 1920s, but nearly everywhere in the Soviet Union. In fact, the prevalence of "banditism" was so widespread that the military sent a strictly confidential report to the top leadership every month during the first half of the 1920s re-lating the progress in the "struggle with banditism." In 1922, that struggle was taking place from Petrograd to Siberia, and back to the western front, where "bandits," in the course of October, had completely destroyed at least one county executive committee building and had committed high-way robbery in the Vitebsk, Mogilev, and Gomel' regions.[73] In 1924, ban-dits were so active in Siberia that the Revolutionary Military Council had to order an extra 103 soldiers from the 18th Rifle Corps to guard tunnels for the Trans-Siberian railroad in the Lake Baikal area, and a total of 440 men to guard railroad bridges over major rivers in the area.[74] By 1926, the situa-tion had eased only slightly, as bandits remained "active" in the Western military district and in Turkestan.[75]

Nor was the violence limited simply to gangs of bandits. Throughout the 1920s, observers complained of an increase in violent crime. They de-scribed a "wave of hooliganism" sweeping major cities in the early 1920s, with special intensity between 1923 and 1926.[76] The violence of the years of World War I and the Civil War had left an indelible imprint upon early Soviet society, an imprint that had not been intended by any of the author-ities, but that had certainly been facilitated by their attempts to use vio-lence as a mechanism of social solidarity and political belonging.

The primary way that violence was tied into notions of social solidarity and political belonging was through the institution of universal military conscription. The massive bureaucratization of the production of violence allowed officials to talk about the performance of "military service" or "mil-itary duty" rather than the performance of "violence" as a central condi-tion of civic belonging. This understandable maneuver normally enabled them to avoid talking about violence directly, but it is possible nevertheless to examine the importance of the act of violence itself to political belong-ing by addressing two topics. The first deals with the performance of vio-lence in its positive aspect, in particular how acts of violence proved able to overcome lost belonging. The second way to deal with this issue is to study violence in its negative aspect, by showing how the refusal to perform vio-lence was understood to be a refusal to join the political community.

The first relationship is quite straightforward. Throughout the early twentieth century, the performance of violence was seen to be an act of civic recovery. Despite the fact that violence was normally downplayed, it was no secret either to commanders or to soldiers that the central task of being a soldier was to conduct violent activities, and that when push came to shove, it was the performance of violence that mattered. This fact is per-haps most clearly seen in instances when soldiers got themselves in serious trouble. Almost without fail, both before and after the revolution, their last-ditch attempt to save their own lives consisted in performing "heroic," indeed often flamboyant, acts of violence.

In 1915, for instance, Nikofor Fedorov was condemned to death by a court-martial, but the carrying out of the sentence was delayed. In a battle that ensued soon after, Fedorov conducted himself with particular "brave-ness and courage" despite having an opportunity to flee the battlefield (and his punishment). His commanding officer recommended that Fedorov's sentence be commuted to one year in a disciplinary battalion at the end of the war, but the tsar went further still, giving him a full pardon for his bravery. Fedorov was not alone in being pardoned. Indeed, requests to have punishments lessened seem to have been granted by Nicholas II as a matter of course when petitioners either offered to "go to forward positions" or displayed "bravery," as Mefodii Vashchenko learned to his delight after his death sentence was also mistakenly delayed. Despite the fact that he had been convicted of desertion or flight from arrest three times (or perhaps be-cause of this), he threw himself into combat with vigor and "bravery" and was rewarded with the tsar's pardon for his effort in 1916.[77]

The practice of promising or performing violence as a method of escaping serious punishment carried over into the Soviet era. Pavel Tsymbal begged for the opportunity to "blot out his guilt" before his brothers-in-arms by re-turning to the front and fighting honorably, while Konstantin Belov promised to "prove" that he was an "honorable citizen" by returning to the front and fighting once again.[78] Several more petitioners pleaded for the chance to "expiate" their sins, to "put them in the very first row [of sol-diers]," all in order to do battle with "bloody oppressors."[79]

Indeed, the belief that doing battle would expiate sins was so strong that the state itself picked up on it in its favorite innovation for dealing with military crimes: conditional sentences. For a wide range of offenses (but especially desertion), soldiers would be conditionally sentenced to death and thrown back into the front lines, where, if they performed well, they could get off without punishment. If they slipped up again, however, their conditional sentence would be carried out. These punishments were almost always framed in terms of giving a soldier a second chance to "blot out" his guilt. In Trotskii's formulation, conditional sentences were created so that soldiers would have a two-month period of "correction" on the front lines.[80]

This practice soon became the favored one. In the first two weeks of September 1919, nearly ten times as many men were conditionally sen-tenced to death (449) as were actually sentenced to death (48). Over the whole course of the second half of 1920, the ratio was about three condi-tional sentences (3831) for every death sentence (1278).[81] The practice of using the front line as a "correctional" facility in which miscreants could expiate their sins through socially useful violence was thus tremendously popular for central and local commanders alike throughout the Civil War. It made a quick return in World War II, when the Gulag was emptied to shore up the army.[82]

Thus, for state and soldier alike, it was accepted that the performance of violence was not only a central facet of being a citizen, but also a means by which to recover lost belonging. That the performance of violence was the center of the nexus between citizen and state is shown in even more stark relief by the experience of conscientious objectors under the tsarist and Soviet regimes.

Refusing Violence

Conscientious objection, though a phenomenon of Russian life for some time prior to the implementation of universal military service, took on new life after 1874.[83] The state's insistence that the performance of violence was the individual duty of every Russian citizen fueled growing resentment among the many small pacifist groups in the empire. This unhappiness coincided with both a widespread religious revival in fin-de-siècle Russia and Lev Tolstoi's rise to prominence as an international prophet of nonviolence. As a result, fundamentalist religious approaches clashed with the determined policies of the state in spectacular ways throughout the late nineteenth and early twentieth century.

Religious and civic protests were intertwined among the sectarian religious groups that dotted the Russian landscape. The Orthodox church, along with most other major churches that had been co-opted by European states, consistently held that it was a religious as well as a civic duty to serve in an army that protected "faith, tsar, and the fatherland." Religious objection to military service therefore had to take place outside of the Orthodox church, which, in fact, it did. Dissident religious groups of both foreign and domestic origin had been a fact of life in Russia throughout its history, but the sectarian movement blossomed in the last half of the nineteenth century and the first few decades of the twentieth century.

The sectarian movement has been the subject of renewed interest in recent years, an interest that promises to produce significant insights into conscientious objection during the period. Many of the sects in late imperial and Soviet Russia officially subscribed to a credo of nonviolence, including the Molokans, Dukhobors, Baptists, Evangelical Christians, Mennonites, and Tolstoians.[84] It was from this small but continually growing movement that the vast majority of conscientious objectors would come.

The turn toward organized civic pacifism that was occurring in western Europe and the United States in the same period was largely absent in Russia.[85] It was present among some members of the educated elite, however, most notably in Jan Bloch, a Polish magnate who wrote a book on modern war that became famous throughout Europe for its argument that war had become "impossible." No reasonable statesman, he argued, could seriously contemplate conducting a long war of attrition that would ruin the economy, destroy a generation, and lead inevitably to revolution. Even if politicians launched such wars, he argued, the populace would in fact rise up and end these wars by themselves.[86] Other members of the Russian "intelligentsia," most notably Pavel Miliukov, were at times as attracted to civic pacifism as Bloch was, but it is not clear how many people were secular pacifists.[87]

In 1874, state and military officials had little sympathy for either of these pacifist positions. In line with the Miliutin program of making military service universal, no provisions for conscientious objection for conscripts were considered. The only sticking point was the lone case of the Mennonites, who had been promised by Catherine II when they emigrated to Russia that they would not be asked to serve in the military because of their religious views. In initial discussions about the law in 1871, state leaders intended a small compromise: Mennonites would be drafted but assigned to noncombat posts. The politically savvy Mennonite leadership, which had connections in the tsarist bureaucracy, repeatedly traveled to St. Petersburg to press for a special exemption, warning that many of their flock would emigrate if forced to serve, but these protests were not sufficient. The 1874 law called for a draft of Mennonites, but only into hospital or supply units. The plans for emigration continued, and as the specter of losing some of the best grain producers in the empire became more and more real, the tsarist government backed down and changed the law in 1875 to allow the Mennonites to be drafted into special forestry units to be run and administered by fellow Mennonites. The details were worked out over the course of the 1870s and the plan was implemented in 1881, when the first Mennonites went off to harvest lumber for the state.[88] Until 1919, the Mennonites were the only group given an exemption for conscientious objection.

Other would-be conscientious objectors faced the wrath of the state, most notably the "Large Party" of the Dukhobor sect, the members of which declared their refusal to serve in the military in 1895. In response, the tsarist government authorized the torture of Dukhobors already in military service and forcibly drove civilians from their homes, whipping small children and adults alike into malarial valleys in Transcaucasia. Homeless and starving, they relied on the good will of other neighboring Russian sectarians, Georgians, and Armenians for nearly four years before a public relations blitz led by Lev Tolstoi pressured the tsarist government to allow them to emigrate to Canada.[89]

Prior to 1905, conscientious objection was, for most pacifists, not only a military crime, but a religious crime as well, for members were in violation both by not serving the armed forces and by being members of illegal sects. The persecution therefore was aimed both at the objection and at the conscience. Throughout the nineteenth century, and particularly from the 1880s onward, when Konstantin Pobedonostsev (chief procurator of the Holy Synod) launched an attack upon sectarianism, offenders were seen as being at the intersection of military and religious codes. With the legalization of alternative religions in 1904–1905, though, that aspect of the definition of conscientious objection as a religious crime faded away.[90] It was replaced by an increased focus on the violation of civic responsibilities as an inherent part of refusing to serve. The transfer did little to mitigate the state's response to the crime. National heretics were just as dangerous as religious ones.

Despite persecution, dozens of men proclaimed that they refused on principle to serve in the armed forces, and many more must have simply chosen to evade by using the traditional means of all Russian citizens, through health, educational, or occupational deferrals, or by simply not showing up. From 1905–1911, according to a compendium of cases saved by Pavel Miliukov, 73 men declared their refusal to serve in the military for reasons of conscience. Many of these suffered the same fate as the Dukhobors. Pavel Bezverkhii, a merchant from Khar'kov province, refused to serve in 1906 and was sent to a disciplinary battalion, where he was "brutally beaten to a pulp and suffered an exceptionally harsh retribution, as a result of which he became severely mentally ill."[91] Bezverkhii was eventually released after an appeal from Tolstoi.

The crime of conscientious objection was viewed as a dereliction of civic duty. Thus, in those cases where individuals had special civic privileges, military courts regularly stripped these individuals of the privileges. Sergei Prozretskii, an "honored citizen," was drafted in 1907 but refused to serve. As a result, he was sentenced by the Warsaw military district court to be "deprived of his military title, and all his rights and privileges, and to be sent to a [civilian] correctional arrest department for five years."[92] This tactic of punishing objectors in civilian institutions rather than in military ones was inconsistently applied, but it was greatly desired by military men who feared the contamination of other soldiers in their disciplinary battalions. Conscientious objection was a dual crime: it was a violation of civic duty as well as military duty.

As troublesome as the problem was between 1905 and 1914, it became even more of an issue during the course of World War I. Just as most military men and radical socialists saw the war as a test, so too did most pacifist propagandists see it as a moment when the righteous would have to make their stand. Pacifists around the country tried to convince soldiers to lay down their arms, telling them that peace would "not be achieved with any sort of diplomatic means and not by the victory of one people over another, but only on the basis of a fraternal unification of all people."[93] No huge pacifist groundswell resulted, but there was a sharp increase of refusals to serve compared to the peacetime years. Whereas Miliukov's file yielded about 10 conscientious objectors each year from around the empire, and pacifist activists later would calculate that the number actually punished for conscientious objection prior to the war was about 20–50 a year,[94] the numbers shot up in the war years. In the Kiev military district there were 5 objectors convicted of refusing to serve in 1914 and 44 in 1915. In the Moscow military district, the numbers were 4 and 71 respectively, of whom the vast majority (53) were peasants.[95] By 1916, the number of men who had declared that they were refusing to serve as a matter of conscience had reached nearly 500 and the rate of refusals, according to the minister of internal affairs in May of that year, was "gradually increasing."[96]

The response to this refusal to serve was familiar. In one case, a conscript who refused was sentenced to death, but the peculiarly popular "fictive punishment" was performed instead. The young man was tied up, and ten men rushed at him with bayonets, stopping just short of stabbing him, and then beat him senseless rather than kill him.[97] Elsewhere, military judges began to levy extremely heavy sentences for refusing to serve. In 1916, the corps court of the 3rd Army sentenced Konstantin Smirnov to exile and forced labor for twelve years, in addition to stripping him of all his rights.[98] The strengthening of punishments did little to slow the rate of refusal. By the time of the February Revolution, 837 men had been convicted of refusing to serve for their religious convictions, and many more were still in the midst of the legal process. Even more pacifists must have avoided service in the ways described in chapter 1.[99]

Multiple factors compounded the perceived threat of pacifism during the war. In addition to worrying that pacifist propaganda in the troops or, even worse, in military hospitals under the sway of pacifist nurses (both male and female), would lower the fighting spirit of the army,[100] military officials suspected conscientious objectors of treason as well. This suspicion stemmed in part from the sectarian base of the conscientious objector movement, for many of the pacifist sects that inhabited the empire had come to Russia from German-speaking lands. In addition to the Mennonites, both the Baptists and the Evangelical Christians carried the taint of "Germanism" during the course of the war. Conservatives around the empire, including representatives of the MVD, wailed to the tsar that sectarianism was an "attack on the Orthodox church" and that sects taught values that ran counter to "true Russian foundations." They hinted darkly that groups such as the Baptists had "foreign ties" and were run by "foreign, especially German, organizations."[101] By 1915, the MVD was beyond hinting; the minister himself stood up in the Duma to announce that "Baptists serve as a weapon of the German government right here among us," citing monetary support from the Kaiser as proof of their treasonous activity.[102] The link between treason and pacifism, never far from the surface within a political system that links military service with civic duty, was now out in the open.

The hostility to conscientious objectors was popular as well as official. There was little sympathy on the home front for "cowards" who refused to go to the front when brothers, fathers, and husbands were dying there. The antipathy to conscientious objectors is most clearly evident in the response encountered by a group of Tolstoians in Tula under the leadership of Sergei Popov. Tula was the center of the Russian munitions industry and as such had been placed under martial law very early in the war. In addition to armaments factories, the 76th Infantry Reserve Battalion was stationed in Tula. It was this militarized milieu that Popov entered to preach the cause of peace. On 25 October 1914, he posted a flyer on the gates of the steel rolling mill telling his "dear brothers and sisters" that "[a]ll people on earth are brothers and sisters," and pleading with his readers to oppose the war and to "love one another." The workers who read the flyer as Popov walked away were not in a loving mood. One commented that "they should arrest those sorts of people," while another declared that it was clearly the "work of a spy." The spy call was quickly taken up. One of the workers shouted, "Boys, follow me, it's a spy!" at which point a mob began to chase Popov, shouting "Catch him!" As one peasant passer-by recounted, the scene looked like real trouble in the making, as a pack of industrial workers ran after the long-bearded Popov, who, shod only in bast shoes and cloth wrappings, was losing ground quickly and was looking around frantically for somewhere to hide.

Popov proved lucky. Before the mob caught him, a local policeman on his beat grabbed him. The policeman was accompanied by several members of the 76th Reserve Battalion. Popov, apparently undaunted, tried to convince the enlisted men to "refuse to participate in the war," by claiming, "Brothers, you don't have to go to the war and fight, we are all identical brothers and everyone's soul is the same, both for Germans and for us." This appeal fell on deaf ears, as did most of the pacifist propaganda produced in Russia during the war.[103]

The general hostility shown toward conscientious objectors was not universal, though. Indeed, as noted above, a significant and growing number of Russians were attracted to nonviolence as a way of life, and an even greater number admired these individuals from afar. Aside from Tolstoi, pacifists had perhaps their biggest support from the Russian liberals, whose belief in freedom of conscience made them natural allies. A. I. Shingarev, in fact, argued strenuously during the debates on the conscription reform in 1912 that conscientious objection should be incorporated into the military code. When reading about the persecution of conscientious objectors he felt "great embarrassment" and "a feeling of moral suffering." "A very deep conflict," he incisively argued, "occurs between the conscience of a man, between the precepts of his religion, the precepts of his faith, and the demands of state duty. . . . Our legislation either did not foresee these instances, or forgets about them; we end up with an impossible situation: in a Christian state, there have arisen martyrs for the Christian faith." After reminding his listeners in the Duma both of the "horrible drama" that occurred with the Dukhobors in the 1890s, when "our motherland lost highly honorable and work-loving people," and of the existing exemption for Mennonites, Shingarev concluded with a call to extend forest service as an option for people of "any sect," who felt that military service violated their conscience.[104]

Shingarev's call was seconded by many liberals. Even the militarily minded leader of the centrist Octobrist party, Aleksandr Guchkov, suggested that they give serious consideration to the issue, but he urged the Duma to push through the reform bill first and discuss the sectarian question later.[105] The conservative Third Duma was not prepared to pass such a radically liberal bill as the one Shingarev proposed, but the debate revealed both an ambivalence about the question and the fact that liberals were prepared to support conscientious objection as a matter of freedom of conscience.

Thus there was excellent reason for sectarians and pacifist activists to hope that the February Revolution, which launched men like Shingarev into high governmental positions (minister of agriculture, in Shingarev's case), would bring about a sea change in attitude toward conscientious objection. Sects from around the country joined the nationwide trend and sent gushing congratulatory telegrams to the Duma after the revolution, talking lovingly about their "dear motherland," and asking the new leadership to free those jailed for their political or religious convictions.[106] The Provisional Government, for its part, moved quickly to establish the right of free conscience by removing all disabilities from alternative religions and freeing those who had been jailed for religious convictions.[107]

In this climate, pressure arose almost immediately to legalize conscientious objection. The first "test case" for the Provisional Government came as the result of a petition from Petr Bugaev, a 26-year-old peasant from Kursk province who did not belong to a sect. Bugaev wrote to the minister of justice (Kerenskii) in March 1917, saying that although he was supposed to have been in the army since October 1916, he had never shown up because of his religion. "I am a follower of the great teacher Jesus Christ, and that conviction, which I have long maintained, does not allow me to cold-bloodedly look at the death of a human being from the hand of another human being, and the voice of conscience within me tells me that it is better to suffer and withstand any offenses than to be the reason of the death of another." Bugaev did not, however, seek a complete exemption, saying he wanted to work in the interior of the country at "any job other than a military one." "I'm not seeking a life on holiday," he maintained. "God loves the working man."[108]

Bugaev made his request not only on the basis of his own convictions, but also upon the clear signals the Provisional Government had sent that it supported freedom of conscience. "I hope that you will allow me to live and work freely," he wrote, "just like all citizens of the great free Russia. I stayed quiet all this time because there was no one to tell and to ask for mercy from. But now I dare to turn to you, who are leading the country to freedom and its spiritual revival." He concluded, "I therefore do not wish to hide myself from the People's Government, but I wish to openly request a free life from it."[109]

Bugaev was articulating an alternative vision of the nation from the one discussed throughout this book, one in which the "people's government" did not require military service and the performance of violence as a prerequisite for citizenship. He was perfectly willing to accept the sovereignty of the Provisional Government as the voice of the people, and indeed was willing to perform any service for it, as well as for the rather more permanent "country" (strana), but he was not willing to be put in the position of "cold-bloodedly" killing someone. This concept of civic duty, as evident in the words of Shingarev above, was not unique to isolated pacifist peasants. The question of conscientious objection, therefore, revealed as much about the concept of nation in 1917 as it had earlier. Not surprisingly, it was occasion for heated debate. Just as unremarkably, the Provisional Government did a lot of talking and very little deciding. Throughout the year, not only conscientious objectors, but the officials in charge of mobilization and other aspects of internal affairs as well, were confused about the official stance toward the question.

This confusion was apparent in the reply of civilian and military officials to Bugaev's letter. The Ministry of Justice forwarded it to the Mobilization Department, which in turn wrote the MVD's Conscription Administration on 20 April asking what to do. The Conscription Administration was not quite sure how to respond, since it thought that the 1917 decree on religious freedom opened the door for conscientious objection claims (though in fact, there was no specific mention of this at all). Nevertheless, the administration maintained that since conscientious objection "would introduce into the important business of drafting the population a completely unacceptable situation of disorder," the Mobilization Department should rely solely on the old regulations, giving exemptions only to Mennonites.[110]

This was the stance taken by mobilization officials throughout 1917, but it led to a whole series of undesirable occurrences, not least of which was the fact that the conscientious objectors jailed by the tsarist regime had been freed by the amnesty for those convicted of political or religious crimes. But those amnestied criminals became subject to conscription upon their release, leading to an awkward situation: many men were being rearrested for the same crimes for which they had been given an amnesty.[111]

In the midst of this conceptual anarchy, the MVD's Department of Spiritual Affairs, which had fought so hard for the continued use of religion as the basis for preserving the conservative, discriminatory distinctions between the tsar's subjects, now became a strident proponent of Dmitrii Miliutin's old national platform. "If belonging to one or another religion should not serve as the basis for any kind of restriction of one's rights," it argued, "then neither should it create privileges, all the more so because of the possibility of the simulation of religious views by people with an insufficient development of the consciousness of their duty before the motherland.[112] For the first time, the fear of simulation was raised in the debate over conscientious objection, not surprisingly by an institution staffed by men who held a nearly instinctive loathing for sectarians. The Orthodox believers in the Department of Spiritual Affairs were, in this respect, the direct precursors of the fundamentalist atheists in the Commissariat of Justice under the Bolsheviks.

The summer of 1917 saw increased discussion about the issue. Newly validated pacifist activists, led by Vladimir Chertkov and Konstantin Shokhor-Trotskii, two influential Tolstoians, finally had a chance to present their project of a law for conscientious objection.[113] The proposal was sympathetically heard, not least by officials in the military justice system, who officially recommended repealing the statute that mandated punishment for conscientious objection.[114] But no firm policy emerged. As a temporary measure, military leaders ordered commanders to ensure that any soldiers declaring their opposition to violence should be transferred to hospital work (like that conducted by Mennonites throughout the war) until the situation was resolved.[115] Before a decision could be reached, first the October Revolution, and then the end of the war, intervened.[116]

The Bolsheviks came to power with mixed emotions on conscientious objection and the role that sects would play in the immediate postrevolutionary system. On the one hand, as already noted, they were committed both to violence as a necessary, even virtuous, activity, and to an atheist program. About both of these tenets there was very little disagreement. But among a few top leaders there was also a rather well-developed opinion that pacifist sectarians were actually more "advanced" than most of the Russian population because they had been strident oppositionists and had courageously withstood the wrath of the state and the Orthodox church.

The affinity went deeper than the precept that "my enemy's enemy is my friend," an idea that the Bolsheviks rarely believed in any case. Instead, the sympathy derived from an understanding that sectarians were instinctually right to oppose the tsar and the church and to set up communist communities as an alternative but had merely misdiagnosed the reason why they felt compelled to do so. They were in need of enlightenment, not opposition. And given the organizational skills, talent for agitation, and rising popularity that sects possessed, they appeared to be natural allies. Their deep religiosity could be overlooked, for their religion was only a retardant to the development of communism, not a direct threat to it. The immediate danger of religion lay in the institution of the Orthodox church, not in religiosity itself.

The potential for sects to become revolutionary allies was picked up by Vladimir Bonch-Bruevich very early in his career. A member of the Social Democratic Party since the mid-1890s, he accompanied the Large Party Dukhobors when they emigrated to Canada in 1899, served as a rapporteur for their activities to the educated public, Social Democrats included, and collected a great deal of ethnographic and religious data from them. In the first years of the twentieth century, he was an important collaborator with Chertkov and his Tolstoian publishing house in England, before being run out after using Chertkov's mailing list to send out revolutionary flyers. In 1902, Bonch-Bruevich made his goals clear in an article that argued for the necessity to distribute propaganda materials to sectarians in order to lay the groundwork for future peasant revolutionary organizations. In 1904, he even got approval and funding from the Central Committee of the Bolshevik Party to publish *The Dawn*, a newspaper aimed directly at a sectarian audience.[117]

The newspaper was soon closed, however, when the Central Committee decided that the funds would be better spent elsewhere, revealing an attitude that would persist for decades: overall apathy toward the sectarian question. Almost no one, with exceptions mentioned below, was really interested enough in the question either to contest or to support making an appeal to sectarians. The fight against the Orthodox church was world-historical and crucial for the success of the revolution, but the question of the sects was much less so. As a result, in the 1920s and 1930s the Bolsheviks had one person who was unofficially recognized as the specialist on sectarians, someone to whom aggrieved sectarians could write and to whom party members would turn for information and advice on policies that affected the sects. Bonch-Bruevich, who was extremely close to Lenin and served as his secretary in Sovnarkom, was the natural choice until his star waned, in direct proportion to Lenin's health. As Bonch-Bruevich faded from view, P. G. Smidovich came to be acknowledged as the sect specialist. Both played the same role, protecting sectarians when they could and frankly informing sectarian leaders when they had stepped out of line or when events were beyond the sect specialist's control.

In those early revolutionary days, therefore, when Bonch-Bruevich was a regular presence at Lenin's side, the sectarians fared fairly well in the highest corridors of power. Even before the October Revolution, the close link between the two men had an impact. On one occasion, as Lenin and Bonch-Bruevich were walking to Bonch-Bruevich's apartment in Petrograd, they passed the statue of Alexander III, where a crowd normally convened to argue back and forth about the war. The two men stopped and watched the proceedings for about a half an hour; according to Bonch-Bruevich, Lenin was particularly interested in the speeches of two "simply dressed" men of the "teetotaler" sect *(trezvenniki)* who spoke out loudly and articulately against the war.

One of those men, Ivan Koloskov, was the leader of the sect. A few months later, after the Bolsheviks had seized power, Koloskov came directly to speak with Lenin. Over the course of their conversation, they articulated their points of agreement and disagreement. According to Bonch-Bruevich, writing up the account years later, Koloskov agreed to recognize the Bolsheviks as the "people's government," while Lenin agreed to respect the sectarian right "to their own convictions." In practical terms, this meant that Koloskov's group would "do other necessary work rather than fight," and Lenin would support legal provisions for conscientious objectors.[118] These were odd arguments for the two men to make; Lenin was hardly a proponent of pluralism of convictions, and Koloskov, if he believed that a legitimate government of the people's will was aggressively atheist, was a rare sectarian indeed. Nevertheless, whatever the true feelings of the two men, the positions offered in this conversation were remarkably close to the ones articulated throughout the Civil War by sectarian leaders and top Bolsheviks.

Lenin, for his part, moved relatively quickly to fulfill his end of the bargain. In February, Lenin struck paragraph 6 from the draft text of the separation of church and state decree (the decree on "freedom of conscience"), which read that "no one may appeal to his religious views in order to evade his civic responsibilities." He ordered Bonch-Bruevich to keep tabs on the cases of conscientious objection that began to flow in with the first drafts in the summer of 1918, telling him to put the objectors to work in cooperatives, where "we need good workers." When the instances of conflict between local authorities and conscientious objectors grew as the drafts piled up, Lenin ordered the formation of a commission to draft a conscientious objector law. It was headed by Bonch-Bruevich, with three other members: Emel'ian Iaroslavskii (political director of the Moscow military district), P. I. Krasikov (Commissariat of Justice), and Vladimir Chertkov. The commission met six times and drafted the conscientious objection decree.[119]

The debates within the commission foreshadowed the debate that would last throughout the 1920s on the issue of conscientious objection. Bonch-Bruevich and Chertkov supported a lenient law. Krasikov, who was to spend much of the Civil War as the point man for separating church and state and for persecuting religion throughout the land, argued along with another member of his commissariat that "different responsibilities" were unacceptable in a republic where there was the "equality of all before the law." Iaroslavskii (whose future career was colored by his stance as a militant atheist) surprised Bonch-Bruevich, however, by supporting the "widest possible application of the decree, definitively stating that these 'unsteady' elements were always pernicious in an army."[120]

The military position should not have been a surprise, despite the fact that the military had consistently pressed for casting the conscription net broadly and had argued for so long that military service must be the duty of all citizens, who were equal before the law. For the military, since 1905, had wanted a broad application precisely so that it could select the strongest men, both physically and morally. "Unsteady" elements were not desired. It was a position that top military leaders would consistently hold, from the Revolutionary Military Council's decree in October 1918, which preempted the decision of Sovnarkom and allowed for conscientious objectors to serve in sanitary units,[121] right through the 1920s, when PUR remained ever vigilant about the extent of sectarianism in the army and in each incoming class of conscripts.[122]

The disagreement between the Commissariat of Justice and the rest of the commission was not resolved, and the dispute was taken to Lenin directly. Krasikov wrote emphatically to Lenin on 13 December 1918 to support the ideal of the militarized nation: "He who does not want to defend the land from the thugs of imperialism should not have the right to use that land, he also should not be able to vote and be elected to Soviet institutions and to enjoy the benefits of social security laws. There is even a question as to whether this passive element should be exiled from the territory of the Soviet Republic as an antisocial element."[123] But Lenin had already decided that this was a fight the embattled Bolsheviks didn't need. A month earlier he had told one gathering of workers that the battle against religious prejudices had to be conducted "exceedingly cautiously" so as not to "anger the masses." He followed his own advice and threw his support behind the conscientious objector decree.[124]

After Lenin's weighty intervention, the only real questions remaining were the procedures to determine who was a legitimate conscientious objector and whether a "complete" exemption could be granted to those people who not only refused to carry arms but also refused to be a part of the war machine. The answers were provided in the decree establishing conscientious objection that came from Sovnarkom on 4 January 1919. This decree allowed sectarians themselves (through the United Council of Religious Communes and Groups) to offer expert testimony on the applications of conscientious objectors before people's courts, which had the responsibility for determining whether a man was a real conscientious objector. "Complete" exemptions were also allowed, but they had to be decided by the unanimous vote of United Council experts and be approved by VTsIK (the All-Russian Central Executive Committee of Soviets).[125]

In principle, then, the question was resolved. There was general consent among government, military, and pacifist elites about the proper course to take and a procedure for doing so. The only fly in the ointment appeared to be the grumbling militant atheists in the Commissariat of Justice, who continually made life difficult for conscientious objectors, refusing in some cases to file appeals of convictions if objectors could not prove they had rejected tsarist military service and belonged to an acknowledged sect, proof they did not have to offer according to the 4 January 1919 law.[126] In addition, the commissariat harassed members of the United Council, examining cases very closely and making not-so-subtle hints that the members were being too soft and were giving exemptions to fakers. Within a year, officials from the Commissariat of Justice charged that members of the United Council were advocating exemptions based on personal declarations alone and were generating "distrust in their expertise." Worse, they maintained that the United Council was protecting men who "not only refused military service, but also conducted open agitation against the performance of military service, disorganizing the Red Army and clearly facilitating counterrevolution."[127] Charges of treason once again swirled around pacifists and conscientious objectors.

Though these officials in Moscow were hindering implementation of the decrees, it was in the countryside that the real abuses were happening. As was the case before the revolution, the ambivalence among elites regarding conscientious objection was not shared by the rank and file. Like the Tula workers who chased Popov, most Russians thought that conscientious objection was unmanly and treasonous. Thus, when local officials made decisions about conscientious objectors, the response was a familiar one: persecution, torture, and execution. Conscientious objectors were denied appearances before people's courts and were sent to Revolutionary Tribunals instead; accused of desertion, they were in many cases beaten and tortured.[128] Between June and December 1919, at least 11 conscientious objectors were shot by Revolutionary Tribunals, in clear violation of the law.[129] Not surprisingly, the United Council and Bonch-Bruevich personally, who received many of the complaints, turned not to the Commissariat of Justice for relief but to military officials, who clarified the law and explained it to their subordinates on a regular basis. Nevertheless, the situation had gotten so bad by August 1919 that Rattel', the head of Vseroglavshtab, felt it necessary to send out a circular noting that though "citizens who submit declarations of refusal to serve in the military for religious convictions are frequently arrested and looked at as deserters," they were not in any situation to be inducted into the army.[130] The frustration of Rattel' stemmed at least in part from the fact that top officials had to keep repeating themselves: this August order was nearly identical to one sent in April by Sklianskii.[131]

Clarifications from the center proved ineffective, and 1920 turned out to be an even worse year for conscientious objectors than 1919 had been. A report submitted in August 1920 by the United Council listed 72 men who had been shot in violation of the 4 January decree, sometimes in spite of the fact that they had attestations from the United Council.[132] Thus, despite the clear disapproval registered by Sovnarkom and by the Red Army, local officials deployed the framework of the militarized nation to address questions of military service, civic duty, and legality. There were limits to the power of central state officials to define the contours of that national ideology.

In Saratov, for instance, local commanders simply ignored the procedure outlined by the 1919 decree. In October 1919, after a "religious display" by local Tolstoians, 600 pacifists "declared to the people's court their lack of desire to serve in the troops." The provincial military commander himself recounted that he had them arrested as deserters and sent to military tribunals for trial, thereby "liquidating" the movement. Only after these arrests, did the tribunal invite an expert from the United Council.[133] Saratov authorities, in other words, arrested, tried, and eventually "liquidated" before they asked for an opinion from the United Council. They did all of this through local military tribunals rather than the people's court, where it should have been handled, and where the Tolstoians went in the first place. But even here the process is obscured by the language of official communication. A better sense of what "arrested," "tried," and "liquidated" means can be had from the account of a Tolstoian who lived through similar circumstances.

Iakov Dragunovskii was the soldier encountered earlier who wrote about his "brutalization" during World War I and his slow progression toward Tolstoianism. By the Civil War, he no longer had any doubts, and in 1920 he marched (preemptively, as had the Saratov Tolstoians) to the local party office to declare that he was refusing to serve. The response was severe. After calling him a "blockhead" for making a declaration in advance of his call-up, officials accused him of anti-Soviet agitation for refusing military service, interrogated him about his passive resistance to food requisitions for the army, and then rummaged through his things, where they found his letter from the United Council authorizing him as their representative in Smolensk province. His interrogator shouted:

—Who the devil gave this document to a fool like you? What kind of authorized representative can you be? Just look at yourself—you're a complete fool! So he was going to defend other people! He can't even say anything for himself that makes sense. He's talked such devilish gobbledygook that it makes you want to puke. Tell me, you nasty devil: do you confess to being guilty of agitation against the Soviet government?

—No, I don't!

—How is it you don't, when you've admitted you have a library? That in itself is proof of agitation! Now, confess it: if you weren't a troublemaker, there wouldn't be so many objectors to war around here.

Dragunovskii refused to confess, so his interrogators wrote out his confession and told him to sign it. Again, he refused, saying, "No, I won't. Write out a protocol I can agree with, and I will sign it." Infuriated, one of his tormentors shouted, "Oh-h-h! So we have to pamper him, rewrite the protocol, take a lot of time with him when we've got nine more waiting out there! Listen, you idiot! We're giving you one last chance; if you don't sign it, you've got only yourself to blame." After further refusals, another one yelled, "Here's what! Sit down and write instructions to the Provincial Cheka to shoot the hell out of him, and in the protocol we'll write that he has refused to sign."

Dragunovskii's ordeal was not yet over, for the head of the local party organization came along to try his hand at convincing him. Again Dragunovskii refused:

> Before I could say those last words, punches rained on my left cheek. Letayev was of medium height but powerfully built, and his blows were so strong that I could not keep my place. . . . My firm categorical refusal awakened the wild beast within him. He began kicking me with his booted foot, blow after blow, right between my legs. The pain was unbearable. I felt I was just at the point where one more blow would mean death. Everyone knows that this is the most sensitive part of a man's body, where one well-aimed blow can kill him. Tears were flowing from my eyes. Instinctively I took my cap and tried to cover the part of my body he was kicking; but Letayev was savage and agile, and that defense did not stop him. He hit the spot he wanted with a well-aimed kick from below. Several times his boot struck my hands, with which I tried to cover myself, and they started bleeding. I thought the sight of blood would stop him, but it only delighted the beast that had awakened within that man. Without the slightest embarrassment, he kept on kicking me with all his might.

Dragunovskii still refused to sign, at which point they took his brother into the next room, where they beat him into unconsciousness while forcing Iakov to listen.

Still, Dragunovskii was lucky. Only days later, he wrote his parents a letter from his prison cell as he watched condemned prisoners brought into the courtyard:

> Oh, horror—not joy but grief and madness! Either I myself have gone so crazy that I feel this way and feel so horrified, or else those who are bringing on these horrors have gone crazy.
>
> There they have been taken out, all fourteen men—four for banditism and ten for refusing to go to war, condemned to death for refusing to kill people, for their purely human feeling of kindness, because they cannot cause harm and do evil to others. All those living men have walked off on their own feet to the pits that have been prepared for them. They will see with their own kindly, intelligent eyes the bed that has been prepared in the damp earth for their bodies. And with their souls and minds, they feel that they have sacrificed themselves in the cause of love. . . .
>
> Their case was up before the People's Court, and testimony had been received from the United Council in Moscow confirming the sincerity of their convictions. Yeliseyev had even been sentenced by the People's Court to some sort of prison term, but just the same they were all condemned as deserters and shot.
>
> I cannot write any more. If I remain alive, I will write in more detail.[134]

Iakov did remain alive, but his 19-year-old cousin Semen did not. Despite an attestation from the United Council and a stay of execution signed by Lenin himself, he was executed in Smolensk province shortly after throwing a letter to his parents out the prison window that read, in part: "Forgive them, for they know not what they do . . . I suffer in the name of Christ—Death is not terrible to me—just very sad."[135]

Cases like these are indicative not only of the orgy of violence that consumed Russia during the Civil War, but also of the powerful feeling that failure to serve in the army, no matter the reason, was an act of treason. Throughout the correspondence of local officials, both military and civilian, appear comments that the conscientious objectors were "shirkers" or "counterrevolutionaries." The conviction that the performance of violence was necessary for men to belong to the political community, in other words, was stronger even than the direct orders of central authorities. Not even Lenin and Rattel' could stop the brutal retribution against conscientious objectors that occurred during the war.

Furthermore, as the war progressed, the idea that the Bolsheviks could coexist with a band of nonviolent fellow travelers began to seem more and more ludicrous. This became clear at the Seventh Congress of Soviets in late 1919, when Ivan Tregubov, a leading Tolstoian, got up to speak. He began his speech by noting that, though he had planned to give a lengthy description of how pacifist sectarians had built communism under the tsarist regime, the congress organizers had restricted the amount of time he would be allowed to speak. He limited himself to saying that "we communist sec-tarians congratulate you for the great and sacred business that you are com-pleting, that you are serving, and that we also serve." Sectarians would not only not be hindrances in the future, but were prepared to offer help. "Sec-tarian communists," he concluded, "consider it our duty to form a party of sectarian-communists or a party of peaceful communists, because that agrees with our convictions." The assembled delegates laughed out loud and began making a commotion at this statement, prompting a hurt Tregubov to snap back: "I asked you earlier not to judge us, but it's like that laughter itself judges us, we don't judge you, you act according to your convictions, we would like to act according to ours."[136] Seconds later, Tregubov was hooted off the stage.

The end of the Civil War brought two major changes for conscientious objectors. The first one was positive: the military tribunals and bands of armed men seeking conscripts by hook or by crook no longer bothered them, and their petitions for exemption were far more likely to be ad-dressed through legal channels. The second development, unfortunately, was that those channels were progressively narrowing under the pressure of the Commissariat of Justice.

The first move to restrict the 1919 conscientious objection decree came in March 1921, when the Cheka brought a case of a "political character"[137] against the United Council. The United Council members were accused of testifying to the sincerity of a claim of a Red Army deserter named Bocharov that "did not correspond to reality." Bocharov himself was the main witness for the prosecution. He admitted that, being "cowardly by na-ture," he had sought an attestation for purely "personal reasons" and claimed to have been reformed by obtaining a "proletarian revolutionary consciousness."

The court then proceeded to the real reason the trial had taken place by noting that Bocharov's case was "organically linked to the whole structure and spirit of the activities of the United Council as a whole," because the "anarcho-religious organzation" of the United Council could not distin-guish between "true believers" and "the mass of shirkers and deserters." Since the mistaken attestation was the result of the "structure" of the United Council, however, none of the accused, the repentant Bocharov in-cluded, were to be punished personally.[138]

The process of depriving the United Council of its power began with a December 1920 decree mandating that the conscientious objection claims be substantiated with a local witness, and taking the formal role of the United Council away.[139] It was completed with the public discrediting of Shokhor-Trotskii and other top members of the United Council, which Chertkov described as a "declaration of war" against Russian sectarians.[140] The message was heard loud and clear. Less than five months later, the 1919 law was circumscribed further by the Commissariat of Justice in a cir-cular written by Krasikov.

In the circular, Krasikov affirmed that religious groups had no juridical status and no right to give out mandates or attestations. It further stated the problem in terms that the Provisional Government's Department of Spiritual Affairs would instantly have recognized: "no one may, by alluding to his religious conviction, evade the performance of his civic responsibilities." But, since the 1919 law was still in force and conscientious objection was officially approved, Krasikov also admitted that "peasant communist formations built and persecuted under tsarism" were "painlessly" conforming to "civic Soviet laws." Sects were "organically" moving as cells into Soviet construction, "notwithstanding the fact that their communist strivings, because of historical circumstances, are clothed in religious form. The task of Soviet organs in connection with these organizations primarily consists in developing and strengthening these communist organizations."[141] This argument, long the mainstay of the prosectarian Bolsheviks, was adopted by the most antisectarian wing at this juncture in a very sly fashion, for by reaffirming both the impossibility for citizens to evade their responsibilities and the need for the party to develop certain preexisting religious communities that had been "persecuted under tsarism," Krasikov was subtly changing the basis for the conscientious objection decree. No longer was the exemption given by virtue of a personal moral stance against violence, but by virtue of belonging to a previously persecuted and "organically" communist group.

The thin edge of the wedge had been inserted; in November 1923, with Lenin and Bonch-Bruevich effectively out of politics, and just in time for the first peacetime draft in the Soviet Union, the process was completed. Again the vehicle was a circular from the Commissariat of Justice. The circular destroyed the 1919 law by declaring that all provincial courts, when deciding conscientious objector cases, had to take into account only one fact: whether the accused belonged to a sect that had rejected military service under the tsarist regime. It then enumerated those sects. Henceforth, only Dukhobors, Mennonites, Molokans, and Netovtsy would be allowed to claim conscientious objector status.[142] The moral basis of conscientious objection had been definitively overturned, and in the future exemptions were to be granted only to specific groups. Those sects, according to theory, would rather swiftly melt away as they gained "true" consciousness, leaving their religious prejudices behind and rendering the very need for a conscientious objector law obsolete.

Thus, in a fashion very similar to the way the policy toward ethnic minorities in the army was constructed (also in 1923), the moral opposition to violence was defined as a temporarily legitimate but clearly delimited "leftover" from the oppressive tsarist past. The solution to dealing with these leftovers was the same: to let them exercise the rights denied them by the tsars and patiently wait for them to merge into the Soviet whole. From 1923 forward, however, ethnic minorities fared considerably better than pacifist sects. Whereas ethnic belonging became more and more respectable, the situation of sectarians declined rapidly. The upheavals of the country's Cultural Revolution and collectivization hit sectarian groups particularly hard, and state policymakers decided that patience with pacifism was no longer desirable or necessary. The provisions for conscientious objection in the 1925 conscription law (which reaffirmed the basis of the 1923 circular) were short-lived. In 1939, the newly revised conscription law contained no provision for conscientious objection, as state officials declared that no one had applied for an exemption in recent years.[143] The final merging, at least in rhetoric, had taken place. The strand of nonviolent thought in the nation had run its course, and the "natural" basis for belonging now universally included the willingness to perform violence.

In practice, however, pacifists had not been converted but had been obliterated. Sectarian communes suffered grievous losses during collectivization. Those that remained were finished off during the Great Terror. By 1939, most pacifists were either dead or dispersed and forced into silence. Those who still courageously refused to enter the army were sent to labor camps in the last few years before World War II. During the war itself, they were simply shot.[144] The ideology of nonviolence would not make its presence felt again on the national stage until the disastrous wars in Afghanistan and Chechnia were underway and the concomitant weakening of state power had opened up a new space for it to return to once again.

Conclusion

Violence loomed large in the imaginings and practices of the national political community. That there was a strand of national thinking and action that saw the performance of violence as central to citizenship seems fairly clear. Otherwise why the fuss over conscientious objectors, who repeatedly stated that they were willing to do "anything" to support the national regime other than commit violence and that, in Petr Bugaev's words, they wished to be citizens of the nation? The answer was quite explicit, both before and after the Bolshevik revolution: citizens with equal rights had to have equal duties, and the primary duty was to perform military service "with rifle in hand."

Throughout the period, there was also a countercurrent that respected the Christian concept of nonviolence and believed that freedom of conscience was compatible with the national order. That respect was really only dominant for a small group of elites: pacifist leaders on the one hand and liberals on the other. But other groups, including most of the military leadership, were willing to allow temporary manifestations of the freedom of conscience, either for political and economic goals (garnering the support of sectarians) or for military ones (preventing a small number of bad apples from ruining the barrel). In the tsarist period, intolerance and fierce punishment of conscientious objection was the official policy, but the strength of the countercurrent grew nevertheless. In the Bolshevik period, a general consensus that patience and accommodation with pacifists was in the general interest of the regime was reached by high party and military leaders, but this shift at the top was powerless to prevent the policies of intolerance toward nonviolence from dominating the halls of the Commissariat of Justice and the bloody offices and courtyards of men with guns in the provinces. When Lenin became incapacitated and Bonch-Bruevich faded from view, the consensus disappeared, putting policy decisions in the hands of the faction of intolerance and leaving conscientious objectors unprotected from the storms of the next twenty years.

Regardless of the fate of the small minority of conscientious objectors, however, the majority of conscripts throughout the period learned that committing violence was a central precondition for being a citizen and a man. State and military authorities uniformly wanted them to understand that violence within the discursive framework they had so painstakingly constructed and energetically propagandized was an act of virtue in certain situations and of debauchery, disorder, and counterrevolution in others.

Though soldiers and citizens incorporated violence into the construction of their political community, and indeed into the construction of their own subjectivity, they did not incorporate the imagined violence of the political scions, but rather a mixture of that discursive violence and the violence they had experienced and practiced. The violence of the virtuous bayonet charge was combined with the kicks to the groin in a dingy local party office. The cleansing of evil was combined with the beating of bad peasant cooks. The virile beauty of a cavalry charge was combined with the whipping of small children who refused to evacuate their own homes. It was this combination of legitimacy and brutality that was permanently impressed into the psyches of those who survived the Great War and the Civil War, that became a constitutive part of Russian and Soviet society and political practice, and that exercised immense influence on the bloody political future and political practices of the ensuing years.

Conclusion

The distinguished British historian Geoffrey Hosking, at the outset of his recent book *Russia: People and Empire*, makes a familiar distinction between the two Russian words for "Russia." The word *Rossiia*, he claims, denoted not only the empire but also the alien state; it was "cosmopolitan, secular, and *pace* grammarians, masculine." *Rus'*, on the other hand, was the people; it was "humble, homely, sacred, and definitely feminine." Given these definitions, it is hardly surprising that the story Hosking tells of the relationship between empire and nation and between state and people is an antagonistic one. In Russia, at least, "the building of an empire impeded the formation of a nation." This failure at nation building had baneful consequences in Hosking's account. Since the nation was the "most effective political unit" in the modern era, one that was "compatible with creating and sustaining a feeling of community and solidarity, such as induces loyalty and reduces the need for coercion," the inability of Russians to consolidate their nation made their evolution more "unstable, polarized, and violent."[1]

Hosking's account is in many respects persuasive. His framework easily accommodates an exposition of some of the great themes of Russian history, such as the split between a westernized state elite and the "people," the inconsistent and troubling relationship between center and periphery, and the increasing anachronism of Russia's political institutions in the late nineteenth and early twentieth centuries. Hosking's analysis is notable for its erudition and its clarity; it lays out the basic case that the tragedy of modern Russia was the consequence of healthy sociological developments retarded by inappropriate political forces. Elite politicians stunted the normal development of Russian society. As a result, when the bracing waves of modern mass economies, mass militaries, and mass societies washed over the Russian landscape the result was disintegration rather than integration.

My argument with Hosking's analysis is not so much with his account of Russian social development as with his assumption that the key to the phenomenon of the nation lies in the realm of social and cultural solidarity. This assumption, which is shared by most national-ists and nation-builders, is not supported by the historical record. If nations are marked by greater degrees of solidarity and therefore reduce the "need for coercion," then we can expect that nation-states will be significantly less prone to civil strife than other kinds of states. But the modern era tells quite a different story, a story of endemic violence and endemic instability in nation-states and nationalizing states. The democratization of the copro-duction of politics and violence has led to the transformation of "imperial-ist wars to civil wars," though not at all in the way that Lenin hoped when he called for this transformation in 1915. In places where affluence has not mercifully dulled the edge of politics, the sparks of international conflict have blown up into firestorms of internecine violence before burning themselves out. Eager civil warriors have emerged nearly everywhere that national mass politics has. Their graves and the graves of their victims blan-ket the globe, from Gettysburg to Belfast, from Kampala to Delhi, from San Salvador to St. Petersburg. If the nation is the answer to the question, "How do we create social solidarity in the modern world?" then the nation is a failed project, not just in Russia but virtually everywhere.

The nation instead answers a different question: "How do we create po-litical authority in the modern world?" It is the rupture of political relation-ships that the nation mainly addresses. The national ideology was part of the broader "authoritarian response" to the emergence of modern individu-alism and mass politics occasioned by the Enlightenment and the revolu-tionary era.[2] The articulation of the nation throughout Europe, though founded on the egalitarian bases promoted by mainstream Enlightenment thinkers, was in essence conducted by men who wished to restore a single source or "author" of power.

The Enlightenment had upset those with an authoritarian bent primar-ily because it attacked the underpinnings of absolutist thought by defocus-ing power, by claiming that power welled from individuals who were en-dowed with worth and with definable rights.[3] Thus the Enlightenment entailed a full reconceptualization, not only of man as an ideal but also of men as they actually existed: dirty, lice-ridden, and illiterate. Modern poli-tics and modern social science came into the world hand in hand. This was a permanent shift. Europe never returned to a *status quo ante revolution*. Au-thoritarians, in order to respond, had therefore a seemingly impossible task, to sew together the rich tapestry of their cherished unitary authority and the varied coarse cloth of Enlightened demotic individualism. Against the odds, they succeeded all across Europe, starting in France in the Napoleonic Era and ending in Russia during World War I. The thread that held these two fabrics together was the nation, and violence was the needle that did the stitching.

Russia's twentieth century cannot be understood without taking this na-tional stitching project into account. It is of course hardly new to point out that the Soviet system that defined Russia's twentieth century mixed coarse populism with firm authoritarianism. Indeed, one could argue that it is precisely this seemingly paradoxical combination that has defined the agenda for Soviet history as a whole. On the left, the question of how (social) democrats became authoritarian has consumed historians from Trotskii forward. On the right, a great deal of attention has been paid to the early development of Bolshevism explicitly in order to show that social democrats were *always* authoritarian. For both camps, it has been communism, not nationalism, that has been on trial.

As a result, studies of prerevolutionary authoritarian thought and prerevolutionary authoritarians have generally been consigned to the category of "the road not taken," a sort of scholarly scavenging from the dustbin of history. My argument, quite to the contrary, is that the position of those making an "authoritarian response" was a road that *was* taken, not only in the late imperial period, but indeed straight through the rest of the twentieth century. In short, it is important to know not only how and why democrats became authoritarian but also how and why authoritarians became democrats.

The process of authoritarians in the military turning their "face to the people" began within small circles of modernizing officers in the first half of the nineteenth century, but it really took off only when these reformers were able to exert control over institutional structures in the period of the Great Reforms. Conscription and training organs were particularly important in this regard. In a few short years, modernizing reformers completely transformed the nature of military training and conscription under Dmitrii Miliutin and Mikhail Dragomirov. Together they introduced the notion that modern armies had to be national armies that both protected and drew their strength from the common people at the heart of every nation. The figure of the citizen-soldier and the national army coalesced quite quickly. Before long, not only popular response but also state policy was reoriented along a radically new axis. The "general" and "personal" obligation to perform military service as a civic duty was established formally, and the volume of draft correspondence shows that this obligation was taken quite seriously by Russian citizens. Military planners, meanwhile, had already identified national security (rather than duty to the tsar) as their primary professional and civic obligation by the end of the 1870s, with consequences that were both subversive to the autocracy and devastating for the country as a whole.[4]

Overall, however, this was a partial transformation. Military modernizers were still outnumbered in state circles. Particularly after the ascension of Alexander III to the throne, state officials in other crucial ministries (especially the Ministry of Internal Affairs) were determinedly conservative and hostile to the mobilizational dreams of military intellectuals. Even in the heyday of the reformers, Miliutin had to make significant concessions when drafting the new military service law. The vast slew of exemptions that Miliutin intended to be "temporary" in 1874 remained virtually untouched after he left office. Conservative officials and the exempt populations themselves grew used to the byzantine regulations and took them to be permanent. The inconsistent hybrid of an inefficient autocratic government with an imperfectly national army combined the worst of both worlds. In 1905, military and state officials alike blanched at the rout that the Russian army suffered at Japanese hands, which seemed to show that the Miliutin/Dragomirov system had failed to produce citizen-soldiers with initiative and enthusiasm. Later that year and into 1906, popular rebellion and military mutiny seemed to show quite the opposite. Perhaps initiative and enthusiasm could be overdone. As I argued in chapter 1, the combined impact of war and revolution made the post–1905 battle lines between modernizers and conservatives quite clear, and the battle took on institutional form. The General Staff clashed with the Ministry of Internal Affairs repeatedly over the next decade. Both sets of officials were authoritarian, but the General Staff appealed to the authority of the nation while the Ministry of Internal Affairs appealed to the authority of the tsar.

World War I dramatically resolved this contradiction in all but the most formal sense. The year 1914 proved to be a watershed moment, the moment when the defining attributes of the nation crystallized. Institutionally, it was the moment when all the accrued impediments to a national system melted away in the heat of mobilization. Entire categories of exemption dissolved instantly, and those that survived either succumbed in the next major wave of mobilization in 1915 or became an item of intense political contestation at all levels of society. Restrictions on the activities of youth training organizations were replaced by government subsidies to those groups. Women and men throughout the land were encouraged to become active parts of the war effort as soldiers and nurses, as voluntary workers in social service organizations, or as civic producers in the fields and factories of the motherland. War bond campaigns and special fund drives for war victims called upon Russians to do their part as responsible citizens in any way they could. In 1915, Nicholas II made one last conservative attempt to stem this wave of public activism by assuming personal command of the army, proroguing the Duma, dismissing moderate ministers, and harassing public organizations. But his desperate move did not stem the tide of the public activism. It simply snapped the thin threads that still tied him and his court to the rest of Russia.

The war was important in another crucial respect. National processes of population categorization came to the fore. As I noted in chapter 2, the varied notions of estate, religion, class, and ethnicity existed in a very complicated relationship prior to 1914. Estate and religion as population markers were important for traditionalists. The imperial, the conservative (or simply the prudent) shied away from attempts to clearly define the boundaries of the nation and to mobilize citizens on the basis of the "new" ascribed population categories of ethnicity and class. In World War I, the traditionalists and conservatives were brushed aside, while the imperial and prudent were overwhelmed. Ethnic units were instantly created as vehicles of mobilization and of "natural" cohesion. Ethnic groups were targeted as bases of support or as victims of persecution on the basis of generalized assumptions about their "natural" behavior or "natural" political predilections. Thus, in 1914, Habsburg Galicians and Poles on all sides of the partition line were targeted as potential allies and given their own units and training in their own languages. Muslims in the Caucasus were tabbed as natural warriors and brought into the army as volunteers soon after the war broke out and were conscripted in 1916. Germans in Moscow had their property and persons destroyed in a massive pogrom in 1915, while Jews suffered both officially sponsored and popular persecution throughout the years of war.[5]

This *process* of categorization (though not always the specific categories themselves) remained in place throughout the Civil War and beyond. Bolshevik officials used class as their primary national category and acted upon their populations according to similarly superficial assumptions about "natural" behaviors and political loyalties. They created national pariahs on a class basis and defined their class nation "inclusively" by attempting to subsume several different Marxist classes under the rubric of "toiler," just as prerevolutionary officials had attempted to bring many different ethnic groups under the umbrella designation of "Russian" *(Rossiiskii)*.

The process of sharp differentiation conflicted with the desire for widespread inclusivity. By defining enemies through naturalized population categories, state officials produced a great deal of mobilizational power. But using those same categories to define inclusion in the nation was at best awkward and at worst impossible. Multiethnic/multi-class nationalists talked and mobilized as if all included groups were included equally. But were Georgians and Russians equally "Russian"? Were factory workers and homestead- owning peasants equal "toilers"? Rhetorically yes, viscerally no.

So if naturalized population categories were awkward to use, how could "positive" national cohesion be built and maintained, both in the ranks and in civilian life? The answer emerged during a period of trial and error, as signals "from below" mixed with mobilizational campaigns "from above." In the end, though, it became clear that the most resonant mobilizational themes were the ones that drew upon local affinities and defined them more broadly. Most of these local affinities were centered around certain ideals of masculine duty, in particular the idea that men had to defend their land and their women in concert with their brothers. This broadening of affinities and priorities defined the national project in both World War I and the Civil War.

At the same time, the notion of masculinity itself was undergoing a dramatic change. As before, true men were to defend their land and family to the last drop of blood. But in other respects, what it meant to be a man was definitively transformed. The most striking aspect of the change was generational. The gender structure in Russia ceased to be patriarchal in the years of war and became aggressively fraternal. Youngsters were to develop the lithe and muscular bodies thought to be essential for the moral quali- ties of aggressive, independent, yet restrained, "new" men. The combina- tion of strength and discipline, initiative and restraint, were the hallmarks of the citizen-soldier, who could flow effortlessly from the workbench to the front and back again, supporting (indeed constituting) the civic com- munity in peace and in war.

As the history of nations and nationalism attests, the institutions, processes, and ideas that I am describing have proved incredibly resonant and powerful throughout the modern world, and so they were in twentieth- century Russia as well. The nation links the local with the general, the indi- vidual with the universal, today with yesterday and tomorrow. It allows for mass politics while retaining the seductive promise of authoritarian control over the centrifugal tendencies of the "mob." The nation is flexible and adaptable. The categories of inclusion and exclusion can change (if only slowly), and the firmness of those categorical boundaries and the conse- quences of being on one side or the other can vary in severity. It allows for individual initiative and provides structures of discipline. It permits public mobilization combined with state control.

All of these improbable connections are made not simply through the transformation of imagination, or by institutions that link the state and the citizenry, or even through the social-scientific processes of population cate- gorization, but through the practices of national citizens. As I stressed in chapter 5, the central national practice is the performance of violence. Mili- tary trainers tried to circumscribe and contain acts of violence in a hierar- chical system of discipline. In this manner, both military and political offi- cials hoped to stabilize this crucial civic act and thereby to stabilize the political community as well.

But violence was not (and could not be) contained by discursive or ideo- logical structures. Violence begun within the framework of civic belonging and disciplined order swiftly flowed over the ideological banks, flooding Russia with murder, rape, brigandage, and pure sadism for a ten-year pe- riod. Thus the principal promise of the nation, the promise of simultaneous equality and order, was subverted by the central practice of the nation. If there was one thing people agreed upon in 1917, it was that disorder reigned. For many authoritarians in the military, 1917 had demonstrated that equality and order could not coexist, at least not in Russia at that time. Given the choice, nearly all of these good authoritarians chose order, though they differed in their assessment of what would bring order about in the shortest period of time. Some went into open opposition and tried to overthrow the communists, while others joined Lenin's party because, in the words of General Mikhail Bonch-Bruevich, it was "the only force capa- ble of saving Russia from collapse and complete destruction."[6]

The new Bolshevik leaders were also profoundly disturbed by the explo- sion of undisciplined violence. The question of how to organize and discipline violence was central for them throughout the Civil War (and of course well beyond). Their consistent answer to this vexing problem was to organize and discipline violence in an expressly national way, mimicking the institutions, "population politics," and mobilizational themes developed by nationalist military officials in the last years of Romanov rule. In so doing, they did much more than simply hire a few ultimately disposable "military specialists." They incorporated the national political framework within the broader spectrum of ideologies through which they communicated and negotiated power with their citizens. Once that ideology was deployed and once citizens engaged with it, it became part of the political identification process. Citizens may very well have engaged explicitly with the anti-capitalist ideology of production and consumption that the Bolsheviks deployed by "speaking Bolshevik,"[7] but they also engaged explicitly with the nationalist ideology of violence. There was no contradiction between these two processes. The combination of total war and communist revolution produced a composite political framework that differed in many significant ways from other political frameworks in the world. This framework, however, was not sui generis and incommensurable. The Soviet nation may have been unhappy in its own way, but it was still a nation in the bigger family of nations.

More precisely, it was a nation-state. If Max Weber was right to define a state as "a compulsory political association with continuous organization [whose] administrative staff successfully upholds a claim to the monopoly of the legitimate use of physical force in the enforcement of its order,"[8] then we should conclude that a nation-state belongs to that subset of compulsory political associations that legitimate the production of violence nationally. This indicates, among other things, a reciprocal relationship between states and nations. States organize nations (or whatever other kind of state they may be) more through the way they organize violence than in the way they educate children or provide for economic trading zones or facilitate the development of a penny press. The national move on the part of the state is to make the performance of violence a constitutive civic act while making the state the only body that can legitimize such acts. In this way, the nexus between the state and the nation is always the performance of violence. As a result, the nation is fundamentally and unavoidably unstable as a political form, since it is centered upon a civic act that cannot be effectively disciplined.

I wish that I could conclude that the political instability of the nation marked it as a temporary phenomenon or that the recent slew of insights into nationalism indicates the arrival of the wise owl of Minerva heralding the "dusk" of the national era, as Eric Hobsbawm has optimistically written.[9] The record of the twentieth century cannot sustain this optimism, however. Individuals and societies seem capable of existing for long periods of time in conditions of volatility and of erupting into violence even after long periods of dormancy. The volcanos of our era remain quite active.

The volatility remains because the problem of national violence cannot be solved within the national form itself. It is even hard to see how such forces as economic globalization might denationalize violence in the foreseeable future. The nationalization of masculinity, of the family, of the land, and of the local community means that any turn away from the nation must entail a restructuring not only of state borders but of "modern" men and women in their deepest forms of identity. The violence at the heart of these identities and social relationships is hidden in plain view. It is hidden in the monumentalization of war heroes, hidden in the kitchen-table instructions to young boys to protect their wives, families, homes, and nation, hidden in the figure of the citizen-soldier. But the violence is there, latent, reproduced daily, and ready for the next spark. Even if the owl of Minerva is flying at the dusk of nationalism, she does not promise the dawn of something better.

Notes

Introduction

1. *Polnoe sobranie zakonov Rossiiskoi imperii,* 2nd series, no. 52982 (1 January 1874).

2. On this view in the early modern period and beyond, see J. G. Pocock, *The Machiavellian Moment: Florentine Political Thought and the Atlantic Republican Tradition* (Princeton: Princeton University Press, 1975).

3. Richard B. Sher, "Adam Ferguson, Adam Smith, and the Problem of National Defense," *Journal of Modern History* 61, no. 2 (June 1989): 240–68; Orville T. Murphy, "The American Revolutionary Army and the Concept of Levée en Masse," *Military Affairs* 23, no. 1 (Spring 1959): 20.

4. See discussion in Linda K. Kerber, "May All Our Citizens Be Soldiers and All Our Soldiers Citizens: The Ambiguities of Female Citizenship in the New Nation," in *Women, Militarism, and War: Essays in History, Politics, and Social Theory,* ed. Jean Bethke Elshtain and Sheila Tobias (Savage, Md.: Rowman and Littlefield, 1990): 89–103.

5. Meyer Kestnbaum, "Citizenship and Compulsory Military Service: The Revolutionary Origins of Conscription in the United States," *Armed Forces and Society* 27, no. 1 (Fall 2000): 7–36.

6. Simon Schama, *Citizens: A Chronicle of the French Revolution* (New York: Knopf, 1989), 640.

7. John Hall Stewart, ed., *A Documentary Survey of the French Revolution* (New York: Macmillan, 1951), 472–74.

8. See Daniel Moran, "Arms and the Concert: The Nation in Arms and the Dilemmas of German Liberalism," in *The People in Arms: Military Myth and National Mobilization Since the French Revolution,* ed. Daniel Moran and Arthur Waldron (Cambridge: Cambridge University Press, 2002).

9. Holger Afflerbach, "'Bis zum letzten Mann und letzten Groschen?' Die Wehrpflicht im Deutschen Reich und ihre Auswirkungen auf das militärische Führungsdenken im Ersten Weltkrieg," in *Die Wehrpflicht: Entstehung, Erscheinungsformen und politisch-militärische Wirkung* (Munich: R. Oldenbourg Verlag, 1994), 89.

10. Peter Paret, *Understanding War: Essays on Clausewitz and the History of Military Power* (Princeton: Princeton University Press, 1992), 69.

11. On this process, see Barry R. Posen, "Nationalism, the Mass Army, and Military Power," *International Security* 18, no. 2 (Autumn 1993): 80–124.

12. David Saunders, *Russia in the Age of Reaction and Reform, 1801–1881* (London and New York: Longman, 1992).

13. See Frederick W. Kagan, *The Military Reforms of Nicholas I: The Origins of the Modern Russian Army* (New York: St. Martin's, 1999).

14. Cited in P. A. Zaionchkovskii, *Voennye reformy 1860–1870 godov v Rossii* (Moscow: Izdatel'stvo Moskovskogo Universiteta, 1952), 49–50.

15. The best book on the military reforms is Zaionchkovskii's, but there are several excellent works in English as well. See Robert F. Baumann, "The Debates over Universal Military Service in Russia, 1870–1874" (Ph.D. diss., Yale University, 1983); E. Willis Brooks, "Reform in the Russian Army, 1856–1861," *Slavic Review* 43, no. 1 (1984): 63–82; Forrestt A. Miller, *Dmitrii Miliutin and the Reform Era in Russia* ([Nashville], Tenn.: Vanderbilt University Press, 1968).

16. Paret, *Understanding War*, 41, 44.

17. M. I. Dragomirov, "Vliianie rasprostraneniia nareznogo oruzhiia na vospitanie i taktiku voisk," in *Sbornik original'nykh i perevodnykh statei, 1858–1880* (St. Petersburg: Balashev, 1881), 1:31.

18. On status in Russia, see Peter von Wahlde, "Military Thought in Imperial Russia," (Ph.D. diss., Indiana University, 1966), 117–22; Bruce Menning, *Bayonets Before Bullets: The Imperial Russian Army, 1861–1914* (Bloomington and Indianapolis: Indiana University Press, 1992), especially chap. 1, "The Army of D. A. Miliutin and M. I. Dragomirov." On international reputation, see Azar Gat, *The Development of Military Thought: The Nineteenth Century* (Oxford: Clarendon Press, 1992), 139–40.

19. This was a pan-European understanding as well. To place Russian thought on this question within the European context, see S. Kozlov, "Voennaia nauka i voennye doktriny v pervoi mirovoi voine," *Voenno-istoricheskii zhurnal* 6, no. 11 (1964): 31–41.

20. E. I. Martynov, *Strategiia v epokhu Napoleona I i v nashe vremia* (St. Petersburg: Voennaia tipografiia, 1894), 35, 283.

21. On the rise of military statistics and ethnicity as a component of those statistics, see David Alan Rich, *The Tsar's Colonels: Professionalism, Strategy, and Subversion in Late Imperial Russia* (Cambridge: Harvard University Press, 1998). See also Peter Holquist, "To Count, To Extract, and To Exterminate: Population Statistics and Population Politics in Late Imperial and Soviet Russia," in *A State of Nations: Empire and Nation-Making in the Age of Lenin and Stalin*, ed. Ronald Grigor Suny and Terry Martin (New York and Oxford: Oxford University Press, 2001), 111–44.

22. N. P. Mikhnevich, *Osnovy russkogo voennogo iskusstva: Sravnitelnyi ocherk sostoianiia voennago iskusstva v Rossii i Zapadnoi Evrope v vazhneishiia istoricheskiia epokhi* (St. Petersburg: Tip. Shtaba otdielnogo korpusa pogranichnoi strazhi, 1898), 172.

23. For an early and influential articulation of this idea, see Chaadaev's 1836 First Philosophical Letter. Peter Yakovlevich Chaadayev, *Philosophical Letters and Apology of a Madman*, trans. Mary-Barbara Zeldin (Knoxville: University of Tennessee Press, 1969).

24. The standard used was "mother tongue." In 1897, 55,667,469 people were classified as Russian, 22,380,551 as Ukrainian, and 5,885,548 as Belorussian of a total imperial population of 125,640,021. Extensive statistics on nationality from the 1897 census are available in Henning Bauer, Andreas Kappeler, and Brigitte Roth, eds., *Die Nationalitäten des Russischen Reiches in der Volkszählung von 1897* (Stuttgart: Franz Steiner, 1991). Statistics cited here in volume B, 73.

25. The file containing this correspondence is RGVIA, f. 2000, op. 3, d. 88.

26. D. A. Miliutin, "O glavnykh osnovaniakh lichnoi voennoi povinnosti," RGIA, f. 906, op. 1, d. 28, ll. 35–36, quoted in Robert F. Baumann, "Universal Service Reform and Russia's Imperial Dilemma," *War and Society* 4, no. 2 (September 1986): 31.

27. Mark von Hagen has been most explicit about this project of the 1920s. See his *Soldiers in the Proletarian Dictatorship: The Red Army and the Soviet Socialist State, 1917–1930* (Ithaca, N.Y.: Cornell University Press, 1990). The metaphor of the

army as the "school of the nation" predated the Bolsheviks, however. See for instance, Aleksandr Neznamov, *Oboronitel'naia voina (teoriia voprosa). Chast' 1: Strategiia* (St. Petersburg: Izd. Nikolaevskoi akademii General'nogo Shtaba, 1909), 219.

28. von Wahlde, "Military Thought," 212.

29. E. I. Martynov, "V chem sila Iaponii i slabost' Rossii?" in *". . . Khorosho zabytoe staroe": Sbornik statei*, ed. O. A. Bobrakov (essay, 1904; Moscow: Voenizdat, 1991): 8–9.

30. Martynov mentioned these works by name in his somber "Iz pechal'nogo opyta russko-iaponskoi voiny," in *"Khorosho zabytoe staroe,"* 62–63.

31. Donald P. Wright, "The Cultivation of Patriotism and the Militarization of Citizenship in Late Imperial Russia, 1906–1914" (Ph.D. diss., Tulane University, 2001). Thanks to Dr. Wright for letting me see parts of this work prior to its submission to University Microfilms.

32. Slavoj Zizek, *The Sublime Object of Ideology* (London and New York: Verso, 1989), 165. Emphasis in original.

33. For the former, Hobbes, Locke, and Rousseau serve as good examples. For the latter, Freud, Lacan, and Zizek.

34. More recently, see the influential work by Louis Althusser on this topic in his *Essays on Ideology* (London and New York: Verso, 1984).

35. See here, Stephen Kotkin, *Magnetic Mountain: Stalinism as a Civilization* (Berkeley: University of California Press, 1995), esp. 224–25.

36. Zizek, *Ideology*, 45.

37. Václav Havel, "The Power of the Powerless," in *Open Letters: Selected Writings, 1965–1990* (New York: Vintage, 1992), 125–214.

38. Rogers Brubaker, *Nationalism Reframed: Nationhood and the National Question in the New Europe* (Cambridge: Cambridge University Press, 1996), 17.

39. Benedict Anderson, *Imagined Communities: Reflections on the Origin and Spread of Nationalism*, rev. ed. (London and New York: Verso, 1991); Eugen Weber, *Peasants into Frenchmen: The Modernization of Rural France, 1870–1914* (Stanford: Stanford University Press, 1976); Hans Kohn, *The Idea of Nationalism: A Study of Its Origins and Background* (New York: Macmillan, 1944); Carlton J. H. Hayes, *The Historical Evolution of Modern Nationalism* (New York: R. R. Smith, 1931).

40. See here, for instance, John Plamenatz, "Two Types of Nationalism," in *Nationalism: The Nature and Evolution of an Idea*, ed. Eugene Kamenka (New York: St. Martin's, 1973), 23–36; Liah Greenfeld, *Nationalism: Five Roads to Modernity* (Cambridge: Harvard University Press, 1992); and Michael Ignatieff, *Blood and Belonging: Journeys into the New Nationalism* (New York: Farrar, Straus, and Giroux, 1994).

41. This is Johann Gottfried von Herder's influential vision, and it has had an immense impact on nationalists and scholars of nationalism alike. The question of whether modern nationalism is the logical outcome of Herder's principles or its corruption is hotly debated. The most famous investigation is Isaiah Berlin, *Vico and Herder: Two Studies in the History of Ideas* (New York: Viking, 1976). For the view that Herder was the logical precursor of modern nationalism, see Carlton J. H. Hayes, "Contributions of Herder to the Doctrine of Nationalism," *American Historical Review* 32, no. 4 (July 1927): 719–36.

42. Jürgen Habermas, *Between Facts and Norms: Contributions to a Discourse Theory of Law and Democracy,* trans. William Rehg (Cambridge: MIT Press, 1996), 500.

43. See here Gary Gerstle's subtle reading of nationalism in the United States in his *American Crucible: Race and Nation in the Twentieth Century* (Princeton: Princeton University Press, 2001).

44. See statistical tables in Joshua A. Sanborn, "Drafting the Nation: Military Conscription and the Formation of a Modern Polity in Tsarist and Soviet Russia, 1905–1925" (Ph.D. diss., University of Chicago, 1998), 541. These are literacy rates at the time of induction. Reading classes in the army itself meant that by the time a soldier left the army he was less likely to be illiterate.

45. See here Scott J. Seregny, "Zemstvos, Peasants, and Citizenship: The Russian Adult Education Movement and World War I," *Slavic Review* 59, no. 2 (Summer 2000): 290–315; Josh Sanborn, "Conscription, Correspondence, and Politics in Late Imperial Russia," *Russian History/Histoire Russe* 24, nos. 1–2 (Spring–Summer 1997): 27–40.

46. Andrew Verner, "Discursive Strategies in the 1905 Revolution: Peasant Petitions from Vladimir Province," *Russian Review* 54, no. 1 (January 1995): 65–90.

47. An excellent reminder of this fact is Michael Geyer's, "War and the Context of General History in an Age of Total War: Comment on Peter Paret, 'Justifying the Obligation of Military Service,' and Michael Howard, 'World War One: The Crisis in European History,'" *Journal of Military History* 57, special issue (October 1993): 145–63.

1: Forming the National Compact

1. Posen, "Nationalism, the Mass Army, and Military Power."

2. William C. Fuller, Jr., *Civil-Military Conflict in Imperial Russia, 1881–1914* (Princeton: Princeton University Press, 1985), 77 and passim.

3. See report from the troop commander of the Kazan' military district to the war minister, 8 January 1910, RGVIA, f. 2000, op. 3, d. 18, ll. 3–3ob; see also correspondence between Stolypin (minister of internal affairs) and Sukhomlinov (minister of war) in 1911 in RGVIA, f. 2000, op. 3, d. 33.

4. The following details regarding the military service code are taken from S. M. Gorianov and P. P. Lebedev, eds., *Ustavy o voinskoi povinnosti (Svod zakonov, tom 4, kniga 1, izd. 1897 g.), dopolnennye vsemi pozdneishimi uzakoneniiami po 1 iiunia 1913 g.,* 12th ed. (St. Petersburg: Berezovskii, 1913).

5. RGIA, f. 1292, op. 7, d. 522–25; RGVIA, f. 400, op. 19, d. 82, ll. 2–15ob.

6. On these denunciations, see Sanborn, "Conscription."

7. Letter from Anton Orliuk, peasant from Volodarka, to the war minister, 28 April 1910, RGVIA, f. 2000, op. 3, d. 75, l. 50.

8. Circular from MVD Conscription Administration to provincial governors, June 1912, RGVIA, f. 2000, op. 3, d. 3818, l. 103.

9. "O poriadke soobshcheniia ob uvol'nenii nizhnikh chinov po izmenivshemusia semeinomu polozheniiu," circular sent to military district chiefs of staff, 23 June 1910, RGVIA, f. 2000, op. 3, d. 76, l. 68.

10. RGVIA, f. 400, op. 19, d. 82, ll. 2–15ob.

11. For Nizhegorod cases, see report from commander (Col. Parskii) of the 140th Zaraiskii Infantry Regiment, 10 March 1910, RGVIA, f. 2000, op. 3, d. 137, ll. 2–3.

12. Letter from Lukomskii to MVD, 23 December 1910, RGVIA, f. 2000, op. 3, d. 137, ll. 11, 16.

13. In Vilna province alone, men were arrested for being "fixers" in three separate districts. Report of Vilna governor to the minister of internal affairs, 14 March 1914, RGVIA, f. 400, op. 19, d. 39, ll. 31–32; Report of the MVD Conscription Administration to the Main Staff, 25 August 1912, RGVIA, f. 2000, op. 3, d. 36, ll. 116; Report from commander of Vilna military district to the war minister (Rediger), 30 December 1908, RGVIA, f. 2000, op. 3, d. 76, l. 115.

14. "Ukomplektovanie nashei armii nizhnimi chinami," report of the Mobilization Department of the Main Staff signed by Major-General Lopushanskii, 13 August 1905, RGVIA, f. 2000, op. 1, d. 307, l. 1.

15. Anton I. Denikin, *The Career of a Tsarist Officer: Memoirs, 1872–1916,* trans. Margaret Patoski (Minneapolis: University of Minnesota Press, 1975), 179; Fuller, *Civil-Military Conflicet,* 197.

16. This sudden fear of national weakness and physical degeneracy was in fact widespread. Top leaders in both Great Britain and America, for instance, had similar anxieties in the first years of the twentieth century. See Joanna Bourke, *Dismembering the Male: Men's Bodies, Britain, and the Great War* (Chicago and London: University of Chicago Press, 1996), 171; Gerstle, *American Crucible,* 25.

17. See complaints in reports from military district commanders for the year 1908, compiled in RGVIA, f. 2000, op. 3, d. 125; statistic in RGVIA, f. 2000, op. 3, d. 71, l. 113.

18. "Kratkii otchet o chastnykh mobilizatsiiakh, proizvedennykh v Evropeiskoi Rossii v 1904/05 gg.," secret report from the Main Administration of the General Staff, 24 June 1906, RGVIA, f. 2000, op. 1, d. 309, ll. 56–57.

19. Authorization cited in letter from chairman of the State Council on Defense (Grand Duke Nikolai Nikolaevich) to the war minister (Rediger), 24 April 1908, RGVIA, f. 2000, op. 1, d. 67, l. 1.

20. "Voprosy, namechaemye dlia obsuzhdeniia v komissii po peresmotru ustava o voinskoi povinnosti," n.d., n.a., RGVIA, f. 2000, op. 3, d. 71, ll. 5–5ob. This agenda also included the question of drafting exempted ethnic groups, which was later deferred to the second round of reforms.

21. Informational report on work of the commission, signed by Lukomskii (hereafter, Lukomskii, Informational report), 19 December 1909, RGVIA, f. 2000, op. 3, d. 71, l. 17.

22. "Voprosy, namechaemye dlia obsuzhdeniia."

23. Lukomskii, Informational report, 19 December 1909, RGVIA f. 2000, op. 3, d. 71, ll. 17ob–19.

24. Report from the MVD Conscription Administration to the war minister, signed by Stolypin, countersigned by Kukol'-Iasnopol'skii, 27 March 1910, RGVIA, f. 2000, op. 3, d. 71, l. 254.

25. Ibid., ll. 254–55.

26. Speech of Deputy Sinadino at closed Duma session, 30 November 1911, RGVIA, f. 2000, op. 3, d. 79, l. 1154.

27. "Zakon ob izmenenii Ustava o Voinskoi Povinnosti," *Sobranie uzakonenii i rasporiazhenii pravitel'stva,* no. 1197 (9 July 1912).

28. A. S. Lukomskii, *Vospominaniia* (Berlin: Otto Kirchner, 1922), 1:26; secret letter from Palitsyn and Danilov to the war minister, 25 November 1905, RGVIA, f. 2000, op. 1, d. 307, l. 57.

29. They joined more than 1.4 million soldiers already on active duty. *Rossiia v mirovoi voine, 1914–1918 goda (v tsifrakh)* (Moscow: Gosizdat, 1925), 17.

30. For a more detailed description of the 1914 mobilization and the responses to it, see Josh Sanborn, "The Mobilization of 1914 and the Question of the Russian Nation: A Reexamination," *Slavic Review* 59, no. 2 (Summer 2000): 267–89.

31. A. Pireiko, *V tylu i na fronte imperialisticheskoi voiny: Vospominaniia riadovogo* (Leningrad: "Priboi," 1926), 9; daily reports of Plotsk district military commander, 17 July through 26 July 1914, GARF, f. 1745, op. 1, d. 58, ll. 370–421.

32. Nicholas N. Golovine, *The Russian Army in the World War* (New Haven: Yale

University Press, 1931), 204; Iu. N. Danilov, *Rossiia v mirovoi voine, 1914–1915 gg.* (Berlin: Slovo, 1924), 111; S. V. Dobrorol'ski, *Die Mobilmachung der russischen Armee 1914* (Berlin: Deutsche Verlagsgesellschaft für Politik und Geshchichte m.b.H., 1922), 33.

33. Telegram of the governor-general of the Steppe district to Sukhomlinov, 18 August 1914, RGVIA, f. 2000, op. 3, d. 1196, l. 93. See also Golovine, *Russian Army,* 204, for a similar interpretation of the riots.

34. Report of commander of Kazan' military district to the war minister, 8 January 1910, RGVIA, f. 2000, op. 3, d. 18, ll. 6–6ob.

35. Report of the chief of the Lugansk garrison to the war minister, 24 July 1914, RGVIA, f. 2000, op. 3, d. 1154, ll. 242–43.

36. Report of commander of Kazan' military district to war minister, 24 July 1914, RGVIA, f. 2000, op. 3, d. 1154, ll. 238–41.

37. Accounts of these events are collected in RGIA, f. 1292, op. 1, d. 1729, passim.

38. "Ukomplektovanie armii nizhnimi chinami," n.d., n.a., RGVIA, f. 2003, op. 2, d. 273, l. 123ob.; for argument that the crisis was a phenomenon of late 1916 and 1917, see L. M. Gavrilov and V. V. Kutuzov, "Istoshchenie liudskikh rezervov russkoi armii v 1917 g.," in *Pervaia mirovaia voina, 1914–1918,* ed. A. L. Sidorov (Moscow: Nauka, 1968), 145–57.

39. The thinking of conscription planners outlined below is contained in "Otchet o mobilizatsiiakh, proizvedennykh v techenie voiny 1914–1918 gg.," 11 June [1918(?)], n.a., RGVIA, f. 2000, op. 3, d. 4057, ll. 1–25ob.

40. A. N. Iakhontov, "Tiazhelye dni (Sekretnye zasedaniia Soveta Ministrov, 16 iiulia–2 sentiabria 1915 goda)," *Arkhiv russkoi revoliutsii* 18 (1926): 15–17.

41. Norman Stone, *The Eastern Front 1914–1917* (New York: Charles Scribner's Sons, 1975), 12–13.

42. See for instance the letter from Satterup (Mobilization Department) to the city chief of Petrograd, 3 December 1914, RGVIA, f. 2000, op. 3, d. 1170, l. 242.

43. Raymond Pearson, *The Russian Moderates and the Crisis of Tsarism, 1914–1917* (London: Macmillan, 1977), 47.

44. Ibid., 29.

45. Speech of Deputy Savenko in closed session of State Duma, 28 July 1915, RGIA, f. 1278, op. 5, d. 205, ll. 11–12.

46. See for instance the comments of Miliukov and Kerenskii, ibid., l. 83, 155.

47. Ibid., l. 113.

48. Report of B. A. Engel'gardt at meeting of committee of military affairs of the fourth session of Fourth Duma, secret, 9 August 1915, RGIA, f. 1278, op. 5, d. 447, l. 288.

49. Comment by Deputy Dziubinskii. Ibid., l. 289.

50. Comments of M. V. Rodzianko, N. V. Savich, N. N. Opochinin, and A. I. Shingarev. Ibid., ll. 289–90, 296.

51. Speech of Deputy Shingarev at closed session of Fourth Duma, 19 August 1915, RGIA, f. 1278, op. 5, d. 216, ll. 12, 14.

52. Ibid., ll. 20, 47, 73.

53. Letter from "Workers of the Donbass" to the minister of internal affairs, 1 September 1915, RGIA, f. 1292, op. 7, d. 298, ll. 122–122ob.

54. Public announcement by city chief of Petrograd, 4 September 1915, RGIA, f. 1292, op. 1, d. 1775, l. 84.

55. "Perechen' 'besporiadkov,' uchinennykh ratnikami 2–go razriada prizyva 5 sentiabria 1915 g., sostavlennyi v departamente politsii," secret, 2 November 1915, RGIA, f. 1292, op. 1, d. 1729, ll. 144–76.

56. "Kirgiz" was a blanket term used by tsarist authorities to describe many different peoples in Central Asia, in particular the peoples now referred to as "Kazakh" and "Kyrgyz."

57. Edward Dennis Sokol, *The Revolt of 1916 in Russian Central Asia,* The Johns Hopkins University Studies in Historical and Political Science, series 71, no. 1 (Baltimore: Johns Hopkins University Press, 1953), 84.

58. "'Takoe upravlenie gosudarstvom-nedopustimo': Doklad A. F. Kerenskogo na zakrytom zasedanii Gosudarstvennoi dumy. Dekabr' 1916 g.," *Istoricheskii arkhiv,* no. 2 (1997): 12; Martha Brill Olcott, *The Kazakhs,* 2nd ed. (Stanford: Hoover Institution Press, 1995), 120.

59. Sokol, *Revolt of 1916,* 84.

60. Ibid., 86–87; Olcott, *Kazakhs,* 120–21.

61. For a blow-by-blow account of the suppression of the rebellion, see G. Sapargaliev, *Karatel'naia politika tsarizma v Kazakhstane (1905–1917)* (Alma-Ata: Nauka, 1966), 297–373.

62. These statistics are taken from Sokol, *Revolt of 1916,* 158–60.

63. Pireiko, *V tylu i na fronte,* 17.

64. Ibid., 13–19.

65. Aleksandr Dneprovskii, *Zapiski dezertira, voina 1914–1918 gg.* (New York: Izd. "Albatros", 1931), 13.

66. Ibid., 39–54.

67. Telegram from Iaroslavl' governor to Conscription Administration of MVD, 31 May 1916, RGIA, f. 1292, op. 1, d. 2069, l. 1.

68. Account included in letter of the duty general of the General Staff to Dobrorol'skii, 6 September 1914, RGVIA, f. 2000, op. 3. d. 1159, l. 161.

69. On this, see circular from governor of Kiev province to the chief of police of Kiev province and the local justice of the peace *(mirovoi posrednik),* August 1916, RGVIA, f. 2067, op. 1, d. 3838, l. 130.

70. This is Allan Wildman's assessment. See his *The End of the Russian Imperial Army: The Old Army and the Soldiers' Revolt (March–April 1917)* (Princeton: Princeton University Press, 1980), 77.

71. Letter from Polivanov to Shcherbatov, 5 August 1915, RGVIA, f. 2000, op. 3, d. 1196, l. 91.

72. Letter from "wives of reservists," Tat'iana Iaremenko, Sinklatia Bozheiko, and Serafima Totskaia (from Radomysl'), to minister of internal affairs, 8 October 1915, RGIA, f. 1292, op. 7, d. 298, l. 125.

73. Letter from "a recruit of the Borovskii district draft board" to the Main Staff of the army, n.d. but early 1915, RGVIA, f. 400, op. 19, d. 147, l. 1.

74. Letter from "a peasant" to the war minister, 20 January 1915, RGVIA, f. 400, op. 19, d. 147, l. 5.

75. For the most recent argument that peasants did not "become Russians," see David Moon, "Peasants into Russian Citizens? A Comparative Perspective," *Revolutionary Russia* 5, no. 1 (June 1996): 43–81.

76. The definitive account of the army in 1917 is Wildman, *The End of the Russian Imperial Army.*

77. See letter from Verkhovsky to Alekseev, 4 September 1917, excerpted in Golovine, *Russian Army,* 70.

78. Rosa Luxemburg, "Militia and Militarism [1899]," in *Selected Political Writings of Rosa Luxemburg,* ed. Dick Howard (New York and London: Monthly Review

Press, 1971), 139; V. Fedorov, *K voprosu o voinskoi povinnosti v Rossii* (Rostov na Donu: tip. "Donskaia rech'," 1906).

79. Leonard V. Smith, *Between Mutiny and Obedience: The Case of the French Fifth Infantry Division during World War I* (Princeton: Princeton University Press, 1994).

80. Rex A. Wade, *Red Guards and Workers' Militias in the Russian Revolution* (Stanford: Stanford University Press, 1984), 142; Leon Trotsky, *The History of the Russian Revolution* (London: Sphere, 1967), 3:180.

81. M. A. Molodtsygin, *Krasnaia armiia: Rozhdenie i stanovlenie 1917–1920 gg.* (Moscow: Institut rossiiskoi istorii RAN, 1997), 35.

82. Cited in Iu. I. Korablev and M. I. Loginov, eds., *KPSS i stroitel'stvo vooruzhennykh sil SSSR (1918–iiun' 1941)* (Moscow: Voenizdat, 1959), 40.

83. "Rabochaia i krest'ianskaia krasnaia armiia i flot," 31 March 1918, quoted in Korablev and Loginov, *KPSS*, 75–76.

84. See S. M. Kliatskin, *Na zashchite Oktiabria: Organizatsiia reguliarnoi armii i militsionnoe stroitelstvo v Sovetskoi Respublike, 1917–1920 gg.* (Moscow: Nauka, 1965), 171.

85. "Kratkii otchet o deiatel'nosti voennogo otdela vserossiiskogo tsentral'nogo ispolnitel'nogo komiteta sovetov, vtorogo i tret'ego sozyvov," [sic] signed by A. Enukidze, 31 March 1918, GARF, f. r-1235, op. 79, d. 2, ll. 8–9.

86. Wade, *Red Guards*, 325–29; "Khod zapisi po gorodu Petrogradu," 19 February 1918, n.a., RGVA, f. 2, op. 1, d. 8, ll. 10–11; Report of All-Russian Collegium for the Organization and Administration of the Worker-Peasant Red Army (RKKA), 8 May 1918, GARF, f. r-1235, op. 79, d. 7, ll. 105ob–107; figure on volunteers in April 1918 taken from Korablev and Loginov, *KPSS*, 66.

87. L. D. Trotskii, "Krasnaia armiia (Rech' na zasedanii VTsIK, 22 aprelia 1918 g.)," in *Kak vooruzhalas' revoliutsiia* (Moscow: Vysshii voennyi redaktsionnyi sovet, 1923–25), 1:113.

88. M. D. Bonch-Bruyevich, *From Tsarist General to Red Army Commander*, trans. Vladimir Vezey (Moscow: Progress, 1966), 222–23.

89. Ibid., 240.

90. Ibid., 245. Emphasis in original.

91. "Iz za chego idet bor'ba?" in Trotskii, *Kak vooruzhalas' revoliutsiia*, 1:242.

92. V. I. Lenin, *Sochineniia*, 2nd ed. (Moscow: Gosizdat, 1930–1935), 22:13–14, quoted in Edward Hallett Carr, *The Bolshevik Revolution, 1917–1923* (New York: Macmillan, 1961), 3:57.

93. V. I. Lenin, "O revoliutsionnoi fraze," in Lenin, *Sochineniia*, 4th ed. (Moscow: Gosizdat, 1952), 27:1–3. Emphasis in original.

94. See for instance telegram from Trotskii to Dolonskii, with copies to Sklianskii and Lebedev, 4 March 1922, RGVA, f. 9, op. 28, d. 191, l. 123.

95. M. D. Bonch-Bruevich, *Vsia vlast' sovetam* (Moscow: Voenizdat, 1964), 258–59, 273–74.

96. "Kratkaia instruktsiia tsentral'nykh upravlenii NK po voennym delam sootvetstvuiushchim upravleniiam okruzh. kom. po voennym delam dlia pervonachal'nogo pristupa k rabotam na mestakh soglasno dekreta SNK ot 8/4 s.g.," 26 April 1918, RGVA, f. 3, op. 1, d. 49, ll. 60–60ob.

97. Kliatskin, *Na zashchite oktiabria*, 172.

98. Text of this message in Trotskii, *Kak vooruzhalas' revoliutsiia*, 1:126.

99. See "Neobkhodimost' pereimenovaniia Ustava o voinskoi povinnosti v Ustav o voinskoi sluzhbe," submitted to State Council and State Duma by member of State Duma G. A. Lashkarev for consideration during debates over military reform, 1911, RGVIA, f. 2000, op. 3, d. 79, ll. 348–355ob.

100. Transcript of telephone conversation between Berzin (in Ekaterinburg) and Ivanov (in Ufa), 13 June 1918, RGVA, f. 176, op. 3, d. 63, ll. 6–6ob.

101. "Postanovlenie piatogo vserossiiskogo s"ezda sovetov rabochikh, krest'ianskikh, krasnoarmeiskikh, i kazach'ikh deputatov, priniatoe na zasedanii ot 10 iiulia 1918 g. po dokladu narodnogo komissara po voennym i morskim delam tov. Trotskogo ob organizatsii Krasnoi Armii," *Dekrety sovetskoi vlasti* (Moscow: Gosizdat, 1957–1989), 2:541–44.

102. This is Kliatskin's point as well as mine. Kliatskin, *Na zashchite oktiabria,* 193. Mark von Hagen, on the other hand, cites debate prior to and during the Eighth Party Congress and the rapid rise in the size of the army during 1919 to argue that the decisive shift to a peasant army came in spring and summer of 1919. See von Hagen, *Soldiers in the Proletarian Dictatorship,* 30, 61, 79.

103. On troubling aspect, see Podvoiskii quote above.

104. "O sushchestvuiushchem poriadke prizyva v prifrontovoi polose na v.s. grazhdan v silu iskliuchitel'nykh obstoiatel'stv i o poriadke uvol'neniia takovykh grazhdan so sluzhby," report of Mobilization Department, September 1920, RGVA, f. 11, op. 8, d. 1059, l. 250 (misnumbered in *delo* as 150).

105. Telegram, illegible recipient, from temporary chief of staff of 3rd Army, 31 August 1918, RGVA, f. 176, op. 3, d. 139, l. 51.

106. Order no. 4 of the Revolutionary Military Council of the Republic (RVSR), RGVA, f. 3, op. 1, d. 110, l. 104.

107. "Spravka materialy po vozniknoveniiu i razvitiiu krasnoi armii RSFSR," (hereafter, "Spravka materialy") report of the Department of Organization and Battle Training of Vseroglavshtab, 9 March 1920, RGVA, f. 2, op. 1, d. 70, l. 10.

108. "Sostoianie Moskovskogo voennogo okruga k 15 noiabria 1918 g.," secret report from the Supreme Military Inspectorate of the RKKA to the Council of Worker-Peasant Defense and the RVSR, December 1918, RGASPI, f. 17, op. 87, d. 326, l. 27ob.-28.

109. "Spravka materialy," ll. 10–12.

110. In some regions the requests were larger still. In Kaluga, Orel, Tula, Kursk, and Voronezh, the army requested an additional 30 percent levy on top of the original 10 percent draft. Coded circular to military commissariats of provinces listed above, to Field Staff, and to Orel and Moscow district military commissariats from Sklianskii and Rattel', 3 June 1919, RGVA, f. 25883, op. 3, d. 977, l. 35.

111. Urgent telegram to the Moscow district military commissar and military commander from Raevskii (chief of the Mobilization Department of Vseroglavshtab) and Favorskii (his commissar), 30 April 1919, RGVA, f. 25883, op. 3, d. 977, l. 6.

112. Stenogram of telephone conversation between the district staff and Bogdanov, chief of Mobilization Department of Tambov, 19 May 1919, RGVA, f. 25883, op. 3, d. 977, l. 97.

113. Assorted telegrams, RGVA, f. 25883, op. 3, d. 977, ll. 102, 108, 115.

114. Molodtsygin, *Krasnaia armiia,* 134.

115. Report from the leader of the "Roslavl' group," comrade Komissarov, to comrade Lander (member of VTsIK and the Central Committee), 31 May 1919, RGASPI, f. 17, op. 84, d. 26, ll. 2–2ob.

116. Cited in Molodtsygin, *Krasnaia armiia,* 133.

117. Golovine, *Russian Army,* 124. All of these numbers are educated guesses. Every student of the subject agrees that statistics gathered during the war are highly suspect.

118. Orlando Figes, "The Red Army and Mass Mobilization during the Russian Civil War, 1918–1920," *Past and Present,* no. 129 (1990): 168–211.

119. Ibid., 207.

120. Letter from Rattel' to chief of Field Staff (RVSR), 8 September 1919, RGVA, f. 11, op. 8, d. 427, l. 1.

121. "Prikaz predsedatelia RVSR po voiskam i sovetskim uchrezhdeniiam iuzhnogo fronta," 24 November 1918. In Trotskii, *Kak vooruzhalas' revoliutsiia*, 1:358.

122. Telegrams from Trotskii to Lenin, 7–9 August 1918, in Jan M. Meijer, ed., *The Trotsky Papers* (The Hague and Paris: Mouton and Co., 1964–1971), 1:70–71.

123. In addition, he created the Central Desertion Commission *(Tsentral'naia komissiia po bor'be s dezertirstvom)*, which coordinated the battle against desertion for the rest of the war. Resolution signed by chairman of the Council of Defense (Lenin), 25 December 1918, RGVA, f. 11, op. 15, d. 49s, l. 2.

124. Ibid., ll. 62, 62ob.

125. Cheka reports on 3rd Army and region surrounding it, May and June 1919, RGVA, f. 176, op. 6, d. 15, ll. 30, 33, 41ob; "Doklad politicheskogo otdela 3 armii za iiun' 1919," RGVA, f. 176, op. 2, d. 14, l. 2ob.

126. "Chto pishut krasnoarmeitsy," report from the head of the military section of *Bednota* (Baratov) to VTsIK, 28 August [1919], RGVA, f. 65, op. 7, d. 11, ll. 8–15ob.

127. Letter from chairman of the Central Desertion Commission (Danilov) to the Central Committee of the Party, 28 April 1919, RGVA, f. 11, op. 15, d. 49s, l. 4–4ob.

128. Resolution of the Central Desertion Commission, sent to provincial desertion commissions, 10 April 1919, RGVA, f. 11, op. 15, d. 49s, l. 5ob.

129. *Dekrety sovetskoi vlasti*, 5:266.

130. Circular to provincial desertion commissions from the Central Desertion Commission (Danilov), 5 June 1919, RGVA, f. 11, op. 15, d. 49s, l. 81.

131. Letter from Moscow provincial desertion commission to the Moscow district (okrug) desertion commission, 26 June 1919, RGVA, f. 25883, op. 1, d. 271, l. 419. In the same *delo*, telegram from chairman of the Tula provincial desertion commission (Bodnev) to the Moscow district (okrug) desertion commission, 17 July 1919, l. 382.

132. "Otkrytoe pis'mo k tovarishcham krasnoarmeitsam." Published in 10,000 copies by the Political Department of the Riazan' provincial military commissariat, n.d. but summer 1919, RGVA, f. 25883, op. 2, d. 764, l. 626.

133. Broadsheet from the Dankovskii district military commissariat, 21 July 1919, RGVA, f. 25883, op. 2, d. 764, l. 508.

134. "Osoboe mnenie politprosvet. otdela Volokolamskogo uezdnogo voennogo komissariata po prikazu Moskovskogo gubkoma voendela ot 28 iiunia sego goda o bor'be s dezertirstvom," signed by Zharov and sent to Moscow provincial desertion commission, 6 August 1919, RGVA, f. 25883, op. 1, d. 271, l. 684.

135. Telegram from Trotskii to Sklianskii with notation, "for the Central Committee," 26 June 1919, RGASPI, f. 17, op. 109, d. 61, l. 3.

136. "Dezertirstvo (po dannym svodki s 1–21 sent. 1919)," signature illegible, RGASPI, f. 17, op. 109, d. 61, l. 4.

137. Order from the RVSR, 18 January 1919, RGASPI, f. 5, op. 1, d. 2452, l. 8.

138. Order from Central Desertion Commission, 31 January 1919, RGASPI, f. 5, op. 1, d. 2452, l. 10.

139. Order from Central Desertion Commission, 28 February 1919, RGVA, f. 11, op. 15, d. 49s, l. 7.

140. For 1 January 1920 instructions for railway checks, see S. Olikov, *Dezertirstvo v krasnoi armii i bor'ba s nim* (Moscow: Izd. NKVM, 1926), 121–22; for orders to conduct verifications of state institutions in Siberia, see circular telegram from the staff of the Siberian military district to provincial military commissariats in Tiumen',

Barnaul, Semipalatinsk, and Omsk, 21 June 1920, RGVA, f. 25875, op. 1, d. 77, l. 1.

141. Telegram from assistant head of the desertion commission of the western front (Slavatinskii) to the Central Desertion Commission and the RVSR, completely secret, 22 October 1920, RGASPI, f. 5, op. 1, d. 2452, l. 39.

142. Report to the council of Vseroglavshtab from the chief of the Mobilization Administration, secret, 8 August 1920, RGVA, f. 11, op. 8, d. 565, l. 2.

143. Lars Lih notes the same sort of transformation in the understanding of the grain problem during the Civil War from one in which class played the dominant explanatory role to one in which administrative success or failure did. See his *Bread and Authority in Russia, 1914–1921* (Berkeley, Los Angeles, and Oxford: University of California Press, 1990), 204–5.

144. M. A. Molodtsygin, who perused all the protocols of RVSR meetings during the war, asserts that "the questions related to the struggle with desertion in 1919 (and later, of course) were constantly at the center of attention of the RVSR." Molodtsygin, *Krasnaia armiia*, 182.

145. Ibid., 184. Undoubtedly, some of these were repeat offenders.

146. "Postanovlenie Soveta RKOborony ob uchete voennoobiazannykh," signed by Lenin, 27 August 1919, RGVA, f. 11, op. 8, d. 431, l. 231. In the original decree, all the men were ordered to undergo a verification to determine their class position. That requirement was soon deleted, apparently out of fear that the military registration would get bogged down by class-determination procedures. Circular telegram to commanders of military districts from the Mobilization Department, September 1919, RGVA, f. 11, op. 8, d. 848, l. 24.

147. "Spravka materialy po vozniknoveniu i razvitiiu krasnoi armii RSFSR," report of Vseroglavshtab Department of Troop Formation and Preparation, 9 March 1920, RGVA, f. 2, op. 1, d. 70, l. 16.

148. Results of verification gatherings, 17 February 1920, RGVA, f. 11, op. 8, d. 1022, ll. 279–80.

149. "Otchet o deiatel'nosti Mobilizatsionnogo Upravlenie Vserossiiskogo Glavnogo Shtaba s 25 Oktiabria 1917 goda po 15-e avgusta 1920 goda," secret, RGVA, f. 11, op. 8, d. 36, ll. 38–40.

150. Report from Tsentkomuchet (Osobaia tsentral'naia komissiia po proizvodstvu poverochnykh sborov pri RVSR), secret, 17 February 1920, RGVA, f. 11, op. 8, d. 1022, l. 277.

151. Molodtsygin, *Krasnaia armiia*, 178.

152. "Otchet o deiatel'nosti Mobilizatsionnogo Upravlenie Vserossiiskogo Glavnogo Shtaba s 25 Oktiabria 1917 goda po 15-e avgusta 1920 goda," secret, RGVA, f. 11, op. 8, d. 36, ll. 38–40.

153. "Svedenie ob ispolnenii prizyva 1901 goda s nachala mobilizatsii po 1 maia 1920 g.," report from staff of Moscow military district to the Mobilization Department of Vseroglavshtab, 14 May 1920, RGVA, f. 25883, op. 3, d. 1013, ll. 61–62.

154. "Otchet o deiatel'nosti Mobilizatsionnogo Upravlenie Vserossiiskogo Glavnogo Shtaba s 25 Oktiabria 1917 goda po 15–e avgusta 1920 goda," secret, RGVA, f. 11, op. 8, d. 36, ll. 38–40.

155. Figure cited in N. F. Kuz'min, *Na strazhe mirnogo truda (1921–1940)* (Moscow: Voenizdat, 1959), 6.

156. Korablev and Loginov, *KPSS*, 190.

157. "Ob obiazatel'noi voinskoi povinnosti dlia vsekh grazhdan RSFSR muzh-skogo pola," *Sobranie uzakonenii i rasporiazhenii rabochego i krest'ianskogo pravitel'stva*,

izdavaemoe Narodnym Komissariatom Iustitsii, 61:786 (20 October 1922). Originally published in *Izvestiia,* 30 September 1922.

158. *Desiatyi s"ezd RKP(b), mart 1921 goda. Stenograficheskki otchet* (Moscow: Gosizdat, 1963), 616. Unfortunately the stenographic reports of the debates on the military question, which took up three full sessions of the congress, have never been published, and, according to officials at RGASPI, they do not exist in manuscript form either. Reports from participants after the fact suggest that the debates were wide-ranging and acrimonious, not least because of an attack on Trotskii by Sergei Gusev and Mikhail Frunze, who publicly and transparently warned of a danger of "Bonapartism" in their theses on reorganizing the army. These were distributed to party delegates, suppressed by Lenin on the urging of Trotskii, and later published by Gusev. They are included in *Desiatyi s"ezd RKP(b),* 710–14. See a detailed discussion of the congress in von Hagen, *Soldiers in the Proletarian Dictatorship,* 137–48.

159. I. B. Berkhin, *Voennaia reforma v SSSR (1924–1925 gg.)* (Moscow: Voenizdat, 1958), 84.

160. Ibid., 85–86.

161. Ibid., 90. See chapter 3 for more discussion about ethnic units.

162. Ibid., 245–47.

163. Circular to all provincial military commanders from Mikulovich (Staff of the West Siberian military district), 31 July 1923, RGVA, f. 25893, op. 1, d. 793, l. 1.

164. von Hagen, *Soldiers in the Proletarian Dictatorship,* 233. von Hagen also cites evidence provided by Berkhin to support this claim.

165. "Territorial'nye formirovaniia." Report delivered by Frunze to plenary session of RVS, 11 November 1924, RGVA, f. 4, op. 1, d. 54, l. 26.

166. "Prizyv 1902 goda," report by unknown individual to plenary session of RVS, 11 November 1924, RGVA, f. 4, op. 1, d. 54, l. 33. Rabkrin was the "Worker-Peasant Inspectorate," the main state auditing organ.

167. Letter from Unshlikht to Stalin. 25 August 1924. RGASPI, f. 17, op. 84, d. 851, l. 45.

168. Circular from Novikov (assistant head of PUR) to all district (okrug) heads of PUR, 12 August 1924, RGVA, f. 9, op. 28s, d. 435, l. 9.

169. Ibid., l. 8ob.

170. The best source for the context and content of these reforms is Berkhin, *Voennaia reforma.*

171. "Zakon ob ob"izatel'noi voennoi sluzhbe," in *Sobranie zakonov i rasporiazhenii raboche-krest'ianskogo pravitel'stva SSSR,* 62:463 (September 1925).

172. Order of RVS, signed by deputy chairman Frunze, 8 December 1924, RGVA, f. 9, op. 28s, d. 477, l. 7.

173. "Perechen' voprosov po kodeksu voennoi sluzhby." Appendix in RGVA, f. 9, op. 28s, d. 477, ll. 8–8ob.

174. Ibid.

175. Draft of the codex of military service. RGVA, f. 9, op. 28s, d. 477, l. 10.

176. "Proekt ustava obiazatel'noi voennoi sluzhby," appendix to circular to all administration heads within the army from the Mobilization Department, authored by Pektorov and Movchin, 12 June 1923, RGVA, f. 7, op. 7, d. 700, l. 3; also same document in RGVA, f. 9, op. 28s, d. 477, l. 114. No indication who made comments on manuscript copies in either instance.

177. Appendix to project submitted by Petin commission to RVS, RGVA, f. 4, op. 1, d. 133, l. 600ob.

178. Report from Levichev (chief of GURKKA) to the RVS SSSR, 6 April 1925, RGVA, f. 4, op. 1, d. 133, l. 604.

179. Excerpt from protocol no. 29 of the meeting of the presidium of the RVS SSSR (Unshlikht, Voroshilov, Bubnov, Kamenev, Baranov, and Zof), 13 April 1925, RGVA, f. 4, op. 1, d. 133, l. 608. List numbers in this *delo* do not correspond to document order.

180. "Zakon ob obiazatel'noi voennoi sluzhbe," article 1.

181. von Hagen, *Soldiers in the Proletarian Dictatorship,* 166–67.

182. "Kodeks zakonov o l'gotakh i preimushchestvakh dlia voen-nosluzhashchikh Raboche-Krest'ianskoi Krasnoi Armii i Raboche-Krest'ianskogo Krasnogo Flota Soiuza SSR i ikh semei," *Sobranie zakonov i rasporiazhenii raboche-krest'ianskogo pravitel'stva SSSR,* 21:198 (28 November 1924).

183. L. Malinovskii and I. Gludin, *Otchet o prizyve na deistvitel'nuiu voennuiu sluzhbu v 1925 godu grazhdan rozhdeniia 1903 goda* (Moscow: Upravlenie stroevoe i po ukomplektovaniiu, 1926), l. 39–40.

184. V. Levichev, *Krasnaia armiia i prizyv 1904 goda: Doklad na sobranii agita-torov pri MK VKP(b) s predisloviem P. Petunina, tezisami dlia dokladov, lozungami i sprav-ochnoi literaturoi* (Moscow and Leningrad: Moskovskii rabochii, 1926), 22.

185. "Zakliuchenie na otzyv TsKK o rabote PURa," 28 February 1924, RGVA, f. 9, op. 28s, d. 477, l. 285.

186. Circular to all national, district, and provincial party central committees, signed by Andreev (TsK RKP), secret, 17 March 1924, RGVA, f. 9, op. 22, d. 44, l. 83.

187. Guchkov was pressing to increase career mobility for soldiers by offering civil service posts upon leaving the army to NCOs who served more than their legal term. Report by Lukomskii, 27 October 1910, RGVIA, f. 2000, op. 3, d. 73, l. 1ob.

2: The Nation and the Dilemma of Difference

1. An erudite exploration of the progression from categorization to policy to practice may be found in Rich, *The Tsar's Colonels;* see also Holquist, "To Count, to Extract, and to Exterminate," 111–44.

2. See especially Elise Kimerling Wirtschafter, *Social Identity in Imperial Russia* (DeKalb: Northern Illinois University Press, 1997).

3. Peter Gatrell, *A Whole Empire Walking: Refugees in Russia During World War I* (Bloomington and Indianapolis: Indiana University Press, 1999).

4. For European views, see George W. Stocking, Jr., *Victorian Anthropology* (New York: Free Press, 1987).

5. M. A. Slavinskii, "Voina i natsional'nyi vopros," in *Chego zhdet Rossiia ot voiny: Sbornik statei,* 2nd ed. (Petrograd: Prometei, 1915), 108–9.

6. On the problem of time in discussions of assimilation in late imperial Rus-sia, see also Robert Geraci, "Russian Orientalism at an Impasse: Tsarist Education Pol-icy and the 1910 Conference on Islam," in *Russia's Orient: Imperial Borderlands and Peoples, 1700–1917,* ed. Daniel R. Brower and Edward J. Lazzerini (Bloomington and Indianapolis: Indiana University Press, 1997), 138–61.

7. The most explicit discussion of the shift from religion to nationality in the late imperial period is in John Willard Slocum, "The Boundaries of National Identity: Religion, Language, and Nationality Politics in Late Imperial Russia," (Ph.D. diss., University of Chicago, 1993).

8. Miliutin, "O glavnykh osnovaniiakh lichnoi voennoi povinnosti," quoted in Baumann, "Universal Service Reform," 31.

9. "Doklad 2–go otdela ob otbyvanii voinskoi povinnosti naseleniem Sibiri," 5 March 1872, RGIA, f. 1246, op. 1, d. 35, ll. 741ob-742; Baumann, "Universal Service Reform," 38–39.

10. Alexander Vucinich, *Darwin in Russian Thought* (Berkeley, Los Angeles, and London: University of California Press, 1988).

11. M. I. Dragomirov, "Zametka o russkom soldate," in *Ocherki* (Kiev: Ia. A. Ogloblina, 1898), 139.

12. On the broader complications of Soviet identity and categorization as it related to class, see Sheila Fitzpatrick, "Ascribing Class: The Construction of Social Identity in Soviet Russia," *Journal of Modern History* 65 (December 1993): 745–70.

13. Memorandum from R. A. Fadeev to Alexander II, 1872. Cited in P. A. Zaionchkovskii, *Voennye reformy 1860–1870 godov v Rossii* (Moscow: Izd. Moskovskogo universiteta, 1952), 290.

14. Nikolai Butovskii, *O sposobakh obucheniia i vospitaniia sovremennago soldata (prakticheskiia zametki komandira rota)*, 3rd ed. (St. Petersburg: Berezovskii, 1893), 1:10–12.

15. On this understanding (within a broader framework) of workers contaminating peasants, see Stephen P. Frank, "Confronting the Domestic Other: Rural Popular Culture and Its Enemies in Fin-de-Siècle Russia," in *Cultures in Flux: Lower-Class Values, Practices, and Resistance in Late Imperial Russia*, ed. Stephen P. Frank and Mark D. Steinberg (Princeton: Princeton University Press, 1994), 74–75.

16. Letter from the duty general of the Main Staff to Lukomskii, 20 February 1912, RGVIA, f. 2000, op. 3, d. 167, l. 3.

17. Letter from MVD to Sukhomlinov (war minister), 22 March 1912, RGVIA, f. 2000, op. 3, d. 167, l. 4.

18. Letter from Lukomskii to the commander of the 25th Army Corps, March 1912, RGVIA, f. 2000, op. 3, d. 167, l. 6ob.

19. Butovskii, *O sposobakh obucheniia*, 1:10–14.

20. On the mutinies, see John Bushnell, *Mutiny amid Repression: Russian Soldiers in the Revolution of 1905–1906* (Bloomington: Indiana University Press, 1985); on angst regarding staunchness, see General [A. N.] Kuropatkin, *The Russian Army and the Japanese War*, trans. Captain A. B. Lindsay (London: John Murray, 1909), 2:72–73.

21. For a brief summary of the ethnic aspect of the 1905 Revolution, see Abraham Ascher, *The Revolution of 1905: Russia in Disarray* (Stanford: Stanford University Press, 1988), 152–61.

22. Secret report from Mobilization Department of the Main Staff to the Council of State Defense, 8 November 1906, RGVIA, f. 2000, op. 1, d. 309, l. 74.

23. Ibid. A year later, for reasons unclear to me, this governor, Prince Vorontsov-Dashkov, radically changed his tune. See below for his plan to have Caucasian Muslims serve in the Caucasus in times of war and peace.

24. For an examination of this process in the realm of education policy in the same period, see Slocum, "Boundaries of National Identity."

25. Memo from Main Staff to Main Administration of the General Staff, June 1906, RGVIA, f. 2000, op. 1, d. 369, ll. 14–16. Most of these discriminatory policies were decreed in an 1888 secret order from the war minister, and included, in addition to Jews and Catholics, natives of the Baltic region, Finns, and Caucasian natives (Armenians in particular). RGVIA, f. 2000, op. 3, d. 7, ll. 38–43a.

26. Internal War Ministry memo, 14 June 1906, RGVIA, f. 2000, op. 1, d. 369, l. 17.

27. Cited in secret telegram from the Service Department of the Main Staff (Baranov) to the chief of the Military-Sanitation Administration, 26 August 1916, RGVIA, f. 400, op. 19, d. 175, ll. 19–20.

28. Sidney B. Fay, *Before Sarajevo: The Origins of the World War*, 2nd ed. (New York: Free Press, 1966), 1:39. See also David G. Herrmann, *The Arming of Europe and the Making of the First World War* (Princeton: Princeton University Press, 1996); David Stevenson, *Armaments and the Coming of War: Europe, 1904–1914* (Oxford: Clarendon Press, 1996).

29. "Perechen' pozhelanii biudzhetnoi komissii Gosudarstvennoi Dumy, vyskazannykh v 1908 i 1909 gg.," n.d., RGVIA, f. 2000, op. 3, d. 4, ll. 21–24.

30. I borrow this definition from Cynthia Enloe. See her *Ethnic Soldiers: State Security in Divided Societies* (Athens, Ga.: University of Georgia Press, 1980), 25.

31. Secret letter from Vorontsov-Dashkov to Stolypin, 14 February 1911, RGVIA, f. 2000, op. 3, d. 88, l. 136ob.

32. Secret memo from the Main Administration of the General Staff to the Main Staff, signature illegible, 26 February 1908, RGVIA, f. 2000, op. 1, d. 326, l. 2.

33. Ibid.

34. For an agenda of the second-order reforms, see the 23 October 1910 circular from Lukomskii to members of his commission, RGVIA, f. 2000, op. 3, d. 80, ll. 20–20ob.

35. Letter from Lukomskii to S. V. Tseiliu (chief of the Asian Department of the Main Staff), 15 April 1911, RGVIA, f. 2000, op. 3, d. 80, l. 49.

36. *Komplektovanie krasnoi armii* (Berlin: Evraziiskoe knigoizdatel'stvo, 1926), 36–37.

37. Secret letter from Zhilinskii (and countersigned by Lebedev) to the Priamurskii governor-general, 22 June 1911, RGVIA, f. 2000, op. 3, d. 88, ll. 25–25ob.

38. On the "great differences" in relations between separate peripheries and the Russian metropole, see Dietrich Geyer, *Russian Imperialism: The Interaction of Domestic and Foreign Policy, 1860–1914*, trans. Bruce Little (New Haven and London: Yale University Press, 1987), especially 318–37.

39. On these frontier conditions, as well as the exasperation of local state officials with Russian settlers, who were often derided as "shiftless" by provincial authorities, see Daniel Brower, "Kyrgyz Nomads and Russian Pioneers: Colonization and Ethnic Conflict in the Turkestan Revolt of 1916," *Jahrbücher für Geschichte Osteuropas* 44, no. 1 (1996): 45.

40. A. Tsurikov, "Bor'ba s nevezhestvom," *Rossiia*, 1 July 1911, RGVIA, f. 2000, op. 3, d. 88, l. 247.

41. Theodore R. Weeks, *Nation and State in Late Imperial Russia: Nationalism and Russification on the Western Frontier, 1863–1914* (DeKalb: Northern Illinois University Press, 1996), 5.

42. Letter from the commander of the Turkmen Cavalry Division to Colonel P. M. Ostrianskii, 30 August 1911, RGVIA, f. 2000, op. 3, d. 88, l. 60.

43. Ibid., ll. 61–62.

44. All of these responses and protocols of military meetings around the empire on this issue are in RGVIA, f. 2000, op. 3, d. 88.

45. Speech by Deputy Khakh-Mamedov to closed 33rd session of Third Duma, 30 November 1911, RGVIA, f. 2000, op. 3, d. 79, ll. 1163ob–64.

46. Ibid.

47. Speech by Deputy Maksudov to closed 35th session of Third Duma, 2 December 1911, RGVIA, f. 2000, op. 3, d. 79, l. 1179ob.

48. Speech by Deputy Kropotov to closed 33rd session of Third Duma, 30 November 1911, RGVIA, f. 2000, op. 3, d. 79, ll. 1165–65ob. Note here also the stress on the class ("peasantry") factor, which is folded into discussions of ethnic limitations.

49. "Po voprosu o vvedenii osobogo voennogo naloga dlia lits, osvobozhdaemykh ot voinskoi povinnosti," Lukomskii report from Mobilization Department, 13 March 1910, RGVIA, f. 2000, op. 3, d. 24, ll. 1–2.

50. Report from the Main Administration of the General Staff's quartermaster-general to the Mobilization Department, 22 May 1914, RGVIA, f. 2000, op. 3, d. 2608, l. 33. At the outbreak of the war, only three ethnic units were present in the army, the Turkmen Cavalry Division, the Dagestan Cavalry Regiment, and the Ossetian Cavalry Division. Ventsov theses to the RVS SSSR, 10 February 1924, RGVA, f. 9, op. 28s, d. 441, l. 196. List numbers in this *delo* do not correspond to document order.

51. On this see also Mark von Hagen, "The Great War and the Mobilization of Ethnicity in the Russian Empire," in *Post-Soviet Political Order: Conflict and State Building*, ed. Barnett R. Rubin and Jack Snyder (London and New York: Routledge, 1998), 34–57.

52. N. V. Podpriatov, "Natsional'nye men'shinstva v bor'be za 'chest', dostoin-stvo, tselost' Rossii . . .': Sozdanie i ispol'zovanie natsional'nykh formirovanii v russkoi armii," *Voenno-istoricheskii zhurnal*, no. 1 (1997): 56.

53. Appeal of the supreme commander of the Russian army, 1 August 1914, RGVIA, f. 2067, op. 1, d. 2878, l. 1. The battle of Grünwald took place in 1410; it was the site of a victory of a coalition of the Muscovite and the Polish-Lithuanian states against the Teutonic Order of Knights.

54. Secret letter from Ianushkevich to N. I. Ivanov, 30 October 1914, RGVIA, f. 2067, op. 1, d. 2878, l. 9.

55. Secret report from Col. Seredin (chief of the General Division of Adminis-tration of the quartermaster-general of the staff of the commander of the southwest-ern front) to the quartermaster-general, 26 December 1914, RGVIA, f. 2067, op. 1, d. 2878, ll. 13–14.

56. Letter from the chief of staff of the southwestern front to the main com-mander of the southwestern front, 28 December 1914, secret, RGVIA, f. 2067, op. 1, d. 2878, l. 20; circular from duty general at Stavka, secret, 21 March 1915, RGVIA, f. 2003, op. 2, d. 323, l. 85.

57. The legion was a volunteer force—Poles who were in the reserves or due to be drafted in 1915 or 1916 were not allowed to join.

58. Letter from Ianuskhevich to Sukhomlinov, 20 April 1915, RGVIA, f. 2003, op. 2, d. 323, l. 154; see also ibid., l. 178.

59. Report from the Service Department of the Main Administration of the General Staff, "O sformirovanii iz tuzemtsev Kavkaza 5–ti konnykh polkov, odnogo batal'iona i upravleniia Kavkazskoi tuzemnoi konnoi divizii," 6 August 1914, RGVIA, f. 29, op. 3, d. 1530, ll. 1–4. Approved on 16 August 1914 by Military Council (l. 13), and ordered on 27 October 1914 by Grand Duke Nikolai Nikolaevich (l. 16). This cavalry division soon became known as the *dikaia diviziia* or the "wild [savage] divi-sion." On forming Armenian units, telegram from General Bolkhovitinov to the quartermaster-general of the Stavka, 1 June 1915, RGVIA, f. 2003, op. 2, d. 323, l. 177; Podpriatov, "Natsional'nye men'shinstva," 56.

60. "O sformirovanii iz tuzemtsev Kavkaza," l. 1.

61. On this, see the report from Baron Brinken (the commander of the 22nd Army Corps) to the Finnish governor-general, 26 July 1914, RGVIA, f. 400, op. 19, d. 86, ll. 52–53.

62. Report from Service Department of the Main Administration of the Gen-eral Staff to the Military Council, 13 January 1915, RGVIA, f. 29, op. 3, d. 1530, l. 21, and the Military Council agreement of 15 January 1915, l. 23. For a brief discussion of the Adjar incident, see Eric Lohr, "Enemy Alien Politics Within the Russian Em-pire During World War I" (Ph.D. diss., Harvard University, 1999), 128–31.

63. Speech of General Beliaev to the State Duma's Committee on Military and Naval Affairs, 10 August 1915, RGIA, f. 1278, op. 5, d. 447, l. 296.

64. Excerpts from a letter from Ia. Nikolenko to the Ministry of Internal Affairs, n.d. but prior to 9 July 1915, RGVIA, f. 2000, op. 3, d. 1194, l. 23.

65. "Ubezhashche," clipping from *Russkoe znamia*, 12 November 1915, RGIA, f. 1292, op. 1, d. 1337, l. 8.

66. Letter from Tobol'sk peasants and merchants to War Ministry, with copy to Ministry of Internal Affairs, 8 October 1915, RGIA, f. 1292, op. 1, d. 1337, ll. 99–100.

67. Speech of Deputy Tregubov to closed third meeting of the fourth session of the Fourth State Duma, 28 July 1915, RGIA, f. 1278, op. 5, d. 205, ll. 211–12.

68. Speech of Deputy Shingarev delivering report of State Duma's Committee on Military and Naval Affairs to the closed 12th meeting of the fourth session of the Fourth State Duma, 19 August 1915, RGIA, f. 1278, op. 5, d. 216, ll. 13–14.

69. There are further complications, of course. Shingarev did assume, for instance, that Russian had to be the single language of command and training in the army.

70. Speech of War Ministry representative to the closed 12th meeting of the fourth session of the Fourth State Duma, 19 August 1915, RGIA, f. 1278, op. 5, d. 216, l. 20.

71. Report of the Pension and Service Department of the Main Staff, 19 September 1915, RGVIA, f. 2000, op. 3, d. 1194, l. 79.

72. Letter from Khvostov to the war minister (A. A. Polivanov), 10 October 1915, RGIA, f. 1292, op. 1, d. 1337, ll. 3ob-4.

73. Report from Kukol'-Iasnopol'skii, 26 November 1915, RGIA, f. 1276, op. 11, d. 840, ll. 32–33.

74. "Proekt o privlechenii k otbyvaniiu voinskoi povinnosti nekotorykh chastei naselenii, osvobozhdennogo ot nei do nastoiashchago vremeni." Submitted to Council of Ministers by minister of war and chief of General Staff, November 1915, RGIA, f. 1276, op. 11, d. 840, l. 11ob.

75. Ibid., ll. 14ob–15.

76. Ibid., ll. 16–17, 21–22.

77. "Osobyi zhurnal sovet ministrov," 27 November 1915, RGIA, f. 1276, op. 11, d. 840, ll. 7–9.

78. "Osobyi zhurnal sovet ministrov," 3 May, 6 May, and 14 June 1916, RGVIA, f. 400, op. 19, d. 152, ll. 40–41ob.

79. Ibid., l. 72. Serious resistance was met to the decree only in Central Asia. The labor draft in the Caucasus went much more smoothly.

80. Brower, "Kyrgyz Nomads," 52, 53.

81. See the explicit linkage in the report of the Semirechie governor to Nicholas II for the year 1910, secret excerpt, RGVIA, f. 400, op. 19, d. 39, l. 4. Conscription exemptions were used as social "carrots" for ethnic Russians as well. Migrants to Turkestan and their children were excused from military service until the manpower demands of World War I forced a change.

82. Gorodovikov, *Vospominaniia*, 23–31.

83. Order no. 135 to all military institutions, 16 March 1917, RGVIA, f. 400, op. 19, d. 175, l. 6.

84. Telegram from Muslim Bureau of Novonikolaevsk to Guchkov, 19 April 1917, RGVIA, f. 2003, op. 2, d. 336, l. 1. Satterup request on obverse.

85. Report from the Main Administration of the General Staff to the duty general of Stavka, 21 October 1917, RGVIA, f. 2003, op. 2, d. 336, ll. 60–62. On agreement of war minister and continuation of plan, see report of M. D. Bonch-Bruevich (chief of Stavka), 27 November 1917, l. 93. For further allowances for Muslim units in late 1917, see ll. 102, 112, 117.

86. Separate telegrams in RGVIA, f. 2003, op. 2, d. 343, ll. 20–21, 22, 24, 25, 29, 61–62, 117–18.

87. The best account of this episode is Mark von Hagen, "The Russian Imperial Army and the Ukrainian National Movement in 1917," *Ukrainian Quarterly* 54, no. 3–4 (Fall–Winter 1998): 220–56.

88. Telegram from Oboleshev (staff of Kiev military district) to duty general of southwestern front, 11 May 1917, RGVIA, f. 2067, op. 2, d. 445, l. 1. It is unclear from this material whether the soldiers themselves wanted "Ukrainization" or simply wanted to be stationed with their friends. Military officials certainly interpreted it as a desire for ethnic units.

89. Circular telegram from duty general of southwestern front, 23 May 1917, RGVIA, f. 2067, op. 2, d. 445, l. 7.

90. Telegram from General Mel'gunov to "Georgii Ivanovich," 3 June 1917, RGVIA, f. 2067, op. 2, d. 445, l. 76.

91. Letter from General Muzhilov (chief commander of the 7th Army) to "Nikolai Osipovich," 26 June 1917, RGVIA, f. 2067, op. 1, d. 2986, l. 1.

92. Report from Sergeant Baturin, representative of the Army Committee of the 7th Army in the 34th Army Corps, n.d. but after 17 July 1917, RGVIA, f. 2067, op. 1, d. 2986, ll. 21–24.

93. The question of the importance of the primary group is one of some debate. For a classic statement of its importance, see E. A. Shils and M. Janowitz, "Cohesion and Disintegration in the Wehrmacht in World War II," *Public Opinion Quarterly* 12 (1948): 280–315. For a sophisticated critique of the primary group concept, see Omer Bartov, *Hitler's Army: Soldiers, Nazis, and War in the Third Reich* (Oxford: Oxford University Press, 1992), 57–58.

94. *Sovetskie vooruzhennye sily: Istoriia stroitel'stva* (Moscow: Voenizdat, 1978), 22; "Nastavlenie dlia verbovki dobrovoltsev vo vnov' sozdavaemuiu armiiu," secret, sent in conjunction with 8 April 1918 Sovnarkom decree, RGVA, f. 11, op. 8, d. 53, l. 120ob.

95. "Doklad o formirovanii Musul'manskikh batal'ionov i tsel' poezdki Tataro-Bashkirskogo batal'iona v Samaru," secret, 3 June 1918, RGVA, f. 11, op. 5, d. 234, l. 134.

96. There was, for instance, a five-day student revolt in Kiev in October 1916, begun due to dissatisfaction with the draft of university students, in which crowds of up to 700 people faced off with police and sang both nationalist hymns. See the report from the chief of the Kiev military district to the chief of requisitions for the armies of the southwestern front, n.d., RGVIA, f. 2068, op. 1, d. 316, ll. 535–36.

97. See for instance, Cathy A. Frierson, *Peasant Icons: Representations of Rural People in Late Nineteenth-Century Russia* (New York and Oxford: Oxford University Press, 1993), 41–47; Laura Engelstein, *The Keys to Happiness: Sex and the Search for Modernity in Fin-de-Siècle Russia* (Ithaca, N.Y. and London: Cornell University Press, 1992), especially 165–211, 265.

98. Leonard Smith, in his intriguing study of the French army mutinies, explicitly draws a parallel between the mutinies in Russia and in France. Smith, *Between Mutiny and Obedience*, 253.

99. Letter from the Mobilization Department to the Commissariat of Internal Affairs, 12 August 1918, GARF, f. r-393, op. 1, d. 41, l. 86.

100. On this "urban contraction," see Diane P. Koenker, "Urbanization and Deurbanization in the Russian Revolution and Civil War," in *Party, State, and Society in the Russian Civil War*, ed. Diane P. Koenker, William G. Rosenberg, and Ronald G. Suny (Bloomington: Indiana University Press, 1989), 81–104.

101. See statistics telegrammed to the Mobilization Department of All-Russian Main Staff from the Moscow District Mobilization Administration, 30 October 1918, RGVA, f. 25883, op. 3, d. 950, l. 531.

102. Molodtsygin, *Krasnaia armiia,* 136.

103. "Otchet o deiatel'nosti Mobilizatsionnogo Upravleniia Vserossiiskogo Glavnogo Shtaba s 25 Oktiabria 1917 goda po 15-e avgusta 1920 goda," secret, RGVA, f. 11, op. 8, d. 36, ll. 38–40.

104. N. Podvoiskii, "Programma rabot kommunisticheskoi partii po sozdaniiu trekhmillionnoi armii," in *Revoliutsionnaia voina,* ed. N. Podvoiskii and M. Pavlovich (Moscow: Izd. VTsIK, 1919), 86.

105. Francesco Benvenuti, *The Bolsheviks and the Red Army, 1918–1922,* trans. Christopher Woodall (Cambridge: Cambridge University Press, 1988), 28, 31.

106. Mentioned in letter from Lebedev (Mobilization Administration) to the Department of Organization and Battle Preparation, 1 November 1918, RGVA, f. 11, op. 8, d. 787, l. 5. Also mentioned in "Plan formirovanii pekhotnoi divizii pod nabliudeniem i otvetstvennost'iu moskovskogo okruzhnogo komissariata po voennym delam," n.d. but after 2 July 1918, RGVA, f. 3, op. 1, d. 45, l. 85ob.

107. Report from TsIK of Turkestan Republic to military commissariat, 30 September 1918, RGVA, f. 11, op. 8, d. 787, l. 2, and telegram from Lebedev to TsIK of Turkestan Republic, 8 November 1918, l. 3.

108. "Ob uchrezhdenii otdela po formirovaniiu kirgizskikh chastei," report from All-Russian Main Staff, Department of Organization and Battle Training to Military-Legal Council, August 1918, RGVA, f. 11, op. 5, d. 96, l. 332.

109. Report from the special commissar of the Steppe Kirgiz krai, 21 May 1919, RGASPI, f. 17, op. 109, d. 16, l. 4; "O mobilizatsiia 1901 goda," n.a., n.d., RGVA, f. 25875, op. 1, d. 298, l. 24; telegram from Frunze (RVS of southern front) to Sklianskii, 29 April 1919, RGVA, f. 33988, op. 1, d. 110, l. 48; report from commissar of Registration Department (A. Pudan') to Mobilization Department (Iurenev), completely secret, 8 May 1919, RGVA, f. 2, op. 1, d. 70, l. 45; circular telegram from chief of the Mobilization Administration to district (okrug) military commissariats, 30 August 1920, RGVA, f. 11, op. 8, d. 692, l. 247.

110. See Yuri Slezkine, "The USSR as a Communal Apartment, or How a Socialist State Promoted Ethnic Particularism," *Slavic Review* 53, no. 2 (Summer 1994): 414–52; Terry Martin, *The Affirmative Action Empire: Nations and Nationalism in the Soviet Union, 1923–1939* (Ithaca, N.Y.: Cornell University Press, 2001); Gerhard Simon, *Nationalism and Policy Toward the Nationalities in the Soviet Union: From Totalitarian Dictatorship to Post-Stalinist Society,* trans. Karen Forster and Oswald Forster (Boulder, San Francisco, and London: Westview Press, 1991); Ronald Grigor Suny, *The Revenge of the Past: Nationalism, Revolution, and the Collapse of the Soviet Union* (Stanford: Stanford University Press, 1993).

111. The best discussion of the struggle among ethnographic viewpoints and the importance of Stalin's 1950 article is in Yuri Slezkine, "N. Ia. Marr and the National Origins of Soviet Ethnogenetics," *Slavic Review* 55, no. 4 (Winter 1996): 826–62.

112. See for instance Mikhail Agursky, *The Third Rome: National Bolshevism in the USSR* (Boulder and London: Westview Press, 1987), 305–41; Peter Zwick, *National Communism* (Boulder: Westview Press, 1983), 64–67.

113. Telegram from Antonov-Ovseenko to Trotskii, 25 December 1922, RGVA, f. 9, op. 28s, d. 191, l. 317.

114. Telegram from Trotskii to comrades Danilov and Antonov-Ovseenko, 3 February 1923, RGVA, f. 9, op. 28s, d. 191, l. 79.

115. Report of Mobilization Administration to the Council of the All-Russian Main Staff, September 1920, RGVA, f. 11, op. 8, d. 692, l. 254.

116. Ibid., ll. 254–54ob.

117. Decree of Council of Labor and Defense, signed by Lenin, 10 May 1920. RGVA, f. 16, op. 3, d. 420, l. 4.

118. On this movement, see "Zhurnal soveshchaniia pri Mobuprav VGSh po voprosu o prizyve na voennoi sluzhbe inorodtsev Sibiri," 23 October 1920, RGVA, f. 11, op. 8, d. 692, l. 282ob. For particular mention that the criteria of exemption would include "backwardness," see information sheet from the Siberian Staff to the chief of the Mobilization Administration, 16 November 1920, RGVA, f. 7, op. 7, d. 570, l. 33, and l. 117 for understanding that tsarist exemption policy was based on desire for faster assimilation.

119. Circular telegram from the Mobilization Administration to the commander of troops of the Caucasian Separate Army, the Turkestan front, the Transvolga military district, and the Priural military district, 15 July 1921, RGVA, f. 7, op. 10, d. 1, l. 31.

120. See here George W. Stocking, Jr., *Race, Culture, and Evolution: Essays in the History of Anthropology* (1968; Chicago: University of Chicago Press, 1982).

121. See report from the Military Sanitation Administration of the Leningrad military district to the Military Sanitation Administration of the Red Army, 3 October 1924, RGVA, f. 34, op. 2, d. 81, l. 8–11.

122. Secret report from Staff of the People's Military-Naval Commissariat of the GSSR to the chief of staff of the Separate Caucasian Army, 7 September 1922, RGVA, f. 25873, op. 1, d. 2116, l. 47.

123. Georgians, Armenians, and Azerbaidzhanis all had their own divisions. Bukhara had two regiments, and Khorezm had several units that varied in number between 1,000 and 2,000 men. Ventsov theses at plenum of RVS SSSR, 10 February 1924, RGVA, f. 9, op. 28s, d. 441, l. 199. List numbers do not correspond to order of documents in this *delo*.

124. On the Trotskii directive, his article in *Pravda*, and Stalin's theses at the Twelfth Party Congress prompting the reconsideration of the national question in the army, see "Spravka o direktivakh, dannykh PURom po voprosu o natsional'noi formirovanii krasnoi armii," n.d. but after June 1924, RGVA, f. 9, op. 28s, d. 704, l. 13. For a similar acknowledgment that Trotskii's letter and the Twelfth Party Congress were the catalysts for change in the military, see RGVA, f. 54, op. 1, d. 1039, l. 9ob.

125. Antonov-Ovseenko communicated the content of Trotskii's letter in a circular from the Political Administration on 24 March 1923. He also specifically recommended that political workers read Trotskii's article in issue 61 of *Pravda* and Stalin's theses for the upcoming congress in the 65th issue. RGVA, f. 9, op. 28s, d. 704, ll. 15–15ob. Trotskii's article in *Pravda* was similar in tone, though not in content, to his missive to Antonov-Ovseenko. L. Trotskii, "Natsional'nyi vopros i vospitanie partiinoi molodezhi," *Pravda*, issue 61 (20 March 1923), 2.

126. The resolutions of the congress, as Gerhard Simon notes, were not a radical break with earlier nationality policies, but did serve to confirm them, and also ended further public debate on the questions involved. Simon, *Nationalism*, 24.

127. Secret letter from Trotskii to Antonov-Ovseenko, with copies sent to members of the RVS, 20 March 1923, RGVA, f. 9, op. 28s, d. 191, l. 52.

128. Ibid.

129. Ibid., 52–52ob.

130. The pre-Congress theses were published in I. Stalin, "Natsional'nye momenty v partiinom i gosud. stroitel'stve (Tezisy tov. Stalina odobrennyi TsK partii)," *Pravda,* issue 65 (24 March 1923), 2. The description of these policies as "affirmative action" is Martin's in *Affirmative Action Empire.*

131. *Dvenadtsatyi s"ezd rossiiskoi kommunisticheskoi partii (bol'shevikov). Stenograficheskii otchet, 17–25 aprelia 1923 g.* (Moscow: Krasnaia nov', 1923), 523.

132. Ibid., 548.

133. Ibid., 649.

134. Secret circular from Antonov-Ovseenko to PUR, 30 June 1923, RGVA, f. 9, op. 28s, d. 324, l. 89.

135. Draft article by Moisei Rafes entitled "Natsional'nyi vopros v Krasnoi armii," 2 July 1923, RGVA, f. 9, op. 28, d. 324, ll. 95–96.

136. Ibid.

137. Protocol no. 4 of RVS SSSR, completely secret, 28 November 1924, RGVA, f. 4, op. 1, d. 54, l. 220.

138. Novikov report to Frunze, 8 July 1924, RGVA, f. 9, op. 28s, d. 441, l. 105.

139. Ibid. On pre-draft training, see Rafes, "Plan raboty PURa v oblasti natsional'nykh formirovanii i uregulirovaniia natsional'nykh otnoshenii v chastiakh KA," secret, 24 January 1924, RGVA, f. 54, op. 1, d. 1039, ll. 22–23.

140. Telegram from Sklianskii to the commanders of troops of the North Caucasus military district and Turkestan front, 8 September 1923. RGVA, f. 9, op. 28s, d. 324, ll. 512, 513.

141. *Pochemu gortsy Severnogo Kavkaza prizyvaiutsia na sluzhbu v RKKA. (Material dlia dokladchikov na obshchikh sobraniiakh grazhdan v aule).* (Novocherkassk: Politupravleniia SKVO, 1927), 3.

142. "Obzor o natsional'nykh formirovaniiakh," from chief of the Informotdel of PUR, secret, 13 May 1926, RGVA, f. 9, op. 28s, d. 803, ll. 70–71. Kishliaks are "villages" in Central Asia.

143. "Zakliucheniia po dokladu GURKKA v RVS SSSR o piatiletnem plane natsformirovanii, izmeneniia, i dopolnitelnye predlozheniia PURa," n.d., n.a., RGVA, f. 9, op. 28s, d. 501, l. 95.

144. On this diverging path of "former allies," see Moshe Lewin, *Russian Peasants and Soviet Power: A Study of Collectivization* (New York: W. W. Norton, 1968), 134.

145. "Reorganizatsiia Raboche-krest'ianskoi Krasnoi Armii (Materialy k X s"ezdu RKP," in *Desiatyi s"ezd RKP(b),* 710–14; "Rezoliutsii Vserossiiskogo soveshchaniia nachal'nikov politupravlenii okrugov," 16–18 December 1921, in *Vsearmeiskie soveshchaniia politrabotnikov, 1918–1940 (rezoliutzii)* (Moscow: Nauka, 1984), 41. Quoted in von Hagen, *Soldiers in the Proletarian Dictatorship,* 144, 158.

146. M. I. Kalinin, *O kommunisticheskom vospitanii i voinskom dolge: Sbornik statei i rechei* (Moscow: Voenizdat, 1962), 128–29.

147. Lewis Siegelbaum skeptically notes E. H. Carr's argument that NEP made the peasant the "spoilt child of the proletarian dictatorship" and as such the object of governmental favoritism. Lewis H. Siegelbaum, *Soviet State and Society Between Revolutions, 1918–1929* (Cambridge: Cambridge University Press, 1992), 91.

148. For one attempt of this kind, see the report from the Mobilization Administration to the Council of Labor and Defense, 3 July 1921, RGVA, f. 7, op. 7, d. 186, l. 35.

149. Circular from the assistant head of PUR (Novikov) to all district PUR heads, 12 August 1924, RGVA, f. 9, op. 28s, d. 435, l. 8ob.

150. "Kratkaia obshchaia kharakteristika pribyvshego iz Ukrainy v Petrograd-skii VO popolneniia doprizyva 1901 goda," 15 November 1922, completely secret, RGVA, f. 9, op. 28s, d. 403, l. 76.

151. "O populiarnoi voenno-propagandistskoi literature (izdan TsK RKSM)," n.d., but almost certainly in 1924, TsKhDMO, f. 1, op. 23, d. 467, l. 88.

152. "Kratkaia obshchaia kharakteristika."

153. All quotes taken from PUR survey, 14 March 1927, RGVA, f. 4, op. 2, d. 233, ll. 24ob, 28ob.

3: The Nation and the Challenge of Unity

1. The term "dual revolution" refers to the combined impact of the industrial revolution and the French Revolution. Eric Hobsbawm, *The Age of Revolution, 1789–1848* (London and New York: Mentor, 1962), xv. On the anachronism of autocracy and the dilemmas faced by Nicholas II, see Andrew M. Verner, *The Crisis of Russian Autocracy: Nicholas II and the 1905 Revolution* (Princeton: Princeton University Press, 1990). On the variety of failed ways that Nicholas II tried to become a national tsar without undermining the traditional base of the autocracy see Richard S. Wortman, *Scenarios of Power: Myth and Ceremony in Russian Monarchy,* vol. 2 (Princeton: Princeton University Press, 2000).

2. See for instance the letter from General N. von Kol'ts (chief of Tula Gendarmes Administration) to S. P. Beletskii (minister of internal affairs), 9 January 1916, included in "Perepiska pravykh i drugie materialy ob ikh deiatel'nosti v 1914–1917 godakh," *Voprosy istorii,* no. 3 (1996): 159.

3. On this split of political vision in other areas of policy, see Lih, *Bread and Authority in Russia, 1914–1921,* especially 33–44.

4. See for instance Kuropatkin, *The Russian Army,* 1:209, 215.

5. On the mass mobilizations of the populace in the economic sphere during World War I, see Lewis H. Siegelbaum, *The Politics of Industrial Mobilization in Russia, 1914–17: A Study of the War-Industries Committees* (New York: St. Martin's, 1983), esp. 49–53. On public mobilization more broadly, see Pearson, *Russian Moderates,* 21. The MVD, of course, tried to continue its policy of containment of public forces, but it was fighting a losing battle. It was, moreover, the army that always stepped in to defend public organizations when they were besieged by MVD forces. On this, see Pearson, 25, and Siegelbaum, 186.

6. I take this notion of a Bolshevik "monopoly" over mobilizational resources from Jane I. Dawson, *Eco-nationalism: Anti-Nuclear Activism and National Identity in Russia, Lithuania, and Ukraine* (Durham, N.C., and London: Duke University Press, 1996).

7. Lesh commission journal, 26 February 1911, RGVIA, f. 2000, op. 2, d. 795, ll. 347–48.

8. See Wortman, *Scenarios of Power,* on this theme.

9. On Miliukov's views in this vein, see Melissa Kirschke Stockdale, *Paul Miliukov and the Quest for a Liberal Russia, 1880–1918* (Ithaca, N.Y., and London: Cornell University Press, 1996), 247–48.

10. "Vozzvanie soiuza upolnomochennykh ofitserov i soldat chastei i uchrezhdenii Stavki Verkhovnogo Glavnokomanduiushchago," n.d. but prior to 22 April 1917, RGVIA, f. 1, op. 1, t. 44, d. 647, l. 37.

11. *Krasnaia zvezda* (Moscow: VTsIK, 1918), 3–4.

12. This suggestion from circular of Service Department of GUGSh to military district commanders, 10 May 1911, RGVIA, f. 2000, op. 2, d. 795, l. 57.

13. On the parallel process in Germany, see Alon Confino, *The Nation as a Local Metaphor: Württemberg, Imperial Germany, and National Memory, 1871–1918* (Chapel Hill and London: University of North Carolina Press, 1997).

14. Telegram from 6th Siberian Rifle Regiment to Rodzianko (Duma), n.d. but likely March 1917, RGIA, f. 1278, op. 5, d. 1257, l. 105.

15. See Lohr, "Enemy Alien Politics Within the Russian Empire during World I," 210–12; for primary account of land discussions, see Iakhontov, "Tiazhelye dni," 18:23–24.

16. "Petrograda ne otdadim! Rabochie, krest'iane, krasnoarmeitsy. Petrograd v opasnosti!" PUR broadsheet (1919) included in N. E. Eliseeva, ed., *Listovki grazhdanskoi voiny v SSSR, 1918–1922 gg.: Komplekt dokumentov iz fondov RGVA* (Moscow: RGVA, 1994), 18.

17. Excerpt from circular of the Political Administration of the Petrograd military district, 25 September 1922, RGVA, f. 9, op. 28s, d. 403, l. 62.

18. Handwritten marginalia, signed by Rafes (chief of PUR Agitprop Department) and dated 21 October (likely 1923) on report from Korol' (chief of the Agitation Unit) entitled "Osnovnye momenty polozheniia v agitproprab v voennoe vremia," RGVA, f. 9, op. 28s, d. 331, l. 3.

19. Letter from the chair of the Front Commission of VTsIK to comrade Loshchenko, 27 January 1918, GARF, f. r-1235, op. 79, d. 27, l. 107.

20. Report from the Central Desertion Committee for period from 1 January 1921 to 31 January 1921, submitted to Lenin, completely secret, 11 March 1921, RGASPI, f. 5, op. 1, d. 2452, l. 41. The type of property confiscated in these cases is not specified, but it includes all cases of confiscation other than monetary fines, which were calculated separately. Usually the confiscation was of movable property, livestock in particular, but whole homesteads were also taken.

21. Letter from "Krasnoarmeets-frontovik N. Nosov" to the Central Desertion Committee, n.d. but prior to 27 May 1919, RGVA, f. 25883, op. 1, d. 271, l. 398.

22. Sovnarkom decree signed by Lenin, 20 July 1918, RGVA, f. 3, op. 1, d. 120, l. 36.

23. Speech of Rodzianko (chairman) to first meeting of third session of Fourth State Duma, 27 January 1915, RGIA, f. 1278, op. 5, d. 201, l. 3.

24. V. A. Zam'sov (assistant to the chief of the Red Cross), "Gimn svobodnoi rossii." n.d. but in March or April 1917, RGIA, f. 1278, op. 5, d. 1360, l. 10.

25. Text of the first oath, reprinted in Korablev and Loginov, *KPSS*, 75.

26. N. P. Vishniakov and F. I. Arkhipov, *Ustroistvo vooruzhennykh sil SSSR*, 2nd ed. (Moscow: Voennyi vestnik, 1926), 142.

27. "Neskol'ko slov o komplektovanii armii molodymi soldatami," n.a., November 1912, RGVIA, f. 2000, op. 3, d. 1114, l. 47.

28. Ibid.

29. As one recruitment slogan in Petrograd military district in 1922 proclaimed, "The Red Army and all the laborers of the Soviet Republic are one tight family." "Spisok lozungov otpravliaemykh na agitpunkty PVO i chastiam," 1922, RGVA, f. 9, op. 28s, d. 403, l. 64ob.

30. Report from the military censor of the 3rd Army, compiled from correspondence of the Red Army examined from 1–15 June 1919, RGVA, f. 16, op. 6, d. 3, l. 59ob.

31. "Otchet o deiatel'nosti Mobilizatsionnogo Upravleniia Vserossiiskogo Glavnogo Shtaba s 25 oktiabria 1917 goda po 15-e avgusta 1920 goda," secret, RGVA, f. 11, op. 8, d. 36, l. 15ob.

32. "Instruktsiia inspektiruiushchim Vseobshchee Voennoe Obuchenie [*sic*] na mestakh," signed by chief of Vsevobuch L. Mar'iasin, 26 October 1918, RGASPI, f. 5, op. 1, d. 2417, l. 2.

33. Orlando Figes, *Peasant Russia, Civil War: The Volga Countryside in Revolution, 1917–1921* (Oxford: Oxford University Press, 1989), 178, 309. Likewise, bands of local peasants often attacked any army entering their territory as a purely defensive maneuver. Vladimir N. Brovkin, *Behind the Front Lines of the Civil War: Political Parties and Social Movements in Russia, 1918–1922* (Princeton: Princeton University Press, 1994), 148–49.

34. A. Rediger, comp., *Komplektovanie i ustroistvo vooruzhennoi sily,* 3rd ed. (St. Petersburg: Voennaia tipografiia, 1900), 91. Emphasis in original.

35. Replies of the MVD to proposed changes in the military service law, n.d. but probably 1905, RGVIA, f. 2000, op. 1, d. 307, l. 46.

36. "Protokol chrezvychainoi komissii, naznach. NK po voendel dlia provedeniia v zhizn' dekreta VTsIK o prinuditel'nom prizyve na voennuiu sluzhbu rab. nas. goroda Moskvy," 3 June 1918, RGVA, f. 11, op. 8, d. 56, ll. 5–5ob.

37. Ibid., ll. 4–6.

38. "O l'gotakh po semeinomu polozheniiu," report from the Military Council of Vseroglavshtab and the chief of the Mobilization Administration (Lebedev) to the deputy chairman of the RVSR (Sklianskii), 31 December 1918, RGVA, f. 11, op. 8, d. 788, l. 1.

39. Report from Muralov to Sklianskii, 13 December 1918, RGVA, f. 11, op. 8, d. 788, l. 21.

40. Telegram from RVS (Kostiaev and Aralov) to Mobilization Administration of Vseroglavshtab, 18 December 1918, RGVA, f. 11, op. 8, d. 788, l. 22.

41. Some wavering on the issue does seem to have occurred. In Kostroma in 1919, officials were instructed to wait until after spring fieldwork was completed before they drafted only sons, and the Council of Worker-Peasant Defense itself even drafted (but did not issue) a directive in May 1919 saying that "in order to protect working families" it would offer exemptions to only sons, though the decree would not be extended to those already drafted into the army or navy. Telegram from Rattel' to Kostroma province military commissar, 14 March 1919, RGVA, f. 11, op. 8, d. 788, l. 87; decree (postanovlenie) of Council of Worker-Peasant Defense, May 1919, RGVA, f. 11, op. 8, d. 788, l. 95.

42. Answer to question from Gerasimov of the 3rd Kazan' Rifle Division, n.a., n.d. but likely 1920, RGVA, f. 7, op. 7, d. 564, l. 45.

43. Circular to all political organs from the deputy chief of PUR (Landa), 11 December 1922, RGVA, f. 9, op. 28s, d. 186, l. 34.

44. For more on the implementation of the *paika,* see Emily E. Pyle, "Village Social Relations and the Reception of Soldiers' Family Aid Policy in Russia, 1912–1921" (Ph.D. diss., University of Chicago, 1997).

45. See below for the only exception to this rule: the period of the volunteer army, when all soldiers were required to sign binding contracts that outlined their duties and what they would receive. The fear of mercenaries loomed large during the volunteer period, for Bolshevik officials suspected that "criminal elements" would jump at the chance to kill for pay. See letter from troop inspector F. Kostianev to the military director of the Northern Territory and Petrograd District, 20 May 1918, RGVA, f. 11, op. 8, d. 53, l. 118ob.

46. Version in force during war printed in D. F. Ognev, comp., *Voinskii ustav o nakazaniiakh (S.V.P. 1869 g., XXII, izd. 3)* (St. Petersburg: Berezovskii, 1912), 298–99.

47. Report from the chief of staff of the main commander of armies of the southwest front to Stavka, 6 March 1915, RGVIA, f. 2003, op. 2, d. 784, l. 9.

48. Report of the Pension Department to the Stavka, 16 March 1915, RGVIA, f. 2003, op. 2, d. 784, ll. 13–14.

49. "Osobyi zhurnal soveta ministrov," 27 March 1915, notation of emperor's agreement attached, RGVIA, f. 2003, op. 2, d. 784, l. 17.

50. See for example, RGVIA, f. 2003, op. 2, d. 784, ll. 33, 34.

51. RGVIA, f. 2003, op. 2, d. 784, passim.

52. Here the personnel continuity in the upper ranks of the army seems to have played at least some role. In M. D. Bonch-Bruevich's crucial memo on the need for a standing army and the proper bases of army formation, he makes it clear that families of soldiers need to be provided for during wartime at a level at least that of "other professions." M. D. Bonch-Bruevich report to Lenin, secret, 15 March 1918, RGASPI, f. 5, op. 1, d. 2415, l. 5.

53. Copy of contract *(kontrakt)* given to volunteers to sign, April 1918, RGVA, f. 11, op. 8, d. 53, l. 122.

54. "Instruktsiia po organizatsii RKKA," 18 February 1918, RGVA, f. 2, op. 1, d. 8, l. 193.

55. Circular to all military district commanders from Lenin and Trotskii, 5 August 1918, RGVA, f. 2, op 1, d. 33, l. 198.

56. In Kostroma province alone, 63 families were fined a total of over 97,000 rubles over a two-week period in 1919. "Svodka deiatel'nosti tsentral'noi [*sic*] i mestnykh komitetov po bor'be s dezertirstvom," 1–15 September 1919, RGASPI, f. 5, op. 1, d. 2452, l. 17. For the instruction to strike family members from labor exchange rolls, see telegram from Central Desertion Committee to Lenin, 4 January 1919, see l. 1ob.

57. Circular of the Central Desertion Committee to provincial commissions, 10 April 1919, RGVA, f. 11, op. 15s, d. 49s, l. 5ob.

58. See for instance, the telegram from Rattel' (Vseroglavshtab) to all district, provincial, and local military committees, 13 June 1920, RGVA, f. 11, op. 8, d. 48, ll. 41–46; Olikov, *Dezertirstvo v krasnoi armii*, 48; von Hagen, *Soldiers in the Proletarian Dictatorship*, 73, 78.

59. von Hagen, *Soldiers in the Proletarian Dictatorship*, 78.

60. "Organizatsiia oblav," signed by Timofeev (chairman of the Moscow District Desertion Committee), n.d. but probably 1919, RGVA, f. 25883, op. 1, d. 271, l. 602ob.

61. This argument is forwarded in Pyle. For concrete evidence that the property taken from deserters was actually given to soldier families, see her "Village Social Relations," especially 334–43.

62. Report from Central Desertion Commission, completely secret, 11 March 1921, RGASPI, f. 5, op. 1, d. 2452, l. 41.

63. Appeal of Iosif Sergeevich Drozhzhin to Appeals Court of Supreme Court of RSFSR, 19 October 1919, GARF, f. r-1005, op. 2, d. 11, l. 19b.

64. von Hagen, *Soldiers in the Proletarian Dioctatorship*, 78, 282.

65. V. Akulinin, *Znachenie voennoi sluzhby i obiazannosti soldata: Molodym liudiam, prizyvaemym na sluzhbu tsariu i otechestvu*, 2nd ed. (Kherson: Gub. tip., 1913), 28–29.

66. M. I. Dragomirov, "Iz soldatskoi pamiatki," in *Izbrannye trudy: Voprosy vospitaniia i obucheniia voisk*, ed. L. G. Beskrovnyi (Moscow: Voenizdat, 1956), 43.

67. This is the terminology (borrowed in turn from Freud) used by Lynn Hunt, *The Family Romance of the French Revolution* (Berkeley and Los Angeles: University of California Press, 1992). See also Elizabeth Jones Hemenway, "Mother Russia and the Crisis of the Russian National Family: The Puzzle of Gender in Revolutionary Russia," *Nationalities Papers* 25, no. 1 (1997): 103–21. I thank Peter Holquist for bringing this article to my attention.

68. Most of these men graduated the General Staff Academy within about five years of each other (1898–1903), and this group includes many of the *voenspetsy* already mentioned: Bonch-Bruevich, Lebedev, Svechin, and Neznamov to name just a few. The indispensable source for biographical details on *voenspetsy* is A. G. Kavtaradze's lovingly detailed *Voennye spetsialisty na sluzhbe respubliki sovetov, 1917–1920 gg.* (Moscow: Nauka, 1988).

69. A. Neznamov, "K nachalu zimnikh zaniatii [1906]," in *Tekushchie voennye voprosy (sbornik statei)* (St. Petersburg: Tip. Khudozhestvennoi pechati, 1909), 105–6.

70. Ibid., 106.

71. Kuropatkin, *Russian Army,* 1:94.

72. "Ob"iavlenie voiny doblestnoi i velikoi russkoi armii." Circular from Stepanov (duty general of the Staff of Armies on the northern front), 18 January 1916, RGVIA, f. 2003, op. 2, d. 784, l. 261.

73. Petition from reservists stationed in the city of Nikolsk-Ussurite, n.d. but after the September 1915 reservist mobilization, RGVIA, f. 2000, op. 3, d. 2694, l. 73.

74. "Zemnaia pros'ba krest'ianstva," sent to State Duma, 5 August 1915, RGIA, f. 1278, op. 5, d. 1193, l. 106.

75. Telegram from representatives of 15 counties near Karkaralov to the chair of the State Duma, 30 August 1916, RGIA, f. 1278, op. 5, d. 1234, l. 41, 42. See also speech by Khakh-Mamedov to the Duma in 1911 on same theme using the same familial metaphors in chapter 2.

76. Wildman, *The End of the Russian Imperial Army,* 225.

77. On fraternal ideas in new volunteer units, see "Plan formirovaniia revoliutsionnykh batal'ionov iz volonterov tyla." Approved by Brusilov, 23 May 1917. RGVIA, f. 400, op. 19, d. 182, l. 6.

78. Wildman, *The End of the Russian Imperial Army,* 279, 379–80.

79. All these included in "Polozhenie o demokratizatsii armii," order signed by the supreme commander N. Krylenko, 3 December 1917, RGASPI, f. 5, op. 1, d. 2, ll. 27–28.

80. Instruction to the delegate of the transport division of the 136th Infantry Division in Petrograd and to the comrade people's commissar for the explanation of questions raised by a general meeting of citizens in the transport division of the 136th Infantry Division, 23 January 1918, GARF, f. r-1235, op. 79, d. 27, l. 125.

81. "Pervyi den' iavki," n.a., in newspaper *Krasnyi novobranets* (one-day newspaper published by the Political Department of the Saratov Rifle Division and the political secretary of the provincial military commissariat), 3 May 1924, RGVA, f. 9, op. 28s, d. 865, l. 229.

82. See for instance, "Otchet o deiatel'nosti voennogo komissariata goroda Moskvy s 9 marta 1918 po 1 oktobria 1919," RGVA, f. 33988, op. 1, d. 25, l. 61; also see appeal to all officials in the "free and independent Soviet republic of Latvia," n.d. but late 1918 or early 1919, GARF, f. r-393, op. 1, d. 37, l. 8ob.

83. Resolution of the 148th Rifle Regiment of the 17th Rifle Division, 6 December 1918, GARF, f. r-1235, op. 79, d. 2, l. 137.

84. For examples of the use of brotherhood as a model for ethnic relations, see resolutions on national question in the Red Army affirmed at a conference of leading political workers of the Caucasian Red-Banner Army, 13 October 1923, RGVA, f. 9, op. 28s, d. 324, ll. 205–205ob.

85. Letter from the Poltava detachment of Young Pioneers to Stalin, n.d. but received in Moscow on 30 May 1927, RGASPI, f. 17, op. 85, d. 504, l. 17. As Stalin consolidated power, it became less and less clear how he should be addressed. Most Pio-

neers stayed with the safe "comrade," some went with "brother," like the Poltava children, others went with "grandfather," like a group from Astrakhan in 1926 (l. 118), or "uncle," like a group from Minsk (l. 48). None that I read used "father," however.

86. This immortality and infallibility are stressed by Rousseau, for instance, in his discussion of the general will. Jean-Jacques Rousseau, *The Social Contract,* trans. Maurice Cranston (New York and London: Penguin, 1968), 72–73, 149–50.

87. Partha Chatterjee, *The Nation and Its Fragments: Colonial and Postcolonial Histories* (Princeton: Princeton University Press, 1993), 119–20.

88. Tim McDaniel, *The Agony of the Russian Idea* (Princeton: Princeton University Press, 1996), 49.

89. Engelstein, *The Keys to Happiness,* 299.

90. "O nedopushchenii stroevykh nizhnikh chinov evreev k proizvodstvu v unter-ofitsery i ob ogranichenii proizvodstva v unter-ofitserskoe zvanie (starshii razriad) muzykantov i nestroevykh nizhnikh chinov iz evreev," secret circular no. 2110 signed by Lukomskii, 18 October 1910, RGVIA, f. 2000, op. 3, d. 69, l. 5.

91. See for instance report from Staff-Captain Vasil'kov to Stavka, secret, 4 June 1915, RGVIA, f. 2003, op. 2, d. 802, l. 2ob.

92. Letter from Main Administration of the General Staff to chief of staff of Warsaw military district, 11 January 1912, GARF, f. 1745, op. 1, d. 30, l. 5.

93. "O nedopushchenii," l. 5.

94. Jacob G. Frumkin, "Pages from the History of Russian Jewry (Recollections and Documentary Material)," in *Russian Jewry 1860–1917,* ed. Jacob Frumkin, Gregor Aronson, and Alexis Goldenweiser, trans. Mirra Ginsburg (New York and London: Thomas Yoseloff, 1966), 58; Salo W. Baron, *The Russian Jew under Tsars and Soviets* (New York: Macmillan, 1964), 187.

95. Draft tables, RGIA, f. 1292, op. 7, d. 525.

96. The fine was widely applied. Between 1906 and 1910, 109,209 families were fined a total of 31,221,108.55 rubles, though the state was only able to collect 813,051.90 rubles of fines. See 10 October 1911 report of Ministry of Finance to War Ministry, RGVIA, f. 2000, op. 3, d. 86, ll. 241–43. On photographing Jews, see "O fotografirovanii ispytaemykh novobrantsev, prisylaemykh voinskimi prisutstviiami v gospitali i mestnye lazarety," report from the staff of the Kiev military district to the Main Staff, 8 February 1910, RGVIA, f. 2000, op. 3, d. 76, l. 123.

97. Report reviewing action on Jewish question from Main Administration of the General Staff to the chief of the General Staff, 28 October 1911, RGVIA, f. 2000, op. 3, d. 86, l. 265.

98. S. M. Dubnow, *History of the Jews in Russia and Poland from the Earliest Times until the Present Day,* trans. I. Friedlaender (Philadelphia: Jewish Publication Society of America, 1920), 3:155.

99. Hans Rogger, *Jewish Policies and Right-Wing Politics in Imperial Russia* (Berkeley and Los Angeles: University of California Press, 1986), 96.

100. Report of Mobilization Department, 21 May 1911, RGVIA, f. 2000, op. 3, d. 86, ll. 1–2; "Perechen' voprosov o sluzhebnykh kachestvakh nizhnikh chinov iudeiskago veroispovedaniia, a ravno o polozhenii ikh v armii," RGVIA, f. 2000, op. 3, d. 86, ll. 3–6.

101. Letter from Sukhomlinov to Kokovtsov, November 1911, RGVIA, f. 2000, op. 3, d. 86, ll. 268ob-269; letter from Dobrorol'skii to Kokovtsov, October 1912, RGVIA, f. 2000, op. 3, d. 86, ll. 293–293ob.

102. Letter from the chief of the sanitary units of the armies of the southwestern front (Ianitskii) to the chief of the 4th main evacuation point, 5 September 1915.

In "Dokumenty o presledovanii evreev," *Arkhiv russkoi revoliutsii* 19 (1928): 264. This was the same wording used by Ianushkevich in his original circular. See secret letter from Ianushkevich to M. V. Alekseev (chief of the northwestern front), 5 August 1915, RGVIA, f. 2000, op. 3, d. 2694, l. 14.

103. On removal of restrictions, see order no. 135 signed by war minister Guchkov, 16 March 1917, RGVIA, f. 400, op. 19, d. 175, l. 6; on amnesty, see MVD circular to provincial officials, 15 April 1917, RGVIA, f. 2000, op. 3, d. 1245, l. 29.

104. Speech of Protopopov (reporter for Duma Defense Committee) at closed Duma session, 30 November 1911, RGVIA, f. 2000, op. 3, d. 79, l. 1152.

105. Officer Dalinskii, *"Evrei v armii"* (St. Petersburg: Tip. Glavnogo upravleniia udelov, 1911), 49. Pamphlet included in RGVIA, f. 2000, op. 3, d. 77, ll. 315–39.

106. See here also Eric Lohr, "The Russian Army and the Jews: Mass Deportations, Hostages, and Violence during World War I," *Russian Review* 60, no. 3 (July 2001): 404–19.

107. Rogger, *Jewish Policies*, 112.

108. I borrow this term from Peter Holquist. See his "'Information is the Alpha and Omega of Our Work': Bolshevik Surveillance in its Pan-European Context," *Journal of Modern History* 69 (September 1997): 415–50.

109. Dozens of these orders to resettle Jews are included in "Dokumenty o presledovanii evreev." For a longer discussion of the refugee issue, Jewish refugees included, see Peter Gatrell, *A Whole Empire Walking: Refugees in Russia During World War I* (Bloomington and Indianapolis: Indiana University Press, 1999).

110. Order of 18th Army Corps, 14 May 1915, in "Dokumenty o presledovanii evreev," 258.

111. For eyewitness and second-hand accounts of some of these incidents, see Florence Farmborough, *Nurse at the Russian Front: A Diary 1914–18* (London: Constable, 1974), 151, 179–81.

112. Order to the police from Kurland province from Stavka, n.d. but May 1915, *Arkhiv russkoi revoliutsii* 19 (1928): 258–59.

113. Dalinskii, "Evrei v armii," 48–49.

114. L. Voitolovskii, *Po sledam voiny: Pokhodnye zapiski, 1914–1917*, 2nd ed. (Leningrad: Gosizdat, 1926), 14.

115. Ibid., 15.

116. Lohr, "Enemy Alien Politics within the Russian Empire during World War I," 181.

117. Frumkin, "Pages from the History of Russian Jewry," 58.

118. Vladimir S. Littauer, *Russian Hussar: A Story of the Imperial Cavalry, 1911–1920* (1965; reprint, Shippensburg, Penn.: White Mane Publishing, 1993), 153.

119. Frumkin, "Pages from the History of Russian Jewry," 70.

120. Alfred Knox, *With the Russian Army, 1914–1917* (London: Hutchinson and Co., 1921), 1:120, 145; Frumkin, "Pages from the History of Russian Jewry," 63.

121. Rogger, *Jewish Politics*, 107.

122. Frumkin, "Pages from the History of Russian Jewry," 66.

123. Taken from anonymous perlustrated letter and reported in "Svodka svedenii, sobrannykh iz otchetov voennykh tsenzorov Kazanskogo voennogo okruga," August 1916, RGVIA, f. 2000, op. 3, d. 2694, l. 45.

124. Letter from Intelligence Department at Stavka to the quartermaster-general at Stavka, completely secret, 31 October 1915, RGVIA, f. 2003, op. 2, d. 784, l. 45; explanation sent further from Alekseev (chief of staff at Stavka) to Polivanov (war minister) in 22 December 1915 letter, RGVIA, f. 2003, op. 2, d. 784, l. 50.

125. The idea that wars were the tests of nations was common throughout the period. See A. M. Zaionchkovskii, *Oborona Sevastapolia: Podvigi zashchitnikov*, 2nd ed. (St. Petersburg: Izd. Vysochaishe utverzhdennnago Komiteta po vozstanovleniiu pamiatnikov Sevastopol'skoi oborony, 1904), 12; A. Bubnov, *Voennaia reforma, prizyv 1902, i politrabota* (Moscow: Krasnaia zvezda, 1924), 32.

126. Letter from Rodzianko to Alekseev, 18 November 1915, RGVIA, f. 2003, op. 2, d. 784, l. 52.

127. See, for instance, Robert Conquest, *The Great Terror: A Reassessment* (New York and Oxford: Oxford University Press, 1990), 25, 111.

128. V. Molotov, *Molotov Remembers: Inside Kremlin Politics: Conversations with Felix Chuev* (Chicago: University of Chicago Press, 1993), 254.

129. For a detailed discussion of Soviet "outcasts" and the mechanisms by which citizens were excluded from the national community, see Golfo Alexopolous, *Stalin's Outcasts: Aliens, Citizens, and the Soviet State, 1926–1936* (Ithaca, N.Y.: Cornell University Press, forthcoming).

130. The rear militia was established by Sovnarkom decree on 20 July 1918. A copy of the decree, along with appendixes including rules for determining who should be placed in it, are in RGVA, f. 3, op. 1, d. 120, ll. 36–39.

131. "Registratsionnaia kartochka litsa, podlezhashchago zachisleniiu v tylovoe opolchenie," 20 July 1918, RGVA, f. 3, op. 1, d. 120, l. 39ob.

132. "Otchet o deiatel'nosti Mobilizatsionnogo Upravlenie Vserossiiskogo Glavnogo Shtaba s 25 Oktiabria 1917 goda po 15-e avgusta 1920 goda," secret, RGVA, f. 11, op. 8, d. 36, ll. 38–40. Overall, excluding rear militia men, former officers, former military bureaucrats, former NCOs, and former medical personnel, 3,866,009 men were conscripted between the October Revolution and 15 August 1920. Typical estimates of the percentage of the population categorized as class enemies in the 1920s (after the first wave of war against class enemies) ranged from 3–5 percent.

133. Telegram from the chairman of the Zamoskvoretskii mobilization induction commission to the [Moscow] district military committee, 30 August 1918, RGVA, f. 25883, op. 3, d. 947, l. 15.

134. Unsigned document, 4 November 1918, RGVA, f. 3, op. 1, d. 92, l. 169.

135. "Voennyi zagovor shpionov i belogvardeitsev," *Izvestiia VTsIK*, 18 June 1919, p. 1. Rex A. Wade, ed., *Documents of Soviet History*, vol. 1 (Gulf Breeze, Fla.: Academic International Press, 1991), 213.

136. See the heated, even acidic, debates on the *voenspets* question during closed sessions of the Eighth Party Congress (March 1919), in which Voroshilov and Stalin faced off against Lenin and military officials sent by Trotskii, with assorted others taking sides during the debate. RGASPI, f. 41, op. 2, d. 3, esp. Ll. 34–62.

137. Letter to Sovnarkom from Aleksandr Shliapnikov and three others, 22 November 1917, RGASPI, f. 5, op. 1, d. 2412, l. 2. A member of the Black Hundreds was a part of the ultra-chauvinist right in tsarist Russia. Bonch-Bruevich belonged to none of those radical organizations.

138. Telegram from Trotskii to Lenin, 21 August 1918, RGASPI, f. 5, op. 1, d. 2412, l. 21.

139. Telegram from Trotskii to Bonch-Bruevich, 21 August 1918, RGASPI, f. 5, op. 1, d. 2412, l. 21; telegram from Trotskii to Sklianskii notifying him of Bonch-Bruevich's permanent departure, 23 August 1918, RGASPI, f. 5, op. 1, d. 2412, l. 22.

140. "Doklad chlena voennogo revoliutsionnogo soveta iuzhnogo fronta i soveta 10 armii Okulova," 22 December 1918, RGASPI, f. 17, op. 109, d. 38, l. 2.

141. Ibid., l. 3.

142. Ibid., l. 16.

143. "Otchet o deiatel'nosti Moskovskogo okruzhnogo komissariata po voen-nym delam s 25 oktobria 1917 do noiabria 1918 g.," November 1918, RGVA, f. 33988, op. 1, d. 4, l. 43.

144. Report of the Political Department of the 3rd Army for June 1919, RGVA, f. 176, op. 2, d. 14, l. 37ob.

145. "Znaite pravdu: pochemu my vedem voinu!" PUR publication (1920) in-cluded in Eliseeva, Listovki, 13.

146. Telegram from Efimov (Riazan') to the VVS (Moscow), 8 November 1918, RGVA, f. 3, op. 1, d. 92, l. 209.

147. See for instance, the completely secret protocol no. 7 of the district politi-cal conference of the Western Siberian military district, 12 January 1924, RGVA, f. 9, op. 28s, d. 441, l. 19.

148. Telegram from Political Department of the 10th Rifle Division to the Military Council of the 3rd Army, 1 July 1919, RGVA, f. 176, op. 6, d. 5, l. 4.; "Kratkaia instruktsiia o bor'be s banditzmom i kulacheskimi vosstaniiami," signed by chairman of Sovnarkom of Ukraine (Rakovskii), completely secret, 20 April 1920, RGVA, f. 11, op. 8, d. 1059, l. 167.

149. Telegram from Gusev (member of the RVS of the southern front) to Trot-skii, subsequently forwarded to Lenin, 20 October 1920, RGASPI, f. 5, op. 1, d. 2435, l. 12; memorandum from the Jewish Communist Party (Poalei-Zion) to Sovnarkom, 10 June 1922, RGASPI, f. 17, op. 84, d. 451, l. 11.

150. "Predvaritel'nye itogi prizyva 1903 goda," secret, addressed directly to Stalin, n.a., n.d. (but no earlier than November 1925), RGASPI, f. 17, op. 84, d. 1013, l. 39.

151. "Kratkaia vypiska iz svodki PURa o khode prizyva 1904 g.," 21 November 1926, RGVA, f. 4, op. 2, d. 233, l. 30.

152. Telegram from Krichev (chairman of soviet of 4th district in city of Temkin) to People's Commissar of Military Affairs (Moscow), 30 April 1919, RGVA, f. 11, op. 8, d. 928, l. 9; declaration from the organization of Red Army men older than 30 years in the Shock Artillery Group of the 3rd Army to the administrator of affairs of the RVSR, 27 April 1920, RGVA, f. 11, op. 8, d. 1059, l. 33ob.; "Svodka materialov o rabote s natsmen'shinstvami prizyve 1903 g.," secret, from chief of the Informa-tion Unit of PUR (Iordanskii), 13 May 1926, RGVA, f. 9, op. 28s, d. 804, l. 14ob.

153. "Kratkaia obshchaia kharakteristika pribyvshego iz Ukrainy v Petrograd-skii voennyi okrug popolneniia doprizyva 1901 goda," completely secret, signed by A. Gusev, 15 November 1922, RGVA, f. 9, op. 28s, d. 403, l. 76; "Natsmen'shinstvo v KA," PUR report signed by Milov and Chernevskii, secret, 21 April 1925, RGVA, f. 9, op. 28s, d. 704, ll. 40–42.

154. Akulinin, Znachenie voennoi sluzhby, 29–30.

155. Order to PUR no. 138/12, signed by Trotskii, Pavlovskii (assistant chief of PUR), and Steingart (head of the Organization and Instruction Department of PUR), 27 March 1922, RGVA, f. 9, op. 28s, d. 1023, l. 161.

156. See for instance instructions on combatting spying sent from General Baluev (commander of the 5th Army Corps) to the commander of the 10th Infantry Division, secret, 12 June 1915, RGVIA, f. 2653, op. 2, d. 367, l. 1ob; also instructions for counterintelligence on the home front during Civil War in "Programma zaniatii v shkole mladshikh nabliudatelei pri Riazanskom otdelenii registratsionnoi sluzhby Moskovskogo raiona," 12 August 1918, RGVA, f. 3, op. 1, d. 71, l. 19.

157. Appeal of the war minister (Guchkov), n.d. but March or April 1917, RGVIA, f. 2067, op. 1, d. 3838, l. 13.

158. Sheila Fitzpatrick, *The Russian Revolution,* 2nd ed. (Oxford and New York: Oxford University Press, 1994), 58; Richard Pipes, *The Russian Revolution* (New York: Alfred Knopf, 1990), 431–33.

159. "K naseleniiu Arkhangel'skoi, Vologodskoi, i Olonetskoi gubernii," appeal from M. Kedrov (people's commissar), 6 August 1918, GARF, f. r-1235, op. 79, d. 7, l. 5.

160. Stenographic report of closed session of Eighth Party Congress, Stalin speech, RGASPI, f. 41, op. 2, d. 3, l. 42.

161. Space does not permit a full explication of White mobilizational strategies, but they were consonant with those of the tsarist period, and often with those of the Reds. Whites used the discourse of family and fraternity, and tried to tar the Bolsheviks as "foreign," not just because of the German connection, but also because many of their leaders were Jewish, and because they used foreign volunteers in the Red Army, of whom the Koreans and Japanese were the most offensive to White sensibilities.

162. Anonymous letter, 1914, RGIA, f. 1276, op. 10, d. 826, l. 35.

163. Eduard M. Dune, *Notes of a Red Guard,* trans. and ed. Diane P. Koenker and S. A. Smith (Urbana and Chicago: University of Illinois Press, 1993), 144–45.

164. Telegram from chief of the Line and Staffing Department of Moscow military district (Sozontov) to the chief of the Line Administration of the Main Administration of the Red Army, immediate, secret, 16 October 1925, RGVA, f. 25883, op. 2, d. 1160, l. 10.

165. See for instance "Programma politzaniatii s krasnoarmeitsami peremennogo sostava 12 terdiv na period ikh trekhnedel'nykh sborov," n.d. but 1924, RGVA, f. 25893, op. 1, d. 136, ll. 93–95.

166. On these units, see RGVIA, f. 2000, op. 3, d. 2647, ll. 35, 47; f. 2003, op. 2, d. 325 passim; RGIA, f. 1276, op. 10, d. 843b, ll. 1–10; RGVA, f. 11, op. 15, d. 20, 22 passim; RGASPI, f. 17, op. 109, d. 51, ll. 1–2.

167. Order to PUR no. 138/12, signed by Trotskii, Pavlovskii (assistant chief of PUR), and Steingart (head of the Organization and Instruction Department of PUR), 27 March 1922, RGVA, f. 9, op. 28s, d. 1023, l. 161.

168. Robert Conquest, *Stalin: Breaker of Nations* (New York: Viking, 1991).

4: The Nationalization of Masculinity

1. On these, see Jeffrey Brooks, *When Russia Learned to Read: Literacy and Popular Literature, 1861–1917* (Princeton: Princeton University Press, 1985); Louise McReynolds, *The News Under Russia's Old Regime: The Development of a Mass-Circulation Press* (Princeton: Princeton University Press, 1991); Ben Eklof, *Russian Peasant Schools: Officialdom, Village Culture, and Popular Pedagogy, 1861–1914* (Berkeley and Los Angeles: University of California Press, 1986). The notion of "print-capitalism" as an important feature in national development comes from Anderson's *Imagined Communities.*

2. For similar concerns in Britain, and similar responses to those concerns, see Bourke, *Dismembering the Male.*

3. Report of the Mobilization Department of the Main Staff, 13 August 1905, RGVIA, f. 2000, op. 1, d. 307, l. 3.

4. Report from consulting physician of Kiev Military Hospital, n.d. but probably 1908 or 1909, RGVIA, f. 2000, op. 3, d. 76, l. 134.

5. Reviews of militia training camps, 1912, RGVIA, f. 2000, op. 3, d. 865, ll. 16, 25ob., 49.

6. Report of the Main Military-Sanitation Administration to the chief of the General Staff, 30 September 1911, RGVIA, f. 2000, op. 3, d. 86, l. 2.

7. Cornelie Usborne has much the same argument regarding Germany. According to her, state intervention into the bodies of its citizens was a trend begun in the Wilhelmine period, expanded during World War I, and developed in Weimar Germany long before it became a Nazi obsession. Cornelie Usborne, *The Politics of the Body in Weimar Germany: Women's Reproductive Rights and Duties* (London: Macmillan, 1992), 202–4.

8. Eklof, *Russian Peasant Schools*, 125.

9. "Otchet o pervykh kratkosrochnykh kursakh gimnastiki dlia uchashchikhsia v nizshikh i srednykh uchebnykh zavedeniiakh Kavkazskogo uchebnago okruga sostoiavshikhsia letom 1909 goda," 1909, RGVIA, f. 2000, op. 2, d. 794, ll. 415–457ob.

10. Excerpts from the 1910 report to the tsar on the condition of Semirechenskaia oblast', RGVIA, f. 2000, op. 2, d. 800, ll. 44–45. At the time, there were 831 boys and 11 girls in "native schools" in the region, and 5,939 boys and 1,629 girls in "Russian schools."

11. See "Zhurnal zasedaniia mezhduvedomstvennoi Komissii, uchrezhdennoi dlia detal'noi razrabotki voprosov o fizicheskom razvitii molodezhi i obuchenii ee voennomu stroiu," 26 February 1911, RGVIA, f. 2000, op. 2, d. 795, ll. 347–348.

12. "K s"ezdu po fizicheskomu razvitiiu i sportu," 1911, RGVIA, f. 2000, op. 2, d. 795, l. 120. List numbers in this *delo* do not correspond to document order.

13. See the declarations of the Holy Synod and the MNP to this effect, 29 December 1911 and 19 June 1912, RGVIA, f. 2000, op. 2, d. 795, ll. 2ob, 7ob.

14. See for instance, Major-General Dmitrii Dubenskii, *Uchebnik dlia vedeniia stroevykh i gimnasticheskikh zaniatii v narodnykh shkolakh i drugikh uchebnykh zavedeniiakh* (St. Petersburg: Morskoe ministerstvo, 1911). Included in toto in RGVIA, f. 2000, op. 2, d. 794, ll. 239–322.

15. The first Boy Scout troop was formed in Tsarskoe Selo by army officers in 1909. James Riordan, *Sport in Soviet Society: Development of Sport and Physical Education in Russia and the USSR* (Cambridge: Cambridge University Press, 1977), 35.

16. Vasili Klyuchevsky, *Peter the Great*, trans. and with an introduction by Liliana Archibald (New York: Vintage, 1961), 10–12.

17. Order to military bureaucracy no. 299, signed by Sukhomlinov (war minister) and approved by the tsar, 28 June 1910 (tsar's approval 21 June 1910), RGVIA, f. 2000, op. 2, d. 794, l. 5.

18. Report from governor of St. Petersburg to the chairman of the Council of Ministers, 18 July 1910, RGVIA, f. 2000, op. 2, d. 794, l. 5ob. See similar expressions of hope and fear regarding *poteshnye roty* in "Osobyi zhurnal soveta ministrov," 29 January 1911, RGVIA, f. 2000, op. 2, d. 794, ll. 58–61.

19. "Polozhenie o vneshkol'noi podgotovke russkoi molodezhi k voennoi sluzhbe," 18 July 1911. In Gorianov and Lebedev, *Ustavy o voinskoi povinnosti*, Appendix section, pp. 3–7. See also RGVIA, f. 2000, op. 2, d. 794, ll. 228–230.

20. "Osnovaniia formirovaniia 'poteshnykh rot' v Moskovskom voennom okruge," 31 August 1910, RGVIA, f. 2000, op. 2, d. 794, l. 16ob.

21. "Plan mobilizatsii molodezhi i sporta," report of Temporary Council on Physical Development and Sport, 7 September 1915, RGVIA, f. 2000, op. 2, d. 2377, ll. 2–4.

22. "Polozhenie o mobilizatsii sporta," approved by tsar on 8 December 1915, RGIA, f. 1292, op. 5, d. 323, ll. 4–8ob.

23. General Voeikov, "O razrabotke mer o fizicheskomu vospitaniiu lits do-

prizyvnogo vozrasta," approved by tsar and submitted to Council of Ministers on 10 October 1915, RGIA, f. 1276, op. 11, d. 931, l. 3.

24. Letter from administrator of affairs of Council of Ministers to Voeikov, 20 December 1915, RGIA, f. 1276, op. 11, d. 931, l. 29. On cost calculation, see "Zhurnal osobago mezhduvedomstvennago soveshchaniia, obrazovannago Sovetom Ministrom 23 Oktiabria dlia soobrazheniia meropriiatii, sviazannykh s mobilizatsiei sporta," 26 October 1915, RGIA, f. 1292, op. 5, d. 322, l. 11.

25. "Chto takoe vsevobuch," n.d., n.a., manuscript copy intended for eventual publication in Petrograd, RGVA, f. 65, op. 13, d. 27, l. 54.

26. Slogans from the Moscow military district Vsevobuch Administration, 23 January 1920, RGVA, f. 65, op. 7, d. 63, l. 224.

27. Report to the Central Administration of Vsevobuch, n.a., 29 October 1918, RGVA, f. 65, op. 13, d. 104, l. 59.

28. "Otchet deiatel'nosti glavnogo upravleniia vsevobuch s nachala uchrezhdeniia vsevobuch po 1 sent. 1920," n.a., n.d., RGVA, f. 33988, op. 1, d. 28, ll. 2, 7, 7ob.

29. Telegram from Sheshukovskii to Muralov, 5 February 1919, RGVA, f. 25883, op. 2, d. 764, ll. 135–135a.

30. "Programma doprizyvnoi podgotovki" n.d. but probably early 1919, RGVA, f. 65, op. 7, d. 1, l. 39.

31. "Kratkii otchet uchebno-org. otdela [Vsevobuch] za 1919 god," n.a., n.d., RGVA, f. 33988 op. 1 d. 28, l. 49.

32. "Programma blizhaishikh meropriiatii," head of Vsevobuch Administration, n.d. but probably late 1918, RGVA, f. 65, op. 7, d. 1, l. 68ob.

33. "Otchet o deiatel'nosti Moskovskogo okruzhnogo komissariata po voennym delam s 25 okt. 1917 g. po noiabr' 1918 goda," n.a., n.d. but clearly in November or December 1918, RGVA, f. 33988, op. 1, d. 4, l. 34ob.

34. "Programma blizhaishikh meropriiatii," head of Vsevobuch Administration, n.d. but probably late 1918, RGVA, f. 65, op. 7, d. 1, l. 66ob.

35. "Vtoroi vserossiiskii s"ezd RKSM. Stenotchet," 5 August 1919, in RGVA, f. 65, op. 13, d. 1, ll. 12–44. Material on scouts: ll. 27, 37.

36. Secret report to the party's Central Committee, with copies to PUR, RVS, and Vseroglavshtab from Nachvsevobuch, September 1919, RGVA, f. 65, op. 1, d. 2, l. 99.

37. Unlabeled document, but very likely speech of Podvoiskii to All-Russian Conference of Responsible Organizers in the Countryside, n.d. but clearly soon after the Ninth Party Congress (which concluded in April 1920), RGVA, f. 65, op. 13, d. 1, ll. 65ob-67.

38. Decree of Sovnarkom of Georgian Socialist Soviet Republic printed in *Pravda gruzii*, 26 November 1922. Excerpt preserved in TsKhDMO, f. 1, op. 23, d. 102, l. 48; "Otchet o rabote po sportu i doprizyvnoi podgotovke v vologodskom polkovom okruge," 25 May 1921, RGVA, f. 25883, op. 5, d. 2207, l. 185ob.

39. A. M. Viaz'mitinov, ed., *Russkie skauty* (Madrid: Central Staff of the National Organization of Russian Scouts, 1969), 106.

40. Quote here from N. K. Krupskaia, "Iunye pionery (1923)," in *Vospitanie molodezhi v leninskom dukhe* (Moscow: Pedagogika, 1989), 201. Her more extended critique is "RKSM i boiskautizm," in *Pedagogicheskie sochineniia v desiati tomakh* (Moscow: Izd. akademii pedagogicheskikh nauk, 1957–63), 5:25–61.

41. Depending on the era, Pioneers included boys and girls aged between 10 and 15 or 11 and 16. N. Verchenko et al., eds., *Leninskii komsomol (ocherki po istorii VLKSM)*, 3rd ed. (Moscow: Molodaia gvardiia, 1963), 265–68. These historians of the

Komsomol make clear that the Pioneers were formed explicitly as a Communist answer to the tasks that the Scouts answered in bourgeois countries, 264. By 1939, there were more than 13 million Pioneers in the USSR. *Bol'shaia sovetskaia entsiklopediia,* 1st ed., s.v. "Pionerskaia organizatsiia."

42. M. I. Dragomirov, "Vliianie rasprostraneniia nareznogo oruzhiia na vospitanie i taktiky voisk" (1861). Reprinted in his *Sbornik original'nykh i perevodnykh statei,* 1:36–37.

43. "Perechen' voprosov o sluzhebnykh i nravstvennykh kachestvakh nizhnikh chinov iudeiskago veroispovedaniia, a ravno o polozhenii ikh v armii," 1911, RGVIA, f. 2000, op. 3, d. 86, l. 3.

44. "Metodicheskoe ukazanie k materialom programmy doprizyvnoi podgotovki shkol'nogo vozrasta pervoi stupeni," n.a., n.d. but likely late 1918, RGVA, f. 65, op. 7, d. 1, ll. 80ob-81.

45. Slogans from Moscow District Administration of Vsevobuch, 9 October 1920, RGVA, f. 65, op. 7, d. 63, l. 36.

46. "Zakony i obychai iunykh pionerov," approved by the Komsomol Central Committee, 17 September 1923, TsKhDMO, f. 1, op. 3, d. 8, l. 58ob.

47. The injunctions to brush teeth, not spit on the floor, and bathe regularly were constants in Red Army training from the very beginning of the regime. See for instance *Instruktsiia krasnoarmeitsu,* 2nd ed. (Moscow: VTsIK, 1918), 7.

48. "Zakony i obychai iunykh pionerov."

49. See *Nastavlenie dlia strel'by iz vintovok, karabinov, i revol'verov* (Kiev: N. Ia. Ogloblina, 1916), 66.

50. List of military property transferred to Plotsk magistrate, 26 July 1914, GARF, f. 1745, op. 1, d. 58, ll. 435ob-440ob.

51. "Nemetskaia pechat' o 'poteshnykh,'" *Rossiia* (7 August 1911). Excerpt in RGVIA, f. 2000, op. 2, d. 678, l. 2.

52. See, for instance reports of formation of show troops in the Moscow military district in 1920, RGVA, f. 25883, op. 5, d. 2112, ll. 17, 20ob.

53. Sergei Varin, "Tri sportivno-gimasticheskikh agitatsionnykh vechera [*sic*]," 1 June 1921, RGVA, f. 65, op. 1, d. 45, l. 134.

54. Front page of *Fizicheskaia kul'tura i vsevobuch* [Organ Sibirskogo Soveta Fizicheskoi Kul'tury i Sibirskogo Upravleniia Vsevobucha] 1, no. 1 (July–August 1921). Copy of paper located in RGVA, f. 16, op. 1, d. 11, l. 17.

55. G. Norvid, "Kuda my vedem," *Fizicheskaia kul'tura i vsevobuch* [Organ Sibirskogo Soveta Fizicheskoi Kul'tury i Sibirskogo Upravleniia Vsevobucha] 1, no. 1 (July–August 1921), RGVA, f. 16, op. 1 d. 11, l. 17.

56. Ibid., l. 17ob.

57. Ibid.

58. "Tezisy doklada po sportu i doprizyvnoi podgotovki," n.a. but likely Podvoiskii, n.d., RGVA, f. 65, op. 1, d. 45, l. 38. I take the term "New Hellenism" from a report of Vsevobuch workers in Viatka. "Doklad po sektsii agitatsii i populiarizatsii idei vsevobucha v zasedanii 1–go viatskogo obshchegubernskogo s"ezda deiatelei po vsevobuchu," 27 November 1919, RGVA, f. 65, op. 4, d. 107, l. 57ob.

59. Report from Vsevobuch, n.a., 29 October 1918, RGVA, f. 65, op. 13, d. 104, l. 60.

60. Letter from Al'bert Kiram received by Vsevobuch, 22 July 1921, RGVA, f. 65, op. 1, d. 45, l. 30.

61. "Lozungi i plakaty dlia detei (Kursk)," n.d. but probably 1920, RGVA, f. 65, op. 7, d. 63, l. 42.

62. Slogans in Orel military district, 21 October 1920, RGVA, f. 65, op. 7, d. 63, l. 60.

63. Order to the 23rd Army Corps in Warsaw, General Baron Raush von Traubenberg, 15 March 1911, RGVIA, f. 2000, op. 2, d. 1160, l. 15.

64. Anton I. Denikin, *The Career of a Tsarist Officer: Memoirs, 1872–1916*, trans. Margaret Patoski (Minneapolis: University of Minnesota Press, 1975), 32.

65. Ibid., 40. For a similar sentiment, see also Donald Raleigh, ed., *A Russian Civil War Diary: Alexis Babine in Saratov, 1917–1922* (Durham, N.C., and London: Duke University Press, 1988), 23.

66. Order of the administration of Vsevobuch of the Western Army in the Western military district, 15 December 1920, RGVA, f. 65, op. 7, d. 63, l. 19.

67. M. Sovetnikov, "Tezisy dokladov o rabote OblSFK i ocherednykh zadachakh po fizkul'ture," 16 February 1926, TsKhDMO, f. 1, op. 23, d. 652, ll. 43–44.

68. *Instruktsiia po obucheniiu voennomu stroiu i gimnastike v nizshikh uchebnykh zavedeniiakh Kievskago uchebnago okruga* (Kiev: N. N. Kushnerev, 1911), 6.

69. See for instance E. V., "Novaia oblast' sovetskogo stroitel'stva," manuscript submitted to *Novyi put'* (Riga), 27 August 1921, RGVA, f. 65, op. 13, d. 27, l. 1.

70. Ibid., l. 6.

71. N. Ganchikov, "Sovremennye problemy fizicheskoi kul'tury," *Fizicheskaia kul'tura i vsevobuch*. RGVA, f. 65, op. 1, d. 11, l. 18.

72. Ibid.

73. "Vsepoddanneishii otchet o sostoianii S-Peterburgskoi gubernii za 1909 god." Governor Aleksandr Zinov'ev, excerpt included in RGVIA, f. 2000, op. 3, d. 71, l. 419. Emphasis added.

74. V. Raikovskii, *Voennoe vospitanie* (Moscow: A. I. Snegirevoi, 1908), 33. Emphasis added.

75. See for instance "O dukhe obucheniia voisk (1868)" and "Domashnye mery vospitaniia soldata (1868)." Both reprinted in V. N. Lobov, ed., *O dolge i chesti voinskoi v rossiiskoi armii: Sobranie materialov, dokumentov, i statei* (Moscow: Voenizdat, 1991), 101–3.

76. M. Galkin, "Novyi put' sovremennogo ofitsera [1906]," in Lobov, *O dolge i chesti voinskoi v rossiiskoi armii*, 203–4. The quote in pt. 6 is taken from Dragomirov's famed "Soldier's handbook" *(Soldatskaia knizhka)*. Emphasis in original.

77. Draft tables, RGIA, f. 1292, op. 7, d. 594–596.

78. On the rapid rise of literature for soldiers in the late nineteenth and early twentieth century, see S. V. Belov, "Izdatel'stvo V. A. Berezovskogo (iz istorii izdaniia voennoi literatury v Rossii)," *Voenno-istoricheskii zhurnal* no. 11 (1989): 85–90. On the role of military service in increasing literacy and exposing young men to popular literature, see Brooks, *When Russia Learned to Read,* 22.

79. Akulinin, *Znachenie voennoi sluzhby,* 5.

80. Ibid., 5–6.

81. N. Gorbov, comp., *Russkaia istoriia dlia nachal'nykh shkol,* 18th ed. (Moscow: Izd. Tikhomirova, 1914), 109–10.

82. *Instruktsiia po obucheniiu,* 3. See an almost identical list of qualitites for the same goal in the "Programma k voennoi sluzhbe v uchebnykh zavedeniiakh i vne ikh," 1910, RGVIA, f. 2000, op. 2, d. 794, l. 75.

83. Instructions to military commissars on eastern front, 14 April 1919, in *Partiino-politicheskaia rabota v Krasnoi Armii (mart 1919–1920 gg.)* (Moscow: Voenizdat, 1964), 172.

84. Vigilance and consciousness, indeed, were the theme of a short morality piece for soldiers published in the late nineteenth century. See K. Tkhvorzhevskii, *Nadezhnye soldaty,* Soldatskaia biblioteka (St. Petersburg: Berezovskii, 1897).

85. Telegram from Trotskii to the chairman of VTsIK, n.d., RGASPI, f. 17, op. 109, d. 8, l. 45.

86. Telegram from Trotskii to Lenin (and Press Bureau), 11 September 1918, RGASPI, f. 17, op. 109, d. 8, l. 34.

87. Order from chairman of RVSR (Trotskii), 7 October 1918, RGASPI, f. 5, op. 1, d. 2452, l. 7.

88. "Beite polskikh panov! Gonite dezertirov," agitational pamphlet from the RVS of the western front, 1920, Smolensk Archive, roll 51, d. 467, l. 3.

89. Material from Kaluga province, July 1920, RGASPI, f. 17, op. 10, d. 47, l. 28. See here also Elizabeth A. Wood, *The Baba and the Comrade: Gender and Politics in Revolutionary Russia* (Bloomington and Indianapolis: Indiana University Press, 1997), 60.

90. "Obshchie ukazaniia po vedeniiu zaniatii po voennoi doprizyvnoi podgotovke," n.a., n.d., RGVA, f. 65, op. 7, d. 1, l. 79ob. See below for a discussion of the masculine coding of "activeness" in distinction to women's "passiveness."

91. "Zakony i obychai iunykh pionerov," approved by the Komsomol Central Committee, 17 September 1923, TsKhDMO, f. 1, op. 3, d. 8, l. 58ob.

92. I stress the caveat here, since conscription was extremely decentralized in certain regions during the Civil War, and it is entirely plausible that a local commander put unwilling women on the front line at that time.

93. Circular to provincial committees from MVD, 18 May 1917, RGVIA, f. 400, op. 19, d. 171, l. 83.

94. Lists of doctors sent to front from Moscow military district, 1919, RGVA, f. 25883, op. 6, d. 619, ll. 15ob., 37ob, 55ob. For statistics in 1913, see *Zdravookhranenie v SSSR: Statisticheskii sbornik* (Moscow: Medgiz, 1957), 51. I thank Chris Burton for this reference.

95. "Polozhenie ob otriadakh osob. nazn. RSFSR," completely secret, 24 March 1921, RGASPI, f. 17, op. 84, d. 263, l. 14.

96. An initial stab at the topic has been made in Iurii Khechinov, *Angely khraniteli: Stranitsy istorii otechestva* (Moscow: Agenstvo "Vmeste," 1993). For passing references, see Hubertus Jahn, *Patriotic Culture in Russia during World War I* (Ithaca, N.Y., and London: Cornell University Press, 1995), 21, 42; W. Bruce Lincoln, *Passage Through Armageddon: The Russians in War and Revolution, 1914–1918* (New York: Simon and Schuster, 1986), 96–97. For an excellent treatment of British nurses prior to World War I, see Anne Summers, *Angels and Citizens: British Women as Military Nurses, 1854–1914* (London and New York: Routledge and Kegan Paul, 1988). In the Civil War, Sisters of Mercy (an organization with "bourgeois" roots) were replaced by Red Sisters.

97. Jahn, *Patriotic Culture*, 42.

98. F. Stepun, *Iz pisem praporshchika artillerista* (Prague: Plamia, n.d.), 159–60.

99. "Vyderzhki iz vyvodov Samarskogo tsentral'nogo punkta, po soderzhaniiu pisem proishedshikh v period vremeni s poloviny oktiabria do poloviny noiabria," 15 October–15 November 1915, RGVIA, f. 2653, op. 2, d. 367, l. 6ob.

100. Telegram from main commander of western front to V. V. Smirnov (commander of 2nd Army), 20 November 1915, RGVIA, f. 2653, op. 2, d. 367, l. 17.

101. Secret telegram from Evacuation Administration of the Main Administration of the General Staff (Beliaev) to commander of Petrograd military district, 6 November 1914, RGVIA, f. 1, op. 1, t. 44, d. 647, l. 6.

102. Telegram from Petrograd local committee to Mobilization Committee of Petrograd Main Administration of Red Cross and response, 12 September 1914 and 13 September 1914, RGVIA, f. 12651, op. 1, d. 1125, ll. 4, 7.

103. Report from doctor on military-sanitary train no. 2228 to the chief of the

130th evacuation point, secret, 23 August 1916, RGVIA, f. 12651, op. 1, d. 1125, l. 139. Emphasis added.

104. Accounts of awards to women in frontline Red Cross units, 11 and 12 December 1914, RGVIA, f. 12651, op. 10, d. 21, ll. 8, 12.

105. Iu. N. Khristinin, "Ne radi nagrad, no radi tokmo rodnogo narodu," *Voenno-istoricheskii zhurnal* no. 1 (1994): 92–93. This uneasiness about women displaying active courage was the norm, but it was not universally felt. One patriotic short book released in 1914 (and approved by the military censor) in Kiev even lauded and glorified its fictional female hero for her ability to shoot, bayonet, and withstand injury just as well as men. See *Zhenshchina-voin* (Kiev: Izd. Rubanova, 1914).

106. On the role of active *virtù* in republican thought, see Pocock, *Machiavellian Moment,* especially p. 203.

107. Other women fought as combat soldiers in Russia prior to World War I, but they posed as men to do so. The most famous example of this type was Nadezhda Durova, who dressed as a man to fight in the Napoleonic Wars. Nadezhda Durova, *The Cavalry Maiden: Journals of a Russian Officer in the Napoleonic Wars,* trans. Mary Fleming Zirin (Bloomington and Indianapolis: Indiana University Press, 1988). Scholarship on the role of women in Russia's armed forces prior to World War II is exceedingly thin. For a brief history, which begins with the acceptance of women into sanitary services in 1716 and concludes with the Russo-Turkish War, see Iu. N. Ivanova, "Zhenshchiny v istorii rossiiskoi armii," *Voenno-istoricheskii zhurnal,* no. 3 (1992): 86–89. For a discussion of women in the Red Army during the Civil War see Wood, *The Baba and the Comrade,* 52–60.

108. Maria Botchkareva, *Yashka: My Life as Peasant, Officer, and Exile,* as set down by Isaac Don Levine (New York: Frederick Stokes, 1919), 73–74.

109. Order of supreme commander, 5 August 1914, RGVIA, f. 2003, op. 2, d. 28, l. 10.

110. Botchkareva, *Yashka,* 74.

111. Ibid., 75–77.

112. The other potentially disruptive force in this relationship is homosexuality among soldiers. There is little that can be said on that issue, however, since homosexuality is notably absent from all the discussions regarding conscription and basic training that I have seen.

113. Botchkareva, *Yashka,* 82.

114. Ibid., 157, 160.

115. Ibid., 217. Freudians may make of the bayoneting scene what they wish. Note also that the bayonet was the repository of proper military morals in Russian military theory. The final bayonet charge was a display of moral strength and moral dominance that was necessary to achieve victory in battle. The favorite pithy phrase of late imperial military theorists was from Suvorov: "The bullet is a fool, but the bayonet is a fine fellow."

116. Ibid., 80.

117. Ibid., 157. That said, the motives for the individual women who joined the women's battalions (there were more than one) seem to have been based at least as much on patriotism as on shaming. The General Staff noted that requests by women to join the army were pouring in during the summer of 1917, and that they expressed a "burst of high patriotism" in addition to "a desire to raise the presently wavering spirit of the Russian army," letter from General Administration of the General Staff to the Military Council, 21 July 1917, RGVIA, f. 29, op. 3, d. 1603, l. 20.

118. Viktor Shklovsky, *A Sentimental Journey: Memoirs, 1917–1922,* trans. and

ed. Richard Sheldon, rev. ed. (Ithaca, N.Y., and London: Cornell University Press, 1984), 30.

119. Botchkareva, *Yashka*, 165–67.

120. Petition from Elena Iost in report of the duty general of the Stavka, 12 June 1916, RGVIA, f. 2003, op. 2, d. 28, ll. 69ob-70. Capitalization in original.

121. "O rasformirovanii voinskikh chastei iz zhenshchin-dobrovol'tsev," from the Main Administration of the General Staff to the Military Council, 19 November 1917, RGVIA, f. 29, op. 3, d. 1603, ll. 24–24ob.

122. On Red Guards accepting women, see I. V. Pavlova, *Krasnaia gvardiia v sibiri* (Novosibirsk: Nauka, 1983), 50.

123. Dmitrii Furmanov, *Sochineniia* (Leningrad: "Khudozhestvennaia literatura," 1971), 1:23.

124. Telegram from Novonikolaevsk to Omsk district staff, 20 June 1920, RGVA, f. 25875, op. 1, d. 290, l. 51.

125. Letter from the chief of the Riazan' Infantry Division to the military commander of Moscow, 20 July 1918, RGVA, f. 11, op. 5, d. 234, ll. 373–373ob.

126. Dune, *Notes of a Red Guard*, 167–68.

127. Report of the Iaroslavl' military district to the All-Russian Main Staff, 18 December 1918, RGVA, f. 11, op. 8, d. 784, ll. 2ob-3.

128. "Instruktsiia po Vseroglavshtabu, no. 6," 2 March 1919, RGVA, f. 11, op. 8, d. 784, l. 4.

129. See for instance the request of Zaida Shtobbe of Omsk to the Omsk district commissariat on 27 January 1920, which noted that she was in dire straits after the death of her husband and asked for work, a request that was quickly granted. RGVA, f. 25875, op. 1, d. 63, l. 30.

130. There was resistance to this idea among some in the Zhenotdel as well. On this, see Wood, *The Baba and the Comrade*, 53–54.

131. Telegram from Vseroglavshtab to the military council of the Tver' Detachment, 13 August 1918, RGVA, f. 11, op. 5, d. 234, l. 374.

132. Telegram from military council of the Tver' Detachment to the military commander of Moscow military district, 6 July 1918, RGVA, f. 11, op. 5, d. 234, l. 377ob.

133. Report of Vseroglavshtab, 7 August 1918, RGVA, f. 11, op. 5, d. 234, l. 378.

134. Dune, *Notes of a Red Guard*, 168–69.

135. Report from Kirillov (military commander of the city of Verei, Moscow province) to chairman of Sovnarkom, 29 April 1918, RGVA, f. 2, op. 1, d. 8, l. 274. The decree that established Vsevobuch stated that military training was obligatory for all "citizens," but that though "female citizens" *(grazhdanki)* would follow the same training program, they would only be trained if they volunteered. "Dekret ob obiazatel'nom obuchenii voennomu iskusstvu," 22 April 1918, from VTsIK, signed by Sverdlov and Avanesov. In *Dekrety sovetskoi vlasti*, 2:151–53.

136. "Tezisy doklada vsevobucha v zhenotdel TsK RKP," n.d. but during Polish War (1920), RGVA, f. 65, op. 1, d. 45, l. 37.

137. "Militsionnaia sistema i zhenshchiny," n.a, n.d., RGVA, f. 65, op. 13, d. 27, ll. 339–40.

138. Report from Levichev (chief of Main Administration of the Red Army) to RVS SSSR on proposed new law of military service, 6 April 1925, RGVA, f. 4, op. 1, d. 133, l. 604ob. List numbers in this *delo* do not correspond to document order. The state retained the right to draft women in wartime.

139. Letter from Military-Sanitation Administration of the Red Army to the

administrator of affairs of Commissariat of Military Affairs and RVS SSSR, 25 October 1926, RGVA, f. 4, op. 1, d. 217, l. 12.

140. A. Kollontai, "Krasnyi front i rabotnitsa," in *Revoliutsionnaia voina (sbornik pervyi)*, ed. N. Podvoiskii and M. Pavlovich (Moscow, Izd. VTsIK, 1919), 103.

141. Ibid., 115–17.

142. Ibid., 122.

143. Ibid.

144. See for instance proceedings of the Gomel' provinicial conference of the Department of Women Workers, 5 July 1920, RGASPI, f. 17, op. 10, d. 47, l. 12.

145. Resolutions of All-Russian Conference of Women Workers on report of comrade Podvoiskii, RGVA, f. 65, op. 1, d. 27, l. 145.

146. For an intriguing parallel with the American Revolutionary case, see Kerber, "May All Our Citizens Be Soldiers and All Our Soldiers Citizens," 89–103.

147. "Prikaz Glavnogo nachal'nika vseobshchego voennogo obucheniia, doprizyvnoi podgotovki i kommunisticheskikh kominstruktorskikh chastei RSFSR," 1 June 1921, RGVA, f. 65, op. 13, d. 19, l. 5ob.

148. Photographs of physical culture performances on Red Square, n.d., RGVA, f. 65, op. 7, d. 6, ll. 75, 76.

149. See for example, Usborne, *Politics of the Body*, 16–17.

150. A. Laptev, "Zhenshchina i fizicheskaia kul'tura," *Fizicheskaia kul'tura i vsevobuch* 1, no. 2 (Sept. 1921), in RGVA, f. 16, op. 1, d. 11, l. 27.

151. Ibid.

152. "Tezisy doklada v plenume otdela raboty sredi zhenshchin pri TsK," n.d., RGVA, f. 65, op. 1, d. 27. l. 238.

153. Kalinin, *O kommunisticheskom vospitanii i voinskom dolge*, 61.

154. "Tezisy po dokladu 'Rabotnitsa i KA,'" n.d. but likely 1922, RGASPI, f. 17, op. 60, d. 392, l. 14.

155. "Svedeniia ob ispolnenii prizyva trudiashchikhsia dlia Vseob. Voen. Obuch. po 96 chas. programme v Riazan'skom territorialnom okruge v periode s 1 okt. 1919 do 25 dek. 1919," RGVA, f. 65, op. 1, d. 2, l. 39.

156. Material from localities, n.d. but likely 1924, TsKhDMO, f. 1, op. 23, d. 477, ll. 87, 93–94.

157. "Informatsionnyi biulleten' no. 1 za period s 1/4 do 1/10 1926 Ural. obl. SF pri Oblispolkome," 1 October 1926, TsKhDMO, f. 1, op. 23, d. 652, ll. 45–55.

158. Littauer, *Russian Hussar*, 30, 45, 117; for 1914, see V. Aramilev, *V dymu voiny: Zapiski vol'noopredeliaiushchegosia (1914–1917)* (Leningrad: Molodaia gvardiia, 1930), 15.

159. Tkhvorzhevskii, *Nadezhnye soldaty*, 11–12.

160. Dmitrii Kudrin, "Novobrantsy," *Krasnyi novobranets* (one-day paper published by the Political Department of the Saratov Rifle Division and the Political Secretariat of the Provincial Military Committee), 3 May 1924. Included in RGVA, f. 9, op. 28s, d. 865, l. 229.

161. Report from the chief of staff of the 10th Infantry Division to the commander of the 39th Tomsk Infantry Regiment, secret, 24 December 1915, RGVIA, f. 2653, op. 2, d. 367, l. 33.

162. "Ofitsery i soldaty russkoi armii!" from "Russkie materi," n.d., RGVA, f. 9, op. 28s, d. 313, l. 48. Capitalization in original.

163. Reports from the Cheka's "Special Section" (OO VChK) in the 3rd Army, 20–22 October 1919, RGVA, f. 176, op. 6, d. 4, ll. 146ob–47.

164. George L. Mosse, *The Image of Man: The Creation of Modern Masculinity* (New York and Oxford: Oxford University Press, 1996), 3.

165. George L. Mosse, *Nationalism and Sexuality: Respectability and Abnormal Sexuality in Modern Europe* (New York: Howard Fertig, 1985), 10–11, 29, 78.

166. Ibid., 23.

167. See for instance the poignant account of the decision of one young student to volunteer in World War I in V. L. Abramov, *Na ratnykh dorogakh* (Moscow: Voenizdat, 1962).

5: Violence and the Nation

1. The fixation of soldiers and citizens alike upon violence and its effects is noticeable in nearly all primary accounts of the war periods. For two especially interesting works in this vein, see Stepun, *Iz pisem praporshchika artillerista;* and Raleigh, *A Russian Civil War Diary.*

2. John Keegan, *The Face of Battle* (New York: Barnes and Noble, 1976), 20.

3. To see examples of this, refer to *Nastavlenie dlia strel'by;* Butovskii, *O sposobakh obucheniia,* vol 1.

4. "Raspredelennaia po nedeliam programma vos'mi-nedel'nogo obucheniia nizhnikh chinov v zapasnykh chastiakh pekhoty." Revised program signed by Shuvaev (war minister), 3 June 1916, RGVIA, f. 2000, op. 2, d. 2379, ll. 1–13.

5. Stepun, *Iz pisem praporshchika artillerista,* 7.

6. Dragomirov, *Izbrannye trudy,* 610.

7. Ibid., 158, 184.

8. This was a pan-European military understanding. See Michael Howard, "Men against Fire: The Doctrine of the Offensive in 1914," in *The Lessons of History* (New Haven: Yale University Press, 1991), 97–112.

9. For examples from quite different military-theoretical perspectives, including from those who favored paying more attention to the role of technology and modern weaponry, from a member of the "nationalist" school, and from an official training manual, see A. G. Elchaninov, *Vedenie sovremennykh voiny i boia* (St. Petersburg, Tip Gr. Skachkova, 1909), 19; Mikhnevich, *Osnovy russkago voennago iskusstva,* 3; *Nastavlenie dlia deistvii pekhoty v boiu* (St. Petersburg: Voennaia tipografiia Imperatritsy Ekateriny Velikoi, 1914), 5.

10. "Violentization" is a phrase used by Athens to describe the entire process of transformation that an individual undergoes before becoming a dangerous violent criminal. "Brutalization" is the first stage of this process. I have relied mainly on the pathbreaking work of Athens to understand the ways in which individuals become violent actors. See Lonnie H. Athens, *The Creation of Dangerous Violent Criminals* (Urbana and Chicago: University of Illinois Press, 1992); and his *Violent Criminal Acts and Actors Revisited* (Urbana and Chicago: University of Illinois Press, 1997). See in addition Hans Toch, *Violent Men: An Inquiry Into the Psychology of Violence,* rev. ed. (Hyattsville, Md.: American Psychological Association, 1992); Marvin E. Wolfgang and Franco Ferracuti, *The Subculture of Violence: Towards an Integrated Theory in Criminology* (London and New York: Tavistock, 1967); Dane Archer and Rosemary Gartner, *Violence and Crime in Cross-national Perspective* (New Haven and London: Yale University Press, 1984).

11. Most criminologists, Athens included, study illegal violence, and hence social conditions that lead to the creation of violent criminals. There has been little attention paid by psychologists to the role of "legal" state-sanctioned violence, a fact

sadly noted by Archer and Gartner, *Violence and Crime* (95): "This deference to the legitimacy of governments has resulted in the near omission of wars and other forms of official homicide from discussions of violence." Richard Rhodes, in his discussion of the theories and career of Lonnie Athens, does try to link military and civilian violence. See Richard Rhodes, *Why They Kill: The Discoveries of a Maverick Criminologist* (New York: Knopf, 1999), 286–312.

12. Athens, *Creation of Dangerous Violent Criminals,* 47.

13. Ibid., 48.

14. Littauer, *Russian Hussar,* 13.

15. Ibid., 26.

16. On corporal punishment, which was legally outlawed between 1904 and 1914 (but still consistently practiced, as scores of letters to Duma members attested), see Wildman, *The End of the Russian Imperial Army,* 34. For further confirmation of continuing physical abuse, see A. A. Ignatyev, *A Subaltern in Old Russia,* trans. Ivor Montagu (London, New York, and Melbourne: Hutchinson and Co., 1944), 146.

17. List of evacuated materials from Plotsk, July 1914, GARF, f. 1745, op. 1, d. 58, ll. 438–440. See also explicit instructions to trainers to use evening periods to discuss the heroic deeds of soldiers, famous battles, and the lives of commanders. Butovskii, *O sposobakh obucheniia,* 1:68.

18. "Raspredelennaia po nedeliam programma vos'mi-nedel'nogo obucheniia nizhnikh chinov v zapasnykh chastiakh pekhoty," n.a., n.d., RGVIA, f. 2000, op. 2, d. 2379, ll. 1–13.

19. Athens, *Creation of Dangerous Violent Criminals,* 60.

20. According to Richard Pipes, Russian peasants had a "primitive mind," were unable to think abstractly, and "shared with other primitive men a weakly developed sense of personal identity." Richard Pipes, *Russia Under the Old Regime,* 2nd ed. (New York: Macmillan, 1992), 157–58.

21. William Edgerton, trans. and ed., *Memoirs of Peasant Tolstoyans in Soviet Russia* (Bloomington and Indianapolis: Indiana University Press, 1993), 184–85.

22. Ibid., 190, 194.

23. See for instance Pireiko, *V tylu i na fronte,* 17; for similar recollections, see M. N., *Na voinu! Zapiski krest'ianina prizyvnogo 1904 goda* (Christchurch, Hants, England: Svobodnoe slovo, 1905).

24. For a critical and constructive survey of these thinkers, combined with a new theory, see Lonnie Athens, "The Self as a Soliloquy," *The Sociological Quarterly* 35, no. 3 (1994): 521–32.

25. Stepun, *Iz pisem praporshchika artillerista,* 19–20.

26. Order of 24th Army Corps, 13 August 1914, RGVIA, f. 2067, op. 1, d. 2904, l. 113.

27. Voitolovskii, *Po sledam voiny,* 34.

28. Littauer, *Russian Hussaar,* 149, 153. For more on attacks on Jews, see chapter 4.

29. Telegram from General Rychkov to Stavka, 9 December 1915, RGVIA, f. 2003, op. 2, d. 810, l. 12; and report from the head of mobile field bakery no. 11 to the duty general of the Stavka, 7 March 1916, l. 35; Shklovsky, *A Sentimental Journey,* 101.

30. For a first stab at this topic, see Lohr, "The Russian Army and the Jews," 404–19.

31. Stepun, *Iz pisem praporshchika artillerista,* 107–8.

32. "Spiski korrespondentsii zaregistrovannoi v Novorossiiskoi voennoi tsenzuroi," 15 August–1 September 1917, RGVIA, f. 1300, op. 1, d. 99, l. 6.

33. Anonymous letter to V. A. Maliuch, 29 July 1917, RGVIA, f. 1300, op. 1, d. 99, l. 43ob.

34. Telegram from estate steward to Podol'sk provincial commissar, 25 May 1917, RGVIA, f. 2067, op. 1, d. 572, l. 66.

35. Tsuyoshi Hasegawa, "Crime, Police, and Mob Justice in Petrograd during the Russian Revolutions of 1917," in *Religious and Secular Forces in Late Tsarist Russia*, ed. Charles E. Timberlake (Seattle: University of Washington Press, 1992), 249–51.

36. Telegram from Gobechii to the chief of the southwestern front, 25 July 1917, RGVIA, f. 2067, op. 1, d. 570, l. 407.

37. Telegram from El'sner (chief of supplies of the southwestern front) to Proskurov district commissar, copy to chief of southwestern front, 29 July 1917, RGVIA, f. 2067, op. 1, d. 570, l. 431.

38. Telegram from the Food Supply Administration chairman of Proskurov district (Kiselev) to the chief of staff of the 7th Army, 26 October 1917, RGVIA, f. 2067, op. 1, d. 2939, l. 110.

39. See for instance the resolutions of the Beskatovskii county Zemstvo Administration sent to VTsIK on 27 December 1917, GARF, f. r-1235, op. 79, d. 27, l. 6; also telegram from Lastovskii (commissar of Dunilovich county) to Sovnarkom, 10 December 1917, GARF, f. r-393, op. 1, d. 40, l. 16.

40. For the tangible feeling of Saratov being run by "dirty" men with guns in late 1917, see Babine's diary entries in Raleigh, *A Russian Civil War Diary*, 1–40.

41. "Doklad o polozhenii na fronte i ekstrennykh merakh dlia usileniia oborony i formirovaniia novykh krepkikh chastei," secret, submitted to Lenin by chief of the operational division, 22 April 1918, RGASPI, f. 5, op. 1, d. 2515, l. 18.

42. Telegram from the Commissariat of Military Affairs to the Commissariat of Internal Affairs, 27 April 1918, GARF, f. r-393, op. 1, d. 41, l. 30.

43. "Svodka telegramm s vnutrennego fronta Mosk. obl. kom. po voennym delam," 25 April 1918, GARF, f. r-1235, op. 79, d. 7, l. 217.

44. Brovkin, *Behind the Front Lines of the Civil War*, esp. 321–25.

45. For a report of an attack on a single woman conducted by "Red partisans," see complaint from Mikhail Mikhailovich Cherzhov to the Western district Soviet Executive Committee, 19 August 1918, GARF, f. r-1005, op. 1a, d. 1297, ll. 3–3ob. The complaint about raping and pillaging was levied against White troops in a letter to an unidentified White commander, n.d., from a "Russian mother" from Elisavetpol or Ekaterinoslav, RGVA, f. 9, op. 28s, d. 313, l. 190. These are just examples; soldiers from both armies engaged in all kinds of violent activity.

46. The most famous defense of state terror is Leon Trotsky, *Terrorism and Communism: A Reply to Karl Kautsky* (Ann Arbor: University of Michigan Press, 1961).

47. Ibid., 25.

48. *Partiino-politicheskaia rabota v krasnoi armii (aprel' 1918–fevral' 1919); Dokumenty* (Moscow: Voenizdat, 1961), 44.

49. "Cheka," in *Krasnyi mech (organ politotdela osobogo korpusa voisk V. U. Ch. K.)*, 18 August 1919. Reprinted in Yuri Felshtinsky, comp., *VCHK-GPU* (Benson, Vt.: Chalidze, 1989), 65.

50. Ibid.

51. N. Podvoiskii, *Iz kazarmy v boi. Pamiatka. (Chto nuzhno znat' kazhdomu voinu molodoi Rossiiskoi Sotsialisticheskoi Armii)* (Kiev: Izd. Polituprav. RVS 12-i armii, 1919), 7.

52. M. N. Tukhachevskii, "Strategiia natsional'naia i klassovaia [1920]," in *Voprosy strategii i operativnogo iskusstva v sovetskikh voennykh trudakh (1917–1940 gg.)* (Moscow: Voenizdat, 1965), 74.

53. Letter from comrade Samoilev to the party's Central Committee, completely secret, 25 August 1919, RGASPI, f. 17, op. 84, d. 12, l. 18ob.

54. Telegram from from the military commissar of the special detachment for the partial reinforcement of cavalry units to the commissar of Vseroglavshtab, secret, 24 March 1920, RGVA, f. 11, op. 15, d. 6, l. 43. For more on peasant brutality directed at communists, see Oliver H. Radkey, *The Unknown Civil War in Soviet Russia: A Study of the Green Movement in the Tambov Region, 1920–21* (Stanford: Hoover Institution Press, 1976).

55. "Tezisy o politicheskoi vospitanii (O sushchnosti politicheskogo vospitanii pri osushchestvlenii vsevobucha" report from Podvoiskii to Komsomol Central Committee, n.d., RGVA, f. 65, op. 13, d. 5, ll. 2–4.

56. Ibid.

57. "Programma po kursu metodiki obucheniia." n.d, written by instructor Khelturin, RGVA, f. 65, op. 13, d. 2, l. 96ob.

58. "Programma 96–ti chas. obuch." RGVA, f. 65, op. 13, d. 2, l. 142ob.

59. Cited in Korablev and Loginov, *KPSS*, 63.

60. S. I. Aralov, *V. I. Lenin i Krasnaia Armiia* (Moscow: Znanie, 1958), 8, quoted in Korablev and Loginov, *KPSS*, 68.

61. "Programma zaniatii voisk," signed by A. Beloborodov (chief of PUR), 24 July 1919, RGVA, f. 11, op. 5, d. 56, l. 2ob.

62. For a useful comparative angle, see many of the works on the experience of American soldiers in Vietnam, for instance, Michael Bilton and Kevin Sim, *Four Hours in My Lai* (New York: Viking, 1992), especially 70–83.

63. On this, see report from Vatsetis to Lenin, 24 June 1919, RGASPI, f. 5, op. 1, d. 2425, ll. 47–50ob.

64. Resolution of Kuban Revolutionary Tribunal, 14 September 1920, GARF, f. r-1005, op. 2, d. 70, l. 19.

65. Trotsky, *History of the Russian Revolution*, 1:125–28.

66. Resolution of the 1st Railroad Battalion, sent to Lenin, 24 November 1917, RGASPI, f. 5, op. 1, d. 2549, ll. 2ob-3.

67. Protest from sailors in the Baltic Fleet, sent to Sovnarkom, 25 March 1918, RGASPI, f. 5, op. 1, d. 2549, l. 6.

68. See for instance report of a battle at the Firovo train station between deserters and Red Army troops in June 1919. "Voennaia svodka otdela voennoi tsenzury," June 1919, RGVA, f. 176, op. 6, d. 3, l. 71ob.

69. "Sdavaite oruzhie!" Published by the Skopinskii district committee for the collection of weapons, July 1919, RGVA, f. 25883, op. 2, d. 764, l. 530. People were in fact executed for "illegally keeping weapons like open counterrevolutionaries." Trial of Briantsev, 5 September 1920, GARF, f. r-1005, op. 2, d. 70, l. 5.

70. L. Trotskii, "Grazhdane, sdavaite oruzhie," *Izvestiia VTsIK* (26 December 1918): 1.

71. V. I. Shishkin, "Krasnyi banditizm v sovetskoi sibiri," in *Sovetskaia istoriia: Problemy i uroki*, ed. V. I. Shishkin (Novosibirsk: "Nauka", 1992), 75. The "militsioner" was a member of the local militia that served as a police force, the "chekist" was a member of the Cheka, and the "chonovets" was a member of the all-communist Red Army units, the "ChONy."

72. On "banditism" in Siberia well into the 1920s, see also I. A. Abramenko, *Kommunisticheskie formirovaniia—chasti osobogo naznacheniia (ChON) zapadnoi sibiri (1920–1924 gg.)* (Tomsk: Izd Tomskogo Universiteta, 1973), 14.

73. "Bor'ba s banditizmom," information sheet, completely secret, October 1922, RGASPI, f. 17, op. 84, d. 444, l. 109.

74. Telegram from RVS SSSR to Siberian military district, secret, 26 October 1924, RGVA, f. 25873, op. 1, d. 799, ll. 1, 4.

75. "Operativno-razvedyvatel'naia svodka shtaba RKKA o sostoianii banditizma," 15 February 1926, RGVA, f. 9, op. 28s, d. 246, ll. 51–51ob.

76. N. B. Lebina, "Tenevye storony zhizni sovetskogo goroda 20–30kh godov," *Voprosy istorii*, no. 2 (1994): 31. Whether this increase in violent crime was due to an objective rise in that crime or to a heightened sensitivity to the issue remains unclear, however.

77. For numerous examples, see the 650-page file of these requests for mercy from the tsar. RGVIA, f. 2003, op. 2, d. 806. Fedorov case on ll. 35–36; Vashchenko on l. 236.

78. Petitions from Tsymbal and Belov, GARF, f. r-1005, op. 2, d. 11, ll. 6, 18.

79. Ibid., 25ob, 43a-ob.

80. Telegram from Trotskii to Rakovskii and Podvoiskii, 28 May 1919, RGASPI, f. 17, op. 109, d. 8, l. 19.

81. Desertion statistics, RGASPI, f. 5, op. 1, d. 2452, l. 18; RGASPI, f. 17, op. 87, d. 26, ll. 153–54.

82. John Barber and Mark Harrison, *The Soviet Home Front, 1941–1945: A Social and Economic History of the USSR in World War II* (London and New York: Longman, 1991), 117.

83. The literature on pacifism and conscientious objection in Russia is fairly small. A recent article on this theme is Nicholas B. Breyfogle, "Swords into Plowshares: Opposition to Military Service Among Religious Sectarians, 1770s to 1874," in *The Military and Society in Russia: 1450–1917*, ed. Eric Lohr and Marshall Poe (Boston: Brill, 2002). There are a few short studies of policies of conscientious objection during the Soviet era. For an early example, see chapter 18 of Roger N. Baldwin, *Liberty Under the Soviets* (New York: Vanguard, 1928); more recently see Alexei Zverev and Bruno Coppieters, "V. D. Bonch-Bruevich and the Doukhobors: On the Conscientious Objection Policies of the Bolsheviks," *Canadian Ethnic Studies/Etudes Ethniques au Canada* 27, no. 3 (1995): 72–90.

84. See Nicholas Brenton Breyfogle, "Heretics and Colonizers: Religious Dissent and Russian Colonization of Transcaucasia, 1830–1890" (Ph.D. diss., University of Pennsylvania, 1998); Heather Coleman, "The Most Dangerous Sect: Baptists in Tsarist and Soviet Russia, 1905–1929," (Ph.D. diss., University of Illinois, 1998). The Dukhobors, in addition, have been the subject of a small cottage industry, particularly in Canada. The standard text (which is coming under increasing criticism) is George Woodcock and Ivan Avakumovich, *The Doukhobors* (Toronto and New York: Oxford University Press, 1968). See also the special issue of *Canadian Ethnic Studies/Etudes Ethniques au Canada* 28, no. 3 (1995); and Andrew Donskov et al., eds., *The Doukhobor Centenary in Canada* (Ottawa: Institute of Canadian Studies, 2000) for a sample of the more recent research on the Dukhobors in Russia and Canada. The Mennonites also have their own specialized scholars, who have published extensively on Mennonite experiences in Russia. See in particular James Urry, *None But Saints: The Transformation of Mennonite Life in Russia, 1789–1889* (Winnipeg: Windflower, 1989); and John B. Toews, "The Russian Mennonites and the Military Question (1921–1927)," *Mennonite Quarterly Review* 43, no. 2 (1969): 153–68. Finally, a tremendous source for and a short history of the Tolstoians is Edgerton, *Memoirs of Peasant Tolstoyans in Soviet Russia*. The standard source for all these groups is A. I. Klibanov, *History of Religious Sectarianism in Russia (1860s–1917)*, trans. Ethel Dunn, ed. Stephen P. Dunn (New York: Pergamon Press, 1985).

85. On this development, see Sandi E. Cooper, *Patriotic Pacifism: Waging War on War in Europe, 1815–1914* (Oxford and New York: Oxford University Press, 1991).

86. Ivan S. Bloch, *Is War Now Impossible?* (1899; Reprint, Hampshire, England: Gregg Revivals, 1991).

87. Miliukov thought the numbers were small, while Richard Stites argues that the appeal was fairly broad. Stockdale, *Paul Miliukov,* 212; Richard Stites, *Revolutionary Dreams: Utopian Vision and Experimental Life in the Russian Revolution* (New York and Oxford: Oxford University Press, 1989), 33.

88. Urry, *None but Saints,* 211–47.

89. For an excellent collection of documents about the 1895 events, see OR RGB, f. 369, k. 44, d. 1. Quotes here are from ll. 19, 20. I thank Nick Breyfogle for informing me of this source. On the torture of Dukhobor soldiers, see V. Chertkov and A. Chertkov, eds., *Dukhobortsy v distsiplinarnom batal'one,* Materialy k istorii i izucheniiu russkogo sektantsva series, no. 4 (Christchurch, England: Svobodnoe slovo, 1902). The details of the Dukhobor interaction with Tolstoi are described in Josh Sanborn, "Pacifist Politics and Peasant Politics: Tolstoy and the Doukhobors, 1895–99," *Canadian Ethnic Studies/Etudes Ethniques au Canada* 28, no. 3 (1995): 52–71.

90. This process was begun by imperial decree on 12 December 1904. It called for a review of laws on religion in a spirit of "religious toleration," and declared that discriminatory religious policies not covered under law would be immediately overturned by administrative fiat. For a copy of this decree, see *Zhurnaly komiteta ministrov po ispolneniiu ukaza 12 dekabria 1904 g.* (St. Petersburg: Izd. Kantselarii Komiteta Ministrov, 1905), 3–7. It was followed the next April by an official decree of religious toleration.

91. "Kratkie svedeniia ob otkazavshikhsia ot voennoi sluzhby v Rossii po religioznym ubezhdeniiam," n.a., January 1912, GARF, f. 579, op. 1, d. 2568, l. 21. Thanks to Nick Breyfogle for alerting me to this source.

92. Ibid., l. 25.

93. "Nashe otkrytoe slovo k liudiam-bratiam vsego mira," pamphlet produced in Russian, French, and German and distributed in Poltava by Nikolai Dudchenko and 37 other signatories, July 1914, GMIR, f. 7, op. 1, d. 1, ll. 7–8.

94. "Kratkaia zapiska o litsakh, otkazyvavshikhsia ot v.s. po relig. ubezhd. pri tsarskom i vrem. prav.," report from United Council of Religious Organizations and Groups, 18 August 1919, RGVA, f. 11, op. 8, d. 924, l. 29.

95. The numbers reflect the total convictions in a given year, so part of the large jump between 1914 and 1915 may reflect the possibility that cases from 1914 were not concluded until 1915. Statistics from correspondence between military courts and the MVD's Department of Spiritual Affairs, RGIA, f. 821, op. 133, d. 325, ll. 20–29.

96. Quote from circular "Ob usilenii nadzora za sektanstskim dvizheniem," from Shtiurmer (minister of internal affairs) to all governors and city chiefs, 18 May 1916, RGIA, f. 821, op. 133, d. 314, l. 22. Statistic from l. 78.

97. "Dokladnaia zapiska ob otnoshenii k otkazyvaiushchimsia po religioznym pobuzhdeniiam ot voennoi sluzhby," materials compiled by Vladimir Chertkov and Konstantin Shokhor-Troitskii, submitted to the Provisional Government, 15 April 1917, RGIA, f. 821, op. 133, d. 314, ll. 48ob-50.

98. Correspondence of the military prosecutor of corps of the 3rd Army, 29 April 1916, RGIA, f. 821, op. 133, d. 325, l. 203.

99. This statistic was generated by the MVD and did not include those men whose cases were still under consideration at the time of the revolution. For figures and discussion, see "Kratkaia zapiska o litsakh."

100. See worried letter on this theme from Beliaev (quartermaster-general) to the city chief of Petrograd, 9 December 1914, RGVIA, f. 1, op. 1, t. 44, d. 647, l. 10.

101. All of these quotes from Maklakov's letter to the tsar, 12 December 1914, RGIA, f. 821, op. 133, d. 314, ll. 8–9.

102. Cited in *Nastroenie sektantov Kievskoi eparkhii i povedenie ikh vo vremia voiny (k voprosu o russkom sektanstve, kak odnom iz vidov nemetskogo zasiliia v Rossii* (Kiev: Tip. Imp. Univers. Sv. Vladimira, 1915). Included in RGIA, f. 821, op. 133, d. 314, ll. 10–17, quote on l. 11.

103. The court case of Popov and other Tolstoians who were also disseminating literature on the same day is included in GMIR, f. 13, op. 1, d. 376.

104. Speech of A. I. Shingarev at Duma session, 30 January 1912, included in "Dokladnaia zapiska ob otnoshenii k otkazyvaiushchimsia po religioznym pobuzhdeniiam ot voennoi sluzhby," materials compiled by Vladimir Chertkov and Konstantin Shokhor-Troitskii, submitted to the Provisional Government, 15 April 1917, RGIA, f. 821, op. 133, d. 314, ll. 44–44ob.

105. Speech of Guchkov at Duma session, 8 March 1912, RGIA, f. 821, op. 133, d. 314, l. 46.

106. See telegrams in RGIA, f. 1278, op. 5, d. 1328, ll. 25, 38.

107. "Postanovlenie vremennogo pravitel'stva ob otmene veroispovednykh i natsional'nykh ogranichenii," *Sobranie uzakonenii i rasporiazhenii pravitel'stva*, no. 70, st. 400 (20 March 1917).

108. Petition from Bugaev to the minister of justice, 24 March 1917, RGVIA, f. 2000, op. 3, d. 1251, ll. 7–7ob.

109. Ibid., l. 7ob.

110. Letter from MVD Conscription Administration to Mobilization Department, 7 May 1917, RGVIA, f. 2000, op. 3, d. 1251, ll. 5–6.

111. See the befuddled despair evident on this question in the letter to the chief of the General Staff from the commander of the Kazan' military district, 9 April 1917, RGVIA, f. 2000, op. 3, d. 1251, l. 11.

112. Letter from the MVD Department of Spiritual Affairs to the chief of the General Staff, 29 April 1917, RGVIA, f. 2000, op. 3, d. 1251, l. 12ob.

113. For more details, see 1917 Shokhor-Trotskii proposal in RGVIA, f. 2000, op. 3, d. 1251, ll. 57–67. Chertkov had been Tolstoi's closest confidant for decades prior to Tolstoi's death

114. Letter from the chief of the Main Military Justice Administration to the chief of the General Staff, 20 May 1917, RGVIA, f. 2000, op. 3, d, 1251, l. 16.

115. Letter from the chief of staff of the Moscow military district to the Mobilization Department (citing decision of conference in Main Military Justice Administration), 10 June 1917, RGVIA, f. 2000, op. 3, d. 1251, l. 39.

116. The issue was still unresolved in October. See letter from the Ministry of Confessions (Department of Non-Slavic and Other-faith Confessions) to the Mobilization Department, 18 October 1917, RGVIA, f. 2000, op. 3, d. 1251, l. 95ob.

117. For an excellent brief summary of Bonch-Bruevich's activities in this period, see Zverev and Coppieters, "V. D. Bonch-Bruevich," 74–78. On the journal *Rassvet*, see RGASPI, f. 381, op. 1, d. 1–4.

118. "O tom, kak sozdalsia dekret ob osvobozhdenii ot voinskoi povinnosti po religioznym ubezdeniiam," unpublished manuscript written by V. D. Bonch-Bruevich, 4 May 1933, OR RGB, f. 369, k. 37, d. 2, ll. 30–32.

119. Ibid., l. 33–34.

120. Ibid., 35.

121. For mention of this, see protocol for meeting no. 179 of "little Sovnarkom," 2 January 1919, GARF, f. r-130, op. 3, d. 64, l. 1ob.

122. See for instance, "O religioznykh nastroeniiakh i sektantakh," report from Milov (chief of the Information and Statistics Department of PUR), secret, March 1925, RGVA, f. 9, op. 28s, d. 704, ll. 30–34.

123. Letter from Krasikov to Lenin, 13 December 1918, excerpted in V. A. Alekseev, *Illiuzii i dogmy* (Moscow: Politizdat, 1991), 70. Thanks to Heather Coleman for alerting me to this source.

124. Ibid.

125. *Dekrety sovetskoi vlasti*, 4: 282–84.

126. See for instance, order from Kurskii (Commissariat of Justice) to all justice departments and people's courts, 27 July 1919, GARF, f. a-353, op. 3, d. 783, l. 146; and the protocol of the conference of the provincial justice commissariat in Samara, 18 September 1919, l. 66.

127. Protocol no. 222 of the Commissariat of Justice Collegium, 2 January 1920, GARF, f. a-353, op. 3, d. 783, l. 114.

128. Letter from Chertkov to RVSR, 18 August 1919, RGVA, f. 11, op. 8, d. 924, l. 28.

129. Letter from Gorbunov-Posadov (United Council member) to Lenin, 12 December 1919, RGVA, f. 11, op. 8, d. 686, l. 89ob.

130. Telegram from Rattel' to all district military commanders and commissars, urgent, 21 August 1919, RGVA, f. 11, op. 8, d. 924, l. 50.

131. Telegram from Sklianskii to all district military commanders and commissars, 29 April 1919, RGVA, f. 11, op. 8, d. 686, l. 3.

132. "Kratkie svedeniia ob izvestnykh Ob"edinennomu Sovetu sluchaiakh rasstreli pri sovetskoi vlasti lits, otkazavshikhsia ot voennoi sluzhby po religioznym ubezhdeniiam," written by Shokhor-Trotskii, GMIR, f. 2, op. 23, d. 16, ll. 6–30.

133. Telegram from provincial military commissar Kapivin and provincial military commander Ivnovksii (Saratov province) to the chief of the Mobilization Administration of the Main Staff, 29 January 1920, GARF, f. a-353, op. 3, d. 780, l. 7.

134. Edgerton, *Memoirs of Peasant Tolstoyans*, 202–10.

135. "Kratkie svedeniia ob izvestnykh Ob"edinennomu Sovetu sluchaiakh rasstreli pri sovetskoi vlasti lits, otkazavshikhsia ot voennoi sluzhby po religioznym ubezhdeniiam," written by Shokhor-Trotskii, n.d., GMIR, f. 2, op. 23, d. 16, l. 10.

136. Speech of comrade Tregubov at the Seventh Congress of Soviets, 9 December 1919, RGASPI, f. 5, op. 1, d. 1901, ll. 1–3.

137. Protocol of Orgbiuro no. 101, 3 March 1921, GARF, f. a-353, op. 4, d. 414, l. 13.

138. Decision of the Moscow People's Court, case no. 31, 21 March 1921, GARF, f. a-353, op. 4,d. 414, ll. 14–14ob.

139. *Sobranie zakonov i rasporiazhenii raboche-krest'ianskogo pravitel'stva SSSR*, 99:527 (14 December 1920).

140. Zverev and Coppieters, "V. D. Bonch-Bruevich," 83.

141. Circular from Krasikov (Commissariat of Justice), Leplevskii (Commissarait of Internal Affairs), Kozyrev (Commissariat of Agriculture), Avanesov (Worker-Peasant Inspectorate), 15 August 1921, OR RGB, f. 369, op. 85, d. 52, l. 2.

142. "O poriadke razbora del ob osvobozhdenii ot voennoi sluzhby po religioznym ubezhdeniiam," circular no. 237 of the Commissariat of Justice, signed by

Kurskii and Stuchka, sent to all provincial, supreme, regional courts and all provincial prosecutors, 5 November 1923, GARF, f. a-353, op. 8, d. 8, l. 79.

143. Zverev and Coppieters, "V.D. Bonch-Bruevich," 85.

144. On this process, see Edgerton, *Memoirs of Peasant Tolstayans*, 92–108.

Conclusion

1. Geoffrey Hosking, *Russia: People and Empire, 1552–1917* (Cambridge, Mass.: Harvard University Press, 1997), xix–xxi.

2. Ludmilla Jordanova, "The Authoritarian Response," in *The Enlightenment and its Shadows,* ed. Peter Hulme and Ludmilla Jordanova (London and New York: Routledge, 1990), 202–16.

3. Ibid., 206.

4. Rich, *The Tsar's Colonels.*

5. On these processes, see Lohr, "Enemy Alien Politics Within the Russian Empire During World War I."

6. Bonch-Bruyevich, *From Tsarist General to Red Army Commander,* 222–23.

7. This is Kotkin's argument in *Magnetic Mountain.*

8. Max Weber, *Sociological Writings,* ed. Wolf Heydebrand (New York: Continuum, 1994), 24.

9. Eric Hobsbawm, *Nations and Nationalism Since 1780: Programme, Myth, Reality* (Cambridge: Cambridge University Press, 1990), 183.

Works Cited

Archival Sources

State Archive of the Russian Federation (GARF)
    Fond 579—Personal papers of P. N. Miliukov
    Fond 1745—Plotsk district military commander
    Fond 6281—Documents relating to World War I
    Fond a-353—People's Commissariat of Justice of the RSFSR
    Fond r-130—Council of People's Commissars (Sovnarkom)
    Fond r-393—People's Commissariat of Internal Affairs of the RSFSR
    Fond r-1005—Supreme Court of the RSFSR
    Fond r-1235—All-Russian Central Executive Committee of Soviets (VTsIK)

State Museum of the History of Religion (GMIR)
    Fond 2—Personal papers of V. D. Bonch-Bruevich
    Fond 7—Personal papers of M. S. Dudchenko
    Fond 13—Personal papers of I. M. Tregubov

Manuscript Division of the Russian State Library (OR RGB)
    Fond 369—Personal papers of V. D. and M. D. Bonch-Bruevich

Russian State Archive of Socio-Political History (RGASPI)
    Fond 5—Secretariat of the chairman of the Council of People's Commissars and the Council of Labor and Defense V. I. Lenin
    Fond 17—Central Committee of the Communist Party of the Soviet Union
    Fond 41—Eighth Congress of the Russian Communist Party (Bolsheviks)
    Fond 381—Materials relating to the journal *Rassvet*

Russian State Historical Archive (RGIA)
    Fond 821—Ministry of Internal Affairs: Department of Spiritual Affairs of Foreign Confessions
    Fond 1246—Special office for obligatory military service
    Fond 1276—Council of Ministers
    Fond 1278—State Duma
    Fond 1292—Ministry of Internal Affairs: Administration of affairs relating to obligatory military service

Russian State Military Archive (RGVA)
Fond 2—All-Russian Collegium for the organization and formation of the Worker-Peasant Red Army
Fond 3—Staff of the Supreme Military Council
Fond 4—Administration of affairs for the Revolutionary Military Council of the USSR
Fond 7—Staff of the Worker-Peasant Red Army
Fond 9—Political Administration of the Worker-Peasant Red Army (PUR)
Fond 11—All-Russian Main Staff (Vseroglavshtab)
Fond 16—Staff of troops in Siberia
Fond 54—Main Administration of the Worker-Peasant Red Army
Fond 65—Universal Military Training Administration (Vsevobuch)
Fond 176—3rd Army of the eastern front
Fond 25875—Administration of the Omsk/Siberian/Western-Siberian military district 1919–1920
Fond 25883—Administration of the Moscow military district.
Fond 25893—Administration of the Siberian military district
Fond 33988—Secretariat of the deputy chairman of the Revolutionary Military Council of the Republic

Russian State Military History Archive (RGVIA)
Fonds 1, 29—Chancellery of the war minister
Fond 400—Main Staff
Fond 1300—Staff of the Caucasus military district
Fond 2000—Main Administration of the General Staff
Fond 2003—Staff of the Supreme Commander (Stavka)
Fond 2067—Staff of armies at the southwestern front
Fond 2068—Chancellery of the chief of supplies for armies of the southwestern front
Fond 2653—39th Tomsk Infantry Regiment

Center for the Preservation of Documents of Youth Organizations (TsKhDMO)
Fond 1—Central Committee of the All-Russian Lenin Communist Union of Youth (Komsomol)

Smolensk Archive

Special Collections, Joseph Regenstein Library, Chicago, Illinois
Samuel Harper Papers

Books, Articles, Newspapers, and Dissertations

Abramenko, I. A. *Kommunisticheskie formirovaniia—chasti osobogo naznacheniia (ChON) zapadnoi sibiri (1920–1924 gg.)* Tomsk: Izd. Tomskogo universiteta, 1973.
Abramov, V. L. *Na ratnykh dorogakh.* Moscow: Voenizdat, 1962.
Afflerbach, Holger. "'Bis zum letzten Mann und letzten Groschen?' Die Wehrpflicht im Deutschen Reich und ihre Auswirkungen auf das militärische Führungsdenken im Ersten Weltkrieg." In *Die Wehrpflicht: Entstehung, Erscheinungsformen und politisch-militärische Wirkung.* Munich: R. Oldenbourg Verlag, 1994.

Agursky, Mikhail. *The Third Rome: National Bolshevism in the USSR.* Boulder and London: Westview Press, 1987.

Akulinin, V. *Znachenie voennoi sluzhby i obiazannosti soldata: Molodym liudiam, prizyvaemym na sluzhbu tsariu i otechestvu.* 2nd ed. Kherson: Gub. tip., 1913.

Alekseev, V. A. *Illiuzii i dogmy.* Moscow: Politizdat, 1991.

Alexopolous, Golfo. *Stalin's Outcasts: Aliens, Citizens, and the Soviet State, 1926–1936.* Ithaca, N.Y.: Cornell University Press, forthcoming.

Althusser, Louis. *Essays on Ideology.* London and New York: Verso, 1984.

Anderson, Benedict. *Imagined Communities: Reflections on the Origin and Spread of Nationalism.* Rev. ed. London and New York: Verso, 1991.

Aramilev, V. *V dymu voiny: Zapiski vol'noopredeliaiushchegosia (1914–1917).* Leningrad: Molodaia gvardiia, 1930.

Archer, Dane, and Rosemary Gartner. *Violence and Crime in Cross-national Perspective.* New Haven and London: Yale University Press, 1984.

Ascher, Abraham. *The Revolution of 1905: Russia in Disarray.* Stanford: Stanford University Press, 1988.

Athens, Lonnie H. *The Creation of Dangerous Violent Criminals.* Urbana and Chicago: University of Illinois Press, 1992.

———. "The Self as a Soliloquy." *Sociological Quarterly* 35, no. 3 (1994): 521–32.

———. *Violent Criminal Acts and Actors Revisited.* Urbana and Chicago: University of Illinois Press, 1997.

Baldwin, Roger N. *Liberty Under the Soviets.* New York: Vanguard, 1928.

Barber, John, and Mark Harrison. *The Soviet Home Front, 1941–1945: A Social and Economic History of the USSR in World War II.* London and New York: Longman, 1991.

Baron, Salo W. *The Russian Jew under Tsars and Soviets.* New York: Macmillan, 1964.

Bartov, Omer. *Hitler's Army: Soldiers, Nazis, and War in the Third Reich.* Oxford: Oxford University Press, 1992.

Bauer, Henning, Andreas Kappeler, and Brigitte Roth, eds. *Die Nationalitäten des Russischen Reiches in der Volkszählung von 1897.* Stuttgart: Franz Steiner, 1991.

Baumann, Robert F. "The Debates over Universal Military Service in Russia, 1870–1874." Ph.D. diss., Yale University, 1982.

———. "Universal Service Reform and Russia's Imperial Dilemma." *War and Society* 4, no. 2 (September 1986): 31–49.

Belov, S. V. "Izdatel'stvo V. A. Berezovskogo (iz istorii izdaniia voennoi literatury v Rossii)." *Voenno-istoricheskii zhurnal,* no. 11 (1989): 85–90.

Benvenuti, Francesco. *The Bolsheviks and the Red Army, 1918–1922.* Translated by Christopher Woodall. Cambridge: Cambridge University Press, 1988.

Berkhin, I. B. *Voennaia reforma v SSSR (1924–1925 gg.)* Moscow: Voenizdat, 1958.

Berlin, Isaiah. *Vico and Herder: Two Studies in the History of Ideas.* New York: Viking, 1976.

Bilton, Michael, and Kevin Sim. *Four Hours in My Lai.* New York: Viking, 1992.

Bloch, Ivan S. *Is War Now Impossible?* 1899. Reprint, Hampshire, England: Gregg Revivals, 1991.

Bonch-Bruevich, M. D. *From Tsarist General to Red Army Commander.* Translated by Vladimir Vezey. Moscow: Progress, 1966.

———. *Vsia vlast' sovetam.* Moscow: Voenizdat, 1964.

Botchkareva, Maria. *Yashka: My Life as Peasant, Officer, and Exile.* As set down by Isaac Don Levine. New York: Frederick Stokes, 1919.

Bourke, Joanna. *Dismembering the Male: Men's Bodies, Britain, and the Great War.* Chicago and London: University of Chicago Press, 1996.

Breyfogle, Nicholas B. "Heretics and Colonizers: Religious Dissent and Russian Colonization of Transcaucasia, 1830–1890." Ph.D. diss., University of Pennsylvania, 1998.

———. "Swords into Plowshares: Opposition to Military Service Among Religious Sectarians, 1770s to 1874." In *The Military and Society in Russia: 1450–1917*, edited by Eric Lohr and Marshall Poe. Boston: Brill, 2002.

Brooks, E. Willis. "Reform in the Russian Army, 1856–1861." *Slavic Review* 43, no. 1 (1984): 63–82.

Brooks, Jeffrey. *When Russia Learned to Read: Literacy and Popular Literature, 1861–1917.* Princeton: Princeton University Press, 1985.

Brovkin, Vladimir N. *Behind the Front Lines of the Civil War: Political Parties and Social Movements in Russia, 1918–1922.* Princeton: Princeton University Press, 1994.

Brower, Daniel. "Kyrgyz Nomads and Russian Pioneers: Colonization and Ethnic Conflict in the Turkestan Revolt of 1916." *Jahrbücher für Geschichte Osteuropas* 44, no. 1 (1996): 41–53.

Brubaker, Rogers. *Nationalism Reframed: Nationhood and the National Question in the New Europe.* Cambridge: Cambridge University Press, 1996.

Bubnov, A. *Voennaia reforma, prizyv 1902, i politrabota.* Moscow: Krasnaia zvezda, 1924.

Buchanan, George. *My Mission to Russia and Other Diplomatic Memories.* 3 vols. Boston: Little, Brown, and Co., 1923.

Bushnell, John S. *Mutiny amid Repression: Russian Soldiers in the Revolution of 1905–1906.* Bloomington: Indiana University Press, 1985.

Butovskii, Nikolai. *O sposobakh obucheniia i vospitaniia sovremennago soldata (prakticheskiia zametki komandira rota).* 3rd ed. 2 vols. St. Petersburg: Berezovskii, 1893.

Carr, Edward Hallett. *The Bolshevik Revolution, 1917–1923.* 3 vols. New York: Macmillan, 1961.

Chaadayev, Peter Yakovlevich. *Philosophical Letters and Apology of a Madman.* Translated by Mary-Barbara Zeldin. Knoxville: University of Tennessee Press, 1969.

Chatterjee, Partha *The Nation and Its Fragments: Colonial and Postcolonial Histories.* Princeton: Princeton University Press, 1993.

Chertkov, V., and A. Chertkov, eds. *Dukhobortsy v distsiplinarnom batal'one.* Materialy k istorii i izucheniiu russkogo sektantsva, no. 4. Christchurch, England: Svobodnoe slovo, 1902.

Coleman, Heather. "The Most Dangerous Sect: Baptists in Tsarist and Soviet Russia, 1905–1929." Ph.D. diss., University of Illinois, 1998.

Confino, Alon. *The Nation as a Local Metaphor: Württemberg, Imperial Germany, and National Memory, 1871–1918.* Chapel Hill and London: University of North Carolina Press, 1997.

Conquest, Robert. *The Great Terror: A Reassessment.* New York and Oxford: Oxford University Press, 1990.

———. *Stalin: Breaker of Nations.* New York: Viking, 1991.

Cooper, Sandi E. *Patriotic Pacifism: Waging War on War in Europe, 1815–1914.* Oxford and New York: Oxford University Press, 1991.

Danilov, Iu. N. *Rossiia v mirovoi voine, 1914–1915 gg.* Berlin: Slovo, 1924.

Dawson, Jane I. *Eco-nationalism: Anti-Nuclear Activism and National Identity in Russia, Lithuania, and Ukraine.* Durham, N.C., and London: Duke University Press, 1996.

Dekrety sovetskoi vlasti. 13 vols. Moscow: Gosizdat, 1957–89.

Denikin, Anton I. *The Career of a Tsarist Officer: Memoirs, 1872–1916.* Translated by Margaret Patoski. Minneapolis: University of Minnesota Press, 1975.

Desiatyi s"ezd RKP(b), mart 1921 goda. Stenograficheskii otchet. Moscow: Gosizdat, 1963.

Dneprovskii, Aleksandr. *Zapiski dezertira, voina 1914–1918 gg.* New York: Izd. "Albatros," 1931.

Dobrorol'skii, S. V. *Die Mobilmachung der russischen Armee 1914.* Berlin: Deutsche Verlagsgesellschaft fur Politik und Geschicht m.b.H., 1922.

"Dokumenty o presledovanii evreev." *Arkhiv russkoi revoliutsii* 19 (1928): 245–84.

Donskov, Andrew, et al., eds. *The Doukhobor Centenary in Canada.* Ottawa: Institute of Canadian Studies, 2000.

Dragomirov, M. I. *Izbrannye trudy: Voprosy vospitaniia i obucheniia voisk.* Edited by L. G. Beskrovnyi. Moscow: Voenizdat, 1956.

———. *Ocherki.* Kiev: Ia. A. Ogloblina, 1898.

———. *Sbornik original'nykh i perevodnykh statei M. Dragomirova, 1858–1880.* 2 vols. St. Petersburg: Balashev, 1881.

Dubenskii, Dmitrii. *Uchebnik dlia vedeniia stroevykh i gimnasticheskikh zaniatii v narodnykh shkolakh i drugikh uchebnykh zavedeniiakh.* St. Petersburg: Morskoe ministerstvo, 1911.

Dubnow, S. M. *History of the Jews in Russia and Poland from the Earliest Times until the Present Day.* Translated by I. Friedlaender. 3 vols. Philadelphia: Jewish Publication Society of America, 1920.

Dune, Eduard M. *Notes of a Red Guard.* Translated and edited by Diane Koenker and S. A. Smith. Urbana and Chicago: University of Illinois Press, 1993.

Durova, Nadezhda. *The Cavalry Maiden: Journals of a Russian Officer in the Napoleonic Wars.* Translated by Mary Fleming Zirin. Bloomington and Indianapolis: Indiana University Press, 1988.

Dvenadtsatyi s"ezd rossiiskoi kommunisticheskoi partii (bol'shevikov). Stenograficheskii otchet, 17–25 aprelia 1923 g. Moscow: Krasnaia nov', 1923.

Edgerton, William, trans. and ed. *Memoirs of Peasant Tolstoyans in Soviet Russia.* Bloomington and Indianapolis: Indiana University Press, 1993.

Eklof, Ben. *Russian Peasant Schools: Officialdom, Village Culture, and Popular Pedagogy, 1861–1914.* Berkeley: University of California Press, 1986.

Elchaninov, A. G. *Vedenie sovremennykh voiny i boia.* St. Petersburg: Skachkov, 1909.

Eliseeva, N. E., ed. *Listovki grazhdanskoi voiny v SSSR, 1918–1922 gg.: Komplekt dokumentov iz fondov RGVA.* Moscow: RGVA, 1994.

Engelstein, Laura. *The Keys to Happiness: Sex and the Search for Modernity in Fin-de-Siècle Russia.* Ithaca, N.Y.: Cornell University Press, 1992.

Enloe, Cynthia. *Ethnic Soldiers: State Security in Divided Societies.* Athens: University of Georgia Press, 1980.

Farmborough, Florence. *Nurse at the Russian Front: A Diary, 1914–18.* London: Constable, 1974.

Fay, Sidney B. *Before Sarajevo: The Origins of the World War.* 2nd ed. New York: Free Press, 1966.

Fedorov, V. *K voprosu o voinskoi povinnosti v Rossii.* Rostov na Donu: tip. "Donskaia rech," 1906.

Felshtinsky, Yuri, comp. *VCHK-GPU.* Benson, Vt.: Chalidze, 1989.

Figes, Orlando. *Peasant Russia, Civil War: The Volga Countryside in Revolution, 1917–1921.* Oxford: Oxford University Press, 1989.

———. "The Red Army and Mass Mobilization during the Russian Civil War, 1918–1920." *Past and Present,* no. 129 (1990): 168–211.

Fitzpatrick, Sheila. "Ascribing Class: The Construction of Social Identity in Soviet Russia." *Journal of Modern History* 65 (December 1993): 745–70.

———. *The Russian Revolution.* 2nd ed. Oxford and New York: Oxford University Press, 1994.

Frank, Stephen P. "Confronting the Domestic Other: Rural Popular Culture and Its Enemies in Fin-de-Siècle Russia." In *Cultures in Flux: Lower-Class Values, Practices, and Resistance in Late Imperial Russia,* edited by Stephen P. Frank and Mark D. Steinberg, 74–107. Princeton: Princeton University Press, 1994.

Frierson, Cathy A. *Peasant Icons: Representations of Rural People in Late Nineteenth-Century Russia.* New York and Oxford: Oxford University Press, 1993.

Frumkin, Jacob G. "Pages from the History of Russian Jewry (Recollections and Documentary Material)." In *Russian Jewry, 1860–1917,* edited by Jacob Frumkin, Gregor Aronson, and Alexis Goldenweiser, and translated by Mirra Ginsburg, 18–84. New York and London: Thomas Yoseloff, 1966.

Fuller, William C., Jr. *Civil-Military Conflict in Imperial Russia, 1881–1914.* Princeton: Princeton University Press, 1985.

Furmanov, Dmitrii. *Sochineniia.* 2 vols. Leningrad: "Khudozhestvennaia literatura," 1971.

Gat, Azar. *The Development of Military Thought: The Nineteenth Century.* Oxford: Clarendon Press, 1992.

Gatrell, Peter. *A Whole Empire Walking: Refugees in Russia During World War I.* Bloomington and Indianapolis: Indiana University Press, 1999.

Gavrilov, L. M., and V. V. Kutuzov. "Istoshchenie liudskikh rezervov russkoi armii v 1917 g." In *Pervaia mirovaia voina, 1914–1918,* edited by A. L. Sidorov, 145–57. Moscow: Nauka, 1968.

Geraci, Robert. "Russian Orientalism at an Impasse: Tsarist Education Policy and the 1910 Conference on Islam." In *Russia's Orient: Imperial Borderlands and Peoples, 1700–1917,* edited by Daniel R. Brower and Edward J. Lazzerini, 138–61. Bloomington and Indianapolis: Indiana University Press, 1997.

Gerstle, Gary. *American Crucible: Race and Nation in the Twentieth Century.* Princeton: Princeton University Press, 2001.

Geyer, Dietrich. *Russian Imperialism: The Interaction of Domestic and Foreign Policy, 1860–1914.* Translated by Bruce Little. New Haven and London: Yale University Press, 1987.

Geyer, Michael. "War and the Context of General History in an Age of Total War: Comment on Peter Paret, 'Justifying the Obligation of Military Service,' and Michael Howard, 'World War One: The Crisis in European History,'" *Journal of Military History* 57, special issue (October 1993): 145–63.

Golovine, N[icholas] N. *The Russian Army in the World War.* New Haven: Yale University Press, 1931.

Gorbov, N., comp. *Russkaia istoriia dlia nachal'nykh shkol.* 18th ed. Moscow: Izd. Tikhomirova, 1914.

Gorianov, S. M., and P. P. Lebedev, eds. *Ustavy o voinskoi povinnosti (Svod zakonov, tom 4, kniga 1, izd. 1897 g.), dopolnennye vsemi pozdneishimi uzakoneniiami po 1 iiunia 1913 g.* 12th ed. St. Petersburg: Berezovskii, 1913.

Gorodovikov, O. I. *Vospominaniia.* Moscow: Voenizdat, 1957.

Greenfeld, Liah. *Nationalism: Five Roads to Modernity.* Cambridge: Harvard University Press, 1992.

Habermas, Jürgen. *Between Facts and Norms: Contributions to a Discourse Theory of Law and Democracy.* Translated by William Rehg. Cambridge: MIT Press, 1996.

Hasegawa, Tsuyoshi. "Crime, Police, and Mob Justice in Petrograd during the Russian Revolutions of 1917." In *Religious and Secular Forces in Late Tsarist Russia,* edited by Charles E. Timberlake, 241–71. Seattle: University of Washington Press, 1992.

Havel, Václav. *Open Letters: Selected Writings, 1965–1990.* New York: Vintage, 1992.

Hayes, Carlton J. H. "Contributions of Herder to the Doctrine of Nationalism." *American Historical Review* 32, no. 4 (July 1927): 719–36.

———. *The Historical Evolution of Modern Nationalism.* New York: R. R. Smith, 1931.

Hemenway, Elizabeth Jones. "Mother Russia and the Crisis of the Russian National Family: The Puzzle of Gender in Revolutionary Russia." *Nationalities Papers* 25, no. 1 (1997): 103–21.

Herrmann, David G. *The Arming of Europe and the Making of the First World War.* Princeton: Princeton University Press, 1996.

Hobsbawm, Eric. *The Age of Revolution, 1789–1848.* London and New York: Mentor, 1962.

———. *Nations and Nationalism Since 1780: Programme, Myth, Reality.* Cambridge: Cambridge University Press, 1990.

Holquist, Peter Isaac. "'Information is the Alpha and Omega of Our Work': Bolshevik Surveillance in its Pan-European Context." *Journal of Modern History* 69(September 1997): 415–50.

———. "To Count, To Extract, and To Exterminate: Population Statistics and Population Politics in Late Imperial and Soviet Russia." In *A State of Nations: Empire and Nation-Making in the Age of Lenin and Stalin,* edited by Ronald Grigor Suny and Terry Martin, 111–44. Oxford and New York: Oxford University Press, 2001.

Hosking, Geoffrey. *Russia: People and Empire, 1552–1917.* Cambridge: Harvard University Press, 1997.

Howard, Michael. "Men against Fire: The Doctrine of the Offensive in 1914." In *The Lessons of History.* New Haven, Conn.: Yale University Pres, 1991.

Hunt, Lynn. *The Family Romance of the French Revolution.* Berkeley and Los Angeles: University of California Press, 1992.

Iakhontov, A. N. "Tiazhelye dni (Sekretnyia zasedaniia Soveta Ministrov, 16 iiulia–2 sentiabria 1915 goda)." *Arkhiv russkoi revoliutsii* 18 (1926): 5–136.

Ignatieff, Michael. *Blood and Belonging: Journeys into the New Nationalism.* New York: Farrar, Straus, and Giroux, 1994.

Ignatyev, A. A. *A Subaltern in Old Russia.* Translated by Ivor Montagu. London, New York, and Melbourne: Hutchinson and Co., 1944.

Instruktsiia krasnoarmeitsu. 2nd ed. Moscow: VTsIK, 1918.

Instruktsiia po obucheniiu voennomu stroiu i gimnastike v nizshikh uchebnykh zavedeniiakh Kievskago uchebnago okruga. Kiev: N. N. Kushnerev, 1911.

Ivanova, Iu. N. "Zhenshchiny v istorii rossiiskoi armii." *Voenno-istoricheskii zhurnal,* no. 3 (1992): 86–89.

Izvestiia VtsIK. Petrograd, 1918.

Jahn, Hubertus F. *Patriotic Culture in Russia during World War I.* Ithaca, N.Y. and London: Cornell University Press, 1996.

Jordanova, Ludmilla. "The Authoritarian Response." In *The Enlightenment and its Shadows,* edited by Peter Hulme and Ludmilla Jordanova, 202–16. London and New York: Routledge, 1990.

Kagan, Frederick W. *The Military Reforms of Nicholas I: The Origins of the Modern Russian Army.* New York: St. Martin's, 1999.

Kalinin, M. I. *O kommunisticheskom vospitanii i voinskom dolge: Sbornik statei i rechei.* Moscow: Voenizdat, 1962.

Kavtaradze, A. G. *Voennye spetsialisty na sluzhbe respubliki sovetov, 1917–1920 gg.* Moscow: Nauka, 1988.

Keegan, John. *The Face of Battle.* New York: Barnes and Noble, 1976.

Kerber, Linda K. "May All Our Citizens Be Soldiers and All Our Soldiers Citizens: The Ambiguities of Female Citizenship in the New Nation." In *Women, Militarism, and War: Essays in History, Politics, and Social Theory,* edited by Jean Bethke Elshtain and Sheila Tobias, 89–103. Savage, Md.: Rowman and Littlefield, 1990.

Kerenskii, Aleksandr. "'Takoe upravlenie gosudarstvom-nedopustimo': Doklad A. F. Kerenskogo na zakrytom zasedanii Gosudarstvennoi dumy. Dekabr' 1916." *Istoricheskii arkhiv,* no. 2 (1997): 4–22.

Kestnbaum, Meyer. "Citizenship and Compulsory Military Service: The Revolutionary Origins of Conscription in the United States." *Armed Forces and Society* 27, no. 1 (Fall 2000): 7–36.

Khechinov, Iurii. *Angely khraniteli: Stranitsy istorii otechestva.* Moscow: Agenstvo "Vmeste," 1993.

Khristinin, Iu. N. "Ne radi nagrad, no radi tokmo rodnogo narodu." *Voenno-istoricheskii zhurnal,* no. 1 (1994): 92–93.

Kliatskin, S. M. *Na zashchite Oktiabria: Organizatsiia reguliarnoi armii i militsionnoe stroitelstvo v Sovetskoi Respublike, 1917–1920 gg.* Moscow: Nauka, 1965.

Klibanov, A. I. *History of Religious Sectarianism in Russia (1860s–1917).* Translated by Ethel Dunn. Edited by Stephen P. Dunn. New York: Pergamon Press, 1985.

Klyuchevsky, Vasili. *Peter the Great.* Translated and with an introduction by Liliana Archibald. New York: Vintage, 1961.

Knox, Alfred. *With the Russian Army, 1914–1917.* 2 vols. London: Hutchinson and Co., 1921.

Koenker, Diane P. "Urbanization and Deurbanization in the Russian Revolution and Civil War." In *Party, State, and Society in the Russian Civil War,* edited by Diane P. Koenker, William G. Rosenberg, and Ronald G. Suny, 81–104. Bloomington: Indiana University Press, 1989.

Kohn, Hans. *The Idea of Nationalism: A Study of Its Origins and Backgrounds.* New York: Macmillan, 1944.

Kollontai, A[leksandra]. "Krasnyi front i rabotnitsa." In *Revoliutsionnaia voina (sbornik pervyi),* edited by N. Podvoiskii and M. Pavlovich. Moscow: Izd. VTsIK, 1919.

Komplektovanie krasnoi armii. Berlin: Evraziiskoe knigoizdatel'stvo, 1926.

Korablev, Iu. I., and M. I. Loginov, eds. *KPSS i stroitelstvo vooruzhennykh sil SSSR, 1918–iiun 1941.* Moscow: Voenizdat, 1959.

Kotkin, Stephen. *Magnetic Mountain: Stalinism as a Civilization.* Berkeley: University of California Press, 1995.

Kozlov, S. "Voennaia nauka i voennye doktriny v pervoi mirovoi voine." *Voenno-istoricheskii zhurnal* 6, no. 11 (1964): 31–41.

Krasnaia zvezda. Moscow: VTsIK, 1918.

Krupskaia, N. K. *Pedagogicheskie sochineniia v desiati tomakh.* 11 vols. Moscow: Izd. Akademii pedagogicheskikh nauk, 1957–63.

———. *Vospitanie molodezhi v leninskom dukhe.* Moscow: Pedagogika, 1989.

Kuropatkin, A. N. *The Russian Army and the Japanese War.* Translated by Captain A. B. Lindsay. 2 vols. London: John Murray, 1909.

Kuz'min, N. F. *Na strazhe mirnogo truda (1921–1940).* Moscow: Voenizdat, 1959.

Lebina, N. B. "Tenevye storony zhizni sovetskogo goroda 20–30kh godov." *Voprosy istorii,* no. 2 (1994): 30–42.

Lenin, V. I. *Sochineniia,* 2nd ed. Moscow: Gosizdat, 1930–1935. 31 vols.

———. "O revoliutsionnoi fraze." In V. I. Lenin, *Sochineniia,* 4th ed., vol. 27. Moscow: Gosizdat, 1952.

Levichev, V. *Krasnaia armiia i prizyv 1904 goda: Doklad na sobranii agitatorov pri MK VKP(b) s predisloviem P. Petunina, tezisami dlia dokladov, lozungami i spravochnoi literaraturoi.* Moscow and Leningrad: Moskovskii rabochii, 1926.

Lewin, Moshe. *Russian Peasants and Soviet Power: A Study of Collectivization.* New York: W. W. Norton, 1968.

Lih, Lars. *Bread and Authority in Russia, 1914–1921.* Berkeley, Los Angeles, and Oxford: University of California Press, 1990.

Lincoln, W. Bruce. *Passage Through Armageddon: The Russians in War and Revolution, 1914–1918.* New York: Simon and Schuster, 1986.

Littauer, Vladimir S. *Russian Hussar: A Story of the Imperial Cavalry, 1911–1920.* 1965. Reprint, Shippensburg, Penn.: White Mane Publishing, 1993.

Lobov, V. N., ed. *O dolge i chesti voinskoi v rossiiskoi armii: Sobranie materialov, dokumentov, i statei.* Moscow: Voenizdat, 1991.

Lohr, Eric. "Enemy Alien Politics Within the Russian Empire During World War I." Ph.D. diss., Harvard University, 1999.

———. "The Russian Army and the Jews: Mass Deportations, Hostages, and Violence during World War I." *Russian Review* 60, no. 3 (July 2001): 404–19.

Lukomskii, A. S. *Vospominaniia.* 2 vols. Berlin: Otto Kirkhner, 1922.

Luxemburg, Rosa. "Militia and Militarism." In *Selected Political Writings of Rosa Luxemburg,* edited by Dick Howard, 135–58. New York and London: Monthly Review Press, 1971.

Malia, Martin. *The Soviet Tragedy: A History of Socialism in Russia, 1917–1991.* New York: Free Press, 1995.

Malinovskii, L., and I. Gludin. *Otchet o prizyve na deistvitel'nuiu voennuiu sluzhbu v 1925 godu grazhdan rozhdeniia 1903 goda.* Moscow: Upravlenie stroevoe i po ukomplektovaniiu, 1926.

Martin, Terry. *The Affirmative Action Empire: Nations and Nationalism in the Soviet Union, 1923–1939.* Ithaca, N.Y.: Cornell University Press, 2001.

Martynov, E. I. "Iz pechal'nogo opyta russko-iaponskoi voiny." In *". . . Khorosho zabytoe staroe": Sbornik statei,* edited by O. A. Bobrakov, 10–66. Essay, 1904. Moscow: Voenizdat, 1991.

———. *Strategiia v epokhu Napoleona I i v nashe vremia.* St. Petersburg: Voennaia tipografiia, 1894.

———. "V chem sila Iaponii i slabost' Rossii?" In *". . . Khorosho zabytoe staroe": Sbornik statei,* edited by O. A. Bobrakov, 8–9. Essay, 1904. Moscow: Voenizdat, 1991.

McDaniel, Tim. *The Agony of the Russian Idea.* Princeton: Princeton University Press, 1996.

McReynolds, Louise. *The News Under Russia's Old Regime: The Development of a Mass-Circulation Press.* Princeton: Princeton Univeristy Press, 1991.

Meijer, Jan M., ed. *The Trotsky Papers.* 2 vols. The Hague and Paris: Mouton and Co., 1964–1971.

Menning, Bruce W. *Bayonets before Bullets: The Imperial Russian Army, 1861–1914.* Bloomington and Indianapolis: Indiana University Press, 1992.

Mikhnevich, N. P. *Osnovy russkago voennago iskusstva: Sravnitelnyi ocherk sostoianiia voennago iskusstva v Rossii i Zapadnoi Evropie v vazhneishiia istoricheskiia epokhi.* St. Petersburg: Tip. Shtaba Otdielnago korpusa Pogranichnoi strazhi, 1898.

Miller, Forrestt A. *Dmitrii Miliutin and the Reform Era in Russia.* [Nashville, Tenn.]: Vanderbilt University Press, 1968.

Molodtsygin, M. A. *Krasnaia armiia: Rozhdenie i stanovlenie, 1917–1920 gg.* Moscow: Institut rossiiskoi istorii RAN, 1997.

Molotov, V. *Molotov Remembers: Inside Kremlin Politics, Conversations with Felix Chuev.* Chicago: University of Chicago Press, 1993.

Moon, David. "Peasants into Russian Citizens? A Comparative Perspective." *Revolutionary Russia* 5, no. 1 (June 1996): 43–81.

Moran, Daniel. "Arms and the Concert: The Nation in Arms and the Dilemmas of German Liberalism." In *The People in Arms: Military Myth and National Mobilization Since the French Revolution,* edited by Daniel Moran and Arthur Waldron. Cambridge: Cambridge University Press, 2002.

Mosse, George L. *The Image of Man: The Creation of Modern Masculinity.* New York and Oxford: Oxford University Press, 1996.

———. *Nationalism and Sexuality: Respectability and Abnormal Sexuality in Modern Europe.* New York: Howard Fertig, 1985.

Murphy, Orville T. "The American Revolutionary Army and the Concept of Levée en Masse," *Military Affairs* 23, no. 1 (Spring 1959): 13–20.

N., M. *Na voinu! Zapiski krestianina-prizyvnogo 1904 goda.* Christchurch, Hants, England: A. Chertkov, 1905.

Nastavlenie dlia deistvii pekhoty v boiu. St. Petersburg: Voennaia tipografiia Imperatritsy Ekateriny Velikoi, 1914.

Nastavlenie dlia strel'by iz vintovok, karabinov, i revol'verov. Kiev: N. Ia. Ogloblina, 1916.

Neznamov, Aleksandr. *Oboronitel'naia voina (teoriia voprosa). Chast' 1: Strategiia.* St. Petersburg: Izd. Nikolaevskoi akademii Generalnago Shtaba, 1909.

———. *Tekushchie voennye voprosy (sbornik statei).* St. Petersburg: Tip. Khudozhestvennoi Pechati, 1909.

Ognev, D. F., comp. *Voinskii ustav o nakazaniiakh (S.V.P. 1869 g., XXII, izd. 3).* St. Petersburg: Berezovskii, 1912.

Olcott, Martha Brill. *The Kazakhs.* 2nd ed. Stanford: Hoover Institution Press, 1995.

Olikov, S. *Dezertirstvo v krasnoi armii i bor'ba s nim.* Moscow: Izd. NKVM, 1926.

Paret, Peter. *Understanding War: Essays on Clausewitz and the History of Military Power.* Princeton: Princeton University Press, 1992.

Partiino-politicheskaia rabota v krasnoi armii (aprel' 1918–fevral' 1919): dokumenty. Moscow: Voenizdat, 1961.

Partiino-politicheskaia rabota v krasnoi armii (mart 1919–1920 gg.). Moscow: Voenizdat, 1964.

Pavlova, I. V. *Krasnaia gvardiia v sibiri.* Novosibirsk: Nauka, 1983.

Pearson, Raymond. *The Russian Moderates and the Crisis of Tsarism, 1914–1917.* London: Macmillan, 1977.

"Perepiska pravykh i drugie materialy ob ikh deiatel'nosti v 1914–1917 godakh." *Voprosy istorii,* no. 3 (1996): 142–65.

Pipes, Richard. *Russia Under the Old Regime.* 2nd ed. New York: Macmillan, 1992.

———. *The Russian Revolution.* New York: Alfred A. Knopf, 1990.

Pireiko, A. *V tylu i na fronte imperialisticheskoi voiny: Vospominaniia riadovogo.* Leningrad: Rabochee izdatel'stvo "Priboi", 1926.

Plamenatz, John. "Two Types of Nationalism." In *Nationalism: The Nature and Evolution of an Idea,* edited by Eugene Kamenka, 23–36. New York: St. Martin's, 1973.

Pochemu gortsy Severnogo Kavkaza prizyvaiutsia na sluzhbu v RKKA (Material dlia dokladchikov na obshchikh sobraniiakh grazhdan v aule). Novocherkassk: Politupravleniia SKVO, 1927.

Pocock, J. G. *The Machiavellian Moment: Florentine Political Thought and the Atlantic Republican Tradition.* Princeton: Princeton University Press, 1975.

Podpriatov, N. V. "Natsional'nye men'shinstva v bor'be za 'chest', dostoinstvo, tselost' Rossii. . . : Sozdanie i ispol'zovanie natsional'nykh formirovanii v russkoi armii." *Voenno-istoricheskii zhurnal,* no.1 (1997): 54–59.

Podvoiskii, N. *Iz kazarmy v boi. Pamiatka (Chto nuzhno znat' kazhdomu voinu molodoi Rossiiskoi Sotsialisticheskoi Armii).* Kiev: Izd. Polituprav. RVS 12–i armii, 1919.

———, and M. Pavlovich, eds. *Revoliutsionnaia voina (sbornik pervyi).* Moscow: Izd. VTsIK, 1919.

Polnoe sobranie zakonov Rossiiskoi Imperii. 33 vols. [St.Petersburg], 1885–1916.

Posen, Barry R. "Nationalism, the Mass Army, and Military Power," *International Security* 18, no. 2 (Autumn 1993): 80–124.

Pravda. Moscow, 1912– .

Pyle, Emily E. "Village Social Relations and the Reception of Soldiers' Family Aid Policy in Russia, 1912–1921." Ph.D. diss., University of Chicago, 1997.

Radkey, Oliver H. *The Unknown Civil War in Soviet Russia: A Study of the Green Movement in the Tambov Region, 1920–21.* Stanford: Hoover Institution Press, 1976.

Raikovskii, V. *Voennoe vospitanie.* Moscow: A. I. Snegirevoi, 1908.

Raleigh, Donald J., ed. *A Russian Civil War Diary: Alexis Babine in Saratov, 1917–1922.* Durham, N.C., and London: Duke University Press, 1988.

Rediger, A., comp. *Komplektovanie i ustroistvo vooruzhennoi sily.* 3rd ed. St. Petersburg: Voennaia tipografiia, 1900.

Rhodes, Richard. *Why They Kill: The Discoveries of a Maverick Criminologist.* New York: Knopf, 1999.

Rich, David Alan. *The Tsar's Colonels: Professionalism, Strategy, and Subversion in Late Imperial Russia.* Cambridge: Harvard University Press, 1998.

Riordan, James. *Sport in Soviet Society: Development of Sport and Physical Education in Russia and the USSR.* Cambridge: Cambridge University Press, 1977.

Rogger, Hans. *Jewish Policies and Right-Wing Politics in Imperial Russia.* Berkeley and Los Angeles: University of California Press, 1986.

Rossiia v mirovoi voine, 1914–1918 goda (v tsifrakh). Moscow: Tsentral'noe statisticheskoe upravlenie, 1925.

Rousseau, Jean-Jacques. *The Social Contract.* Translated by Maurice Cranston. New York and London: Penguin, 1968.

Sanborn, Joshua A. [Josh]. "Conscription, Correspondence, and Politics in Late Imperial Russia." *Russian History/Histoire Russe* 24, nos. 1–2 (Spring–Summer 1997): 27–40.

———. "Drafting the Nation: Military Conscription and the Formation of a Modern Polity in Tsarist and Soviet Russia, 1905–1925." Ph.D. diss., University of Chicago, 1998.

———. "The Mobilization of 1914 and the Question of the Russian Nation: A Reexamination." *Slavic Review* 59, no. 2 (Summer 2000): 267–89.

———. "Pacifist Politics and Peasant Politics: Tolstoy and the Doukhobors, 1895–99." *Canadian Ethnic Studies/Etudes Ethniques au Canada* 28, no. 3 (1995): 52–71.

Sapargaliev, G. *Karatel'naia politika tsarizma v Kazakhstane (1905–1917).* Alma-Ata: Nauka, 1966.

Saunders, David. *Russia in the Age of Reaction and Reform, 1801–1881.* London and New York: Longman, 1992.

Seregny, Scott J. "Zemstvos, Peasants, and Citizenship: The Russian Adult Education Movement and World War I." *Slavic Review* 59, no. 2 (Summer 2000): 290–315.

Schama, Simon. *Citizens: A Chronicle of the French Revolution.* New York: Knopf, 1989.

Sher, Richard B. "Adam Ferguson, Adam Smith, and the Problem of National Defense." *Journal of Modern History* 61, no. 2 (June 1989): 240–68.

Shils, E. A., and M. Janowitz. "Cohesion and Disintegration in the Wehrmacht in World War II." *Public Opinion Quarterly* 12 (1948): 280–315.

Shishkin, V. I. "Krasnyi banditizm v sovetskoi sibiri." In *Sovetskaia istoriia: Problemy i uroki,* edited by V. I. Shishkin, 3–79. Novosibirsk: "Nauka", 1992.

Shklovsky, Viktor. *A Sentimental Journey: Memoirs, 1917–1922.* Translated and edited by Richard Sheldon. 1970. Revised edition, Ithaca, N.Y., and London: Cornell University Press, 1984.

Siegelbaum, Lewis H. *The Politics of Industrial Mobilization in Russia, 1914–17: A Study of the War-Industries Committees.* New York: St. Martin's, 1983.

———. *Soviet State and Society Between Revolutions, 1918–1929.* Cambridge: Cambridge University Press, 1992.

Simon, Gerhard. *Nationalism and Policy Toward the Nationalities in the Soviet Union: From Totalitarian Dictatorship to Post-Stalinist Society.* Translated by Karen Forster and Oswald Forster. Boulder, San Francisco, and London: Westview Press, 1991.

Slavinskii, M. A. "Voina i natsional'nyi vopros." In *Chego zhdet Rossiia ot voiny: Sbornik statei.* 2nd ed., 106–24. Petrograd: Prometei, 1915.

Slezkine, Yuri. "N. Ia. Marr and the National Origins of Soviet Ethnogenetics." *Slavic Review* 55, no. 4 (Winter 1996): 826–62.

———. "The USSR as a Communal Apartment, or How a Socialist State Promoted Ethnic Particularism." *Slavic Review* 53, no. 2 (Summer, 1994): 414–52.

Slocum, John Willard. "The Boundaries of National Identity: Religion, Language and Nationality Politics in Late Imperial Russia." Ph.D. diss., University of Chicago, 1993.

Smith, Leonard V. *Between Mutiny and Obedience: The Case of the French Fifth Infantry Division during World War I.* Princeton: Princeton University Press, 1994.

Sobranie uzakonenii i rasporiazhenii pravitel'stva. [St.Petersburg]: Pravitel'stvuiushchii senat, 1863–1917.

Sobranie uzakonenii i rasporiazhenii rabochego i krest'ianskogo pravitel'stva, 1917–January 1938. Moscow: Iuridicheskoe izdatel'stvo N. K. Iu. RSFSR, [1920–50].

Sobranie zakonov i rasporiazhenii raboche-krest'ianskogo pravitel'stva SSSR, 1924–February 1938. Moscow: [Council of Ministers of USSR].

Sokol, Edward Dennis. *The Revolt of 1916 in Russian Central Asia.* The Johns Hopkins University Studies in Historical and Political Science. Series 71, number 1. Baltimore: Johns Hopkins University Press, 1953.

Sovetskie vooruzhennye sily: Istoriia stroitel'stva. Moscow: Voenizdat, 1978.

Stepun, F[edor Afgustovich]. *Iz pisem praporshchika artillerista.* Prague: Plamia, n.d.

Stevenson, David. *Armaments and the Coming of War: Europe, 1904–1914.* Oxford: Clarendon Press, 1996.

Stewart, John Hall, ed. *A Documentary Survey of the French Revolution.* New York: Macmillan, 1951.

Stites, Richard. *Revolutionary Dreams: Utopian Vision and Experimental Life in the Russian Revolution.* New York and Oxford: Oxford University Press, 1989.

Stockdale, Melissa Kirschke. *Paul Miliukov and the Quest for a Liberal Russia, 1880–1918.* Ithaca, N.Y., and London: Cornell University Press, 1996.

Stocking, George W., Jr. *Victorian Anthropology.* New York: Free Press, 1987.

———. *Race, Culture, and Evolution: Essays in the History of Anthropology.* Chicago: University of Chicago Press, 1982.

Stone, Norman. *The Eastern Front, 1914–1917.* New York: Charles Scribner's Sons, 1975.

Summers, Anne. *Angels and Citizens: British Women as Military Nurses, 1854–1914.* London and New York: Routledge and Kegan Paul, 1988.

Suny, Ronald Grigor. *The Revenge of the Past: Nationalism, Revolution, and the Collapse of the Soviet Union.* Stanford: Stanford University Press, 1993.

Svechin, Aleksandr A. *Strategy.* 2nd ed. Edited by Kent D. Lee. 1927. Revised edition, Minneapolis: East View Publications, 1992.

"'Takoe upravlenie gosudarstvom-nedopustimo': Doklad A. F. Kerenskogo na zakrytom zasedanii Gosudarstvennoi dumy. Dekabr' 1916 g." *Istoricheskii arkhiv,* no. 2 (1997): 4–22.

Tkhvorzhevskii, K. *Nadezhnye soldaty.* Soldatskaia biblioteka. St. Petersburg: Berezovskii, 1897.

Toch, Hans. *Violent Men: An Inquiry Into the Psychology of Violence.* 1969. Revised edition, Hyattsville, Md.: American Psychological Association, 1992.

Toews, John B. "The Russian Mennonites and the Military Question (1921–1927)." *Mennonite Quarterly Review* 43, no. 2 (1969): 153–68.

Trotskii [Trotsky], L. D. *Kak vooruzhalas' revoliutsiia.* 3 vols. Moscow: Vysshii voennyi redaktsionnyi sovet, 1923–25.

———. *Terrorism and Communism: A Reply to Karl Kautsky.* Ann Arbor: University of Michigan Press, 1961.

———. *The History of the Russian Revolution.* Translated by Max Eastman. 3 vols. London: Sphere, 1967.

Urry, James. *None But Saints: The Transformation of Mennonite Life in Russia, 1789–1889.* Winnipeg: Windflower, 1989.

Usborne, Cornelie. *The Politics of the Body in Weimar Germany: Women's Reproductive Rights and Duties.* London: Macmillan, 1992.

Verchenko, N., et al., eds. *Leninskii komsomol (ocherki po istorii VLKSM).* 3rd ed. Moscow: Molodaia gvardiia, 1963.

Verner, Andrew M. *The Crisis of Russian Autocracy: Nicholas II and the 1905 Revolution.* Princeton: Princeton University Press, 1990.

———. "Discursive Strategies in the 1905 Revolution: Peasant Petitions from Vladimir Province." *Russian Review* 54, no. 1 (January 1995): 65–90.

Viaz'mitinov, A. M., ed. *Russkie skauty.* Madrid: Central Staff of the National Organization of Russian Scouts, 1969.

Vishniakov, N. P., and F. I. Arkhipov. *Ustroistvo vooruzhennykh sil SSSR.* 2nd ed. Moscow: Voennyi vestnik, 1926.

Voitolovskii, L. *Po sledam voiny: Pokhodnye zapiski, 1914–1917.* 2nd ed. Leningrad: Izd. pisatelei, 1926.

von Hagen, Mark. "The Great War and the Mobilization of Ethnicity in the Russian Empire." In *Post-Soviet Political Order: Conflict and State Building,* edited by Barnett

R. Rubin and Jack Snyder, 34–57. London and New York: Routledge, 1998.

———. "The Russian Imperial Army and the Ukrainian National Movement in 1917." *The Ukrainian Quarterly* 54, no. 3–4 (Fall–Winter 1998): 220–56.

———. *Soldiers in the Proletarian Dictatorship: The Red Army and the Soviet Socialist State, 1917–1930.* Ithaca, N.Y.: Cornell University Press, 1990.

von Wahlde, Peter. "Military Thought in Imperial Russia." Ph.D. diss., Indiana University, 1966.

Voprosy strategii i operativnogo iskusstva v sovetskikh voennykh trudakh (1917–1940 gg.). Moscow: Voenizdat, 1965.

Vucinich, Alexander. *Darwin in Russian Thought.* Berkeley, Los Angeles, London: University of California Press, 1988.

Wade, Rex A. *Red Guards and Workers' Militias in the Russian Revolution.* Stanford: Stanford University Press, 1984.

———, ed. *Documents of Soviet History.* Vol. 1-5. Gulf Breeze, Fla.: Academic International Press, 1991–2000.

Weber, Eugen. *Peasants into Frenchmen: The Modernization of Rural France, 1870–1914.* Stanford: Stanford University Press, 1976.

Weber, Max. *Sociological Writings.* Edited by Wolf Heydebrand. New York: Continuum, 1994.

Weeks, Theodore R. *Nation and State in Late Imperial Russia: Nationalism and Russification on the Western Frontier, 1863–1914.* DeKalb: Northern Illinois University Press, 1996.

Wildman, Allan K. *The End of the Russian Imperial Army: The Old Army and the Soldiers' Revolt (March–April 1917).* Princeton: Princeton University Press, 1980.

Wirtschafter, Elise Kimerling. *Social Identity in Imperial Russia.* DeKalb: Northern Illinois University Press, 1997.

Wolfgang, Marvin E., and Franco Ferracuti. *The Subculture of Violence: Towards an Integrated Theory in Criminology.* London and New York: Tavistock, 1967.

Wood, Elizabeth A. *The Baba and the Comrade: Gender and Politics in Revolutionary Russia.* Bloomington and Indianapolis: Indiana University Press, 1997.

Woodcock, George, and Ivan Avakumovich. *The Doukhobors.* Toronto and New York: Oxford University Press, 1968.

Wortman, Richard S. *Scenarios of Power: Myth and Ceremony in Russian Monarchy.* Vols. 1–2. Princeton: Princeton University Press, 1995–2000.

Wright, Donald P. "The Cultivation of Patriotism and the Militarization of Citizenship in Late Imperial Russia, 1906–1914." Ph.D. diss., Tulane University, 2001.

Zaionchkovskii, A. M. *Oborona Sevastapolia: Podvigi zashchitnikov.* 2nd ed. St. Petersburg: Izdatel'stvo "Vysochaishe utverzhdennnago Komiteta po vozstanovleniiu pamiatnikov Sevastopol'skoi oborony," 1904.

Zaionchkovskii, P. A. *Voennye reformy 1860–1870 godov v Rossii.* Moscow: Izd. Moskovskogo universiteta, 1952.

Zdravookhranenie v SSSR: Statisticheskii sbornik. Moscow: Medgiz, 1957.

Zhenshchina-voin. Kiev: Izd. Rubanova, 1914.

Zhurnaly komiteta ministrov po ispolneniiu ukaza 12 dekabria 1904 g. St. Petersburg: Izd. Kantselarii Komiteta Ministrov, 1905.

Zizek, Slavoj. *The Sublime Object of Ideology.* London and New York: Verso, 1989.

Zverev, Alexei, and Bruno Coppieters. "V. D. Bonch-Bruevich and the Doukhobors: On the Conscientious Objection Policies of the Bolsheviks." *Canadian Ethnic Studies/Etudes Ethniques au Canada* 27 no. 3 (1995): 72–90.

Zwick, Peter. *National Communism.* Boulder: Westview Press, 1983.

Index